SPECTERS OF ANARCHY

SPECTERS OF ANARCHY

LITERATURE AND THE
ANARCHIST IMAGINATION

JEFF SHANTZ, EDITOR

Algora Publishing
New York

Library of Congress Cataloging-in-Publication Data —

Specters of anarchy: literature and the anarchist imagination / Jeff Shantz, editor.
    pages cm
    Includes bibliographical references and index.
    ISBN 978-1-62894-141-8 (soft cover: alk. paper) — ISBN 978-1-62894-142-5 (hard
cover: alk. paper) — ISBN 978-1-62894-143-2 (eBook) 1. Anarchism in literature. 2.
Literature, Modern—20th century. 3. Literature, Modern—19th century. I. Shantz, Jeff.,
editor of compilation.
    PN56.A567S64 2015
    809'.933581--dc23

                                2015026712

Printed in the United States

Dedicated to Saoirse and Molly Shantz

Acknowledgements

I would like to thank the contributors for their commitment and patience throughout the process of putting the collection together. Special thanks to p.j. lilley for many hours of production work. I would like to acknowledge those local publishers, like pulp magazine at Kwantlen Polytechnic University, that continue to provide venues for anarchist literature, particularly for early stage writers.

Table of Contents

INTRODUCTION. THE ANARCHIST IMAGINATION: LITERATURE/CULTURE/ANARCHY

Culture and politi cs in the first decades of the twenty-first century are once again haunted by a specter that some had declared vanquished only a few decades earlier—the specter of anarchism. This is the very specter that haunted political and economic power holders in the first decades of the twentieth century and against which vast repressive resources (arrest, imprisonment, deportation, and execution) had been deployed in great acts of social exorcism. From the early 1990s, and particularly with the impetus of alternative globalization movements and uprisings against neoliberalism, anarchism as an explicitly self-identified force has enjoyed a rather incredible resurgence. In a period of less than 20 years anarchism has gone from appearing to be dead and buried as a political movement and idea to revive and become perhaps the most significant oppositional political force in Western liberal democracies.

Despite the intervening passage of a century of time, it appears that anarchism remains widely misunderstood. Popular representations and perceptions of anarchism are based largely on fabrication, falsification, and fear as social mythologies continue to construct anarchism as a synonym for chaos and disorder. In some public proclamations political and economic elites present anarchy as even more than this—as another word for terrorism (in the Age of Anti-Terrorism). The image of the anarchist as a frightening presence has been played up in mass media representations that have focused on anarchist activities particularly during protests against meetings of global capital such as the World Trade Organization (WTO), Organization of American States (OAS), and World Bank (WB). Over the last decade and a half, sensationalistic media stories involving angry, black-clad, masked youth demonstrating against the global meetings of government and corporate power holders, often accompanied by property damage and running battles with police, has fueled a moral panic over anarchism similar to that which marked the beginning of the twentieth century and eventually found expression in the first Red Scare. Acts of direct action, or "uncivil" disobedience, especially where it is believed to involve damage to corporate property, attributed to so-called "black bloc" anarchists during global capitalist summits since the 1999 World Trade Organization meetings in Seattle have returned anarchists to the headlines and landed them on the covers of major national and international publications, including *Time* and *Newsweek*, as well as making them the subject of feature stories on leading news programs. In addition to this, police assaults on anarchists during economic summits, including the use of pepper spray, tear gas, and rubber bullets along with mass arrests, shootings, and even killings of anarchists have suggested to the general public that anarchists are indeed something to be feared—something against which force is necessary. This view has been reinforced in mainstream media depictions of anarchists as "criminals," "thugs," and "hooligans."

In the popular imagination, anarchism is largely a phantom. The continued absence of any real, informed analysis and discussion of anarchist politics, popularly, has meant that the actual, as opposed to imagined, perspectives, visions, and activities of this major, and growing, contemporary movement remain obscured. Overlooked or ignored in recent sensationalized accounts are the creative and constructive practices undertaken daily by people who identify as anarchists as they pursue a world free from violence, oppression, and exploitation. A close examination of some of these constructive anarchist visions, which provide examples of politics (and cultures) grounded in everyday resistance, offers needed insights into real world attempts by individuals and collectives to radically transform social relations in the here and now of everyday life (while seeking broader social change).

The works in this collection examine historical and contemporary engagements of anarchism and diverse expressions of cultural production. Together they show that anarchists have used various forms of literary production to express opposition to values and relations characterizing advanced capitalist (and socialist) societies while also expressing key aspects of the alternative values and institutions proposed within anarchism. Among favored themes are anarchist critiques of corporatization, prisons, and patriarchal relations as well as explorations of developing anarchist perspectives on revolution, ecology, sexuality, and mutual aid.

Anarchy

The term "anarchy" comes from the ancient Greek word *anarchos* and means "without a ruler." Anarchism refers to the social perspective that people can run their affairs, individually and collectively, on a positive and generally peaceful basis in the absence of rulers. More than this, people are entitled to make the decisions that affect their lives and are not beholden to the decisions of elites or presumed power holders. Anarchism has long provided a compelling alternative to the false and forced dualism of the exploitative capitalist market and the oppressive totality of the political party and state (of liberal democracy or Leninist communism). Anarchism rejects the rule of either the corporate or the state managers—it rejects managerialism and bureaucracy.

While rulers, not at all surprisingly, claim that the end of their rule will inevitably lead to a descent into chaos and turmoil, anarchists maintain that external rule by elites or professional "decision makers" is unnecessary for the preservation of order. Rather than a descent into Hobbes' hypothetical war of all against all, a society without government suggests to anarchists the very possibility for creative and peaceful human relations—indeed the absence of government is necessary for such relations to be realized. Against the specters of capitalist-driven fear (and xenophobia), "[a]narchism is the great liberator of man from the phantoms that have held him captive" (Goldman xiii). As one commentator remarked in 1912, anarchists are "licensed to taunt us with our moral cowardice, to plant in our souls the nettles of remorse at having acquiesced so tamely in the brutal artifice of present day society" (Dell quoted in Drinnon vii). Pierre-Joseph Proudhon, the first to identify his theoretical position positively as anarchist, neatly summed up the anarchist position in his famous slogan: "Anarchy is Order."

Anarchists oppose all the social ills "for the cure of which governments try to persuade us to accept the greater evils of police and armies, laws and punishments" (Woodcock xxx). For anarchists, the numerous and varied regulatory and supervisory mechanisms of the state are particularly and especially suited to producing docile and dependent subjects. Through institutions like police, courts, and prisons, but also psychology and social work, authorities extend the practices of ruling from control over bodies to influence over minds. Moral regulation provides a subtle means for nurturing regulation, repression, compliance, and conformity. It results, in relations of dependence and deference rather than autonomy and self-determination as the external practices of the state increasingly come to be viewed as the only legitimate mechanisms for identifying social problems, solving disputes, or addressing social needs. For anarchists the "rule of law" administered through the institutions of the state is not the guarantor of freedom, but, rather, the enemy of freedom, closing off alternative avenues for human interaction, creativity, and community while corralling more and more people within its own bounds. Similarly statist systems of legal and criminal justice are not at all capable of securing justice but instead serve to maintain social injustices, inequalities, and exploitation.

Where critics have tried to associate anarchism with disorder, chaos, and violence, anarchists respond that the violence of some despairing individuals is puny in comparison with the everyday activities of states (liberal as well as socialist). As Emma Goldman suggests: "We Americans claim to be a peace-loving people. We hate bloodshed; we are opposed to violence. Yet we go into spasms of joy over the possibility of projecting dynamite bombs from flying machines upon helpless citizens" (xi). Anarchists point out the hypocrisy and falsity of statist expressions of concern about violence. They shine a light on the fact that people tend to organize their communities in ways that are more stable and supportive than the conditions imposed on people through force by states. Indeed, states are responsible for more and greater acts of violence than any, even the most troubled, individual acting within his or her community.

The anarchist imagination has always carried dual characteristics. First, to see and criticize the injustices of the present and, second, to envision a better alternative based on free associations and cooperation. Anarchists object to a programmed present and programmed futures. They also strive to overcome "the burdens of the past" (Drinnon xiii). This gives anarchists general resonance with the artist who shares similar concerns with creating new modes of expression, new forms, new realities. Indeed, anarchists have always pursued and encouraged the creation of new cultural forms and expressions as an integral part of political theory and practice. During the last wave of growing anarchist mobilization, one commentator noted that the anarchist "openness to new beginnings in the arts, to experimental drama, for example, and to jazz" has added an aesthetic quality to revolutionary thought (Drinnon xiii). Against the grey seriousness of revolutionary duty, Emma Goldman once famously proclaimed: "If I can't dance, I don't want to be part of your revolution."

Anarchist theory and practice have proven particularly relevant to cultural revolutionists of the twenty-first century. Systems of economic inequality and inefficiency and political domination and cynical opportunism in each have been unmasked in the period of neoliberal austerity, global crisis, and ecological calamity. Movements from indigenous resistance to alternative globalization to the Arab Spring to Occupy have emerged to confront and address these challenges.

At the same time, the colossal failures, and continued pains, of statist communism have left new generations of people seeking alternatives to both market and statist cruelty. The alternative that stands, almost alone, on the side of equality and social justice is anarchism. For new generations seeking a better future through positive social change, the anarchist alternative is the one that resonates forcefully with their hopes and aspirations—that fires their imaginations.

Anarchy and Criticism

Among the critical or radical perspectives on literary criticism, anarchism has been largely overlooked, until now. Far greater attention and influence have been enjoyed by Marxist criticism which has, in fact, achieved some standing as a broad perspective within established criticism, including within academic venues. With the waning of Marxism broadly in the late 1980s and early 1990s critical approaches came to be dominated by developments identified within a rubric of poststructuralism or postmodernism rather than anarchism (though some have noted the affinity of some postmodern and anarchist perspectives). Yet the marginalization of anarchism is undue and unwarranted. A brief look at anarchist history shows that, from the start, anarchists have developed engaged and insightful approaches to literature. Indeed, major anarchist theorists and activists, including Peter Kropotkin and Emma Goldman, have devoted considerable attention, and substantial writings to analyses of literary production. Even more, their works were well received publicly and their lectures on literature were delivered to packed houses. As anarchism has suffered under violent state repression, and movements have been broken up and diminished, so too has anarchist criticism been written out of intellectual and social histories. That is, however, beginning to change, as the present volume attests.

As anarchism re-emerges as a vital political theory and practice, and provides key inspiration for a new generation of politically active people, the time has come for a re-acquaintance with anarchist criticism and a re-assessment of its place in literary analysis. A glance at some of the contributions made by anarchists shows their ongoing concerns with literary production and provides a beginning for a (re)turn to anarchist criticism for contemporary scholars and/or activists. Criticism was of great consequence for many of the most influential anarchist theorists.

Unlike many later revolutionists, Peter Kropotkin read widely in the contemporary literature of his day. The period during which he was active (as an activist *and* writer) was a period of immense creativity in Russia. In contrast to some Marxist critics, and especially the dire social realists,

Kropotkin sought to give credit and appreciation not only to explicit anarchists or social revolutionists, but to all who challenged and opposed instituted authorities and who offered honest expressions of resistance. Kropotkin "did not, like so many revolutionaries, allow social preoccupations to blunt his literary and artistic preoccupations" (Woodcock xxxiii).

In 1897, Kropotkin undertook a brief lecture tour of the US, speaking in Chicago, Philadelphia, New York, Boston, and Washington. While in New York he offered a single lecture on Russian literature which proved wildly popular. The Lowell Institute lectures in Boston proved so successful that Kropotkin was invited to deliver a series of talks in 1901. These would prove as popular as the ones presented four years before.

Kropotkin's book *Memoirs of a Revolutionist* had already secured a place for him in the annals of Russian literature. In England, where Kropotkin lived many years as an exile, he was well respected in literary circles and counted among his friends William Morris, Oscar Wilde, Bernard Shaw, Patrick Geddes, Frank Harris, and Ford Madox Ford (Woodcock xxvii).

Kropotkin's book *Russian Literature: Ideals and Realities* originated as a series of eight lectures focusing on Russian literature during the nineteenth century that he delivered at the Lowell Institute in Boston during March of 1901. Later that same year he also delivered a lecture on Russian literature at Chickering Hall in New York followed by a final lecture on Turgenev and Tolstoy at the University of Wisconsin in Madison. At that time the Russian literature was hardly known to readers in the United States. Only three or four Russian writers had even been properly translated into English (Woodcock xx–xxxiv).

Kropotkin holds the perspective of the social revolutionary. His position is that in Russia only literature could express real intellectual and political development because of massive repression of explicitly political documents. He focuses on content rather than form and emphasizes aspects that are social in nature (Woodcock xxvi). This is distinct from most anarchist critics who are as concerned with innovations in style. Typically anarchist critics seek the relation of means and end, connections of content and form.

Among anarchist theorists whose works have addressed literary production one whose works has enjoyed a lasting influence is Emma Goldman. Once labeled by governments and media as "the most dangerous woman on the planet" because of her oratorical and organizing skills, Goldman wrote and lectured extensively on literary arts. The longest chapter in her widely read work *Anarchism and Other Essays* is an essay on "The Drama: A Powerful Disseminator of Radical Thought." While in Vienna during 1895, a period of great moment for anarchist social struggles, Emma Goldman immersed herself in the newest literature of Europe. She threw herself into the works of Nietzsche, Hauptmann, Ibsen, Zola, and Hardy. Goldman would make it her goal to introduce these authors and their works to audiences in America.

In fact, Goldman played a primary part in introducing countless North Americans to the works of Strindberg, Shaw, and Ibsen. She regularly lectured in cities across the continent on issues of culture and literature—as much as on topics more typically associated with anarchism such as politics and economics. Indeed, here journal *Mother Earth* would provide the first North American publication for many works of new literature. This is an anarchist politics and theory journal.

Emma Goldman recalls the transformative powers, and the real transformations induced in her, of the fiery anarchist orator. In her case, the incendiary words of the dynamic speaker and propagandist Johan Most seemed enough to spark the social revolution itself. As she relates in *Anarchism and Other Essays*:

> It seemed to me then, and for many years after, that the spoken word hurled forth among the masses with such wonderful eloquence, such enthusiasm and fire, could never be erased from the human mind and soul. How could any one of all the multitudes who flocked to Most's meetings escape his prophetic voice! Surely they had but to hear him to throw off their old beliefs, and see the truth and beauty of Anarchism! (41)

Twenty years later, however, she sensed that her "great faith in the wonder worker, the spoken word," had dissipated (41). She remarks that her perspective shifted noticeably: "Gradually, and with no small struggle against this realization, I came to see that oral propaganda is at best but a means of shaking people from their lethargy: it leaves no lasting impression" (42).

For Goldman the situation, real and imaginal, is entirely different with written modes of expression. In meetings the audience is distracted and restless, too in the moment to adequately or properly attune to issues. Many have come only to be amused by the rhetoric, style, or performance of the speakers. For literature, and other literary arts, it is something different for Goldman. In her view: "The relation between the writer and the reader is more intimate. True, books are only what we want them to be; rather, what we read into them. That we can do so demonstrates the importance of written as against oral expression" (42–43). She preferred reaching those who wished to learn rather than those seeking to be amused.

Perhaps the most notable, respected, and influential anarchist critic to date is Paul Goodman. Not only was Goodman a literary theorist, he was also a poet, novelist, and playwright of some regard. Goodman's critical work began with his doctoral dissertation on *The Structure of Literature* (published in 1954 by the University of Chicago Press). His major works of literary criticism include: *Art and Social Nature* (New York: Vinco Publishing Company, 1946); *Speaking and Language: Defence of Poetry* (New York: Random House, 1971); *Creator Spirit Come!: Literary Essays*, edited by Taylor Stoehr (New York: Free Life Editions, 1977); and *Format and Anxiety: Paul Goodman Critiques the Media*, edited by Taylor Stoehr (Brooklyn, NY: Autonomedia, 1995).

From an anarchist perspective, Goodman examines the domination of expression by format. Format is the constraining and restriction of expression within rigid and limited styles, forms, and meanings. Format involves a policing of language and encourages a self-policing of expression. It is instilled in primary and secondary schools, university courses, workplaces, and government and mass media products. Format is repetitive and unimaginative relying on ready made statements. It is a language of sameness. For Goodman, the decline of literature as a major art corresponds with the growth and expansion of bureaucratization in schools and various media and the associated privileging of format. Not only conventional approaches but radical ones too can be captured by format. Such has been the fate of socialist literature and literary criticism confined to socialist realism. The creativity associated with radical social change is drained and a format of (of false materialism and revolutionary caricatures) remains.

Anarchists must challenge and break format. They must refuse managerialism in language, as in social institutions, and promote instead playful, even transgressive, creativity. Such has been the impetus of the anarchist imagination.

The critique of format is related in some ways to the critique of social and political massification and the reduction of politics to the restricted false choices of elections. Format is the language of massification (and pacification). As an anarchist Goldman repudiates notions of "the mass" and refuses appeals to general palliatives as offered by political opportunists of all stripes (whether socialist or reactionary). Instead she encourages the creativity of freely associating individuals who, in pursuing common purposes with others, develop their cooperative imaginations.

The domination of the mass spirit—of quantity—reflecting the pressures of market exchange value, for profit, overruns concerns for quality, ideals, justice. According to Goldman: "As a mass its aim has always been to make life uniform, gray, and monotonous as the desert. As a mass it will always be the annihilator of individuality, of free initiative, of originality" (78). The mass, as an abstraction, cannot reason. For Goldman: "Without ambition or initiative, the compact mass hates nothing so much as innovation. It has always opposed, condemned, and hounded the innovator, the pioneer of a new truth" (70). For anarchists, the mass must be broken up. Against the mass, the anarchist proposes not the individualism of the market, an abstract construction, but rather individuality—cooperatively self-determining people.

This is not an elitist appeal to "greatness" (abstract and arbitrary) over and against "regular folks" or "commoners." Rather it is a concern that mass production for mass markets (of economics, politics, or culture) tends to privilege production (and exchange) of a certain uncritical sameness (or imposition of a safe center in politics) rather than a challenging creativity or critical sensibility. The language of the mass (or the center in politics) is the language of format. This is perhaps most powerfully felt in the unprincipled posturing, cynical salespersonship, and anonymous insincerity of political elections.

During the 1970s and 1980s, radical criticism came to be dominated by variants of Marxist analysis. The works of Terry Eagleton, Frederic Jameson, and Raymond Williams would make influential contributions to materialist or dialectical analysis of literature. The earlier works of Marxist theorists, such as Leon Trotsky and Georg Lukács, who had written substantial studies of literature found new audiences. The prominence of Marxist criticism reflected the broader movements of activists inspired by and involved in the New Left and counter-cultural movements of the 1960s and 1970s and the rise of academic Marxism as these activists took up positions on campuses.

The twenty-first century has seen a similar growth of activist academics as people inspired by social movements have taken up positions on campuses (though not yet on the same scale as during the 1970s). This time, however, the theoretical tendency that most animates them is not Marxism but anarchism.

With the re-emergence of anarchist movements since the 1990s there has developed also a renewal of interest in anarchist cultural production, especially anarchist art and literature. Contemporary critics have sought to re-evaluate authors who have been influenced by or engaged with anarchism, who have not generally been identified as anarchists, such as Eugene O'Neill and John Fowles. They have also examined contributions to an anarchist vision by authors not recognized as explicitly anarchist, such as Oscar Wilde. Others have sought to bring greater attention to, and more deeply analyze, anarchist writers and works that have until now been overlooked, such as Ursula K. Le Guin. Recently, literary analysis has been brought to bear on alternative modes of expression such as graphic novels, including the works of Alan Moore.

Among the notable recent works of anarchist criticism are *Anarchy and Culture* (1997) by David Weir and *Anarchy and Art* (2007) by Allan Antliff.

Most of these works have offered only tentative steps in anarchist analysis. The first full work of contemporary critical analysis from an anarchist perspective is my own solely authored *Against All Authority: Anarchism and the Literary Imagination* (Imprint, 2011).

New voices, such as some of the contributors to this collection, are striving to address pressing questions about anarchist literary production. The present volume, *Specters of Anarchy: Literature and the Anarchist Imagination*, then, offers a unique contribution to emerging discussions of anarchism and literature. There is no other comparable work available that examines anarchism and literature within the context of contemporary anarchist movements. This is a work that addresses a certain gap in the research both in modern literature, and overlooked connections with anarchist perspectives, and in political theory and theories of contemporary cultural movements. Hopefully it will be of great use for students of literature, politics, sociology, communication and cultural studies. It is also intended to be of interest to activists and members of community movements for whom anarchism represents a vital living movement.

Expressing the Anarchist Imagination: Essays

Of those whose lives moved within or touched anarchist circles few were simultaneously revered and reviled among the broader (international) public. Oscar Wilde was one of the few figures to know a world-wide fame as well as a world-wide disgrace. In the first essay, Agathe Brun expresses the great reward of studying Wilde's life and art in the light of anarchism because he seems to go against all rules and conventions. Condemned for his sexuality, specifically for homosexual practices, this genius of art was rendered as a scapegoat within a society ruled by codes and morals. Brun notes that in the Victorian era, and even more during the *fin de siècle* period, the extraordinary and unconventional Oscar Wilde represented—in the eyes of some—a sort of symbol of decay, or decadence at the center of a supposedly well-ordered and conventional world. In most of his writings, Oscar Wilde directly or indirectly questions the legitimacy of Victorian codes and beliefs while explicitly, in works such as *The Soul of Man under Socialism* espouses an anarchistic (or libertarian socialist) alternative in defense of freedom and liberty.

In the first essay, Brun notes that in *The Decay of Lying*, Wilde praises Art and Imagination to the expense of Mother Nature and the belief in universal truth. In *The Soul of Man under Socialism*, he praises individualism by putting man at the center of all things, while in *De Profundis*, he even calls Christ the "supreme individualist," etc. Everywhere in Wilde's writings, opposition, contradiction and rebellion prevail even though it always remains poetic, light and witty.

Brun notes that the nineteenth century was a century of sudden and great changes: industrialization had brought along a helpless urbanization that endangered economic and social balance. In this context, Nature was praised and symbolized re-birth and the origins of life, but Oscar Wilde thought differently, as he always did. Wilde suggests that for all time, humans have tried to create comfort and security for themselves and their fellow creatures. There is no reason, with modernity, that they would now reject all these efforts and progress in order to bask in ignorance and the discomfort of Nature. But this rebellion against Nature is not the most important step in Wilde's criticism. In *The Picture of Dorian Gray*, he shows his love for beauty and youth through the relationship between Basil Hallward, Lord Henry Wotton, and Dorian Gray. In doing so, Wilde highlights the eternal weakness of men: relying upon appearances. Dorian's beauty and youth give him whatever he wants but his soul is lost and the stupidity of people around him is revealed.

A different approach to nature emerges in the works of so-called individualist anarchists in the context of American anarchism and literature. In the second essay, James Brown offers a brief overview of how American nature writing, beginning with Henry David Thoreau, has been part of an international discourse advocating the abolition of nations and governments for the simple reason that, for many of the writers explored herein, governments are seen as the primary cause behind the desecration of nature and the related oppression of human beings. Brown traces the influence of Emerson and Thoreau on the environmental left from Walden Pond to the Occupy movement. This suggests some of the ethical challenges this anarchist tradition of personal accountability—or self reliance—poses to activists who have, in Brown's view, failed to distinguish anarchism itself—which calls for the abolition of government on behalf of individual liberty—from its symbolic use as a tactic for liberal and progressive reform.

As creations of one of the most important Modernist writers, James Joyce's (1882–1941) works have primarily been taken by critics until recently as purely aesthetic creations with little overt political content. Then came Enda Duffy's *The Subaltern Ulysses* (1994), which begins with the question: "Might an IRA bomb and Joyce's *Ulysses* have anything in common?" (1). This explosive question begins a study which points out that the composition dates of *Ulysses* enshrined in that novel, 1914–1921, coincide with the dates of "the crucial revolutionary period in modern Irish history" (12). In Chapter Three, Josephine McQuail shows that there is ample evidence that Joyce was shaped by the political and philosophical background which preceded

Modernism: the development of the philosophy of anarchy and the turn-of-the-century debates about Irish politics that are so much a part of *Dubliners* (Joyce 1996/1914) and *Portrait of the Artist as a Young Man* (Joyce 2007/1916). For McQuail, Joyce's anti-nationalism and perceived apoliticism actually coincide with key ideas of the philosophy of anarchism, which many personal statements by Joyce testify he was familiar with. Joyce's well-known early devotion to the works of Ibsen, especially regarding the oppression of women in patriarchy, resembles that of the noted American anarchist Emma Goldman (1869–1940). McQuail suggests that like Goldman, again, Joyce's interest in liberation from proscribed gender roles may be conjectured to have gone farther than conventional heterosexuality, at least imaginatively. That Joyce continually chaffed at borders is indicated by the other part of the phrase that follows Molly Bloom's "Yes": "Trieste-Zürich-Paris" (Joyce 1934/1990, 783). Though Joyce preferred not to be identified with any philosophy or movement, his works prove that he, through his characters, explores key concepts of anarchy, which include suspicion of governments, nations and states, in favor of a philosophy of beneficent individualism.

The libertarian movement in Spain was the largest and most advanced example of political anarchism in history. In his chapter, Michael Gilliland examines the relationship between the historical developments of Spanish anarchism and the literature that sought to represent it. The study looks at Spanish anarchism through its varied representations in 20th Century novels. In particular, three distinct and different works of literature are discussed; each with Spanish anarchists as characters. The first, Vicente Blasco Ibañez's *La bodega*, was published in 1905. The second, *Baza de Espadas* by Ramón del Valle-Inclán, was published in 1932, at the outbreak of the Spanish Revolution. Lastly, *Chaos and Night* by Henri de Montherlant was published in 1963. The varied publishing dates allow for an examination of the way anarchism as a social movement was represented at different points in its development. By examining how the descriptions of Spanish anarchists in literature are related to the actual historical rise and development of the movement, we can more easily understand the obstacles and influences such a movement faced in the larger culture. Today, with the growing influence of anarchist activists in such varied examples as the anti-WTO protests in Seattle in 1999, the Greek uprising in 2008, the Occupy movement, the radical ecology movement, and the workers' control and cooperative movements, it is useful to go back and examine political anarchism by asking how such a vision of radical egalitarianism developed in Spain, what its aspirations were, and what were its successes and failures. The answers to these questions can help explain anarchism's continuing appearance and message on the world scene.

Scott Drake notes that the book is an object that has both a material and an aesthetic existence. As such it cannot be accounted for merely by its thematic content. A central claim Drake makes in Chapter Six is that the material and aesthetic components of a book are related. His essay discusses the relations between these two poles of the field of cultural production through an examination of B. Traven's problematic identity as an author. The obscurity of Traven's identity, Drake claims, is an extension of a fictional aesthetic that emphasizes its collective nature. In short, the Traven name is a decentralized text. But while it is a "text" it also functions as a means to regulate material trade relations. Drake argues that Traven's problematic authorship is best understood, not as a source of individuality, but as a site of struggle for collective forms of cultural production.

Critics often claim that Traven's fiction examines the individual in what might be termed a "primitive" sense—that is as s/he exists outside civilization. Civilization is posed as exerting a corrupting force on the individual. Drake seeks to turn this analysis on its head by suggesting that for Traven existence is defined by its social nature. In *The Treasure of the Sierra Madre*, for example, civilization is the codification of a certain relationship that institutionalizes property theft through the law. The adventure of Dobbs, Curtin, and Howard, in this sense, is not so much outside of civilization, but rather an aspect of cultural production. The story itself is not a story of separate individuals, but instead is about the social relations that define their existence both amongst themselves and in those fields which appear external to their immediate interests. In this sense the individual is not an autonomous individual (as in liberal constructions), but a social relation. Through this social relation, defined as a struggle for power, Traven raises questions regarding how authority and ownership are claimed and asserted.

While liberal discourse reinforces the notion that the source of authority and ownership resides within an individual, the textual aesthetic expressed in Traven's work suggests that as the individual is a site of struggle. There is no truly autonomous individuality that could govern without necessarily being part of another relation. Indeed, the notion of the individual is a recent development of capitalist liberal democracies. For Drake, this matter is complicated by the fact that this discourse gets turned back against Traven's own position as an author who owns a particular material literary property. The construction of Traven's obscurity is an extension of this aesthetic and rather than hiding an authentic individuality, his absence forces the critical reader to see how his own identity is intertwined with the issues of authority and ownership that are central to his fiction. But, the author is not merely a fictional figure; it also has a material existence as a regulator of trade relations. For Drake, Traven's authorship straddles the material and aesthetic components of the field of cultural production. At the same time, in emphasizing the social nature of his own literary production, Traven introduces a form of cultural production that privileges its collective aspect. The form, in this sense, imagines cultural production as a collective process whose source is multiple, rather than returning to the romantic notion of the individual author, which underlies the bourgeois subject.

By the last decades of the twentieth century concerns had shifted. Issues of modernity/postmodernity superseded questions of communism/anti-communism. John Fowles described himself as something of an anarchist. His best known work, *The French Lieutenant's Woman*, is often thought of as a novel that marks the passage from modernism to postmodernism because of its narrative technique. This technique also marks the novel as a symptom of the anarchistic rebellion of the 1960s. The novel is set in the Victorian age when the narrator was thought of as more or less god. However, the narrative technique of John Fowles is more consistent with the anarchistic views of god held by Michael Bakunin. Namely, that god must be thought of as "the freedom that allows other freedoms to exist." In this way, according to Bryan Jones, the novel subverts Marxist thought in a very specific way, one that reflects the culture's growing distrust of the authoritarian thrust of Marxism. In doing so, Jones suggests, Fowles constructs a narrator whose techniques highlight the basic framework of anarchistic thought.

The contemporary subject is constituted along various fault lines or fissures of contestation. Notions of gender, like the individual itself, are constructed outcomes of collective struggle. In contrast to the more traditionally "political" anarchism explored in her early works, Ursula K. Le Guin's corpus since the turn of the millennium has echoed and critically reflected on themes of community, democracy, bottom-up struggle, feminist, anti-oppressive, and anti-colonial practice and direct action, themes that have characterized the "new social movements" widely associated with the recent resurgence of anarchist(ic) thought. In Chapter Eight, Max Haiven suggests we can trace these affinities by identifying Le Guin's work as "prefigurative fiction." This approach takes up the best of the traditions of critical speculative and utopian literature to radically blur present tendencies and future potentialities as an endless provocation, one moved by both an unflinching and holistic criticism of the here-and-now and a mature but unrepentant optimism for the undecidable to-come of human possibility.

Further, Le Guin occupies the space of fiction, the meager terrain left to semi-autonomous, socially constitutive stories, to model and call out for a means of writing beyond the mode of bourgeois subjecthood so central to the co-construction of character, author and reader. Instead, Le Guin's stories, while heavily focused on characters and traditional in their casting of author and reader, highlight the critical interdependency of humanity and the fluid and way people and societies constantly recreate each other, themes germane to an anarchist(ic) politics of immanent potential.

Contemporary networks of activism organize around values of autonomy, affinity, radical equality, anti-oppression, experimental community and democracy, and the mutual rejection of both state and capitalist "solutions" to the palimpsest of ongoing and deepening global crises (economic, ecological, humanitarian, etc.). Further, these movements are characterized by a "prefigurative politics" which, on the basis of these values, actively build the relationships, institutions and networks of the world they demand within and against the world they contest.

Haiven's chapter argues that Le Guin's recent work models a *prefigurative anarchist fiction*. Rather than a literature germane to (neo)liberalist projects of "progress" which mobilize utopian or speculative fiction to scout possible futures for colonization by the present order (even when they intend to do otherwise), Le Guin's recent work prefigures a fiction of human potentiality measured with a depth of compassion which "returns" to work on the present. This approach mirrors recent anarchistic attempts to close the gap between the world of social justice to-come and the practices of bringing that world to birth. Haiven suggests that, like these new social movements, Le Guin's "textual direct action" understands capitalist/state power to be intractably intertwined with other levels of social power relations, especially those bound up in race, class, gender, sexuality, friendship, tradition, culture, everyday life and, especially, social narrative and stories. In the end, what Le Guin models and calls into our world is a complicated and seemingly contradictory figure of the anarchist author as prefigurative practice.

Andrew Taylor Loy describes his essay as a cross-genre pilot study in anarchist thought experiments. Loy does not seek to produce an encyclopedic overview of the emergence or function of anarchism in critical dystopias. He describes his objective as less ambitious: to plot the evolution of each rebellion within its own context. In the end, Loy tries to broaden an understanding of anarchy and anarchism. This is not an understanding that congeals and grows more rigid, but rather one that author hopes expands and flows, nearing a point of superfluidity.

The primary focal points of analysis are Ursula K. Le Guin's novel *The Dispossessed*, the graphic novel *V for Vendetta*, created by Alan Moore and David Lloyd, and the film *The Matrix*, written and directed by the Wachowski Brothers. These texts and film have been selected because they each present disparate versions of anarchistic rebellions. Drawing from Thomas Hughes's characterization of the evolution of large technological systems, Loy analyzes the responses of the various protagonist anarchists in these works to the oppressive components of the respective technological infrastructures with which they are confronted.

The aim of the essay is not to conclude definitely what anarchism is but what it does, how it works within the boundaries of each thought experiment. Ultimately, for Loy, each of these texts is a performance, an acting out of anarchistic ideals embodied in each character's response to the demands of their environment.

The anarchist imagination has a long association with drama and theatrical works. In the penultimate chapter, I examine some of the historic and ongoing connections between anarchism and drama. Major anarchist theorists, such as Emma Goldman and Paul Goodman, wrote extensively on drama as a means of revolutionary communication. Goodman was himself a playwright of some note. The intersection of anarchism and drama is shown significantly in the works of Eugene O'Neill. Indeed anarchism is the primary overtly referenced ideological influence on O'Neill's perspective. While O'Neill initially showed some sympathy for social anarchist movements, and looked favorably upon the writings of prominent social anarchist Emma Goldman, his primary personal commitment was to philosophical anarchism, which remained the greatest ideological influence on his thinking. Beyond the works of individual playwrights one can also point to the thriving anarchist community theatres and collective practices such as those of the Living Theatre.

In the final chapter Michelle Campbell utilizes Octavia E. Butler's science fiction trilogy *Xenogenesis* (1987–1989) to develop the beginnings of a theory of post-anarchist feminism (PAF). Campbell, like others in this volume (Haiven and Loy especially) argues that science fiction, as a genre, is particularly apt at describing and portraying radical change. This is certainly because the genre conventions, unlike regular fiction, do not require the author to stay within the realm of what has happened; rather, the author is able to branch out into what could have happened in the past or what could happen in the future. Thus, SF is perfect for experimenting with social conventions and constrictions, for questioning the way things are and the way they could or should be. Using the *Xenogenesis* trilogy as proof-texts, Campbell brings a range of anarchist and gender theories as well as analyses to bear on the alternative world that this author creates.

Butler's trilogy examines a post apocalyptic world in which main characters learn to navigate oppression and forge new identities. Butler's post-nuclear earth is repopulated by human-alien hybrids, which brings to light questions of human nature. Each of the three books follows a different main character, and they each bring new questions and considerations to the table. In *Dawn* (1987), Lilith brings forth questions of agency, manipulation, and the role of traditions of Western thought in subverting relations. Akin adds critical components concerning productive power, resistance, and ontology in *Adulthood Rites* (1988). Finally, in the last book *Imago* (1989), Jodahs creates a space for considering the construction of gender for reproductive means. The narratives of the texts help the reader to consider challenges and opportunities for radical change such as power relations, hierarchy, commodification, informed consent, and reproduction as it relates to constructions of gender. As such, Campbell argues that post-anarchist feminism can help us to consider gender, sex, and sexuality as possibilities for revolution, resistance, subversion, and other radical actions.

Conclusions

In some ways the literary imagination always expresses uniqueness— the creativity of producers. Literary production maintains a certain quality of production for use—of meaning to the producer. These are elements of human activity that are central to anarchist theory. Anarchists stress the cooperative and social aspects of human creativity as a counter to dualisms of society and individual that are presented within capitalist cultures. Against mass production for exchange anarchists tend to see value in more artisanal forms of production for use (though anarchists also argue for worker and community control over mass production for use).

A period of elite rule and market nomination, as under neoliberalism, stifles real individuality as production for exchange dictates uniformity for mass markets. Even individualism itself becomes a mass product. So too rebellion—as in the mass production of images of Che Guevara or the anarchist "circle-A." For Goldman: "The individual educator imbued with honesty of purpose, the artist or writer of original ideas, the independent scientist or explorer, the non-compromising pioneers of social changes are daily pushed to the wall by men whose learning and creative ability have become decrepit with age" (71).

The creative artist too is confronted with the market—publishers and critics concerned predominantly with good sales. The chief literary output becomes output for the market. For the anarchist artist the general fate has been either undue obscurity (as in Kristyn Dunnion or Jim Munroe) or, if one becomes famous, an obscuring of the anarchism in their work (as in Eugene O'Neill or Alan Moore).

A key component of anarchist perspectives is the belief that means and ends must correspond. Thus in anarchist literature as in anarchist politics, a radical approach to form is as important as content. Anarchist literature joins other critical approaches to creative production in attempting to break down divisions between readers and writer, audience and artist, encouraging all to become active participants in the creative process.

Anarchist gatherings, conferences and book fairs regularly include workshops on DIY publishing. Typically such workshops are put on in the neighborhoods (often literally in the streets) in which such gatherings are held. An examination of constructive anarchist projects, in which literature is part of a holistic approach to everyday resistance, provides insights into dreams, desires and concerns of those who pursue alternative worldviews. In this literary production plays a rich part, as brief look at ongoing anarchist histories show.

Kropotkin argues that in Russia literature was the manner for expressing underground political views and intellectual development. Literary criticism and literature (novels, poems, satire) formed the media for communicating ideals and aspirations. In this, literature was more central than explicitly political writings, policy tracts, and polemics. For this, the literary producers, poets, and novelists were exiled, imprisoned, and put to hard labor. Such was the fate of entire generations. Others lived constantly under this threat.

The threat of persecution persists in the neoliberal democracies of the twenty-first century (see Shantz 2012). In Seattle, activists involved with an anarchist bookstore and book fair have been arrested simply for possessing anarchist literature. They face lengthy prison terms. This in a supposed liberal democracy in the year 2012. In the present period, literature still faces what Kropotkin referred to as "the strokes of the censor" and the menaces of...[the] State's police" (viii).

Where political life closes and people are not called upon or equipped to take a real, active part in the shaping of social institutions, literature will exercise an influence—beyond political writings or policy briefs—in the popular social imagination. Literature and criticism become media for expressing aspirations, social visions, and opposition to current social and political relationships. It is to works of creative production rather than newspapers that one must go to understand political, social, and economic ideals.

Jeff Shantz

Surrey, B.C. (Coast Salish Territories)

References

Drinnon, Richard. "Introduction." *Anarchism and other Essays*. New York: Dover, 1969.

Goldman, Emma. *Anarchism and other Essays*. New York: Dover, 1969.

Kropotkin, Peter. *Russian Literature: Ideals and Realities*. Montreal: Black Rose, 1991.

Shantz, Jeff, ed. *Protest and Punishment: The Repression of Resistance in the Era of Neoliberal Globalization*. Durham: Carolina Academic Press, 2012.

Woodcock, George. "Introduction." *Russian Literature: Ideals and Realities*. Montreal: Black Rose, 1991.

1. WILDE AND THE VICTORIAN MOULD: THE ARTIST'S INDIVIDUALISM THROUGH ANARCHY

Agathe Brun

Oscar Wilde was one of the few who knew a world-wide fame as well as a world-wide disgrace. Condemned for homosexual practices, this genius of art served as a scapegoat in a society rul ed by codes and morals. In Victorian age and even more during the fin de siècle period, the extraordinary and unconventional Oscar Wilde turned out to be a kind of symbol of decay—in the eyes of some—at the centre of a well-ordered and conventional world.

On reading biographies about Wilde or recent fictions such as Gyles Brandreth's *Oscar Wilde and the Candlelight Murders*, we can think about something of interest about Wilde that appears in most writings about him: Wilde was famous during his life and everyone knew his skills as a poet, playwright, aesthete and much more. Oscar was everywhere, he was invited in the salons and everyone longed to meet him. This specific aspect of the man seems in contradiction with the idea that he could have something to do with anarchy. And yet, his first play, *Vera*, deals with the fate of Russian anarchists and their czar... How could someone apparently much loved and admired be an anarchist? In fact, the question is not so much about his links with anarchists but his love for freedom of thought and individualism

In most of his writings, Oscar Wilde directly or indirectly questions the legitimacy of Victorian codes and beliefs. The nineteenth century was indeed the century of sudden and great changes: industrialization had brought along a helpless urbanization that endangered economic and social balance. Cities were growing too fast and turned out to be less and less wealthy and healthy.

Pauperism set in; cities became insane and inadequate to the growth of population. Housing, security, hygiene, employment, everything showed the limitations and flaws of the Empire. In this context, Nature was praised and symbolized re-birth and the origins of life. But Oscar Wilde thought different, as he always did. For all time, man has tried to create comfort and security for himself and his fellow creatures, why would he now reject all these efforts and progress in order to bask in ignorance and the discomfort of Nature. In *The Decay of Lying*, Oscar Wilde announces his own theory of art to offer a very disturbing idea: in substance, Art is an expression of man's mind and Nature is without imagination, therefore Nature can only copy the creations of Art. But this rebellion against Nature is not the most important step in Wilde's criticism. In *The Picture of Dorian Gray*, he shows his love for beauty and youth through the relationship between Basil Hallward, Lord Henry Wotton and Dorian Gray. Doing so, Wilde highlights the eternal weakness of men: going by appearances. Dorian's beauty and youth give him whatever he wants but his soul is lost and the stupidity of people around him is revealed.

Wilde has been largely satirized in the press: Wilde the dandy at the centre of a sunflower or Wilde the delicate Irishman holding at arm's length a Stetson from his American tour... Dandy, aesthete, the artist Wilde aroused admiration then disgust, he was loved then despised and fell from the highest spheres of society to the darkest spheres of Dante's hell. That is why no reader can have an interest in English or Irish literature without reading the works of the one who has been regarded as a genius during his lifetime and is now having his image restored after having been the scapegoat of Victorianism. But we can wonder what stirs up that keen interest for Oscar Wilde? We may attribute it to his accurate analysis of society, his caustic irony and eloquence. Or maybe the long-lasting of his success is due to his much contentious life and sexual practices? But if his life and brilliant conversation were the only reason for his fame, then why read his works and not just biographies?

The reason why it is so rewarding to study Wilde's life and art in the light of anarchism is that he seemed to go against all rules and conventions: in the Preface to *The Picture of Dorian Gray*, he explains that morals can't be talked about concerning literature and that Art is useless and has nothing to do with rules; in his *Maxims*, he gives advice to the young against all that they can learn elsewhere; in *The Decay of Lying*, he praises Art and Imagination to the expense of Mother Nature and the belief in universal truth, in *The Soul of Man under Socialism*, he praises individualism by putting man at the centre of all things; in *De Profundis*, he even calls Christ the "supreme individualist", etc. Everywhere in Wilde's writings, opposition, contradiction and rebellion prevail even though it always remains poetic and witty.

From Height to Hell, the Atypical Life and Career of Oscar Wilde

A Brilliant Ascent

Few artists can boast to have known fame during their lifetime; especially such an exceptional fame as that of Wilde. he makes it clear in *De Profundis* that he was indeed an exceptional being: "The gods had given me almost everything. I had genius, a distinguished name, high social position, brilliancy, intellectual daring: [...] there was nothing I said or did that did not make people wonder: [...] I awoke the imagination of my century so that it created myth and legend around me" (Wilde 1017). In his biography of Wilde, Franck Harris explains that "the conditions of English society being what they are, it is but impossible at first to account for the rapidity of Oscar Wilde's social success" (Harris 102). Indeed, Victorian society doesn't give many opportunities to young talented men or if it does they must wait a long time to reap the benefits of their efforts. Fame in England awaits at the end of a long and exhausting journey and Wilde's lightning ascent is quite a feat: "The road up to power or influence in England is full of pitfalls and far too arduous for those who have neither high birth nor wealth to help them" (Harris 102). If Oscar Wilde didn't really have high birth in the sense that his father was not heir of his title but was knighted by the Queen in 1864, he was the son of a famous Irish family and his social status was quite enviable. In fact, Wilde held all the cards to take a good start in the world: his father, Sir William Robert Wills Wilde was the Queen's eye and ear surgeon, and his mother, known under the pseudonym of Speranza, was an activist poetess who fought for the Irish cause. Later, in jail, deprived of name and freedom, he writes in *De Profundis*: "She [my mother] and my father had bequeathed me a name they had made noble and honoured not merely in Literature, Art, Archaeology and Science, but in the public history of my own country in its evolution as a nation" (Wilde 1010).

As a matter of fact, the son of Sir Wilde and Speranza used his artistic genius, his atypical aspect and charisma to create a myth around him. As Harris states it: "From the beginning he set himself to play the game of the popular actor, and neglected no opportunity of turning the limelight on his own doings" (Harris 103). Nowadays, his plays are staged, his novel read, as well as his poems and essays; but we also know the man because of his tragic fate. Therefore, it seems quite impossible to study Wilde's famous writings without taking into account his exceptional life. As a young man, Wilde had already decided that his life was to be public and his name famous. The importance of fame seems to be a recurrent idea in Wilde's life. Trying to be famous in a very conventional society and at the same time criticizing moral values and strictness appear rather contradictory at first and yet Wilde managed to be the idol of this Victorian world. Oscar expresses this vivid desire for fame, notoriety and admiration in *The Picture of Dorian Gray* through Lord Henry Wotton's speech. During Henry and Dorian's first meeting, the former explains that beauty is all that matters as far as—being a form of genius—it allows one to attain a high rank in society. Lord Henry whispers in Dorian's ear: "You have a wonderful beautiful face, Mr. Gray. [...] And Beauty is a form of Genius—is higher, indeed, than Genius, as it needs no explanation. [...] It has its divine right to sovereignty. It makes princes of those who have it" (Wilde 31). As the mentor explains, youth and beauty are everything because they secure for their owner the best seat within society. And what is true about Dorian's beauty in the novel seems true about Wilde's life and art. Since his youth, Wilde had expressed a strong desire for fame. When asked by a friend of his what he wanted to do when an adult, he answered:

> God knows, I won't be an Oxford don anyhow. I'll be a poet, a writer, a dramatist. Somehow or other I'll be famous; and if not famous, I'll be notorious. Or perhaps I'll lead a life of pleasure for a time and then—who knows?—rest and do nothing. What does Plato say is the highest end that man can attain here below? To sit down and contemplate the good. Perhaps that will be the end of me too. (Morley 31)[1]

Actually, we can't deny that the myth of the dandy that surrounded him throughout the evolution of his character certainly gave even more weight to his words. It is well-known that Wilde has been said to have walked down Piccadilly with a sunflower in his hand.[2] He didn't disprove it at first and stated later that to know for sure whether he had actually done it or not was of no importance, but to make people believe it could happen was the real success of the myth. As we can clearly see through this famous example, Wilde was an alien in a world of conventions; yet, he was famous and admired. Some said that his written words were a very pale mirror of his brilliant conversation. Franck Harris mentions that "even as a schoolboy he was an excellent talker" (Harris 24). Talkative, fascinating, the pale-skinned giant slowly became a reference in art and a prince of words. Letters and

---

1 This famous quotation can be found in many other biographies of Wilde, for instance in Ellmann's: "I'll be famous, and if not famous, I'll be notorious" (Ellmann 46).
2 Cf. "the gentleman who wore long hair and carried a sunflower down Piccadilly" (Ellmann 208).

testimonies from that period show what a major figure of Victorian society he was.

Controversy of the Dandy with a Sunflower in his Hand

However, we must not regard his life as a *sine qua non* of his fame. Some of his contemporaries and so-called "friends" have criticized his lack of skills and his being a dandy and a poser. Wilde himself is said to have commented upon his own conduct: "I've put my genius into my life; I've put only my talent into my works,"[1] and Edmund Gosse, in his correspondence with Gide in 1910 wrote: "Of course he was not a 'great writer'... his works, taken without his life, present to a sane criticism, a mediocre figure". In the same manner, Merlin Holland in his introduction to the 1994 edition of the *Complete Works of Oscar* Wilde notes that "Arnold Bennett in 1927 treats him as outmoded and his style as lacking in permanence but grudgingly concedes 'Wilde, even if he was not a first rate writer, had given keen pleasure to simpletons such as my younger self; and he was a first rate figure" (Holland, in Wilde 1). It leads John Sloan to the following comment:

> Oscar Wilde is still widely considered to be a writer of clever but ultimately superficial works whose genius lay in his personality and conversation. This view of Wilde as a gifted raconteur whose writings are a pale and mediocre version of the witty conversation was already current in his lifetime. (Sloan 99)

Of course, such an exceptional being could but stir up jealousy and misunderstanding; and the economical and political situation of the country deepened the gap between Wilde and his detractors. Indeed, at the end of the 19th century, the British Empire seemed to be at its peak: it was a great economic power and could pride itself on having the largest and richest colonies of all. But this ideal situation could not last forever; the Boer Wars—which took place from 1880 to 1881 and from 1899 to 1902—revealed the weaknesses of the Empire. Britain was less strong than in the past and its cohesion was more than questionable. At that point eugenicists denounced the frail constitution of men who were rejected from the army because they were not fit for the service. The British Empire was losing prestige because the nation had fewer men who were able to fight for it. Later in the text, the philanthropist Lord Brabazon, in *Thoughts on Imperial and Social Subjects* (1906) writes that 75% of the men who offered were rejected sooner or later from the Army's ranks. As he points out: "It cannot be denied that these facts point to a most serious condition of the affairs, threatening the very foundations

---

1 Translation from André Gide, *Oscar Wilde: In Memoriam*, 7th edition, Paris : Mercure de France, 1947, 12: "J'ai mon génie dans ma vie, mais je n'ai mis que mon talent dans mes œuvres."

of British social, commercial, and national life." The Boer War revealed something about the Empire that no one wanted to know: Britain was in danger; it was no longer competitive as a great world-power. It was weak; it was crowded with unfit people and unable to defend itself against the raising powers, such as the United States or Germany. Due to industrialization, cities were crowded and unsanitary, pauperism and disease were worrying issues. Eugenics rushed into the breach at a time when people needed to believe again in the strength of the nation. "Degeneration," the term was launched and made the effect of a bomb in Victorian society: some men were unfit; they had defects... for example men who loved men.

Consequently, when Lord Queensberry challenged Wilde with frequent assaults of vulgarity and Wilde finally retorted, the artist's fate was already sealed: the dandy Wilde with his extravagant look and extravagant writings would be the scapegoat of Victorian Puritanism and fear. Because of his love for youth and Greek beauty, his ceaseless efforts to denounce morals and the wrong place of the artist, Oscar Wilde was the perfect victim for a show trial. His fame and following fall then don't seem to derive mere accident or bad luck but rather from his being such an extra-ordinary—in the very literal meaning of the word—being and extra-ordinary writer. As Kohl notices:

> Any critic dealing with the life and works of Oscar Wilde will realise right from the start that his subject was not only an author but, to his contemporaries and also to succeeding generations, an outstanding personality on the English cultural scene of the late nineteenth century. He was ostracised and forced into exile by the guardians of tradition, cast by the liberals in the role of the martyred artist, victimised by puritan prudes and Pharisees, dismissed by literary historians as a brilliant epigon caught between the Victorian Age and modern times, and smugly classified by the critics as a first-class representative of the second division. And yet his works are always in print, his books and bought and read, and his plays are continually being produced. (Kohl 1)

First Commitments: An Ambiguity of Feelings

We have just wrote that Wilde's trials had something to do with his writings but up to now, his writing success only had been mentioned. Thinking about politically and socially committed artists, one would rarely mention Wilde. Even though his mother, Speranza, spent her life fighting for the cause of Ireland, Oscar has rarely shown, in his most known writings, an immense sense of rebellion for the Irish cause. His Irish origins gave him pride but we wouldn't read Wilde's writings in search of political lines. At least, this is the usual view on Wilde's work for the occasional reader of *Dorian Gray* or spectator of *An Ideal Husband*. Indeed, in the non-academic world, his writings are synonymous of laugh and wit. As Merlin Holland puts it in his introduction to the last part of the *Collins Complete Works of Oscar Wilde*, "seriousness and Wilde for the most of his non-academic readers are laughably incompatible" (Holland, in Wilde 907). Nevertheless, Wilde is now regaining the image of an serious writer whose social and political ideas equaled his skills as a poet, playwright and novelist. John Sloan writes about this matter: "Since the 1960s there had been a significant revaluation of Wilde's life and work. In particular, Wilde's writings have been recognized as deeply resonant with the main social questions of the day—anarchy and socialism, poverty and privilege, feminism and gender, imperialism, and prison reform" (Sloan 99).

At the beginning of his career, Oscar Wilde expressed his personal questioning about politics in his poems. "Wilde's political radicalism might easily be dismissed as an artistic pose, as a romantic and emotional rather than a genuinely political commitment. His politics were unquestionably complex and contradictory" (Sloan 100). Indeed, that a young man from a well-off and notorious family should turn towards anarchy all of a sudden is quite inconceivable and we can clearly feel in Wilde's poems a genuine political commitment that vacillates between a desire to free people from monarchical system and an instinctive appeal towards conservatism.

Wilde's Faith in the Empire

Who could best answer the question of Wilde's political convictions than Wilde himself? Mary Watson in 1882, in *The Daily Examiner*[1] reports Wilde's words: "If you would like to know my political creed, read the sonnet *Libertatis Sacra Fames.*"

> Albeit nurtured in democracy,
> And liking best that state republican
> Where every man is Kinglike and no man
> Is crowned above his fellows, yet I see,
> Spite of this modern fret for Liberty,
> Better the rule of One, whom all obey,
> Than the clamorous demagogues betray
> Our freedom with the kiss of anarchy.
> Wherefore I love them not whose hands profane
> Plant the red flag upon the piled-up street
> For no right cause, beneath whose ignorant
> Arts, Culture, Reverence, Honour, all things fade,

---

1 *The Daily Examiner*, San Francisco, March 27, 1882.

> Save Treason and the dagger of her trade,
> And murder with his silent bloody feet. (Wilde 858)

The first verses highlight the ideal of democracy and of equality among men, with the words "every men," "no man," "fellows," and the comparison with the malfunctioning of a monarchy where one is "above." But the end of the fourth verse shows a reversal of ideas and Wilde's ambiguity of feelings: "yet," the fear brought along by the ideas of anarchy leads to an instinctive return towards monarchy. The very first word of the text is also a clue to understand the poem: "albeit," which clearly indicates that Wilde is questioning his political convictions. Anarchy is here shown as the evil system that deprives man of freedom. The poem, whose title translated from the Latin means "The Sacred Hunger for Freedom," points out the risks that lay in anarchy: to Wilde, "the clamorous demagogues" turn towards anarchy and therefore betray the people's need for freedom. In the poem, anarchy is contemplated from a very pessimistic point of view: the "red flag" represents oppression and is violently planted "upon the piled-up streets." Oscar Wilde despises demagogues because their charming words lack meaning and are void of any kind of cause to fight for. Under the mask of anarchy, treason and murder awaits man; the words "dagger" and "blood" suggest once more the violence brought in by anarchy that would eradicate all that Wilde believes in. There is an accumulation of terms linked to intellectual skills and qualities valued by the artist: "Arts, Culture, Reverence, Honor." Thus appears in this text Wilde's perplexity towards his own interests. As John Sloan puts it: "The clash between republican sympathies and fear of violence return him to a conservative resolution" (Sloan 100). Wilde admits this ambiguity and if the poem begins with a clearly stated admiration for democracy, the fear of how it could be dragged into anarchy prevails.

This hesitation is to be found in many of Oscar Wilde poems. In the 53rd stanza of "Humanitad" for instance, Anarchy is compared to "Freedom's own Judas, the vile prodigal / Licence who steals the gold of Liberty" (Wilde 823). Condemned for its violence, ignorance, anarchy is seen as a fast moving devastating force devoid of knowledge and intelligence. Blind with rage and deaf to the people's need for tolerance, freedom, art and culture, it sweeps away will and hope before itself. The reference to Judas is a reminder of the previous poem where anarchy performs in silence and relies on treason.

Even in *Vera or the Nihilists*, Wilde's first play in 1879—and a rather unsuccessful one—violent anarchism, that annihilates, kills, destroys furiously, is embodied by Michael: he is a kind of storm that Vera only can stop and sees no point in trying to understand Alexis's point of view. On the contrary, the young Alexis is a prince, well-behaved, brave and sensible. Using two consecutive lines of dialogue which are written in mirror, Wilde emphasizes the contrast between the two men: "Alexis: It shall not be while I have a tongue to plead with. / Michael: Or while I have hands to smite with." (Wilde 689). Both want to prevent the czar from signing the martial law order but where the former wants to use diplomacy, the latter shows the violent—and prevailing—side of his personality.

The Giant with Feet of Clay: When the Empire Fails to Meet Expectations

If Wilde appears to despise anarchy in "Libertatis Sacra Fames," he has nonetheless a very critical look upon monarchy as well. When we read "Quantum mutate," the artist's resentment leaves no doubt.

> How comes it then that from such high estate
> We have thus fallen, save that Luxury
> With barren merchandise piles up the gate
> Where noble thoughts and deeds should enter by. (Wilde 774)

Even though this critic is not directly aimed at the monarchy, it has to do with the evil brought along by industrialization and capitalism. The bourgeoisie is harshly criticized because it confuses what one has with one what is, as Wilde explains later in *The Soul of Man under Socialism*. Luxury, abundant as it is of no value, keeps off "noble thoughts and deeds." The title of that poem, "Quantum Mutata," means "how much changed" and this is precisely what Wilde regards as a shame: not only has society fallen into capitalism and consumer society but it has also pulled down the whole system of monarchy which is not as strong as it used to be. The opening verse "There was a time in Europe long ago" (Wilde 773) shows the nostalgia of the artist who misses the brilliant past of England because "It was so / While England could a great Republic show" (Wilde 774). Capitalism is also denounced in "Theoretikos" where Wilde insists upon the fact "day by day / Wisdom and Reverence are sold at mart" in "this vile traffic-house" (Wilde 776). Still the same values of wisdom and reverence are mentioned showing Wilde's strong attachment to a certain social position where education is of the utmost importance.

Then we can see that Wilde's poetry contain much critic and questioning. Van de Kamp and Leahy draw this conclusion out of their own study of the poems: "He centres in these poems on the sense of loss of cultural values, on the deprivation of pleasure in modern society and on the debilitating authority of supply and demand" (Van de Kamp and Leahy 149). If his personal convictions are not formed yet, his expression of it is quite a denunciation of both parts: capitalism and present government for their loss of values and pride; anarchism for its violence and bloody means.

If Wilde's poems throw light on his ambiguous feelings concerning politics; his very first play is also quite telling about it. In *Vera, or the Nihilists*, tyranny and violence are not the prerogative of one specific part. The czar is an old man who knows nothing about his people and who would kill anyone on his way, even his son if he had to. Vera describes him and the other representatives of the State as: "A few old men, wrinkled, feeble, tottering dotards whom a boy could strangle for a ducat, or a woman stab in a night-time" (Wilde 690). On hearing that Vera is in Moscow, he seems to go mad and starts a soliloquy about treason and death a part of which we would like to comment upon:

> O God, were it not better to die at once the dog's death they plot for me than to live as I live now! Never to sleep, or, if I do, to dream such horrid dreams that hell itself were peace when matched with them. To trust none but those I have bought, to buy none worth trusting! To see a traitor in every smile, poison in every dish, a dagger in every hand! To lie awake at night, listening from hour to hour for the stealthy creeping of the murderer, for the laying of the damned mine! You are all spies! You are all spies! You worst of all—you, my own son! (Wilde 701)

In this passage, Wilde offers a particularly relevant idea of the dark side of power. The "father of the people" can only feel anger, hatred and fear. At no point does he question his own actions or the reason why he is the target of the Nihilists. He lives in the fear of death, in the fear of his own son's treason. He represents the despised monarch whose sole purpose is to possess: gold, land... he's got it all and yet doesn't even live for pleasure as he always lie in wait for enemies.

As for Michael, he is the perfect embodiment of the form of anarchy that Wilde denounces in "Libertatis Sacra Fames": he is violent, ready to kill his fellow creatures and to spread blood all over Russia. It is hardly imaginable that this blood-thirsty brute and regicide is the man we saw in the first lines of the play. At the beginning of the play, Michael appears as a young farmer quite devoid of animosity, he is in love with Vera and later use this argument to lead her to achieve her duty towards the anarchists and the people. He explains that he joined the Nihilists because it was Vera's will and he loved her:

> You wrote me to follow you her. I did so; first because I loved you; but you soon cured me of that; whatever gentle feeling, whatever pity, whatever humanity, was in my heart you withered up and destroyed, as the canker worm eats the corn, and the plague kills the child. You bade me cast out love from my breast as a vile thing, you turned my

hand to iron, and my heart to stone; you told me to live for freedom and for revenge. I have done so; but you, what have you done? (Wilde 712).

Once a man, he is now a kind of beast. Love is compared to "canker worm" and "plague" that destroy and kill. Yet, what we could read from the Nihilists' oath is much more frightening: poisoning, killing a night, suffering... Michael has turned into a beast and is now as cold as death: iron and stone have replaced hand and heart. The Nihilists' creed, "to annihilate" (Wilde 686), reveals their true nature: rather than pondering on what they should do after the czar's death, the Nihilists hurry towards the object of their hatred in a fit of blind anger. They are no longer able to decide what is right and what their aim is. They want to have the power and once they have it through the intermediary of the czarevitch, they still want to kill him. They don't even seem to notice that the czar is not Ivan but Alexis; to them, both are alike because they belong to monarchy. Their oath shows their complete lack of humanity; though they try to free their fellow creatures, they turn into beasts:

> To strangle whatever nature is in us; neither to love nor to be loved, neither to pity nor to be pitied, neither to marry nor to be given in marriage, till the end is come; to stab secretly at night; to drop poison in the glass; to set father against son, and husband against wife; without fear, without hope, without future, to suffer, to annihilate, to revenge. (Wilde 687).

In the oath we can find no political conviction, no mentioning of a definite enemy but just an enumeration of violent actions, destruction and even self destruction as Nihilism is supposed to deny individualism and deprived of all human feelings. Once the czar is dead and the czarevitch is the new leader, they decide to kill him though he has expressed his strong desire to help the people. Vera is the only one who understands something because she has failed to follow anarchist rules: "neither to love nor to be loved." She is in love, and this love draws her towards a certain awareness of the issue. She is able to analyze the situation properly because from the beginning she listens to her heart: she wanted to talk to the prisoners when she lived at her father's inn, she decides to avenge her brother, she is the leader of anarchists, she has wit and ponders the situation. Nevertheless, she is a monster too because she has changed Michael into a monster. On the contrary, Alexis is wise and devoted. He looks like a kind of Prince Kropotkin, "a man with a soul of that beautiful white Christ which seems coming out of Russia" (Wilde 1038), whose influence on Wilde's political thoughts can't be denied. He is the czarevitch and yet, his education led him to take a fresh look at his position, his social rank and his obligations towards the people.

In *Vera, or the Nihilists,* Wilde makes a vivid testimony of his faith in freedom. However, the portrait he makes of the nihilists is quite negative: after the death of the czar, the nihilists keep on thinking about a revolution even though the new czar is one of them and longs to change the political context of his country. The anarchists remain somehow solemnly bound to their faith: monarchy is hell, anarchy is freedom. In this sense, their blind action against the new, good-hearted czar shows them in a very bad light. In the play, no one is spared, neither the monarchical representatives, nor the anarchists.

The Evils of Property

Poverty and Slavery as the Children of Property-Holding System

In *The Soul of Man under Socialism,* Wilde develops at length his conception of socialism. The working out of this essay takes roots in Wilde's admiration for George Bernard Shaw's vision of socialism. Shaw told that when he asked British artists to sign a petition against the hanging of four American anarchists, Wilde was the only one who met his demand.[1] The reason why he signed might have something to do with the feeling he expresses at the end of "Sonnet to Liberty": "These Christs that die upon the barricades, / God knows it I am with them, in some things" (Wilde 859). They seemed to have quite the same conception of what socialism should be. Then, after a meeting in Westminster where Shaw commented upon his view on socialism, Wilde decided—Robert Ross reports—to gives his opinion about the same topic and to reveal his utopian conception of society. As we can see, Wilde was not the first one to tackle with this issue and he has certainly been influenced by many of his contemporaries who played their role in a definition of socialism, anarchism and individualism as well as gave their opinion concerning burning issues such as gender, imperialism, privilege... and poverty which is the first point we are going to develop.

When we read *The Soul of Man under Socialism,* what strikes us first is Wilde's self-confidence: the writer doesn't seem to have the faintest doubt about the coherence of his theory. To him, property is at the origin of misfortune in Victorian society. To him, poverty is a tragedy but it is wrongly treated: "the majority of people spoil their lives by an unhealthy and exaggerated altruism", Wilde writes, "They find themselves surrounded by hideous poverty, by hideous ugliness, by hideous starvation" (Wilde 1174).

---

1 "In the sphere of political action, Wilde, according to Shaw, was the 'only name' outside of direct socialist circles to sign a petition for the reprieve of four Chicago anarchists sentenced to death in 1886" (Sloan 102).

What is criticized here is the altruistic attitude of men and women who try to give some reason for living to the poor and disadvantaged. It sounds rather disturbing at first in our modern society where solidarity prevails to read such a comment; and yet, Wilde is not the first one who rejects the benefits of altruism. Morris before him had expressed his opinion as follows: "a rich man cannot give to a poor one without both being the worse for it" (Morris 181). Wilde echoes Morris to explain that "the people who do most harm are the people who try to do most good" and adds with a touch of irony: "They try to solve the problem of poverty, for instance, by keeping the poor alive; or, in the case of a very advanced school, by amusing the poor" and draws to the conclusion that "charity creates a multitude of sins" (Wilde 1174). But no poverty would exist under Socialism: the abolition of property Wilde expects would solve the problem by bringing back equality among men. No property, no unsatisfied need or desire. "Socialism would relieve us from that sordid necessity of living for others which [...] presses so hardly upon almost everybody" (Wilde 1174). As a consequence of the abolition of property, men would not have to beg if they are poor or to keep all the destitute afloat if they are rich. The reason why society is so unfair relies upon its being based on a capitalist scheme: workers are overexploited and the system of supply and demand enriches the rich and starves the poor. Once more, we can find in Morris's thought the origin of that of Wilde: "There are people who work so hard that they may be said to do nothing else than work. [...] It is clear that this inequality presses heavily upon the 'working' class, and must visibly tend to destroy their hope of rest at least, and so, in that particular make them worse off than mere beasts of the field" (Morris 100). The word "beasts" is quite significant; far from elevating man, capitalist society digs the gap between classes and turns those who suffer into mere animals. This word is so meaningful that Wilde uses it too when he explains:

> There are a great many people who, having no private property of their own, and being always on the brink of sheer starvation, are compelled to do the work of beasts of burden, to do work that is quite uncongenial to them, and to which they are forced by the peremptory, unreasonable, degrading Tyranny of want. These are the poor; among them there is no grace of manner, or charm of speech, or civilization or culture, or refinement in pleasures, or joy of life. [...] the man who is poor is in himself absolutely of no importance. He is merely the infinitesimal atom of a force that, so far from regarding him, crushes him: indeed, prefers him crushed, as in that case he is far more obedient. (Wilde 1175)

But once "crushed," nothing differentiates the poor from the slaves. Poverty "driven below a certain limit means degradation and slavery pure and simple" (Morris 183). If the poor are the victims of capitalism and can do nothing but work all their life long and feel no pleasure or relief, the slaves, even if there are no slaves in the usual sense of this term at that time in England, are their part to play too. "The fact is, that civilisation requires slaves" (Wilde 1183). He follows Morris's idea that: "our society includes a great mass of slaves, who must be fed, clothed, housed and amused as slaves, and [...] their daily necessity compels them to make slave-wares whose use is the preparation of their slavery" (Morris 104). These slaves are the poor who besides living under bad conditions and have to work for the rich. But neither Morris nor Wilde encourage the reader to an action against those revolting lives of theirs. Instead, Wilde repeats that the more the rich help the poor or the slaves, the more they destroy any hope of improving society. He gives the example of slavery and its abolishment: to him the Abolitionists brought more trouble than relieved it. "When at the close of the war the slaves found themselves free, found themselves indeed so absolutely free that they were free to starve, many of them bitterly regretted the new state of things" (Wilde 1177).

The Question of Crime

The critical state the poor undergo is due to the evils of government and this is what leads some of them to become criminals. Wilde believes that as they have no money, it is what they want most: "There is only one class in the community that thinks more about money than the rich, and that is the poor. The poor can think of nothing else" (Wilde 1180). Even if this sentence can sound a little bit ironical, it is still written in a text arguing his point and developing the main aspects of his theory. Wilde comments on what he believes to be the cause of most crimes and then he explains how to get rid of crime in society. Human beings who make up their mind to steal, for instance, are drawn to this bitter end because of "Tyranny of want", because of need. Therefore, "what are called criminals nowadays are not criminals at all. Starvation, and not sin, is the parent of modern crime. [...] [criminals] are merely what ordinary respectable, commonplace people would be if they had not got enough to eat" (Wilde 1182). Because they lack the most necessary things to live, the poor are almost forced to do it.

But if the need is the cause of crime, it is the consequence of the malaise imposed by the economical system: "Though a crime may not be against property, it may spring from the misery and rage and depression produced by our wrong system of property-holding." As a consequence, Oscar Wilde finds a solution to this long-lasting injustice: the abolition of property. And this is his creed from that moment till the end. To him, "when private property is abolished there will be no necessity for crime, no demand for it; it will cease to exist" (Wilde 1182). And he develops his idea with a new argument: punishment is an easy way but not the solution to criminality; on the contrary, it makes it worse. Wilde puts forward an alternate solution that strengthens his idea about property and socialism: if punishment doesn't dissuade criminals, it is of no use. The author even goes further in his analysis and links crime to punishment in a quite unusual way: "It obviously follows that the more punishment is inflicted the more crime is produced" so that "the less punishment, the less crime" (Wilde 1182). Wilde's ideas are not entirely new and he owes much to other writers, and yet, his manner of outlining his view shows that he believes strongly in his socialism. Wilde wants to get rid of property, to free society from the oppressive restraints of capitalism. He adds that crime is not only a question of need but can also find roots in many other reasons that all derive from property. "Jealousy, which is an extraordinary source of crime in modern life, as an emotion closely bound up with our conceptions of property, and under Socialism and Individualism will die out" (Wilde 1183).

Moreover, Wilde does not mention it but to reuse Pierre-Joseph Proudhon's famous words: "Property is Theft." Two different interpretations can be given to this sentence, in the light of Wilde's socialism. Propriety, created by civilization, has no legitimacy other than what man gives to it. Therefore, it steals what should belong to the whole community. Property is illegitimate as it comes from human laws. The second interpretation would lead us to consider that thief is a consequence of property.

The Proper Use of Machinery

Following Morris, Wilde adds that the poor, the slaves, the destitute could live better lives had they not to earn money and support a family. Quite often, what they do to survive are inhuman tasks, degrading for them and for those who forces them to do so. If industrialization is the root of all that is ugly, as Wilde explains in *The Soul of Man*, still it can be useful as long as it is used to relieve man from unsatisfying tasks. Morris explains:

> I want modern science, which I believe capable of overcoming all material difficulties, to turn... to the invention of machines for performing such labour as is revolting and destructive of self-respect to the men who have to do it by hand. (Morris 160)

Labor enslaves man, deprives him from his individuality and freedom and leaves no time for pleasure. Machinery is the key to solve the problem: "All unintellectual labor, all monotonous, dull labor, all labor that deals with dreadful things, and involves unpleasant conditions, must be done by machinery." Wilde the aesthete was repelled by the sight of ugliness and, to him, labor is ugly because it exhausts man, obliges him to stand in uncomfortable posture for hours and is not intellectually rewarding. "Machinery must work for us in coal mines, and do all sanitary services, and be the stocker of steamers, and clean the streets, and run messages on wet days, and do anything that is tedious or distressing" (Wilde 1183). What Wilde describes here, and Morris before him, sounds like an ideal use of machinery and is just a question of good sense. It seems natural to say that if man has been able to produce machinery, he must now use it to relieve him from repellent harsh labor and to help him in his daily life. However, Wilde, as well as Morris, thinks that under the present situation, machinery is misused and weights on the shoulders of men instead of taking it off. To Morris, the machines "have, instead of lightening the labor of workmen, intensified it, and thereby added more weariness yet to the burden which the poor have to carry" (Morris 193). When machines are badly used, they endanger man because they add to hideous labor the need to equal their capacities. That is to say that man must show that he is as skilled as the machine and that he can work as much; this is not how it should be. Indeed, man, with the help of machinery, should not worry about daily tasks. Wilde adds:

> At present machinery competes against man. Under proper conditions machinery will serve man. There is no doubt at all that this is the future of machinery; [...] while Humanity will be amusing itself, or enjoying cultivated leisure—which, and not labour, is the aim of man—or making beautiful things, or reading beautiful things, or simply contemplating the world with admiration and delight, machinery will be doing all the necessary and unpleasant work. (Wilde 1183)

Labor is indeed a real punishment: it can weaken the body and is even used to enslave those who try to use their brain instead of their hands. In *Vera*, when the young woman implicitly questions the legitimacy of authority, the answer shows that labor in the mines is a punishment for thinkers, or for those who want to put tradition and authority to the test: "Vera: Who are our masters? / Colonel: Young woman, these men are going to the mines for life for asking the same foolish question." (Wilde 684). In this quotation, we can also feel that authority is not recognized as automatically legitimate; it reminds us of Proudhon's comments: "To be GOVERNED is to be watched, inspected, spied upon, directed, law-driven, numbered, regulated, enrolled, indoctrinated, preached at, controlled, checked, estimated, valued, censured, commanded, by creatures who have neither the right nor the wisdom nor the virtue to do so" (Proudhon 293). Wilde's socialism wants to get rid of property to ensure security to man. If the whole community can have the same right to freedom, happiness and pleasure, there will be no crime, no poverty, no jealousy, no starvation or disease. And this ideal socialism, that will have to be built on an entirely new basis, will allow man to live in peace and out of the strictness of social classes. As for this last point, the strictness of Victorian era is to be the next victim of Wilde's political theory.

Socialism for the Artist

If Wilde has shown some sympathy towards anarchists, for instance when he signed Shaw's petition, he disapproved of the violent means used by some of them to reach their purpose. "Disobedience [...] is man's original virtue; It is through disobedience that progress has been made, through disobedience and through rebellion" (Wilde 1176). And yet, Marcel Schwob gives a report of his conversations with Wilde about anarchists: "M. Oscar Wilde... said formerly in a salon that the outbursts of anarchists were nothing but the consequence of an instinct to destroy. And, he added, we can understand that instinct. Man fells surrounded by so many manufactured and civilized things, that he experiences the need to simplify, and he annihilates a part of it."[1] Anyway, Wilde's conception of socialism relies on this disobedience but nothing is mentioned about violence and we might easily think that this very theory of a new society with no government at all is a Utopia: "A map of the world that does not include Utopia is not worth even glancing at, for it leaves out the one country at which Humanity is always landing. And when Humanity lands there, it looks out, and, seeing a better country, sets sail. Progress is the realisation of Utopias" (Wilde 1184), and as Van de Kamp and Leahy state it: "Both Morris and Wilde present a socialism that is essentially Utopian" (Van de Kamp and Leahy 142).

Youth, Art and Beauty: The claims of Wilde's Socialism

In *The Decay of Lying*, Wilde explains through Vivian and Cyril's dialogue his own conception of what art should be. In the essay, he highlights the evils of industrialization to demonstrate—with great ability—that Nature is not the proper place for man. *The Decay of Lying* is a short essay written under the literary form of a dialogue. Vivian and Cyril are the protagonists of a sort of Platonic demonstration where Vivian reads an article about this "decay of lying: a protest." The first element in conflict with tradition is the rejection of Nature: the strong Victorian tendency that pulls everyone towards the marvelous creations of Mother-Nature, the belief in a concept of re-birth through Nature, etc. due to the evils of consumer society, is nothing

---

1 Marcel Schwob, letter to the "Phare de la Loire," May 14th, 1892: "M. Oscar Wilde... disait naguère dans un salon que les explosions des anarchistes n'étaient que les conséquences de [l']instinct de détruire. Et, ajoutait-il, on peut comprendre cet instinct. L'homme se sent environné de tant de choses fabriquées et civilisées, qu'il éprouve le besoin de simplifier, et il en annule une partie."

but a mistake. Nature is not a solution, to Wilde, even though "Industry is the root of all ugliness" (Wilde 1245). Nature "creates" nothing. "What Art really reveals to us is Nature's lack of design, her curious crudities, her extraordinary monotony, her absolutely unfinished condition" (Wilde 1071). Art only can create and give birth because it is the expression of the deepest thoughts of man. At first, saying that Nature is not the most favorable condition for man might not seem a very anarchist thought but we must not forget that, once more, it shows Wilde's deep opposition to commonplace and to cultural so-called "values."

The second element that is in conflict with tradition is that Vivian is the youngest. The master, who delivers his knowledge and brings the disciple to the understanding of what surrounds him is a young man. Usually, in traditional thinking, knowledge is embodied by the old wise, who has learnt much year after year. Thanks to that reversal of situation, Oscar Wilde is able to reinforce his own argument: youth is everything. Far from being a meaningless phrase it serves Wilde's interests: he seems fiercely opposed to platitude and rejects any form of common thinking. Early in the dialogue, we can see the superiority of Vivian's arguments; he refuses to sit on the grass because it is not comfortable, he explains that Cyril is not eligible to The Tired Hedonists club because he is "a little too old" (Wilde 1073).

In *The Picture of Dorian Gray*, Lord Henry Wotton uses the same arguments to persuade the young and handsome Dorian that his youth and beauty are ephemeral and that he must enjoy it when he still has time to do so. Wotton explains to the young Adonis that nothing on earth has more value than beauty and youth: both are not meant to last and both allow man to get what he wants from others. In the novel, this theory will turn out to offer an opportunity to Dorian: unlike his fellow creatures, his youth and beauty are not ephemeral and he becomes a prince of society. The innocence of his face seems to counterbalance the darkness of his heart... until he unmasks.

Getting Rid of Morality and Religion in Art

Once Wilde has shown that the young are the wise and that Nature and not Art is a mere imitation, he uses Cyril's lines to bounce on his new attack: morality. Cyril, as a good apprentice, encourages his new master to go on. He says:

> You have proved it [your theory] to my dissatisfaction, which is better. But even admitting this strange imitative instinct in Life and Nature, surely you would acknowledge that Art expresses the temper of its age, the spirit of its time, the moral and social conditions that surround it, and under whose influence it is produced. (Wilde 1087)

Cyril's statement represents the public opinion; to this, Vivian retorts: "Certainly not! Art never expresses anything but itself. This is the principle of my new aesthetics" (Wilde 1087).

To offer the proper condition of creation to the artist, Wilde explains that Socialism—after getting rid of property—will have to leave aside moral codes. The preface to *The Picture of Dorian Gray* is a praise of amorality. To Wilde, nothing matters but youth, beauty, in a word: appearances. Beauty and pleasure must be the ultimate goal of human beings; as a matter of fact, morals, social rules and all kind of cultural obligations are obstacles on the way towards the accomplishment of the self. In this context, the artist must be freed from moral constraints. Indeed, as Wilde writes in the Preface, "there is no such thing as a moral or immoral book. Books are well written, or badly written. That is all" (Wilde 17). Wilde could not picture when he wrote these lines that his very novel would be used during his trials and interpreted so that his amorality would be denounced and condemned. This recurrent idea of the amorality of art appears in *The Soul of Man under Socialism*: "What is a healthy or an unhealthy work of art?" Wilde asks; "A healthy work of art is one that has both perfection and personality," he answers (Wilde 1187). Art is quite often misunderstood because men try to find meaning in it or a message that has to do with social issue.

What Wilde reproaches with much resent to the public is that they just live in the past, regard art as a kind of performance through which the artist can show his skills in a way that is familiar to them. "When they say a work is grossly unintelligible, they mean that the artist has said or made a beautiful thing that is new; when they describe a work as grossly immoral, they mean that the artist has said or made a beautiful thing that is true" (Wilde 1186). He adds: "In fact, the popular novel that the public call healthy is always a thoroughly unhealthy production; and what the public call an unhealthy novel is always a beautiful and healthy work of art" (Wilde 1187). Morality, like property, is a concept created by man for man and can't thus have any legitimacy apart from that attributed by laws. The problem is that the public have mixed up the works of art and handcrafts so that they believe that both must be useful. "No artist has ethical sympathies. An ethical sympathy in an artist is an unpardonable mannerism of style" (Wilde 17). In that sense, Victorian society looks like a tyrant towards the artist because it imposes on him a great amount of laws and rules and obligations that have slowly turned art into a mere handcraft: a painting, if it is meant for religious purpose and ordered by church, is not a work of art any more but the result of a commission. Art can't contain a message that it not only the expression of the soul of the artist, as Wilde explains, real art comes from an ideal balance between perfection and personality. In this definition of art, no use for the spectator, reader, viewer, or the entire society is mentioned. As a consequence, Wilde can add that "the Renaissance was great, because it sought to solve no social problem" (Wilde 1193).

But art is not the only victim of Victorian morality. Man himself is observed, controlled and forced to follow the rites and code of society. As fate would have it, Wilde's rejection of common conception of good and bad would soon seal the end of his fame and social life. It is even almost disconcerting to read Wilde's comments upon Sin and society in *The Critic as an Artist* as well as in *The Soul of Man under Socialism*. In the first, Gilbert explains:

> What is termed Sin is an essential element of progress. Without it the world would stagnate, or grow old, or become colourless. By its curiosity Sin increases the experience of the race. Through its intensified assertion of individualism it saves us from the monotony of type. (Wilde 1121)

Sin is defended because it is at the origin of much improvement, to Wilde's mind. In the same way, the second text highlights man's individuality s opposed to social conventions:

> A man cannot always be estimated by what he does. He may keep the law, and yet be worthless. He may break the law, and yet be fine. He may be bad, without ever doing anything bad. He may commit a sin against society and yet realise through that sin his true perfection. (Wilde 1180)

To a certain extent, we can fathom that Wilde means the same when he gives advice to the young in *Phrases and Maxims for the Use of the Young*: "Any preoccupation with ideas of what is right or wrong in conduct shows an arrested intellectual development" (Wilde 1245). Wrong or right, moral or immoral, the artist cannot bother with such consideration because, otherwise, he would not be an artist. Wilde thinks that the artist has no responsibility whatsoever in man's life and that art delivers no message.

Journalism, Public Opinion and the Corruption of Words

As for the artist, at some point in history, he found himself caught by the furious mob and was forced to sell himself to public opinion. "It was a fatal day when the public discovered that the pen is mightier than the paving-stone, and can be made as offensive as the brickbat. They at once sought for the journalist, found him, developed him, and made him their industrious and well-paid servant" Wilde writes in *The Soul of Man under Socialism* (Wilde 1188). The writer, instead of expressing his own soul through his words becomes the instrument of a cause, that of the people, or any other group who possesses him. Ironically, he is the property Wilde despises. As we have said previously, Wilde refused any form of mercantilism in art and denounces the tyranny of public opinion which dictates "to the artist the form which he is to use, the mode in which he is to use it, and the materials with which he is to work" (Wilde 1190). Morality, society, need, property, everything that derives from the establishment of authority, has led the people to a bitter end: they are now the tyrants of art. "Homo homini lupus" Plautus would said; indeed man is a wolf to man in this specific context as, by imposing his own view on art, he destroys the very value of it.

> An individual who has to make things for the use of others, and with reference to their wants and their wishes, does not work with interest, and consequently cannot put into his work what is best in him. Upon the other hand, whenever a community or a powerful section of a community, or a government of any kind, attempts to dictate to the artist what he is to do, Art either entirely vanishes, or becomes stereotyped, or degenerates into a low and ignoble form of craft. A work of art is the unique result of a unique temperament. Its beauty comes from the fact that the author is what he is. It has nothing to do with the fact that other people want what they want. Indeed, the moment that an artist takes notice of what other people want, and tries to supply the demand, he ceases to be an artist, and becomes a dull or an amusing craftsman, an honest or a dishonest tradesman. (Wilde 1184)

Once more, on this point, Wilde follows Morris who wrote that "the only handicraftsmen who are free are the artists" (Morris 151). Wilde uses quite harsh terms to speak about the people and compares it to a tyrant: "There are three kinds of despots. There is the despot who tyrannises over the body. There is the despot who tyrannises over the soul. There is the despot who tyrannises over the soul and body alike. The first is called the Prince. The second is called the Pope. The third is called the People" (Wilde 1193). And Wilde's convictions burst out all of a sudden: monarchy, religion, public opinion, all form of authority is a danger for the artist. Apparently he is the one who needs most freedom and calm. Because of the public he can get none: he is deprived of freedom because "that monstrous and ignorant thing that is called Public Opinion, which, bad and well-meaning as it is when it tries to control action, is infamous and of evil meaning when it tries to control Thought or Art" (Wilde 1188). All the same, the artist cannot find calm and the proper environment for creation because "[People's] authority is a thing blind, deaf, hideous, grotesque, tragic, amusing, serious, and obscene. It is impossible for the artist to live with the People" (Wilde 1193). He gives the example of Shelley who left England and thus saved his private life. To

Wilde, the public can do nothing but hurt artists and harass them as soon as they find something they can exploit and adapt to their need.

> Shelley escaped better [than Byron]. Like Byron, he got out of England as soon as possible. But he was not so well known. If the English had realised what a great poet he really was, they would have fallen on him with tooth and nail, and made his life as unbearable to him as they possibly could. (Wilde 1179).

Wilde's opinion on the public shows his hatred of ignorance as well as of what he would consider as over-education. The mind of man is educated to derive a specific feeling and understanding from a certain kind of art; therefore, all that is new is disliked, all that is unconventional is feared. The public refuse to lose control and prefer to appropriate art and thus to devalue it:

> If a man approaches a work of art with any desire to exercise authority over it and the artist, he approaches it in such a spirit that he cannot receive any artistic impression from it at all. The work of art is to dominate the spectator: the spectator is not to dominate the work of art. The spectator is to be receptive. He is to be the violin on which the master is to play. (Wilde 1190)

But Wilde is not pessimistic, the public need to be educated, and the curious thing is rather that they are not. The public are able to improve, to perceive the soul of the artist and to leave his art be revealed to them. Oscar Wilde accepts the idea that some artists have managed to face that awful tyrant called Public Opinion. One of them is Irving. He didn't give up and that is why he could face the public and educate them at the same time:

> [Mr. Irving's] object was to realise his own perfection as an artist [...] that success is entirely due to the fact that [Mr. Irving] did not accept their standard, but realised his own [...] This advance [in drama] is entirely due to a few individual artists refusing to accept the popular want of taste as their standard, and refusing to regard Art as a mere matter of demand and supply. (Wilde 1190)

This success leads Wilde to the further comment: "The problem then is, why do not the public become more civilised? They have the capacity. What stops them?" (Wilde 1190).

But since they have no awareness of the perfection of art, the people constitute a kind of authority thanks to the weight of journalism they have bought: "But what is there behind the leading-article but prejudice, stupidity, cant, and twaddle? And when these four are joined together they make a terrible force, and constitute the new authority" (Wilde 1188). Consequently, "Art should never try to be popular" (Wilde 1184) because if it is popular, it must be devoid of real artistic value.

It is at once too easy and too difficult to be a popular novelist. It is too easy, because the requirements of the public as far as plot, style, psychology, treatment of life, and treatment of literature are concerned are within the reach of the very meanest capacity and the most uncultivated mind. It is too difficult, because to meet such requirements the artist would have to do violence to his temperament, would have to write not for the artistic joy of writing, but for the amusement of half-educated people, and so would have to suppress his individualism, forget his culture, annihilate his style, and surrender everything that is valuable in him. (Wilde 1185)

Anarchism as Individualism

All Governments are Useless and Dangerous

"Wilde would seem to follow the example of other late-Victorian writers, especially Pater and Morris; but in one respect at least he is strikingly different. Both Pater and Morris use tradition and myth to give authority to their radical views. Wilde by contrast drains tradition of all authority" (Sloan 99). In reality, Wilde refuses authority. Property derives from it, as well as all the other evils of society. Religion is as dangerous as political tyranny because its orders turn art into object that can be sold and bought. What Wilde denounces is tyranny under all its forms: the unique tyrant, with his crown and scepter, who can break man and enslave him; religion as we have said previously; and the people whose tyranny is far from being imaginary to Wilde. "All modes of government are failures" Wilde states (Wilde 1181). Indeed, it fails to secure the welfare of its people when it should exist for it.

I can quite understand a man accepting laws that protect private property, and admit of its accumulation, as long as he himself is able under those conditions to realize some form of beautiful and intellectual life. But it is almost incredible to me how a man whose life is marred and made hideous by such laws can possibly acquiesce in their continuance. (Wilde 1176)

His arguments, that we have developed in the previous chapters, lead him to the conclusion that "all authority is quite degrading" (Wilde 1182), "all authority is equally bad" (Wilde 1193) and "the form of government that is most suitable to the artist is no government at all" (Wilde 1192). In fact, Wilde does not look for an alternative solution or the establishment of a new government, his idea is to get rid of government definitively. We can feel that his rejection of government is before all a rejection of conformity:

They are probably thinking other people's thoughts, living by other people's standards, wearing practically what one may call other people's second-hand clothes, and never being themselves for a single moment. 'He who would be free', says a fine thinker, 'must not conform'. And authority, by bribing people to conform, produces a very gross kind of overfed barbarism amongst us. (Wilde 1182).

Individualism as a Keystone of Art

In *Vera, or the Nihilists*, Prince Paul embodies the very first dandy of Wilde's writings. He is a cynical character who is delighted with his own puns even in the most inconvenient circumstances. We can but despise that vile character who manipulates with a bewildering skill the czar, and later, the anarchists. And yet, we must admit that he is what Wilde will later call an individualist: he lives for his own interest. He turncoats easily to secure his best interest, and still he achieves his own personality; he does not care about morality or conventions. As Wilde explains in *The Soul of Man under Socialism*: "It is not selfish to think for oneself" (Wilde 1195). And this is what Prince Paul does. Once in the czar's rooms, once at the Anarchists' spot, he uses all means to reach his goal.

"Individualism, then, is what through Socialism we are to attain" (Wilde 1181). This is what Wilde says in *The Soul of Man under Socialism* and it is the cornerstone of his theory of individualism. "[Individualism] comes naturally and inevitably out of man. It is the point to which all development tends. It is the differentiation to which all organisms grow. It is the perfection that is inherent in every mode of life, and towards which every mode of life quickens" (Wilde 1194). In this essay, Wilde gives to the reader a testimony of what he believes in. Individualism is a complex concept that contains many aspects: To start with, Individualism frees man because there is no reason to worry for others. With the abolition of social classes and government, human beings can be nothing but equal and have thus a personal and legitimate right to be free. However, this must not be taken for selfishness because as Wilde explains: "Selfishness is not living as one wishes to live, it is asking others to live as one wishes to live" (Wilde 1194) and this is not what Individualism wants. And we must not miss the fact that Wilde does not mean that all interaction with people is vain: on the contrary, it is the purpose of the realization of the self: in *The Critic as Artist*, Gilbert explains that "if you wish to understand others you must intensify your own individualism" (Wilde 1131). Pleasure, pain, love, feelings are intensified thanks to Individualism because once man knows himself he is even more open-minded to the feelings of others: "Anybody can sympathise with the sufferings of a friend, but it requires a very fine nature— it requires, in fact, the nature of a true Individualist—to sympathise with a friend's success" (Wilde 1195). Christ is also an essential figure in Wilde's socialism. He is mentioned in *The Soul of Man under Socialism* as well as in *De*

Profundis and is called the "supreme individualist." Indeed, Christ's attitude and advice was to develop oneself in order to become someone who could take part to a community. In *The Soul of Man under Socialism*, Wilde explains that "in its development it will be assisted by Christianity, if men desire that; but if men do not desire that, it will develop none the less surely" (Wilde 1179) and adds: "the message of Christ to man was simply 'Be Thyself.' That is the secret of Christ" (Wilde 1179). Moreover, Individualism can be achieved through pain: "The evolution of man is slow. The injustice of men is great. It was necessary that pain should be put forward as a mode of self-realisation. Even now, in some places in the world, the message of Christ is necessary. No one who lived in modern Russia could possibly realise his perfection except by pain" (Wilde 1196). However, if pain is one possible way to attain and achieve Individualism, Wilde admits that "Pain is not the ultimate mode of perfection. It is merely provisional and a protest" (Wilde 1197).

For the artist, art can only be achieved through Individualism, therefore, it reinforces Wilde's phrase: "All art is quite useless" (Wilde 17). That is to say, art has no social, moral or political use. It is nothing but a means for the artist to express himself, his soul and his need for identity. The artist is, to Wilde, the most important actor of society because he is the one who needs most to be an Individualist. "But the past is of no importance. The present is of no importance. It is with the future that we have to deal. For the past is what man should not have been. The present is what man ought not to be. The future is what artists are" (Wilde 1193).

Conclusion

There is no doubt that Wilde's fame and tragic fate adds to his myth. As Sloan puts it, there is no doubt that Wilde was "a committed writer deeply concerned with the literary and social controversies of his day" (Sloan 99) and he was also the emblem of literary feats of his time. What's more:

> He remains a symbol of the conflict between the middle-class values of the nineteenth century and the artist's need for freedom, and his name will always be linked to the attempt to reconcile the individual's desire for self-realisation with public pressure to conform to social conventions. (Kohl 1)

However, he died in a country that was not his, far from his wife and children and despised by the people who had once admired him. His obituary contains a lot of absurd commonplace that many critics used at that time and later on to characterize a man who is nowadays read with great interest and delight:

> Mr. Wilde [...] took up the aesthetic fashion rather than made it; for its beginning are to be found in the paintings of Rossetti and Burne-Jones, the art work of William Morris, and the writings of Pater. [...] The Irishman's attacks on social conventions recalls, on other respects, that of Disraeli the Younger, though he was a much smaller man. He was audacious in costume, and succeeded through an elaboration of wit. [...] Mr. Wilde had wonderful cleverness, but no substantiality. His plays were full of bright moments, but devoid of consideration as drama. [...] He was content, for the most part, that his characters should sit about and talk paradoxes. [...] Mr. Wilde's gifts included supreme intellectual ability, but nothing he ever wrote had strength to endure. Of his apes the less said the better. His most useful influence was as a corrective to British stolidity, but it was too diffuse to be worth much even at that.[1]

Some critics or journalists have suggested or directly said that Wilde was not a genius but a mere actor in society. This idea is summed up by Norbert Kohl: "The resultant portrait is as crude as it has proved long-lasting: less an artist than a personality, less a personality than a poser" (Kohl 3). Since 1962 and the publication of the entire version of *De Profundis*, we can have a global view on Wilde's work. Far from being a collection of commonplace or frivolous comments as one would like to make us believe, Wilde's writings offer a large range of texts in different styles and forms. And these writings prove to be the clue to understand his ambiguous political ideas. It may be quite disturbing to read about "understanding" when we admit that we can but speak about ambiguity. Nevertheless, the fact is that Wilde's expression of his political and social convictions is intentionally blurred; first because it is part of the artist within him to hold the mask of mystery before him, and second because Wilde must have been torn between an instinctive conservatism and his sympathy for socialism—as he calls it. A socialism that denies all right to property, moral and authority, and that looks rather like anarchism. "The possession of private property is very often extremely demoralizing, and that is, of course, one of the reasons why Socialism wants to get rid of the institution" (Wilde 1175). To sum up what Wilde develops in his theory of socialism throughout his different writings, we can say that he condemned the evils brought by property, such as crime, poverty and slavery: "The recognition of private property has really harmed Individualism, and obscured it, by confusing a man with what he possesses" (Wilde 1178). The only thing that matters is then the achievement of the self apart from any kind of belongings. Once man has understood that "to have" is nothing compared to "to be," socialism has open the path towards individualism: "Man thought that the important thing was to have, and did not know that

---

1 Unsigned obituary notice, *Pall Mall Gazette*, 1 December 1900, p.2.

the important thing is to be" (Wilde 1178). This development of awareness is the key to the understanding of the self and the achievement of one's personality. Therefore, the expression of the self—through art—must obey no human rule except the very limits of the soul and mind. We would join Norbert Kohl in his own analysis: "This nihilistic attitude towards the established social and moral order, together with the anti-realism of his aesthetics, makes it very easy to understand why the paradox—as a means of undermining the validity of conventional beliefs—was one of Wilde's favourite literary choices." (Kohl 5)

This could sum up Wilde's relation to anarchy: a vivid desire to free man and the artist to lead them to the realization of their Individualism. Anarchism—even though Wilde rather calls it socialism—is the only step to attain Individualism, where understanding begins and self-achievement as well. As far as art is an independent expression of an independent soul, it is the perfect manifestation of Individualism: "Art is Individualism, and Individualism is a disturbing and disintegrating force. Therein lies its immense value" (Wilde 1186). Whereas governments only allow people to exist and work and suffer, individualism offers knowledge, pleasure and permits to live. We end this analysis of Wilde's relation to anarchy by quoting Wilde himself when he asserts that "To live is the rarest thing in the world. Most people exist, that is all" (Wilde 1178).

References

Ellmann, Richard. *Oscar Wilde*. London: Penguin Books, 1987.

Harris, Franck. *Oscar Wilde, His Life and Confessions*. New York: printed and published by the author, 1918.

Kohl, Norbert. *Oscar Wilde, the Works of a Conformist Rebel*. Trans. David H. Wilson. Cambridge: Cambridge U P, 1989.

Morley, Sheridan. *Oscar Wilde*. Worthing, West Sussex: Littlehampton Book Services Ltd, 1976.

Morris, William. *The Collected Works*. Ed. May Morris. New York: Russell & Russell, 1966.

Proudhon, Pierre-Joseph. *General Ideas of the Revolution in the Nineteenth Century*. Trans. John Beverly Robinson. London: Freedom Press, 1923.

Sloan, John. *Oscar Wilde*. Oxford: Oxford University Press, 2009.

Van de Kamp, Peter, and Patrick Leahy. "Some Notes on Wilde's Socialism." *The Crane Bag* 7.1 (1983): 141–150.

Wilde, Oscar. *Collins Complete Works of Oscar Wilde* . 5th ed. Introduction by Merlin Holland. London and Glasgow: HarperCollins, 2003.

2. Anarchy, Ecology, and the Care of the Self: The Legacies of Emerson and Thoreau

James Brown

When, in 1917, Emma Goldman, an anarchist activist then considered by the United States federal government the most dangerous woman in America, was brought to tria l for her anti-conscription activism against World War I, she cited in her defense two cornerstones of what would become the American literary canon throughout most of the twentieth century: Ralph Waldo Emerson and Henry David Thoreau. To Goldman, Thoreau and Emerson represented a value that she and her family had emigrated from Russia in hopes of finding in America: the radical right to assert one's individuality against the perceived injustices of the state. In response to her defense, however, the judge presiding over Goldman's case concluded that such individualism was not, in fact, a core American value: "We have no place in this country," he said, "for those who express the view that the law may be disobeyed in accordance with the thoughts of an individual."[1]

Fifty-five years later, on May 11, 1972, John William Ward sat down in front of Westover Air Force Base near Chicopee, Massachusetts, with his wife Barbara, 1,000 students, and 20 faculty members from Amherst College in protest against Richard Nixon's escalation of bombing in Southeast Asia. Like numerous social critics of his era, and like many of his students, John Ward had become opposed to what he considered America's imperialistic foreign policy in Vietnam. Unlike

1 Emma Goldman, "The Verdict," *Berkeley Digital Library Sunsite*, accessed February 3, 2010, http://sunsite.berkeley.edu/Goldman/Writings/Essays/TrialSpeeches/verdict. html.

most of these critics, however, and unlike his students, Ward was also the recently appointed president of Amherst College. Unique among liberal establishmentarians of his generation, he did not just hold that protestors could be right while the establishment could sometimes be wrong. Rather, turning to his reading of Emerson and Thoreau and other nineteenth century writers, Ward, like many student activists of his generation, attributed his decision to protest the war in part to the moral challenges posed to him by anarchist thought in the nature writing tradition.

What these two public figures shared in common was their commitment to an individualistic understanding of the politics of Nature that has a long association with the philosophy of anarchism as well as with a large part of the American and global environmental left. This essays offers a brief overview of how American nature writing, beginning with Henry David Thoreau, has been part of an international discourse advocating the abolition of nations and governments for the simple reason that, for many of the writers explored here, governments were seen as the primary cause behind the desecration of nature and the related oppression of human beings. Briefly tracing the influence of Emerson and Thoreau on the environmental left from Walden Pond to the Occupy movement, it suggest some of the ethical challenges this anarchist tradition of personal accountability—or self reliance—poses to activists who have, I suggest, failed to distinguish anarchism itself—which calls for the abolition of government on behalf of individual liberty—from its use as a tactic for liberal and progressive reform.

Recent critical interpretations of what is essentially America's written radical environmental tradition have devalued, by misrepresenting, the central message of that literature, which is, simply, as follows: That consumerism is the source of human and natural suffering and that a necessary condition for ending environmental and human degradation is to take individual responsibility for the results of one's choices in the capitalist marketplace. Emerson and Thoreau have always been, in fact, part of a globally shared, anti-capitalist, anti-exceptionalist environmental tradition holding this view, one with deep roots in the anti-government politics of the antebellum abolitionist movement.

The relationship between anarchism, a political theory advocating absolute individual liberty and freedom from external governance, and nature writing in the United States is one that Ward and many other scholars recognized in the recent past but that a good deal of scholarship has since forgotten. Much recent post-colonial scholarship, in fact, tends to identify Emerson, Thoreau, and the scholars who originally studied and anthologized them early in the twentieth century with the U.S. nationalist values of cold war liberalism. This is because Emersonian and Thoreauvian "individualism," compared to soviet Communism, seems implicitly "anti-Marxist" and therefore explicitly pro Capitalist, making the reading of Emerson and Thoreau apparently "ideologically self-serving to certain groups, especially to white male elites."[1]

In addition to missing the mark entirely, as this essay will explain, these recent literary histories present inherent historiographical problems. First, they are framed in terms of what the scholar Gene Wise has called "paradigm dramas." Writing in the late 1970s, when a generation of academics was first beginning to forward a series of "complicity critiques" about the relationship between canonical literature and the "establishment," Wise pointed out that the previous generation of cold war scholars who the radicals had been protesting were never the conservatives, or even the liberal American exceptionalists, that the radicals wanted them to seem.

In fact, although the term "paradigm shift" remains an important Humanities meme to indicate forward-thinking criticism, there was no radical paradigm shift in the Humanities in the nineteen sixties for the simple reason that paradigms, by definition, only refer to universally held scientific hypotheses and theories, such as the heliocentric theory of the universe, which scientists believed was law until it was proven objectively false.[2] By comparison, scholars in the Humanities throughout the nineteen fifties and leading into the nineteen sixties never agreed, with anything approaching the finality of a scientific paradigm, that the United States was the center of the world or that it was meant to lead the planet toward a shared vision of democratic, free market prosperity, as the liberal consensus held. The truth is, inspired by their background in radical, "classic" American literature and the criticism of American culture it generated, cold war era liberal scholars in the Humanities tended to actually embraced the anti-war, gender, racial, and environmental justice agendas of the radical scholars in the late nineteen sixties and early nineteen seventies, which is partially how the disciplines became radicalized.[3]

---

1 Cecelia Tichi, "American Literary Studies to the Civil War," in *Redrawing the Boundaries: The Transformation of English and American Studies*, ed. Stephen Greenblatt and Giles Gunn (New York: Modern Language Association, 1992), 218.
2 Gene Wise, "Paradigm Dramas in American Studies: A Cultural and Institutional History of the Movement." *American Quarterly 31* (3), 1979. According to Thomas Kuhn, "A paradigm is what members of a scientific community, and they alone, share," while, by contrast, scholars in the Humanities "are constantly faced with "a number of competing and incommensurable solutions" to problems that they must "must ultimately examine" for themselves. *The Structure of Scientific Revolutions*. Chicago: University of Chicago Press, Fourth Edition, 2012, p. 164.
3 James Brown, "Interdisciplinary American Studies and the Cold War: A New, Archival History from the Records of the Library of Congress." American Studies Association Annual Conference, 2008.

Further, the increasingly shared critical understanding of Emerson and Thoreau as prophets of acquisitive, capitalist individualism and of American empire has not always been assumed, and it is historically unsupported. In the Gilded and Progressive Ages (roughly spanning the years between 1870 and 1920), anarchists in the United States, literary scholars in American academies, and Popular Front radicals were all arguing that Emerson and Thoreau were progenitors of an anarchist political philosophy or some related form of "native" American radicalism. The foremost public figure speaking on behalf of their anarchism was Emma Goldman, but her and other anarchists' interpretations of these authors were strongly seconded by early Americanist scholars like John Macy (1913), Vernon Louis Parrington (1929), and F.O. Matthiessen (1941). Taken together, these scholars and anarchist activists offer what one might call an "anarchist hermeneutic," or an anarchist way of reading the individualism of American nature writers that helps us to how understand their very direct anti-government, anti-capitalist, and anti-nationalist politics poses a direct challenge to how we think (or don't think) of our place as individuals with ethical agency in perpetuating global human and ecological injustice.

What makes anarchism most significant to American nature writing is the literary tradition's uses of the term "Nature" as both a physical and a political space. Politically, for Emerson and Thoreau, and later for Emma Goldman and other immigrant anarchists, the Beats, and the 1960s counterculture, Nature meant—as it did for Rousseau, Thomas Paine, and many others—the foundation of personal freedom, the state into which we are each born before culture introduces the principles of power and authority. As a tangible place, meanwhile, physical nature, which Emerson called the "not me," is the outer world as perceived and understood through human perception. Since nature (i.e., the Other) and the individual (i.e., the self) essentially co-arise, political Nature has been understood in this tradition as part and parcel of an individual's ethical way seeing, apprehending, and understanding the Other in which the Other was at once physical nature, the individuals who populate it, and the self.

This Transcendentalist use of the Nature idea had, for nineteenth century radicals in the U.S. and abroad, obvious political implications. Nature, in nineteenth century American nature writing, was anathema to slavery, to the global shipping trade, to factory production, to paper currency, and to war. It abhorred consumerism and, finally, it abhorred the State that upheld all these constructs. It focused on transnational ethics and considered global suffering to be the direct result of one's immediate, local choices in the world: it thought globally and acted locally. In the nature writing tradition referred to here, the individual becomes a site of personal responsibility (and is not, definitely, an acquisitive capitalist) in which the care of the self is no different from the care of the other, which is no different from the practice of social justice. Unequivocally, when they spoke of the free individual, this type of personal responsibility to the Other was the only thing that Emerson and Thoreau ever meant by "self reliance."

Within his ethics and in his writing, for example, Thoreau made central an anti-capitalist critique of mercantilism and government corruption, and his experiment at Walden Pond was indicative of his anti-establishment politics. Far from rejecting society in favor of egotistical individualism, Thoreau was deeply engaged in seeking solutions to the repression of human freedom that American government in the expansionist nineteenth century represented for him and many of his contemporaries. In Thoreau's view, such solutions began with one's personal ethos—the philosophical ground of one's moral actions, or one's total way of being in the world—as this ethos was informed by self-reflection. To take time out in nature, to limit one's habits of consumption, was to remove oneself as far as possible from the political economy, from exploitative markets, and from governments that rigged and enforced these markets.

This view is clear throughout his work, especially "Civil Disobedience" and "A Plea for Captain John Brown," which distill his essential political philosophy (in response to slavery), but it also appears more subtly in his less read books, like his posthumously published *Cape Cod*, a bleak meditation on the ethics of mercantile capitalism. For Thoreau, among the premier scandals of the mid-nineteenth century, as uncovered in *Harper's* and other journals, was the forcing to sea of unworthy vessels in unsafe conditions by investors and insurance underwriters in the shipping trade. In the text of *Cape Cod*, acknowledging this social context, Thoreau repeatedly refers to two shipwrecks, that of the *St. John* and that of the *Franklin*, associated in his readers' minds with this economic scandal of global proportions.

According to an 1838 article published in the *Edinburgh Review* (a journal read on both sides of the Atlantic), the American and British underwriting (insurance) industries, for several years, had been encouraging shipping investors to maximize their risks because they could earn greater profits from dangerous ships than from safer ones, a practice profitable to the insurance industry because "the premium depends partly on the condition of the ship," with an unsafe ships costing more to insure. "It is in fact established by the records of our judicial proceedings," the reported continued, "that ships and goods have been sent to sea *in order that* they might be cast away, and a profit made at the expense of insurers. Underwriting "procures security, but at the same time [is] apt to generate carelessness, and occasionally fraud." [1]

---

1 "On the Frequency of Shipwrecks," *Edinburgh Review*, January 1835, 340-341.

Later, an 1874 article by *Harper's* writer Charles Nordhoff titled "The Rights and Wrongs of Seamen," written after Thoreau's death, examined the results of three decades of this fraudulent underwriting and shipping practice. "Do men consciously send ships to sea knowing them to be unseaworthy?" the article asks. Indeed, it continues, "There appears to be even a regularly organized business" of doing so. The article then listed nineteen such ships cited before an English investigating committee in 1873 that had been lost by a single Liverpool company, which had "no further interest or aim in the venture than simply to make as much money as they can in the quickest amount of time,"[1] in the course of ten years. Calculated risks by such companies included taking the chance that only one of three of their ships would arrive safely ashore with cargo intact, a practice also common among slave traders. As a result of such practices, seventeen percent of 4,069 American-built ships were lost between 1841 and 1845. Between 1868 and 1872, that number increased to forty percent of 4,387 ships: 2,177 shipwrecks in four years. In addition to fraud, Nordhoff attributed this increase to the cheapness of vessels contracted by ever more money-conscious investors and the "furious competition in trade which has affected all business since the great gold discoveries of California and Australia."[2] Nordhoff, however, held most responsible any man who "owns coffins and sails them."[3]

The appropriation of human life in these practices—human life risked so that investors and underwriters could better procure what Thoreau considered the "facsimile" of nature known as currency—underscored the need, to many, for political regulation of the industry and, by 1858, the incessant shipwrecks along Cape Cod resulting from insurance fraud prompted the residents of Hull, Massachusetts to hold a protest demanding regulation of the underwriting industry.[4] For Thoreau, however, the problem struck deeper than the need for regulation. Rather, it underscored the immorality of trade itself. Thoreau's response to this web of global suffering, which was driven, as he understood it, by consumerism and greed, was to insist upon the need for more self-reliance and less buying and selling. For a

---

1 Charles Nordhoff, "The Rights and Wrongs of Seamen," *Harper's New Monthly Magazine*, March 1874, 557.

2 Ibid., 561–62.

3 Ibid., 557.

4 For a narrative account of the Hull gathering, see Hallie, *Tales of Good*, 135–38. Not attentive to the ironies of power and justice addressed in *Cape Cod*, Hallie looks no further into the relationship between the charity houses and the shipping interests who were causing the wrecks but instead opposes the Hull residents' sense of cooperation and Thoreau's individualism. As a result, Hallie criticizes Thoreau's suspicion of charity while overlooking important contradictions and hypocrisies of which Thoreau and his readers (not to mention the irate people of Hull) would have been aware. This oversight likely emerges from Hallie's Manichean cosmology, in which Thoreau must be evil and harmful.

model of his rejection of consumerist morality, he turned to the tradition of the care of the self in Western democratic ethics, borrowing especially from the Greek Cynical philosopher Diogenes of Sinope, whose ideas and career have been (more recently) examined by Michael Foucault.

For Foucault, in Western democratic ethics, which privilege personal freedom, individuals are continually faced with the choice, when we act freely, between enforcing total "states of domination" in our interactions with others and encouraging the interplay of "relations of power." Although many critics since Foucault have mistaken his use of the word "power" to mean tyranny or oppression, Foucault himself believed that "relations of power" are positive since power is only possible "insofar as the subjects are free."[1] Furthermore, subjects are free only to the extent that those who might otherwise dominate them instead practice control over themselves. Foucault, summarizing this sense of the care of the self in Western philosophy, wrote that "the risk of dominating others and exercising a tyrannical power over them arises precisely when one has not taken care of the self and has become the slave of one's desires."[2] For this reason, Foucault, like the Hermit of Concord, held that, after all, "there is no first or final point of resistance to political power other than in the relationship one has to oneself."[3]

The care of the self as a practice of political resistance in the West has its roots, as Foucault traced them, in Greek Cynical philosophy, especially that of the Cynic Diogenes, whose spirit was later "manifested in a number nineteenth century writers and philosophies, including "Max Stirner, Schopenhauer, Nietzsche, dandyism, Baudelaire, anarchy, [and] anarchist thought."[4] Philosophical Cynicism involves the practice of contemplating oneself as an object one's own knowing for the purpose of "eliminating the dependencies introduced by culture, society, civilization, and so on" that hinder a "natural life."[5] Having eliminated such dependencies, one can then go about the politically engaged business of *parrhesia*, or radical truth-telling, without concern for one's entrenched self interest. For Thoreau and others, such truth-telling (i.e., activism) begins with practices of refusal of the marketplace and, by implication, the structures of state and church that support it. Indeed, the original "foundation from which Cynicism sprang among the Greeks" was "an irresistible urge to say 'no' to the world that

---

1 Michael Foucault, *The Hermeneutics of the Subject: Lectures at the College de France 1981-1982* (New York: Picador, 2005), 292.
2 Ibid., 288.
3 Ibid., 252.
4 Ibid., 251.
5 Michel Foucault, "The Ethics of the Concern for the Self as a Practice of Freedom," in *Ethics: Subjectivity and Truth*, ed. Paul Rabinow (New York: The New Press, 1997).

human beings have constructed, because, in the light of *reason*, such a world is built on faulty foundations."[1]

For Diogenes, the first Cynical philosopher and a student of Plato's, the care of the self involved stripping himself of all but the barest minimum of possessions—a toga, a bowl, a walking-stick—and living as a squatter out of a single empty barrel in the bustle of Athens, begging for his livelihood. The anarchist historian Daniel Guérin traces the roots of anarchist thought back to Diogenes, Thoreau's model for his Walden experiment, with his "deconsecration" of all that was sacred in Greece and his "visceral revolt" against oppressive value systems.[2] What Foucault calls Diogenes' "Cynic *parrhesia*" (i.e., Cynic "truth-telling") resulted from his rejection of materialism and manifested in an ironic and witty reversal of accepted values as well as an abiding disrespect for cultural authority. Once, when asked whether it was true, as Plato had joked, that man was a "featherless biped," Diogenes produced a plucked chicken. In another episode, one that Foucault discusses in detail, when approached by the Emperor Alexander, Diogenes, rather than rising and bowing, asked the emperor to step out of his patch of sunlight.

Appearing in iconography and literature throughout the nineteenth century, the Diogenes figure suggested such ideals as "freedom from prejudice and open criticism of secular and religious authorities" and the "autonomy of the individual and the separation of morality from religious constraints."[3] Diogenes also came to represent the cause of labor against capital, the cause of the people against the state, and the cause of Nature against the law. For the eighteenth and nineteenth century adopter of classical Cynicism, "natural law does not know slaves by birth. By nature, the worker is not distinguished from the master, but all are equal.[4] In Thoreau's nineteenth century, in other words, to be "Cynical" was to be politically enlightened, democratic in the broadest sense, and, more importantly, a radical in one's critique of the relationship between culture and acquisitive capitalism while personally living in accord with Nature's laws.

In fact, when reading Thoreau, as one scholar has noted and as his bourgeois contemporaries were painfully aware, "It is impossible to avoid

---

1 Luis Navia, *Classical Cynicism: A Critical Study* (Westport, CT: Greenwood Press, 1996), 29.
2 Daniel Guérin, *Anarchism* (New York: Monthly Review Press, 1970), 13.
3 Heinrich Niehues-Pröbsting, "The Modern Reception of Cynicism: Diogenes in the Enlightenment," in *The Cynics: The Cynic Movement in Antiquity and Its Legacy*, ed. R. Brach Branham and Marie-Odile Goület-Cazé (Berkeley: University of California Press, 1996), 335.
4 Ibid.

comparing him with Diogenes."[1] In 1854, Charles Frederick Briggs, in an article titled "A Yankee Diogenes," made the same comparison. As a figure of Diogenes, Thoreau's aim, Briggs held, "was the very remarkable one of trying to be something, while he lived upon nothing; in opposition to the general rule of striving to live upon something, while doing nothing." In this sense, Thoreau was pushing against the current of "The New England Character [which] is essentially anti-Diogenic" because New Englanders were typically committed to "bettering their condition by barter."[2] An 1857 review of *Walden* for *Chamber's Journal*, meanwhile, described "Henry D. Thoreau, the American Diogenes" as one whose object, apparently, was "the exaltation of mankind by the utter extinction of civilization."[3]

Indeed, it becomes obvious upon reading Thoreau closely that his goal was not to celebrate nineteenth century capitalist individualism. Rather, it was to expose this individualism as false, as a mythology that masked what he gloomily called "interdependency," or society's reliance upon the interrelated structures of the state, religion, and markets to assuage its individuals' ever increasing wants. Nature, however, had loftier aspirations for humankind. For English Romantics and American Revolutionaries, Nature had always been equated with political equality, even though this equality was often exclusionary (as in the case, for example, of Thomas Jefferson's vision of an agrarian, slave holding America). Thoreau reasserted this radical equation, but with the caveat that, practically speaking, Nature, as a political concept, was not enough. Rather, for real political equality to emerge, he believed, it was necessary that we learn to reduce our needs and to provide those reduced needs with our own hands to the extent possible, leaving others free from the need to submit to exploitative labor practices, to slavery, and to empire.

For Thoreau, in other words, a return to physical nature was a necessary condition for the flowering of political Nature. This primary emphasis of Thoreau's on a return to literal nature as the practical ground of freedom and social justice is what distinguishes him as America's first environmental writer (and it inspires the majority of his allegories in *Walden*). It also helped

---

1 Holbrook Jackson. *Dreamers of Dreams* (New York: Farrar, Strauss and Company, 1950), 123.
2 Charles Frederick Briggs, "A Yankee Diogenes," *Putnam's Monthly Magazine of American Literature, Science and Art*, October 1854, 443–48; Thoreau Institute at Walden Woods, "Walden: Contemporary Notices and Reviews," *Walden Woods Project*, last modified April 30, 2009, http://www.walden.org/Institute/thoreau/writings/walden/Reviews/Putnams%20October%201854.htm
3 *Chamber's Journal*, "An American Diogenes," November 1857, 330-332, The Thoreau Institute at Walden Woods/The Walden Woods Project, "Walden: Contemporary Notices and Reviews," http://www.walden.org/Institute/thoreau/writings/walden/Reviews/Chambers%20Journal%2021%20November%201857.htm.

him to avoid the philosophical excesses of his friend and mentor Emerson, who became a statist at the eve of the Civil War. In making a return to nature, Thoreau drew a defiant line in the sand, daring the state, its executors, and its exploitative markets to force him to surrender his conscience or his labor (including in the form of taxes) to a government that sponsored the consumerist frame of mind that seemed to be leaving a trail of corpses strew along Cape Cod's shores. For radical readers in the nineteenth and twentieth centuries in the U.S. and abroad, this defiance against the state and the values of materialist society would also mark him, as well as Emerson, as among America's first bone fide anarchists.

The idea of the care of the self as the care of the world and the Other (which Emerson called "self reliance") has both domestic and global implications for the ethical behavior of citizens in a consumer driven democracy. It has also bridged national and cultural divides in radical and unexpected ways often misunderstood as constituting American cultural appropriation and colonialism, as in the case of the Beat poets and Zen Buddhism. However, nineteenth century individualist radicalism, and the Transcendentalist literature that propagated it, actually began in, and was a response to, a moment of global moral and political crisis: The war with Mexico and a possible expansion of slavery to the Western states, the Irish potato famine (caused by the British taxation system) leading to a new domestic servant class, and the consumerist culture that drove it all were decisively seen by the authors who began the radical American nature writing tradition as the direct result of government's very existence insofar as government created conditions that demanded a citizen's personal dependence on unacceptable market and social conditions. In coming to this conclusion, Emerson and Thoreau were each strongly influenced by the anti-government rhetoric of the radical abolition movement.

Nowhere was nineteenth anarchist sentiment in the United States more evident than in the emergent U.S. libertarian left's response to government's role in the support of slavery. As William Lloyd Garrison declared in his anti-slavery Declaration of Sentiments, adopted by the Massachusetts Peace Convention in 1838:

> We cannot acknowledge allegiance to any human government. . . .
> We are bound by the laws of a kingdom which is not of this world, the
> subjects of which are forbidden to fight; in which Mercy and Truth
> are met together, and Righteousness and Peace have kissed each other;
> which has no state lines, no national partitions, and no geographical
> boundaries; in which there is no distinction of rank, or division of
> caste, or inequality of sex; the officers of which are Peace, its exactors

Righteousness, its walls Salvation, and its gates Praise; and which is destined to break in pieces and consume all other kingdoms.[1]

Adin Ballou, an abolitionist signatory to Garrison's Declaration, explained the reason for this radical stance by noting that government is only a construct "exercising absolute authority over man, by means of cunning and physical force. It may be patriarchal, hierarchical, monarchical, aristocratic, democratic, or mobocratic—still it answers to this definition. It originates in man, depends on man, and makes man the lord—the slave of man." As a social construct, government had no relation to nature—human or divine—and any cooperation with its offices were strictly voluntary, to be ignored at the dictates of conscience when required.

Ralph Waldo Emerson's concept of "self reliance," as well as Thoreau's, expressed this spirit of antinomianism latent in Christian abolitionist political culture. Thus, in 1841, borrowing directly from this rhetoric, Emerson wrote, in "Self Reliance,"

No law can be sacred to me but that of my own nature. Good and bad are but names very readily transferable to that or this; the only right is what is after my constitution, the only wrong is what is against it. A man is to carry himself in the presence of all opposition as if every thing were titular and ephemeral but he. I am ashamed to think how easily we capitulate to badges and names, to large societies and dead institutions.[2]

Since the law emerges from one's nature, for both Emerson and the radical abolitionists, breaking the earthly law whenever necessary to follow the higher law of conscience was central to self-reliance as an ethical system.

Also like the radical abolitionists, Emerson believed that society, in contrast to self-reliance, imposes a fatal conformity on the moral conscience of individuals. This is because the institutions that shape society are, ethically speaking, bankrupt. Their corruption "makes them," as Emerson writes of the church, "not false in a few particulars, authors of a few lies, but false in all particulars."[3] At the heart of this falseness, furthermore, lay the corrupting influence of property: "The reliance on Property," Emerson insists, "including the reliance on governments which protect it, is the want of self-reliance." Slavery itself, as Emerson and the antinomian abolitionists understood it, was a direct outcome of the property system, in which

1   William Lloyd Garrison, "Declaration of Sentiments, Adopted by the Peace Convention, Held in Boston, September 18–20, 1838," *Nonresistance.org*, accessed April 2, 2012, http://www.nonresistance.org/docs_pdf/Declaration_of_Sentiments.pdf
2   Ralph Waldo Emerson, "Self Reliance," in *The Essays of Ralph Waldo Emerson*, ed. Alfred Kazin (Cambridge, MA: Belknap Press, 1987), 30.
3   Ibid., 32.

men and women "measure their esteem of each other, by what each has, and not by what each is."[1] As he wrote in "Man the Reformer" (1841), the laws protecting our "whole institution of property" supports a "system of selfishness," a "system of distrust, of concealment, of superior keenness, not of giving but of taking advantage."[2] Would it not be better, Emerson asked, "to have few wants and to serve them one's self, so as to have somewhat left to give, instead of being always prompt to grab?"[3] "Can we not learn," instead, "the lessons of self-help?,"[4] Emerson was asking his bourgeois audiences, trying to challenge them out of their social complacency.

With the original admission of slavery into the Union for the sole purpose of supplying the wants of greed, Emerson held that the fundamental, individualist principle of "American justice was poisoned at its fountain,"[5] and that the entire current system of government was therefore discredited. Given the enormous violation of self-reliance that state-sponsored slavery entailed, however, Emerson also came to believe that the state must now act to correct the problem it had created, even if doing so required expanding its own power. Emerson, by 1850, could no longer, he felt, "find an American people able to leave government behind." Such a people, softened by venality and incapable of practicing self-reliance, now needed the guidance of a few "illustrious men"[6]—Emersonian "representative men"—like Lincoln, whose moral guidance would purify the nation through war.

In contrast to his philosophical anarchism in "Self Reliance," Emerson eventually came to embrace the Civil War as part of Nature's great compensation for slavery, one that would justly "punish us" "with burned capitals and slaughtered regiments."[7] Abraham Lincoln, with all the "virtues of a good magistrate," could "undo a world of mischief" by executing this war as quickly as possible. The war itself, meanwhile, would serve to bring out heroism, since war "reinforces manly power a hundred and thousand times."[8] War "always ennobles an age," Emerson intoned as the nation prepared, eventually, for Sherman's March, and it was perfectly fair that "one generation might well be scarified . . . that this continent be purged, and a new era of equal rights dawn on the universe." "Nature says to the

---

1 Ibid., 49.
2 Ralph Waldo Emerson, "Man the Reformer," in *The Political Emerson: Essential Writings on Politics and Social Reform*, ed. David M. Robinson (New York: Beacon, 2004), 38.
3 Ralph Waldo Emerson, "New England Reformers," in *The Political Emerson: Essential Writings on Politics and Social Reform*, ed. David M. Robinson (New York: Beacon, 2004), 45.
4 Emerson, "New England Reformers," 74.
5 Emerson, "Man the Reformer," 132.
6 Ibid., 133.
7 Ibid., 182.
8 Ibid., 195.

American," Emerson concluded, "You are to imperil your lives and fortunes for a principle."[1]

Addressing the nineteenth century American middle class with the sanction of liberal, urban media outlets such as *Harper's*, whose editors had comfortable connections to Boston political authority, Emerson, for all his contributions to American anti-government thought, ultimately spoke of reform in ways that reflect the liberal, not exactly the anarchist, political and ecological mind. One legacy of this liberal ecological imagination has been, unfortunately, from Emerson's time to the present, a tendency for radicals to support economic centralization, colonial expansion, wealth redistribution, and eugenic population control all in the name of social justice. Indeed, Emerson's belief that war and bloodshed were necessary to purge the nation and revitalize Natural heroism and manliness more closely reflects the authoritarian political cosmology of Theodore Roosevelt—police commissioner, military general, President, eugenicist, and conservationist—than of any known free market conservative, in spite of post-nationalist critics' claims about Emerson's capitalist individualism.

After the Civil War solidified the industrial future of the United States and opened the gates to the Gilded Age, writers like Emma Goldman and Rudolf Rocker conjured up the spirits of the early Emerson, Thoreau, and other American nature/Nature radicals to help them resist the newly emergent forms of industrial authority that they found dominating urban American life. They did so for large public audiences numbering in the thousands per night on lecture tours for the purpose of defending their "foreign" radical ideal with reference to an American one: that of individual liberty from authority and oppression. In other words, they were inviting their audiences to understand Emerson and Thoreau as expositors of a global anti-capitalist, anti-government vision of individual liberty.

The individual, Goldman argued, in language echoing the Emerson of "Self Reliance," is "A cosmos in himself" and

> does not exist for the State, nor for that abstraction called "society," or the "nation," which is only a collection of individuals. Man, the individual, has always been and necessarily is the sole source and motive power of evolution and progress. Civilization has been a continuous struggle of the individual or groups of individuals against the State and even against "society," that is, against the majority subdued and hypnotized by the State and State worship.

This kind of individualism, however—which Goldman called "Individuality," or "the consciousness of the individual as to what he is and how he lives"—was not the *laissez-faire* "rugged individualism" of the

---

1 Ibid., 197.

bourgeoisie, which she believed served as "only a masked attempt to repress and defeat the individual and his individuality." As Goldman's comrade Max Baginski wrote, although "the State Socialists" (much like post-nationalist critics) "love to assert that at present we live in an age of individualism," in fact, "individuality was never valued at so low a rate as it is today."

This distinction between bourgeois individualism and anarchist individuality was shared by Voltairine de Cleyre, an American-born descendent of French immigrant parents and friend of Emma Goldman. Born in Michigan in 1866 and named by her father—a French immigrant and freethinker—after Voltaire, de Cleyre, like Goldman, understood the individualism of Emerson and Thoreau as part of an American anarchist tradition of individual accountability to society. Writing in her essay "Anarchism and American Traditions," published as a pamphlet by Mother Earth Press in 1909, De Cleyre argued that American literary and philosophical traditions—America's revolutionary impulse, its Jeffersonian idealism, and its Transcendentalist seeking after higher laws and self governance—all resonated with anarchist idealism.

Drawing attention to the anarchist idealism in Emerson and Thoreau in particular, de Cleyre wrote in her 1914 essay "Anarchism and Literature,"

> None who are familiar with the thought of Emerson can fail to recognize that it is spiritual Anarchism . . . And he who has dwelt in dream by Walden, charmed by that pure life . . . has felt that call of the anarchist Ideal which pleads with men to renounce the worthless luxuries which enslave them, that the buried soul which is doomed to mummy clothes by the rush and jangle of the chase of wealth may answer the still small voice of the Resurrection, there, in the silence, the solitude, the simplicity of the free life.[1]

For de Cleyre, it was evident that Emerson and Thoreau's anarchism included a plea for individual liberation and a scathing critique of capitalist materialism and that it pointed the way toward a personal liberation necessary for social transformation. The values of the Gilded Age, however, stifled this impulse by drowning it beneath a sea of unbridled consumerism.

Indeed, in de Cleyre's vision of history, which closely paralleled Peter Kropotkin's, every age was possessed of a "dominant idea," and "the one great real ideal of our age . . . is the Much Making of Things—"

> not the making of beautiful things, not the joy of spending living energy in creative work; rather the shameless, merciless driving and overdriving, wasting and draining of the last bit of energy, only to

---

1 Voltairine de Cleyre, "Anarchism in Literature," in *Selected Works of Voltairine de Cleyre: Pioneer of Women's Liberation*, ed. Alexander Berkman (New York: Revisionist Press, 1972), 145–46.

produce heaps and heaps of things— things ugly, things harmful, things useless, and at the best largely unnecessary.[1]

Over and against this materialism stood the individual soul, "the mind, or character," an "active modifying agent" that could, if awakened, function as an ethical counterpoint to the new productive and consumptive capitalism that had become a dominant factor in American life and that drew its sustenance from the authority of government. The individual soul must summon the courage to resist and to forge an alternate course: Though "the Society about us is dominated by Thing Worship, and will stand marked so for all time, that is no reason any single soul should be."[2]

In an Emersonian vein, de Cleyre issued a call for new and representative individuals capable of resisting the materialist course of American and Western history:

> Let us have Men [she pleaded]. Men who will say a word to their souls and keep it . . . keep it when the storm roars and there is a white-streaked sky and blue thunder before, and one's eyes are blinded and one's ears deafened with the war of opposing things; and keep it under the long leaden sky and the gray dreariness that never lifts. Hold unto the last: that is what it means to have a Dominant Idea which Circumstance cannot break.[3]

Character in the face of materialism was, for de Cleyre, the meaning of individuality, and true individuality must become the dominant idea of the age if men and women were to reject capitalism and shatter their chains of oppression.

Even as they overlooked Emerson's ultimate progressive anti-individualism, Emma Goldman and Voltarine de Cleyre (along with other public anarchists of the twentieth century, such as Howard Zinn) were largely right in reading the individualism of Emerson and Thoreau as radical rather than conservative; indeed, schooled in the politics of abolition, Emerson at his most "individualistic," like Thoreau, recommended anti-statism, dissidence, and new personal habits, rather than complicity and reform, in response to the domestic, authoritarian regime of state-sponsored consumerism that both of these authors saw beginning to embrace the world, manifesting most viscerally in slavery, the war with Mexico, shipping fraud, and "the Irish question." By finding reflections of their eclectic political philosophy in these American canonical authors, the Gilded Age anarchists

---

1 Voltarine de Cleyre, "The Dominant Idea," in *Anarchy! An Anthology of Emma Goldman's Mother Earth*, ed. Peter Glassgold (New York: Counterpoint Press, 2000), 190.
2 Ibid., 192.
3 Ibid.

helped to inform how a new generation of writers on nature would come to understand the personal, direct character of environmental responsibility.

Gradually, throughout the 1930s, 1940s, and 50s, anarchism as a U.S. domestic philosophy seemed to have receded from the American political scene. This was due, in part, to the successful U.S. suppression and deportation of anarchist immigrants like Emma Goldman after World War I, but it was also due to the powerful draw of Bolshevism in the two decades following the Wall Street crash of 1929. With Franklin Roosevelt's persuasive New Deal nationalism appealing more strongly to the Marxist, progressive, and fellow travelling Left in the United States than competing ideologies, and with the political repression of McCarthyism silencing much dissent, it would seem, as influential critics like Michael Denning have argued, that the radical left itself in the United States was rendered dormant for the entire decade of the nineteen fifties.[1] However, when we look at the cultural politics of the United States in the fifties more closely, we see that anti-government activism on the left was not only vibrant during that decade, but had a strong popular appeal in the form of the Beat writers of the San Francisco Poetry Renaissance and was informed by an international dialogue on the problem of American consumerism.

While post colonial scholars tend to see the Beat generation's well-known adoption of Buddhism as an "orientalist" appropriation of an "exotic," othered culture,[2] the Beat religious conversion was based, in fact, on Japanese missionary Buddhists' actual appeals to the tradition of American anarchist individualism when they explained Zen to their American audiences.[3] Those poets who adopted Zen did so in large part because the critique of Western culture its Japanese expositors in the U.S., especially D.T. Suzuki, offered to them confirmed their anti-authoritarianism and provided an alternative to what they saw as the deadening effects of rationalism on the human spirit, evident in postwar U.S. culture's technocracy and alienation.

Since "Zen is concerned with the absolute individual self," D.T. Suzuki, the most well known of the Zen missionaries to gain converts in the early cold war years, believed, the government "should cast such a pale shadow that one begins to wonder whether it even exists at all," and toward the end of his life, in 1952, Suzuki stated at a symposium, "I think anarchism is best."[4]

---

1 See Michael Denning, *The Cultural Front: The Laboring of American Culture in the Twentieth Century* (New York: Verso, 1997), 77, 446.
2 See, for example, Michael K. Masatsugu, "Beyond This World of Transiency and Impermanence: Japanese Americans, Dharma Bums, and the Making of American Buddhism during the Early Cold War Years," *Pacific Historical Review* 77 (2008): 423–51.
3 In other words, in reality, Buddhist missionaries to the U.S. appropriated American culture, not the other way around.
4 Kirita Kiyohide, "D. T. Suzuki on Society and the State," in *Rude Awakenings: Zen, the Kyoto School, and the Question of Nationalism*, ed. James W. Heisig and John C.

Indeed, as he wrote in his 1934 *An Introduction to Zen Buddhism*, reprinted in 1959 with a foreword by Carl Jung, "Zen aims at preserving your vitality, your native freedom, and above all the completeness of your being. In other words, Zen wants to live from within. Not to be bound by rules, but to be creating one's own rules."[1]

With missionary zeal, Suzuki, who lectured at Buddhist centers around the country, often accompanied by the British theologian Alan Watts, believed that the Zen teaching of immediate, individual enlightenment would awaken Americans to the flaws in their materialist economic system. Westerners, in the words of his long-time friend Nishida Kitarō, were "completely unaware of what is closest to them, the very ground under their own feet. They can analyze and explain all the ingredients in bread and all the elements in water but they can't describe the taste of such bread and water."[2] To become completely aware of "the very ground under their feet," Westerners could not go by the artificial way of dualistic logic and reason, which had dominated their culture and brought it to the brink of ruin. Rather, they must, if they wished to break free of the ego delusion, go by way of *zazen* (meditation) and *satori* (enlightenment).

The writing and talks of Alan Watts echo the anarchist themes in Suzuki's work as well as his occidentalist criticism of American life. Watts, taking his cue from Suzuki, understood Zen as resulting from the contact between Indian Buddhism and Chinese Taoism.[3] Emphasizing the Tao at the heart of Zen, he then related Zen Buddhism to individual liberation from the tyrannical and authoritarian nature of Western theology. Unlike the Western God, "Tao," Watts argued, "does not act as a boss. In the Chinese idea of nature," in fact, "nature has no boss. There is no principle that forces things to behave the way they do. It [Tao] is a completely democratic theory of nature."[4] While Christianity offered a system of social relations most nearly reflected in the modern, antidemocratic workplace, Zen Buddhism, with the Tao at its core, offered true, direct democracy. This democracy, in

Maraldo (Honolulu: University of Hawaii Press, 1995), 65–66.

1 Daisetz Teitaro Suzuki, *An Introduction to Zen Buddhism* (New York: Grove Press, 1964), 63–64.

2 Letter quoted in William R. LaFleur, "Between America and Japan," in *Zen in American Life and Letters*, ed. Robert S. Ellwood (Malibu: Undena, 1987), 73. Ellwood discusses Suzuki's interest in William James's *Varieties of Religious Experience*, which Suzuki believed offered Westerners the hope of sloughing off their cultural trappings in order to experience directly the heart of Zen practice.

3 As Watts wrote in his autobiography, "I had learned from D. T. Suzuki" and others "that Zen is basically Taoism—the water-course way of life. . . ." *Alan Watts, In My Own Way* (Navato, CA: New World Library, 2001), 251.

4 Alan Watts, "Identical Differences," lecture, 1964, on *Alan Watts Live*, Shambhala SLE 15, 1991, audiocassette.

turn, was parallel to nature itself, which Watts called "a system of orderly anarchy."[1]

In Watts' political outlook, the Taoist heart of Buddhism was "high philosophical anarchy," since it implied that nature, including human nature, should be trusted fully.[2] Nature—the Tao—"doesn't have a boss because a boss is a system of mistrust."[3] By contrast, the system of mistrust that upheld the "boss system" inherent to Western culture and theology, Watts argued, leads finally and inevitably to a "totalitarian state." Combining elements reminiscent of Orwell's description of an authoritarian Communist England in *1984* and David Riesman's criticism of psychotherapeutic cold war conformism in *The Lonely Crowd*, Watts argued that in the boss system of Western thought

> everybody is his brother's policeman. Everybody is watching everybody else to report him to the authorities. You have to have a psychoanalyst in charge of you all the time to be sure that you don't think dangerous thoughts or peculiar thoughts and you report all your peculiar thoughts to your analyst and your analyst keeps a record of them and reports them to the government, and everybody is busy keeping records of everything.[4]

As a result of our ways of knowing in the West, he stated in the opening minutes of 1949 series of lectures for San Francisco's public TV station KQED, "Our whole culture, our whole civilization . . . is nuts. It's not all here. We are not awake. We are not completely alive now."[5]

Postwar American culture was not alive primarily because it was "using science and technology, the powers of electricity and steel, to carry on a fight with our external world and to beat our surroundings into submission with bulldozers." Our "religio-philosophical tradition," meanwhile, "has taught us to . . . mistrust ourselves." Taoism and Zen, instead, want us to realign ourselves to nature's "self governing state" and "self organizing pattern" in which "each one of us is that entire pattern."[6] Harmony between the individual, society, and nature was at once a reaffirmation of the individual, in the sense that one's real nature was realized as identical to that of cosmos, and a freeing of the individual from the delusion of the isolated ego. Thus freed, one could more cooperatively engage the world without government.

---

1   Ibid.
2   Ibid.
3   Ibid.
4   Ibid.
5   *4x4 by Watts: Eastern Wisdom and Modern Life* (Seattle: Unapix/Miramar, Inner Dimension, 1995), videocassette
6   Ibid.

Drawing from these anarchist principles, Gary Snyder, who converted to Zen Buddhism and spent much of the years of the San Francisco Poetry Renaissance studying in Japan, hoped that Zen practice would not only reawaken the West but would become part of a revolutionary means of solving the environmental crisis created by capitalist consumerism. This crisis could be solved if we became more place-based in our environments, depending on the land for sustenance in a mass return to Neolithic life that would be aided by the contemplative awareness offered in Zen practice, which grounds us to our environment as well as to the present. Snyder also proposed that the solution to the problem of ecological crisis was less, not more, centralization. The ideal organization of society—local, spiritual, regional—should be driven by an ecological consciousness that Snyder equated with "a political anarchist position: that the boundaries drawn by national states and so forth don't represent any real entity." Instead of clinging to this fiction, "people have to learn a sense of region." They also have to surrender the illusion that the "promiscuous distribution of goods and long-range transportation is always going to be possible."[1]

Snyder held the cold war technocratic state directly responsible for the planetary ecological crisis, and he believed that this state should be overthrown. "There are two kinds of earth consciousness," he wrote, "one which is called global, the other we call planetary," he held. "Global consciousness" was the consciousness of the state: "world-engineering-technocratic-utopian-centralization men in business suits who play world games in systems theory." Planetary consciousness, by contrast, was revolutionary, biocentric, and literary: "planetary thinking is decentralist, seeks biological rather technological solutions," and learns from Western sources as well as "the libraries of the high Occidental civilizations." In contrast, "global consciousness . . . would ultimately impose a not-so-benevolent technocracy on everything via a centralized system."[2] The concept upholding this technocratic dystopia, Snyder told the *Berkeley Bard*, was "the idea of a 'nation' or 'country' [which] is so solidly established in most people's consciousness now that there's no intelligent questioning of it. It's taken for granted as some kind of necessity." Snyder added that the communism inherent to a "tribal social structure" was "one of the ways of breaking out of that nation-state bag."[3]

As Snyder argued in "Buddhism and the Coming Revolution," published in 1961 under the title "Buddhist Anarchism," "The mercy of the West has been social revolution" while "the mercy of the East has been individual insight into the basic self/void. We need both" in order to affect "any cultural

---

1   Ibid., 25.
2   Ibid., 126.
3   Ibid., 10.

and economic revolution that moves toward a free, international, classless world."[1] Meditation—the Eastern key to opening this world—affects social revolution insofar as it attunes one to "wisdom," or "the intuitive knowledge of the mind of love and clarity that lies beneath one's ego-driven anxieties and aggressions." This mind of love and clarity expresses itself socially both in the Buddhist notion of *sangha*—the interdependent community of all beings—and in the theories of the "Anarcho-Syndicalists" who "showed a sense for experimental social reorganization" and who, Snyder reminds us, influenced the "San Francisco poets and gurus" like himself who "were attending the meetings of the 'Anarchist Circle'" hosted by Kenneth Rexroth, the de facto father of the Beat generation and old Left radical friend of Emma Goldman.[2]

Just as, for Emma Goldman, American individualism in the nature writing tradition made America seem like a natural home for European anarchism, for Japanese writers like D.T. Suzuki, the freedom promised by the tradition of American revolutionary individualism coincided exactly with the central message of Zen Buddhism: liberation from the technological into the natural life. Far from an individualistic appropriation of an oriental "Other," the Beat anarchist encounter with Buddhism was a genuine interreligious dialogue in the sense that Martin Buber might use the term: it challenged a cohort of Americans to meet the objectified Other as a self and to view from that perspective the results of American empire, an ethical ideal previously established in both American nature writing, with the practice of "self reliance" as the care of the self, and in anarchist personal ethics.

As one consequence of the wide distribution of dissident Beat writing during the cold war years, this intercultural and interreligious anarchist encounter helped to popularize the environmental frame of mind over the two decades leading up to the first Earth Day, hailed as the single largest political demonstration in human history, on April 22, 1970, followed by the establishment of the EPA in December of the same year. By the 1960s, predating this turning point in the environmental movement, thousands of Americans, like Gary Snyder, began returning to the land to seek ethical alternatives to what they saw as Cold War America's culture of consumerism and exploitation. With several anarchist texts from Goldman's generation in reprint for the first time in decades, Thoreau and Emerson, along with anarchism, would again become common fare in the countercultural Left's politics of nature.

With official recognition of the ecology movement under Richard Nixon, though, what had nineteenth century roots in a radically individualist

---

1 Ibid., 92.
2 Ibid., 106.

critique of government's direct role in environmental and human degradation was quickly becoming a mainstream, though vigorously debated, political worldview. This shift in the public's acceptance of ecology, which emphasized global responsibility far more than the more nationalist, Rooseveltian tradition of conservation that most Americans in the 1950s had known, can be partially explained by the sensational popularity of works like Rachel Carson's *Silent Spring* (1962), which reported, for example, on the discovery of the insecticide and neurotoxin DDT in polar bears, and Paul Ehrlich's *The Population Bomb* (1968), which predicted that human reproduction rates would soon outpace the planet's ability to support life. Before these sensational sellers, however, writing at the same time that the Beats were proclaiming their individualist dissent, Lewis Mumford—architectural critic, Americanist scholar, and frequent Book of the Month Club author—had been writing anarchist-inspired plans for a new, green, sustainable organization of society. With popular books in print on vernacular architecture, urban planning, literature, and the history of technology, Mumford's cultural criticism, focusing on the individual's lived experience in built and planned environments, continues to have an influence on the disciplines of urban planning and environmental design. At the same time, his strong influence in the disciplines of literature and American Studies in the nineteen fifties shaped, in that decade, how many liberally educated college students, an increasingly large percentage of the population, including John William Ward, the Thoreau-and-anarchism inspired college president arrested for protesting the Vietnam War who opened this essay, were taught to understand the collective political meanings of Emerson, Thoreau, and Nature prior to the emergence of the counterculture in the 1960s.

Mumford succinctly proposed an outline for new kind of city and a new kind of society in his 1922 book *The Story of Utopias*. As he explained in his introduction to the book, which was reprinted in 1962 (just in time for the counterculture), *The Story of Utopias* was written "in a terrified and discouraged age . . . to remind the reader of the human attitudes and human hopes that once existed and flourished, and that may burgeon again." [1] For a new kind of society to blossom, Mumford argued, we must first do away with the Utopia of the Nation State, a fiction that "had continually to be willed" through a "persistent projection," a "beautiful fabrication" that was in fact a geographically and anthropologically irrelevant fiction. [2] In America, the Nation-State, Mumford argued, had imposed a single suburban-industrial

---

1 Lewis Mumford, *The Story of Utopias* (New York: Viking, 1962), 10.
2 Ibid., 221–222.

model on the country, one that impoverished the cultural and ecological diversity of America's regions.

Consistent with his anarchism, Mumford argued that the nation-state was a self-serving entity that had designed society not for the good of the population but for its own perpetuation. Like his literary heroes Emerson and Thoreau and his revolutionary contemporaries Goldman and De Cleyre, Mumford believed that "the chief concern of the national utopia is the support of the central government, for the government is the guardian of territory and privilege." Its authority, Mumford added, emanated only from the "paper utopia" of the Megalopolis, the bureaucratic center of the nation-state.[1] The one thing the State asked of its citizens in exchange for this urban-industrial-bureaucratic nightmare, Mumford added, was complete, undying loyalty: "If you and I were perfect citizens of the Megalopolis, we should never let anything come between us and our loyalty to the State," he wrote.[2]

One of the virtues of the alternative plan for society that Mumford proposed was that it would weaken the power and hegemony of nations and, ideally, return power to local communities and the individuals in them. Along these lines, the importance of Emerson and Thoreau, for Mumford, was that they had prevented American towns "from becoming collections of yes-men, with never an opinion or an emotion that differed from their neighbors."[3] They also offered a way of refusing the pioneer ethos of acquisitive capitalism and selfish individualism. The virtue of Emerson in particular was his transcendence of his time and place, his capability "of getting beyond the institution, the habit, the ritual," and finding out what these things really are "afresh in one's own consciousness."[4] As for Thoreau, his simplicity pointed the way toward "a higher civilization."[5] "What Thoreau left behind is still precious," whereas what "the pioneer left behind was only the burden of a vacant life."[6] The individualism of the pioneer and the capitalist, Mumford believed, destroyed all that gave life meaning—community, meaningful work, political participation, direct democracy—because it cared only for personal aims. The individualism of Thoreau and Emerson, by contrast, became a template for the kind of men and women that Mumford's Utopia would create: the kind who seek Nature "in order to arrive at a higher state of culture" and who practice individualism "in order to create a better society."[7]

Given the state of the world under capitalism and consumerism, Mumford wrote, "No wonder Thoreau observed" that most men in society "led lives of

1 Ibid., 225–26.
2 Ibid., 231.
3 Ibid., 58.
4 Ibid., 46.
5 Ibid., 56.
6 Ibid., 59.
7 Ibid., 59.

quiet desperation. By putting business before every other manifestation of life, our mechanical and financial leaders have neglected the chief business of life: namely, growth, reproduction, development, expression."[1] Mumford believed that building a new Eden based on anarchist principles would liberate the individual from the machine by putting the machine in the service of the community. Doing this, however, would merely require the "services of the geographer and the regional planner, the psychologist, the educator, the sociologist, the skilled political administrator."[2] Each of these experts, working together for the common good, would establish Mumford's green, anarchist plan for society.

In this plan, every city would subsist in a bioregion, and every bioregion would be a place large enough to embrace "the diversity of crafts and economic activities needed to sustain a community and small enough so that its members had a direct shared set of interests and direct collective concern."[3] For each regional community, there would also be "a portion of the wilderness" set aside "free for the citizens from all the encroachments of civilization, where the individual could attune himself to the individuality of the landscape, and all land, not just public parks," would be communally owned, "placed in the trusteeship of appropriate municipal and regional authorities"[4] and occupied by those best suited to maintain it for the benefit of all."[5]

The primary impediment to this utopian vision of personal and social wholeness, Mumford believed, was what he called "the power state." The power state was both regressive and "mystic," something that always meant "whatever the ruling classes hold it convenient to mean at the moment."[6] However, there was another, better kind of state: the "service state," one that could operate not as "the arbitrary rule and dictator of regional life, but as the willing agent of that life."[7] Steeped in the idealism of New Deal America, Mumford was convinced that such a state was possible given all that Roosevelt had accomplished: "The triumph of the Public Works Administration" had demonstrated "superior methods of comprehensive planning and design" and had proven "the advantage of large-scale operations and unified technical direction."[8] The New Deal had showed "the desirability

---

1 Ibid., 400.
2 Ibid., 389.
3 Lewis Mumford, *The Culture of Cities* (New York: Harcourt Brace Jovanovich, 1970), 314.
4 Ibid., 328.
5 Ibid., 331.
6 Ibid., 349.
7 Ibid., 365.
8 Ibid., 365.

of planned housing, not for individuals, but for communities."[1] As long as such planning was meant to broaden the scope for individual expression, creativity, and development, Mumford believed, it could lead back to "the restoration of the human scale in government."[2]

There was, however, a shadow side to Mumford's plan, one evident in his emphasis on politics as a form of localized discipline. The service state that Mumford envisioned "democratized" the political process to such an extent that one can feel the weight of the political system in one's daily walk, and the localism of Mumford's political ideal threatens to make national politics an immanent tyranny rather than a distant one: a service state is still a state, and a meddlesome "skilled political administrator" next door is little better, and probably worse, than a national tyrant a thousand miles away. Typical of all such progressive utopias, Mumford's green utopia demands a highly disciplined populace. It would require what he called "the systematic practice of rational discipline through education and co-operative service"[3] to create a culture of the "truly enlightened and disciplined individual."[4] As the citizens become disciplined, political life for everyone would seem "as constant a process in daily living as the housewife's visit to the grocer or the butcher."[5]

The community, meanwhile, run through a system of expertly planned education, would gradually and naturally find itself divided into "the base"— those who were "generic, equalized, standardized, and communal"—and "the emergent," comprised of those who were "specific, unstandardized, individual, [and] aristocratic."[6] These latter would become the architects of the world. To accomplish their long-term goal of liberating the individual from tyranny, they would, in turn, be required to run a eugenics program to root out genetically undesirable elements from the race so that "the most reckless and ill-bred shall not burden the community."[7] Like a public school tasked with raising and socially sorting children, the service state would require "deliberate regulation and direction, in order to ensure continued growth and creativity of the human personalities and groups concerned."[8]

Similar to elements of the New Deal, the planned elements of Mumford's anarchist utopia carried with them a high potential for the abuse of power and are based in a fundamental elitism that is as philosophically removed from anarchism as reform is from revolution. After all, hand-in-hand with

1 Ibid., 373.
2 Ibid., 382.
3 Ibid., 383.
4 Ibid., 458.
5 Ibid., 382.
6 Ibid., 458.
7 Ibid., 333.
8 Ibid., 128.

the New Deal, much of which was either inspired by or directly inspired Italian and German fascism,[1] came the Second World War, which centralized executive power in ways unprecedented since Lincoln and Woodrow Wilson combined. As they had for Emerson, Mumford's love of the nature idea and his attachment to democratic principle of the good life led directly to the reassertion of the tyranny he opposed: that of a state which, whether directed toward power or service, will, by definition, draw boundaries and distinctions between groups and individuals.

Throughout his career as a scholar and public intellectual, Mumford attempted to align these two competing impulses of his thought: his anarchist individualism and his progressive collectivism. Even as he decried the influence of the machine and the mechanistic culture of expertise on American life, Mumford's proposals recapitulated the basic liberal impulse of post World War II America: the belief that planners and experts could best direct the psychic and material lives of the people and that the service state— which, in reality, is financially dependent on the power state—could act as a corrective to the destructive "Pentagon of Power," or the military industrial complex. Mumford's merging of liberal planning and anarchist individualism defines his liberal anarchism—his belief that anarchist principles of individual freedom could best be secured by massive social planning. This outlook has virtually come to define anarchist activism in the United States since the Battle of Seattle, when the meaning of anarchism—a praxis of individual refusal and voluntary communalism—came to be conflated with decentralized protest tactics aimed at calling attention to demands not for the end of government but for the enactment of more liberal and progressive reforms.

The Occupy Movement, for instance, has turned out to strongly represent this liberal turn in anarchist activism. From an actual proletarian standpoint, far more than one percent of American property holders is a class enemy, far fewer than ninety-nine percent of Americans share anything in common with the plight of the U.S. working class (let alone their global counterparts), and Occupy's on-the-ground organization by a Yale professor with the support of liberal celebrity writers like Naomi Klein makes it seem an event basically organized by and for the elite. Indeed, rather than demanding the complete dissolution of Wall Street, the extinction of paper currency, or the end of federal power, Occupy Wall Street's political demands—such as student loan forgiveness, more Congressional regulation of investment firms, and mortgage relief—fairly closely reflected the progressive platforms of mainstream Democrats; more problematically, they reinforced the basic

---

1 See Wolfgang Schivelbusch, *Three New Deals: Reflections on Roosevelt's America, Mussolini's Italy, and Hitler's Germany, 1933–1939* (New York: Picador: 2007).

liberal assumption that freedom requires government intervention. A liberal movement using anarchist tactics—or a liberal anarchist social movement—Occupy Wall Street, like Emerson and Mumford, ultimately relied upon the very progressive theory of government's role in creating freedom that gives power to centralists and their corporate donors.

Influenced by a countervailing message of individual responsibility inherent in the anarchist tradition from which critics like Mumford and Ward drew, for many in the environmental movement in the decades to follow the founding of the EPA, such liberal incorporations of the politics of Nature into national progressive politics would be seen as coming at the cost of a sense of personal accountability for one's choices in the marketplace of goods and values. Among those who have been critical of the liberal tendency to avoid accountability by turning to social policy to smooth over and equalize markets that are unacceptable in and of themselves include anarchist writers, activists, and transnational social and environmental justice organizations such as Edward Abbey, James C. Scott, Earth First!, and Food Not Bombs, and among those strongly advocating for personal ecological accountability include writers like Joanna Macy, Julia Buttery, and a host of anti-WTO protestors who descended on Seattle in 1999, a handful of whom truly wanted to dismantle, rather than fix and reregulate, the machine.

Their basic individualist ethical position has been shared, though, outside the radical margins of society, especially by ex-president Jimmy Carter in his famous "Crisis of Confidence" speech of 1979, in which he cited as a source of the world's financial and fuel crises of the nineteen seventies the problem of the individual's consumerist desires: "Human identity," Carter argued, "is no longer defined by what one does, but by what one owns. But we've discovered that owning things and consuming things does not satisfy our longing for meaning. We've learned that piling up material goods cannot fill the emptiness of lives which have no confidence or purpose." Though Carter, in typical presidential vein, went on to propose reforms to the already entrenched, New Deal inspired, consumer-driven national economy that had dominated the Cold War years, his basic emphasis on the need to first reform the self, reduce one's wants, and redefine one's values in order to live as citizens without relying on government to manage the impacts of our individual lifestyle choices reflects the Transcendentalist ethics of the care of the self, borrowed from the anarchist context of radical abolitionism, exactly.

It might seem paradoxical that an ethical stance central to a long standing individualist anarchist ecological tradition—the idea that personal accountability to the Other begins with reducing one's consumer wants and desires—would emerge from the mind of a U.S. President and be broadcast into millions of American homes, where it would also soon be lambasted by Ronald Reagan. However, like the radical abolitionists of the nineteenth century and like their cultural comrades Emerson and Thoreau, Carter's sense of social justice was influenced by his religious convictions and their emphasis on the human will, an emphasis nearly sufficient to distinguish anarchism from authoritarian communism and its progressive cousins, for whom every individual is actually seen as an economically and socially constructed entity waiting to be liberated by the state and its college educated executors. In Carter's case, like that of William Lloyd Garrison, the most anarchist of the abolitionists, these countervailing convictions—rooted in the view that the exercise of individual will and choice matter—were Baptist, and they had common roots with Emerson and Thoreau in an evangelical, Protestant tradition of personal awakening and salvation.

Carter's radically individual sense of social justice, not uniquely American (for its values have been in conversation with writers and thinkers from America's purported enemies, like D.T. Suzuki) or even uniquely Christian (it has been held by anarchist atheists like Emma Goldman) was based in an emphasis on the centrality of the individual will to effect redemption, both temporal and political. In the end, however, it spoke to this tradition of dissent more effectively than it spoke to the American voters, helping to ensure Ronald Reagan's rise to the presidency on the promise of unlimited material prosperity. Carter, to his political detriment, chose to emphasize the individual as the first site of moral, environmental choice, taking a serious stance against what the New Right Christians would also begin to deride, but from the midst of their contradictory Reaganomics, as the secular humanist world.

The challenge of this tradition of individual accountability is important, regardless of its political feasibility, to framing how we see ourselves as individuals and how we act in our environments and our world. Generally, liberal politicians, and the protesters who ask favors from them, have come to accept that organized, global reform is the primary way out of our collective environmental problems, the most pressing of which is global warming, with carbon representing, essentially, rates of human consumption of the natural world. They are right to the extent that collectively created problems usually require collective solutions. However, these efforts leave unanswered, and sometimes even conceal, the equally important question of our personal environmental values as individuals with ethical agency. Are we surrendering the moral outcomes of our choices to leaders whose very sense of the economy has brought us to this tipping point in human evolution?

I suggest (though I can't, for reasons of ethical consistency, insist that everyone has to agree) that we can begin developing a personal ecological ethics for the global age by exploring the concept of individual liberty in the globally shared ecological tradition of individual natural rights offered here. What we discover is that this tradition's major contribution to social and ecological justice—its strong emphasis on the Other as part and parcel of the self—has enormous implications for how we think about consumer choices in daily life. It draws our attention to the close connection between our individual selves, our consumer and lifestyle choices, and our collective environmental and human outcomes.

In addition to undermining natural systems, the unnatural environments we have created—environments that include our government-directed and subsidized systems of food production, our government-funded learning and government-inspected working spaces, our government-planned urban landscapes, our government-approved homes and government-backed power monopolies, and our government-paved roads as well as our government-sponsored systems of political ideology—are having devastating effects on the mental, physical, and social health of millions in the developed world while creating intolerable working and living conditions for the globalized individuals producing to assuage worldwide consumer desires. The tradition explored here, which offers an alternative ("self reliance"), was begun in a period, more or less like ours, when a form of slavery demanded immediate abolition. It suggests, in response, that the suffering our actions cause can only end when we begin to make personal, ecological choices in our everyday lives that have the consequence of leaving other people free from our indirect, mediated, state-sponsored methods of exploitation.

3. SUSPICIOUS OF THE STATE: THE ANARCHIST POLITICS OF JAMES JOYCE

Josephine A. McQuail

One of the many conundrums of James Joyce (1882–1941) is the fact that his writings focus perennially on Ireland, even though he rejected the potent Irish nationalism promoted by many in his time, like his slightly older contemporary W. B. Yeats (1865–1939). Joyce, having left Ireland in 1904, nonetheless features Dublin or a generalized Ireland, as the scene of all of his works to come: *Dubliners*, obviously, *Portrait of the Artist as a Young Man, Exiles, Ulysses*, and *Finnegans Wake*. Joyce, like his character Gabriel Conroy in "The Dead," was not drawn to Gaelic as a vital aspect of exploring his origins. His suspicion of Irish Nationalism is more than evident in "Ivy Day in the Committee Room" in *Dubliners* and the "Cyclops" chapter of *Ulysses* among many other instances. Why was Joyce not drawn to promote Irish Nationalism? Richard Ellman notes in his biography of Joyce that for a time, Joyce was very taken with the ideas of Benjamin Tucker, American anarchist thinker (Ellman, 1959/1982, 142). Joyce was also influenced by William Blake, whose distrust of British imperialism is obvious in poems like "London" from *Songs of Innocence and of Experience*, and *Marriage of Heaven and Hell*. Following these two writers, as well as perhaps automatically resisting the ideas of his fellow Irishman Yeats, Joyce remains suspicious of the state, at the same time paradoxically celebrating the myths and legends of a people. When Joyce died in 1941 in Zürich, having fled the incursions of Hitler, the Nazis, and Mussolini and the fascists, into Europe, he could feel vindicated, in that he was not tempted by the appeal of ANY nationalism, even Irish Nationalism. Perhaps due to the experience of World War I as well as hearing about such things back home as the Easter Uprising—when Sinn Fein, the Irish nationalist movement, along with the Irish Citizens Army, in league with Germany, attempted to seize Dublin by force in order to establish an independent Irish republic, only to be brutally repressed by the English Navy which shelled Ireland (Levack, 1995, 257–258)—Joyce also did not advocate any particular political ideology very clearly, but he did give several indications of his Anarchist leanings.

Evidence of Joyce's Anarchist Leanings

In some notes for a projected biography by Herbert Gorman, Joyce mentions (speaking in the third person about himself) several key Anarchist writers:

> Among the many whose works he had read may be mentioned Most, Malatesta, Stirner, Bakunin, Kropotkin, Elisée Reclus, Spencer, and Benjamin Tucker, whose *Instead of a Book* proclaimed the liberty of the non-invasive individual. He never read anything by Karl Marx except the first sentence of *Das Kapital* and he found it so absurd that he immediately returned the book to the lender. (Joyce, cited in Ellman 1959/1982, 142, ftnote)

Bakunin, Kropotkin, Reclus and Tucker and Malatesta were all founders of Anarchism. The social movements of anarchy and socialism arose at about the same time, and have many things in common, though their philosophies, of course, finally differ in significant ways. Reclus (1830–1905) initiated the Anti-Marriage Movement in 1882. Ericco Malatesta (1853–1932) was an Italian anarchist/socialist. Max Stirner, (pseudonym for Johann Caspar Schmitt, 1806–1856) was a philosopher and anarchist known for his founding of "egoist-anarchism" ("Stirner, Max," 2009). Even Herbert Spencer (1820–1903), Victorian English philosopher and originator of the phrase "Survival of the Fittest" has been associated with Anarchism, for he asserted "Every individual has the right to ignore the state" ("Spencer, Herbert," 2009). It is remarkable that Joyce identified a retinue of Anarchist writers and philosophers for use in Gorman's biography (begun in 1930 according to Ellman, 1959/1982, 631–632), and this might be seen to belie Joyce's reluctance to be labeled as an anarchist as expressed in an early letter to his brother, around March 1, 1907: "I have no wish to codify myself as anarchist or socialist or reactionary. . . ." (Ellman, 1966, 151–152). Despite this statement, what is obvious is that Joyce gave Gorman a list of the most important founders of the anarchist movement in his description of writers who had influenced him.

One of the great leaders of Anarchism, Michael Bakunin (1814–1876) posits in his *God and the State* that loyalty to state and religion were chief obstacles to social progress and human liberty (Barnes, 1930, 141). Joyce in *Ulysses* eviscerates both Catholicism and Irish Nationalism through the attitudes and thoughts of primarily Stephen Dedalus and Leopold Bloom. Peter Kropotkin (1842–1921), "the chief systematic and constructive writer on modern anarchism" (Barnes, 1930, 142) declared "ideal organization of society is the non-coercive community without private property, and functioning perfectly through the operation of mutual aid or coöperation" (cited in Barnes, 1930, 142). The culminating act of *Ulysses* is the help offered to Stephen by Leopold Bloom, who goes to a great deal of trouble to track down Stephen in the Red Light district of Dublin, and finally brings him home and makes him a simple cup of hot chocolate before sending him on his way. The fact that such a simple act of ordinary human decency would be the apotheosis of a modern day epic seems absurd, and of course, Joyce himself deflates it with the "question and answer"—the "mathematical catechism" (Joyce, cited in Ellman, 1959/1982, 501) as he called it—chapter of "Ithaca."

Apolitical Joyce?

But it is just such an ordinary act of human *indecency* that begins the epic *Ulysses*, since Buck Mulligan betrays Stephen with the condescending Englishman Haines, while the latter mocks the Irish milkwoman as well, speaking Gaelic to her—thus appropriating her own native language which she herself does not speak—while, along with Mulligan, "stiffing" her for twopence of the money owed for the milk she has delivered. At the end of the first chapter, "Telemachus," Mulligan asks Stephen for not only the key to the Martello tower where they are living, thus disenfranchising him, but also for tuppence, which has been withheld from the old milkwoman. In the appropriate fairytale setting of the Martello tower, Stephen thinks of the old woman as the prototypical young princess disguised as an old crone in order to "test" those around her. "A wandering crone, lowly form of an immortal serving her conqueror and her gay betrayer, their common cuckquean, a messenger from the secret morning. To serve or to upbraid, whether he could not tell: but scorned to beg her favour" (Joyce, 1934/1990, 14). The appearance of the enchanted princess in the form of wizened old milkwoman begins Stephen's adventure as surely as Alice's sighting of the White Rabbit in *Alice in Wonderland*.

In *Portrait of the Artist as a Young Man*, the twin subjects of nationalism and religion erupt before Stephen's innocent eyes as a disruptive force which spoils family camaraderie. As the family sit around the Christmas dinner table, which happens to be the first Christmas little Stephen Dedalus is allowed to sit with the grownups, the subject quickly veers from the luscious food in front of them to accusations by the men that priests are meddling in politics, which Dante Riordan refutes. Poor Mrs. Dedalus, Stephen's mother, protests, "—For pity' sake and for pity' sake let us have no political discussion on this day of all days in the year" (Joyce, 1914/2007, p. 27). Around Stephen the men hurl insults at the Catholic Church, while Dante stoutly defends it. Mrs Dedalus begs, "—Mrs Riordan, I appeal to you . . . to let the matter drop now" (Joyce, 1914/2007, 27). She thinks of Stephen overhearing the nasty fight, appealing to her husband,

"—Really, Simon . . . you should not speak that way before Stephen. It's not right" (Joyce, 1914/2007, 29). The dispute continues, with Stephen's father and Mr. Casey insulting the priests who, in their estimation, betrayed Parnell, and Dante asserting, "They behaved rightly" (Joyce, 1914/2007, 29). "[I]t is perfectly dreadful to say that not even for one day of the year . . . can we be free from these dreadful disputes!" says Mrs Dedalus in return. Mr Casey yells, "—No God for Ireland! . . . . We have had too much God in Ireland. Away with God!" (Joyce, 1914/2007, 34). Finally, Dante Riordan violently leaves the table, shouting deprecations at Mr Casey and Parnell as she goes: "—Devil out of hell! We won! We crushed him to death! Fiend!" Sure enough, the young Stephen Dedalus "terrorstricken" observes Mr Casey, who "suddenly bowed his head on his hands, with a sob of pain" (Joyce, 1914/2007, 34).

> —Poor Parnell! He cried loudly. My dead king!
> He sobbed loudly and bitterly.
>
> Stephen, raising his terrorstricken face, saw that his father's eyes were full of tears. (Joyce, 1914/2007, 34)

It is the mark of Joyce's avant-garde style that there is no authorial commentary on the scene, but we can deduce that for Stephen on his first opportunity for "grownup" conversation, it is not the experience he has been looking forward to. However, he is cued into what adults are preoccupied with: nationalism and religion, Bakunin's twin bugbears.

The Evidence of Ulysses

Stuart Gilbert in his *James Joyce's Ulysses*, takes the New Critical view of Joyce's politics. Citing the above passage in *Portrait of the Artist as a Young Man*, he says that

> the author of *Ulysses*, in this as in other matters, shows no bias; he introduces political themes because they are so inherent in the Dublin scene, and also because they illustrate one of the motifs of *Ulysses*, the betrayal or defeat of the man of mettle by the treachery of the hydra-

headed rabble. As far as his own outlook on those matters can be appraised, it is that of weariness and disgust. (Gilbert, 1930/1955, 18)

Gilbert's commentary here is disingenuous; it would be like saying that Ernest Hemingway in *In Our Time* is not critical of the effects of World War I on the Lost Generation he portrays in that work because he never comes out and says it. In contrast, Enda Duffy has recently asserted that *Ulysses* is "*the* book of Irish postcolonial independence" (Duffy, 1994, 3). But perhaps there is some truth in both these extreme opinions: Joyce *was* weary of politics, but he saw the solution to the problem of politics as the end of politics. In the "Ithaca" chapter of *Ulysses* there is also the following question and answer:

Did Bloom discover common factors of similarity between their respective like and unlike reactions to experience?

Both were sensitive to artistic impressions musical in preference to plastic or pictorial. Both preferred a continental to an insular manner of life, a cisatlantic to a transatlantic place of residence. Both indurated by early domestic training and an inherited tenacity of heterodox resistance professed their disbelief in many orthodox religious, national social and ethical doctrines. Both admitted the alternately stimulating and obtunding influence of heterosexual magnetism. (Joyce, 1934/1990, 666) (emphasis mine)

Is it "weariness and disgust" that Joyce shows for the constant quarrels in the Dublin he depicts over politics and religion, or is it a vehement rejection of current realities that he expresses in his depictions of the choleric personalities that argue the matters (sadly similar to the same ilk today in the United States, our Rush Limbaughs, Bill O'Reillys, etc.)?

Early on in *Ulysses* Stephen has declared to the pedantic school superintendant Mr Deasy: "History . . . is a nightmare from which I am trying to awake" (Joyce, 1934/1990, 34). What he perhaps means here is that past wars, movements, quarrels have brought nations and the world where it was in Stephen Dedalus's/Joyce's time and where it is today. How can the quagmires of the past—past resentments, past borders, past injustices—be surmounted? Only by the complete annihilation of history, which is the usual interpretation of Stephen's smashing of the chandelier in the "Circe" episode with his ashplant: "*(He lifts his ashplant high with both hands and smashes the chandelier. Time's livid final flame leaps and, in the following darkness, ruin of all space, shattered glass and toppling masonry)* (Joyce, 1934/1990, 583). Since this is impossible, it may be that simple human kindness is the only place to start.

In *Ulysses*, Jews are singled out and mocked, which we learn of especially through Bloom, but also, as in the "Nestor" chapter, through Stephen's conversation with Mr. Deasy. In fact, it is Deasy's remark about Jews, that "—They sinned against the light" (34) that Stephen answers to with his

"History is a nightmare from which I am trying to awake." Xenophobically, Deasy had just vented to Stephen:

> Mark my words, Mr Dedalus, he said. England is in the hands of the jews. In all the highest places: her finance, her press. And they are the signs of a nation's decay. Wherever they gather they eat up the nation's vital strength. I have seen it coming these years. As sure as we are standing her the jew merchants are already at their work of destruction. Old England is dying. (Joyce, 1934/1990, 33)

When later in "Cyclops" we get the citizen's mean-spirited rant against Bloom, we recognize that this kind of scapegoating is not to be condoned, and Bloom's noble responses refute the citizen's nastiness. Interestingly, in view of the possible influence of Matthew Arnold's *Culture and Anarchy* on Joyce, Ellman theorizes that Joyce got his idea that Jews and Irish were alike, "with perhaps 'Hebraism and Hellenism' in mind, that there were two basic ways of thinking, the Greek and the Jewish, and that the Greek were logical and rational" (Ellman, 1959/1982, 395), while the Irish and the Jews, according to Joyce, were "alike he declared, in being impulsive, given to fantasy, addicted to associative thinking, wanting in rational discipline" (Ellman, 1959/1982, 395). The contrast between "Hebraism" and "Hellenism" is a major conceit in Arnold's *Culture and Anarchy*.

Michael Ferber points out that "all literature has an ideology, or components of an ideology" (Ferber, 1985, p. 8). He implies even, as Duffy points out, what has been up until recently the prevalent view of *Ulysses*, the aesthetic view, misses this crucial level of meaning:

> To put it simply, literature has designs on us, palpable or not, and those designs have social bearings, however remote. All literature teaches, even if it claims only to delight. In fact, the claim only to delight not merely is false but has a fairly evident ideological ring. Certain highly self-conscious works, deliberately critical of prevailing ideologies and alert to their social bases, might make an exception to this rule, though of such works it might be truer to say that they project an anti-ideological viewpoint that is itself partly ideological. So one might argue of James Joyce's *Ulysses* that, while its many narrative stances and styles seem to sweep away all Archimedean points from which to comprehend, or at least speak about, the world, the careful continuity of its "realistic" level beneath all the devices, and the final surfacing of that level in the seemingly artless soliloquy of Molly, endorse after all the standpoint of "life," of empathy, of realism, of something like Albert Camus's anti-ideological decency, whose ideological features are not hard to discern. (Ferber, 1985, 8)

Ferber sees *Ulysses* as affirming "life," but not as affirming any ideological stance, and in this he seems to have been persuaded by the aesthetic school of interpretation that Duffy asserts has been all too dominant in the "Joyce industry." Ferber asserts that even a lack of ideology can have ideological implications. In Joyce's case, his apparent lack of ideology could indicate an Anarchist philosophy.

Placing *Ulysses* in the context of its time it is more and more difficult to ignore its ideological groundings, much as Joyce might have wanted to elude them. It was profoundly disingenuous on Joyce's part to set his novel, which he might have begun writing *pre*-World War I, in the sense that he claimed the germ of the idea came to him while writing *Dubliners*, he certainly worked on the bulk of it post-World War I (the novel includes the postscript 1914-1921 for dates of composition). Setting his novel pre-World War I, Joyce avoids the problems of his generation of writers, the Lost Generation, faced in dealing with the pessimism and angst of life in the aftermath of the "War to End All Wars." June 16, 1904, was a happier time, obviously, than during or after World War I. Joyce's novel is much more optimistic than T. S. Eliot's *The Waste Land*, published in 1922, the same year that the full text of *Ulysses* came out, or the aforementioned *In Our Time* by Ernest Hemingway, published in 1925. However, far from being politically naive in 1904, western nations were very suspicious of possible political challenges to their governments. In 1903 in the U.S., for instance, Congress passed a law prohibiting anarchists—anyone who did not profess to believe in government—to enter the U.S. In turn, one of the key beliefs of Anarchism is the free migration of people which would be allowed by the dissolution of national borders.

And far from being politically neutral, looked at with late 19th century developments in the philosophy of Anarchy in mind, Joyce's *Ulysses* may be seen as reflecting many central ideas of Anarchism, in the areas of not just politics and religion, but also sexuality. And, importantly, though Joyce *sets* his novel pre-World War I, he *dates* its composition 1914-1921. Stephen also questions the monarchy, and this is the event that causes Stephen to smash the gas lamp in his struggle with Private Carr, an English soldier. Stephen had stated to him "I have no king myself at the moment" (Joyce, 1934/1961, 591), an insulting thing to say to a British soldier since he was saying that he did not recognize Britain's authority in occupied Ireland. In addition, Joyce gives us the names of the cities, in three different countries (or four if you count the fact that Trieste would change its country affiliation) he lived in while writing *Ulysses*: Trieste-Zürich-Paris. When Joyce lived in Trieste from 1904-1914 it was part of the Austro-Hungarian empire. After World War I, it became part of Italy. Joyce, forced to flee Trieste (which he called "his second country" (Ellman,1959/1982, 389) according to Ellman) by the outbreak of war in 1914, moved to Zürich, Switzerland for 6 years, then to

Paris in 1920, from which he once again would have to flee because of war in 1939, moving back to Zürich. Another tenet of Anarchy that is, today, very attractive in the draconian regulation of national borders is that restriction on the free movement of people across national borders should be relaxed; this would have been attractive also to Joyce considering both his own experience and that of his brother Stanislaus. According to Ellman, just a few days before he died, Joyce learned that his brother Stanislaus had been forced by the Italians to leave Trieste for Florence (Ellman, 1959/1982, 740).

Joyce himself certainly knew much about emigration and immigration. Of course, he left Dublin for Paris first supposedly to study medicine in 1903, returning to Dublin briefly because of his mother's ill health and finally death, then leaving for Europe again in 1904 with Nora Barnacle, where he lived for the rest of his life. He was inconvenienced by restrictions on the free movement of people by various nations along the way, not to mention the arbitrary assignment of national borders. There was no promised job for him in Zürich, and, promised one in Trieste, Nora and he went there; within a few hours after arriving in Trieste, where he was to find no job waiting again, Joyce was arrested and jailed after trying to help some drunken sailors in an altercation with a policeman. It was only after great difficulty that he could get an official from the British consul to help him, after being accused by the latter of committing suspected crimes in England that he was fleeing from. Ellman (1959/1982) reports that Joyce's disgust for government officials, especially British, was confirmed by this incident (184–185). His brother Stanislaus was actually imprisoned in Trieste as World War I began brewing, because he too loudly advocated Italy's claim to Trieste (Ellman, 1959/1982, 380)—making his later displacement on the eve of World War II more ironic. During World War I and in its aftermath, Joyce certainly saw much arbitrary division of nations and the effect of ancient claims to certain vicinities taken by other nations. Countries, nations and states were in flux. With the fall of the Austro-Hungarian empire modern Europe began to emerge, and with it, more pronounced Nationalistic movements of all kinds. Ellman (1959/1982) points out that even as a teenager Joyce distrusted Nationalism in a pronounced form, following his idol Ibsen (66).

The term "state" is used rarely in *Ulysses*. In "Eumaeus," when Leopold Bloom, trying to change the subject from the country of Ireland, free associates, he cannot think of any good served by the heads of state:

> Briefly, putting two and two together, six sixteen, which he pointedly turned a deaf ear to, Antonio and so forth, jockeys and esthetes and the tattoo which was all the go in the seventies and thereabouts, even in the House of Lords, because early in life the occupant of the throne, then heir apparent, the other members of the upper ten and other high personages simply following in the footsteps

of the head of the state, he reflected about the errors of notorieties and crowned heads running counter to morality . . . (Joyce, 1934/1990, 646)

Bloom thinks, in other words, that neither royalty nor the "upper tenth" of society, the aristocracy, set a good moral example in society. The monarch is setting a bad example for the aristocracy, or the "upper tenth." The "submerged tenth" was a phrase coined by General William Booth, founder of the Salvation Army, to describe the percentage of British people who lived in wretched poverty in England (Gifford and Seidman, 1988, 551). A bit earlier in the setting of the cab shelter where he has taken Stephen, Bloom alludes to his encounter with the intolerant citizen and the way he shut him up by telling him "his God, I mean Christ, was a jew too, and all his family" (Joyce, 1934/1990, 643). Further, Bloom continues:

> All those wretched quarrels, in his humble opinion, stirring up bad blood—bump of combativeness or gland of some kind, erroneously supposed to be about a punctilio of honour and a flag—were very largely a question of the money question which was at the back of everything, greed and jealousy, people never knowing when to stop. (Joyce, 1934/1990, 643)

Stephen also questions the monarchy, and this is the event that causes Stephen to smash the gaslamp in his struggle with Private Carr, an English soldier. As aforementioned, Stephen had stated to him "I have no king myself at the moment" (Joyce, 1934/1990, 591). John Wyse has asked Bloom in the "Cyclops" chapter "—But do you know what a nation means?" (Joyce, 1934/1990, 331). "—A nation? says Bloom. A nation is the same people living in the same place. . . . —Or also living in different places" (Joyce, 1934/1990, 331). He perhaps doesn't sound very wise, but his definition covers that trendy term today, the diaspora. As a Jew, he should well understand that concept.

The word "state," Bloom does not define, and it is perhaps more slippery a term. A key anarchic text by Benjamin Tucker is "The Relation of the State to the Individual," a lecture published in *Liberty* Nov. 15, 1890.

> Take the term "State," for instance, with which we are especially concerned to-day. It is a word that is on every lip. But how many of those who use it have any idea of what they mean by it? And of the few who have, how various are their conceptions! We designate by the term "State" institutions that embody absolutism in its extreme form and institutions that temper it with more or less liberality. . . . the Anarchists, whose mission in the world is the abolition of aggression and all the evils that result therefrom, perceived, that to be understood, they must attach some definite and avowed significance to the terms which they are obliged to employ, and especially to the words "State" and "government." Seeking, then, the elements common to all the

institutions to which the name "State" has been applied, they have found them two in number: first, aggression; second, the assumption of sole authority over a given area and all within it, exercised generally for the double purpose of more complete oppression of its subjects and extension of its boundaries.

The lack of prominence of such catchwords as "state" in *Ulysses* has led critics like Curran to overlook the implicit political content of Joyce's book. The sympathetic and pacifistic Leopold Bloom is contrasted with the extreme nationalism of the citizen in the "Cyclops" chapter. In the world of Joyce's *Ulysses*, "right" behavior comes from one individual aiding another, as Bloom aids Stephen. In the "Eumaeus" chapter, Stephen and Leopold discuss Ireland, and Leopold remembers the citizen's insults, and reveals his ultimate equanimity:

> Of course, Mr Bloom proceeded to stipulate, you must look at both sides of the question. It is hard to lay down any hard and fast rules as to right and wrong but room for improvement all round there certainly is though every country, they say, our own included, has the government it deserves. But with a little goodwill all round. It's all very fine to boast of mutual superiority but what about mutual equality? I resent violence or intolerance in any shape or form. It never reaches anything or stops anything. A revolution must come on the due instalments plan. It's a patent absurdity on the face of it to hate people because they live round the corner and speak another vernacular, so to speak. (Joyce, 1934/1990, 643)

Bloom's moderation is remarkable in a country which inspired the violence and intolerance charted in Ulysses and Joyce's earlier works. Tucker's "The Irish Situation in 1881," is a piece which Joyce must have read with interest, and it forecasts the sad future of Ireland's struggle towards nationhood. Joyce in *Dubliners*, *Portrait of the Artist as a Young Man*, and *Ulysses* illustrates Tucker's points below in various of his characters:

> Ireland's chief danger: the liability of her people—besotted with superstition; trampled on by tyranny; ground into the dust beneath the weight of two despotisms, one religious, the other political; victims, on the one hand, of as cruel a Church and, on the other, of as heartless a State as have ever blackened with ignorance or reddened with blood the records of civilized nations—to forget the wise advice of their cooler leaders, give full vent to the passions which their oppressors are aiming to foment, and rush headlong and blindly into riotous and ruinous revolution.

Tucker admired the Land League of Ireland (1879–1892), which he defined as "Ireland's true order: the wonderful Land League, the nearest approach, on a large scale, to perfect Anarchistic organization that the world has yet seen"

(1880). Charles Stewart Parnell was elected president of the Land League on October 21st 1879 in the county of Mayo in Ireland. Parnell as the lost hope of the Irish cause is a figure who recurs in Joyce's writing. The Land League deplored violence but tried to win ownership of land to its exploited tenant farmers at the same time as reducing the rent charged for the land they tilled.

In "Eumaeus," Stephen wishes to change the subject of conversation from Ireland, and declares

"We can't change the country. Let us change the subject" (Joyce, 1934/1990, p.645). But Leopold has given an important definition "patriotism": "I call that patriotism. *Ubi patria*, as we learned a small smattering in our classical day in Alma Mater, *via bene*. Where you can live well, the sense is, if you work" (Joyce, 1934/1990, p.644). What he meant to say, Gifford and Seidman (1988) conjecture, is: "'Ubi bene, ibi patria'" (where I am well or prosperous, there is my country." (550)

Stephen, though, is neither politician nor worker, in the sense that Leopold means when he declares country to be the place "Where you can live well, the sense is, if you work" (Joyce, 1934/1990, 644). As a nascent writer, Stephen might well be one of the "others who had forced their way to the top from the lowest rung by the aid of their bootstraps. Sheer force of natural genius, that. With brains sir" (646). Seeing he has offended Stephen with his declaration that all must work, Leopold includes "literary labour" (644) in his definition of work: ". . . You have every bit as much right to live by your pen in pursuit of your philosophy as the peasant has. What? You both belong to Ireland, the brain and the brawn. Each is equally important" (Joyce, 1934/1990, 644–645). Stephen's reply in the subsequent exchange is also telling, though:

You suspect, Stephen retorted with a sort of a half laugh, that I may be important because I belong to the faubourg Saint Patrice called Ireland for short.

I would go a step farther, Mr Bloom insinuated.

But I suspect, Stephen interrupted, that Ireland must be important because it belongs to me. (Joyce, 1934/1990, 645)

Imaginatively, Stephen—and of course, Joyce—will create his own vision of Ireland, based on historical fact and existential experience, no doubt, but filtered through his own words and imagination and those of his characters. By telling Leopold that Stephen himself is important not because he belongs to Ireland but because Ireland belongs to him, Stephen is denying that the nation of Ireland has shaped him, ultimately. Instead, in the infamous words of Stephen in *A Portrait of the Artist as a Young Man*, "I go to encounter for the millionth time the reality of experience and to forge in the smithy of my soul the uncreated conscience of my race" (Joyce, 1914/2007, 224). As briefly quoted earlier, Joyce declared in a letter to his brother Stanislaus, " . . . I have certain ideas I would like to give form to: not as a doctrine but as the continuation of the expression of myself which I now see I began in *Chamber Music.* These ideas or instincts or intuitions or impulses may be purely personal. I have no wish to codify myself as anarchist or socialist or reactionary. . . . " (Ellman, 1966, 151–152). Yet, Joyce's character Stephen wishes to speak for his "race" or people at the end of *A Portrait.*

Still, the fact that Joyce chose Leopold Bloom, the Jew, to be a protagonist of *Ulysses* makes it clear that "race" does not have a narrow meaning, and "uncreated" might mean innate, again, not shaped by upbringing. "Conscience" is also a word with more than one connotation, including not only the more common meaning of one's moral sense, but also, according to the *Compact Oxford English Dictionary*, "Inmost thought, mind, 'heart.' " Joyce's attitude toward Irish Nationalism makes it unlikely that by "race" he means simply the Irish people. Indeed, in *Finnegans Wake* Joyce expands "race" to the human race, with his multiple puns in numerous different languages.

Nineteenth Century Discussions of Anarchy

Why does Joyce insist so vehemently, "*I have no wish to codify myself as anarchist or socialist or reactionary*" (emphasis mine)? The fact that he mentions Anarchy, though, is both surprising and revealing. Like most artists, Joyce hated being labeled. He didn't want to be thought of as a propagandist or anything like it. Beginning with the Irish National movement, he disdained being part of a movement. Despite so many coincidences between his narratives (even *Finnegans Wake*) and the highlights of Freudian theory (dream-interpretation, primal scene, Oedipal complexes, etc.) he always disavowed the influence of Freud (Ellman 1959/1982, 126; 436). Unlike Irish nationalism, German nationalism or any other nationalism, or communism or socialism, there is no prominent, obvious practitioner of Anarchy at a national level; indeed, the idea of an Anarchic state is an oxymoron! Anarchy, when it is practiced, is practiced at a level difficult to observe, for anyone not participating in it, at events like Burning Man or Rainbow Gatherings. Today, and even in the 19th century, the philosophy of anarchy is confused with individuals who may be disrupting events like the World Bank meetings or the World Climate meetings at Kyoto or Geneva. Even in the 19th century this confusion existed. T. H. Huxley explains in a footnote to his "Government: Anarchy or Regimentation" (1890): "Let me remind the reader that I use 'anarchy' in its philosophical sense. Heaven forbid that I should be supposed to suggest that Mr. Herbert and his friends have the remotest connection with those too 'absolute' political philosophers who desire to add the force of dynamite to that of persuasion" (ftnote 1, 214).

Even today there is little understanding of the philosophy of Anarchy. Huxley (1890) explains the object to Law very well and in such a way that understanding of Anarchy in its pure sense may be conveyed:

> the sole sanction of the law being the will of the majority, which is a mere name for a draft upon physical force, certain to be honoured in case of necessity; and 'absolute political ethics' teaching us that force can confer no rights; it is plain that state-compulsion involves the Citizen as slavery, as completely as if any other master was compeller. Wherever and whenever the individual man is forced to submit to any rules, except those which he himself spontaneously recognises to be worthy of observance, there liberty is absent. (414)

Huxley's explanation clarifies Emma Goldman's definition of anarchism: "the philosophy of a new social order based on liberty unrestricted by man-made law; the theory that all forms of government rest on violence, and are therefore wrong and harmful, as well as unnecessary" (Goldman, as cited in Falk, 1984/1990, 1).

Matthew Arnold's *Culture and Anarchy* also brings up the "Irish situation." Arnold's *Culture and Anarchy* was a major contribution to the negative connotations of the word "anarchy." Interestingly, his book was published in January 1869, shortly before Gladstone disestablished the Episcopal Church of Ireland. A great deal of Ch. vi of Arnold's book, "Our Liberal Practitioners," had to do with the question of disestablishing the Irish Church, and influenced the outcome (Wilson, 1960, xxxi), especially since it was published in the *Cornhill Magazine* in July and September 1868, and was "almost an electioneering pamphlet" (Wilson, 1960, xxxi). Arnold declared (1868/1960) emphatically: "*The State is of the religion of all its citizens without the fanaticism of any of them*" (166). After the disestablishment of the Irish Church, Gladstone in the British Parliament introduced Irish land laws. The Home Rule League was organized in Ireland so that the Irish themselves could work to establish independence from England. In 1886 Gladstone tried to get Parliament to cede to Ireland its own parliament, unsuccessfully. These issues come up, of course, in Joyce's works, as we have seen. As Enda Duffy points out, it was in 1914 that the Home Rule bill was passed by Parliament, and in 1922 that the Irish Free State was established. Joyce not only refers to these events and conflicts in his works, he dates composition of *Ulysses* from 1914–1921. It took a long time, and, sadly, a lot of violence, for Arnold's reasonable words to be heeded by the Parliamentary faction that dithered about giving any new endowments to religion:

we shall never awaken love and gratitude by this mode of operation; for it is pursued, not in view of reason and justice and human perfection, and all that enkindles the enthusiasm of men, but is pursued in view of a certain stock notion, or fetish, or the Nonconformists, which proscribes Church-establishments. And yet, evidently, one of the main benefits to be got by operating on the Irish Church is to win the affections of the Irish people. Besides this, an operation performed in virtue of a mechanical rule, or fetish, like the supposed decision of the English national mind against new endowments, does not easily inspire respect in its adversaries, and make their opposition feeble and hardly to be persisted in, as an operation evidently done in virtue of reason and justice might. For reason and justice have in them something persuasive and irresistible; but a fetish or mechanical maxim, like this of the Nonconformists, has in it nothing at all to conciliate either the affections or understanding. (Arnold, 1868/1960, 169)

Women in Joyce

Early on in his childhood, Stephen had seen the effect of political squabbles on the equanimity of his family and community at Christmas time. Interestingly, in the story "The Dead" which closes *Dubliners*, Gabriel Conroy finds himself at loggerheads with his former fellow university student, Molly Ivors, who upbraids him for being a "West Briton," or siding with the British rather than Ireland, since he writes reviews for (in her view) a British-leaning newspaper. Gabriel allows Miss Ivors's jibes to get to him in a milder version of the scene in the novel in a sort of reversal of Mrs Riordan's hysterical baiting of Simon Dedalus and Mr Casey. Nonetheless Gabriel is extremely upset by Miss Ivors's criticism of him, and the much anticipated night alone with his wife in a hotel room is marred also by the memories called up in his wife Greta when she hears the ballad *The Lass of Aughrim* at his aunts' annual Christmas party. Miss Ivors may not be too far removed from Yeats's depiction of Maude Gonne in "No Second Troy":

Why should I blame her that she filled my days
With misery, or that she would of late
Have taught to ignorant men most violent ways,
Or hurled the little streets upon the great.
Had they but courage equal to desire?
What could have made her peaceful with a mind
That nobleness made simple as a fire,
With beauty like a tightened bow, a kind
That is not natural in an age like this,
Being high and solitary and most stern?
Why, what could she have done, being what she is?

Was there another Troy for her to burn? (Yeats, 1910/1983, 91)

There can be little doubt that Joyce hated nationalism, and this is evident even in the story "The Dead" where Gabriel doesn't at first seem to be a sympathetic character when we might think that he is to be criticized in his rejection of Miss Ivors's brand of nationalism. The loaded exchange between Miss Ivors (another Molly, interestingly) and Gabriel is important to recount here. People who do not know Joyce's politics, or, some would say, lack thereof, might be tempted to think that Joyce is on Miss Ivors' "side."

—O, Mr Conroy, will you come for an excursion to the Aran Isles
   this summer? . . .
—The fact is, said Gabriel, I have already arranged to go —
—Go where? asked Miss Ivors.
—Well, you know, every year I go for a cycling tour with some
   fellows and so—
—But where? asked Miss Ivors.
—Well, we usually go to France or Belgium or perhaps Germany,
   said Gabriel awkwardly.
—And why do you go to France or Belgium, said Miss Ivors, instead
   of visiting your own land?
—Well, said Gabriel, it's partly to keep in touch with the languages
   and partly for a change.
—And haven't you your own language to keep in touch with—Irish?
   asked Miss Ivors.
—Well, said Gabriel, if it comes to that, you know, Irish is not my
   language. . . .
—And haven't you your own land to visit, continued Miss Ivors, that
   you know nothing of, your own people, and your own country?
—O, to tell you the truth, retorted Gabriel suddenly, I'm sick of my
   own country, sick of it! (Joyce, 1914/1994, 31–32)

Miss Ivors leaves before the Christmas dinner at Gabriel's aunts' is served, before Gabriel's words especially inserted in his after dinner speech aimed at her overheated nationalism can be heard. She also refuses Gabriel's gentlemanly offer to accompany her home. Miss Ivors resembles that decidedly "new woman" that Yeats loved to hate, Maude Gonne. In that all too accepted sense of the word "anarchism," perhaps Maude Gonne could be thought to be an anarchist. And perhaps this is Joyce's "point"—if he can be said to have a "point"—as an artist. Besides violent change there are other ways to effect change in society and to fulfill anarchist ideals. Even Yeats expresses revulsion for Gonne in the poem "No Second Troy." "The Second Coming" may also refer to the Easter Uprising of 1916, just as his "Easter 1916" refers to John MacBride, Gonne's second husband whom Yeats despised. "The Second Coming" declares that "Everywhere the ceremony of innocence is drowned" and "Mere anarchy is loosed" (Yeats, 1921/1983, 187–188). Here Gonne's rabble-rousing and (to Yeats) similar popular uprisings represent "anarchy" in the nonphilosophical sense.

Perhaps as a New Woman Miss Ivors is not to be admired, but Molly Bloom also has more than a touch of her independence and gumption, though none of her political rabble-rousing. Like Maude Gonne, who acted in Yeats's dramas, though, Molly Bloom has performed in Blazes Boylan's musical productions. She is not much like Emma Goldman, except, perhaps, in the matter of her sexuality. Goldman's lecture on "Marriage and Love" criticized marriage and concluded:

> In our present pygmy state love is indeed a stranger to most people. Misunderstood and shunned, it rarely takes root; or if it does, it soon withers and dies. Its delicate fiber can not endure the stress and strain of the daily grind. Its soul is too complex to adjust itself to the slimy wool of our social fabric. . . . If the world is ever to give birth to true companionship and oneness, not marriage, but love will be the parent. (Goldman, as cited in Falk 77)

Arnold had shown his support for marriage, not coincidentally, in his opposition to the Deceased Wife's Sister Bill, also discussed in *Culture and Anarchy*. He supported the continued prohibition of marriage to one's deceased wife's sister which had been passed in 1835 because of his respect for the institution of marriage. G. W. E. Russell emphasizes "his strong sense . . . that the sacredness of marriage, and the customs that regulate it, were triumphs of culture which had been won, painfully and with effort, from the unbridled promiscuity of primitive life. To impair that sacredness, to dislocate those customs, was to take a step backwards into darkness and anarchy" (Russell, cited in Wilson, 1960, xxxi-ii). To some degree, Joyce differed from Arnold on this point of the institution of marriage.

Leopold and Molly do have an "open" marriage in the sense that they do not stifle each other, which apparently becomes more "open" on June 16, 1904 when Molly takes a lover. True, Bloom is impotent, but that impotence allows Molly to avert further childbearing—advocacy of birth control being one of the major focuses of Goldman's life work. Molly's husband Leopold, "the new womanly man," has sympathy for women in every arena, including this issue of childbearing—for he thinks of the Dedalus family—and also in the pain of labor, for which he advocates the "Twilight sleep idea" (Joyce, 1934/1990, 161)—early anaesthesia, utilized by none other than Queen Victoria. The notion of a woman asserting her sexual freedom was one which engaged Joyce's imagination, since he brings up a "second" man in the marriages of Gabriel and Gretta Conroy (in the spectral Michael Furey), in *Exiles* with Robert Hand, and here in *Ulysses* with Blazes Boylan.

Anarchy and Sexuality in Joyce

For anyone familiar with the life and works of Oscar Wilde, when contemplating *Portrait of the Artist as a Young Man* or *Ulysses* it is hard to deny echoes of Oscar Wilde's and Walter Pater's aestheticism, but also homosexual and homoerotic nuances are noticeable as well. When Emma Goldman read Frank Harris's *My Life*, she commented: "Well, Frank dear, when I read your first volume, I realized, at once, how utterly impossible it is to be perfectly frank about sex experiences and to do so in an artist and convincing manner" (Goldman, as cited in Falk, 1984/1990, 232). Harris's account was of male sexuality, of course, as the title implies, and provoked a furor, but according to Falk, Goldman thought that "complete honesty about female sexuality would cause a far worse scandal" (232). Much of the scandal that erupted over *Ulysses* and caused it to be banned in the U.S. involved the Molly Bloom soliloquy, as well as the Night Town segment, but surely another aspect that stands out to today's readers is the same sex camaraderie of Stephen and Bloom. In some ways, perhaps the sensational ending of the novel with Molly Bloom's soliloquy is a sort of (what Jacques Lacan would call) lure— the heterosexual distraction from the homosexual bonding of Stephen and Leopold. Bloom urinates after masturbating to the sight of Gerty MacDowell in "Nausicaa," and he and Stephen enjoy a dual piss in "Ithaca." This is the chapter containing, as Joyce called it, a mathematical catechism, with the amorphous narrator's inane questions, followed by a reply:

> Were they indefinitely inactive?

> At Stephen's suggestion, at Bloom's instigation both, first Stephen, then Bloom, in penumbra urinated, their sides contiguous, their organs of micturition reciprocally rendered invisible by manual circumposition, their gazes, first Bloom's, then Stephen's, elevated to the projected luminous and semi-luminous shadow.

> Similarly?

> The trajectories of their, first sequent, then simultaneous, urinations were dissimilar: Bloom's longer, less irruent, in the incomplete form of the bifurcated penultimate alphabetical letter who in his ultimate year at High School (1880) had been capable of attaining the point of greatest altitude against the whole concurrent strength of the institution, 210 scholars: Stephen's higher, more sibilant, who in the ultimate hours of the previous day had augmented by diuretic consumption an insistent vesical pressure. (Joyce, 1934/1990, 702–703)

More than one critic has seen homosexual implications in Joyce's works, including Ellman, who said of Prezioso, an Italian journalist living in Trieste whose admiration of Nora Barnacle, Joyce's common-law wife, edged into seduction:

> Prezioso's admiration for Nora was combined with an admiration for Joyce, whose musical and literary knowledge he tried to absorb. It was probably this peculiar relationship with Prezioso that Joyce drew upon in the later chapters of *A Portrait*, where, with homosexual implications, Stephen's friend is as interested in Stephen as in Stephen's girl. (Ellman, 1959/1982, 316)

Another critic, Joseph Valente, points out the homoerotic implications of *A Portrait of the Artist as a Young Man* in his "Thrilled by His Touch: Homosexual Panic and the Will to Artistry in *A Portrait of the Artist as a Young Man*." Valente points out that Joyce reports reading Wilde's *A Picture of Dorian Gray* (and notes the similarities in the titles of the two works) in a letter to his brother from 1906. Certainly Joyce's remarks in this letter are interesting, but Valente doesn't mention the context of Joyce's remark on Wilde, which is sandwiched between two observations about Oliver Gogarty, the model for Buck Mulligan, but also, as Ellman remarks, along with Prezioso, the model for Robert Hand, and even for Blazes Boylan.

There is some evidence for coded references to homosexuality in both Joyce's remarks about Gogarty, as here in this letter, and also in Gogarty's remarks about Joyce. First, Joyce remarks upon Gogarty's very recent marriage, which had evidently surprised him greatly, then mentions reading Wilde's novel and thinking how much evidence it must have offered in Wilde's trial for sodomy, then again recurs to the subject of Gogarty. The association is remarkable:

> No advt from Gogarty. I suppose his writing to me was some drunken freak. I suppose he wouldn't dare present me to his wife. Or does the poor mother accompany them on the honeymoon? . . . I have just finished *Dorian Grey* (sic). . . . I can imagine the capital which Wilde's prosecuting counsel made out of certain parts of it. It is not very difficult to read between the lines. Wilde seems to have had some good intentions in writing it—some wish to put himself before the world—but the book is rather crowded with lies and epigrams. If he had had the courage to develop the allusions in the book it might have been better. I suspect he has done this in some privately-printed books. Like his Irish imitator. (Ellman, 1966, 96).

In a footnote to this letter Ellman identifies the "Irish imitator" as Gogarty, who wished to win the Newdigate prize at Oxford, which Wilde had won—but Gogarty came in second and did not win the prize (Ellman, 1966, p. 96, ftnote 4). Joyce had broken off his friendship with Gogarty in 1904, which worried Gogarty, who kept writing him in an attempt at reconciliation (in *Ulysses* Stephen thinks of Milligan that "He fears the lancet of my art as I fear that of his. The cold steelpen" (Joyce, 1934/1990, 7), and indeed the two would spar with words until literally the end of their lives—Joyce, according to Ellman, (1959/1982) died with Gogarty's book, *I Follow Saint Patrick*, on his desk (742). Probably just to put him off, Joyce suggested that they might meet again in Italy, and Gogarty wrote back while on his honeymoon, "'I suppose I will be gladder to see you than you to see me, but I miss *the touch of a vanished hand and the sound of a voice that is still*'" (Ellman, 1966, 236; emphasis mine). Gogarty alludes in the italicized lines to Tennyson's *In Memoriam: A.H.H.*, in which Tennyson expresses his, by today's standards, homoerotic longings for his dead friend Arthur Henry Hallam. For sophisticates like Gogarty and Joyce, the homosexual implications of Tennyson's poem must have been obvious, especially after Oscar Wilde's trial for sodomy in 1895.

Though homosexuality is not by any means a tenet of anarchism, it is a challenge to state control of sexuality and the civil and religious regulation of human behavior through the institution of marriage. Though they eloped in 1904, Joyce and Nora Barnacle did not marry for many years, not until 1931, when Joyce was 49 and Nora 47, after the birth of their two children. He wrote Miss Weaver, his patroness, that it was when "'reading a book on the legal position of women'" (Ellman, 1959/1982, 637), he had discovered that the legal status of both his "common law" union with Nora and his "illegitimate" children was in doubt, and a civil marriage ceremony in England was his answer. Emma Goldman, in her own campaign for women's rights, encountered many lesbians and possibly had homosexual relationships. She met the editors of the *Little Review*, Margaret Anderson and Harriet Dean, where, of course, Joyce's *Ulysses* was first serialized. Goldman noted that their lesbian relationship broke "the shackles of their middle-class homes to find release from family bondage and bourgeois tradition" (Goldman, as cited in Falk, 1984/1990, p. 130). Ellman doesn't discuss this, but Joyce was surrounded by lesbians in Paris, and they were his most helpful allies and patrons: Harriet Shaw Weaver and Sylvia Beach, and, in America, through the intermediary Ezra Pound, Margaret Anderson and Harriet Dean. As Valente points out, Joyce had no more courage, in fact, perhaps less, than Wilde, with *Portrait* and its scaled down homoeroticism, and one could say even less courage is shown in *Ulysses*, where the anticipated meeting between Bloom and Dedalus, which is so crucial, is understated and anticlimactic as relayed, at least, in the "Ithaca" chapter. If Joyce's anarchic vision includes alternative sexualities they are most obviously confined to Bloom's masturbation, erotic correspondence as "Henry Flower," and his masochism as portrayed in "Circe."

Reconciliation of Dualities and the Crossing of Borders

In Book 13 of *The Odyssey* Odysseus had tested Telemachus upon his return home in disguise, and Bloom's conversation with Stephen about Ireland is at least meant to draw Stephen out. At the end of the chapter, Bloom warns Stephen against Buck Mulligan, his irreverent and false friend. The "real life" parallel of Mulligan, Oliver Gogarty, remained a hanger-on to the Irish Nationalists, Yeats, AE, etc. Joyce, on the other hand, broke away, as, now, at the end of *Ulysses*, presumably, Stephen is ready to do, having become reconciled to his symbolic father, Leopold, and symbolic mother, Molly. The father has "come home" in this comedy, and so the tragic fate of Hamlet is averted. The son's reconciliation to the father as played out in *The Odyssey* makes it possible for the son, Stephen, to go forth without fear of usurpation. Through confrontation with Private Carr, Stephen has had an ultimate confrontation with Nationalism. Interestingly, Joyce seems to have modeled this incident on William Blake's encounter with the soldier Scofield, who was trespassing in Blake's garden in Felpham. Scofield's claims that Blake had said treasonous words against the king while summarily dragging the soldier out of his garden and down the street were taken seriously enough that Blake underwent a trial for sedition, for which he was acquitted. This was a creative turning point for Blake, who left Felpham and what he perceived as the slavery demanded by his patron William Hayley, moving back to London and dedicating himself anew to his own visionary projects, which resulted eventually in *Milton* and *Jerusalem*, his two great epic poems.

Joyce's very reluctance to be categorized, like the desire of Gabriel Conroy to escape the Nationalist Molly Ivors's relentless probing by his declaration that he is sick of his own country might indicate his deepest anarchist position as a profoundly free individual, but there are many expressions of Anarchic feeling in all of Joyce's works. The death of the egoistic self is implied at the end of both "The Dead" and *Ulysses*, and with that erasure of the individual ego seems to come erasure of nationhood as well. Molly, shaped by her upbringing in the territory of Gibraltar, has the last word, and the place dates at the end of *Ulysses* in themselves point to the transgression of borders by Joyce himself: *Trieste-Zürich-Paris*, 1914–1921" (Joyce, 1934/1990, 783). The three cities are melded into one entity, as perhaps Joyce means his vision of Molly, Leopold and Stephen to merge in the reader's mind. After all, Shakespeare had done the same in the sonnets, with his speaker, the Young Man and the Dark Lady, though the three play a complicated dance rather than ever coming together. The characters of *Ulysses* represent people living their lives with not much thought of acting to bring about true political change. Yet, Stephen's encounter with the old woman in the Martello tower reminds one of the old woman who was the figure for Ireland in *Catherine*

Ni Houlihan by Yeats. The old woman shows up on the doorstep on a young man's wedding day in Yeats's play. Stephen is in quest of her just as he is (unknowingly) seeking Leopold as substitute father. In fact, in the "Circe" chapter the old woman comes back in the form of "Old Gummy Granny" (Joyce, 1934/1990, 600) urging Stephen on to refute the obnoxious soldier Private Carr. Handing him a dagger, she orders: "Remove him, acushla. At 8:35 a.m. you will be in heaven and Ireland will be free. (She prays.) O good God, take him!" (Joyce, 1934/1990, 600).

It is difficult to say whether Joyce knew of Emma Goldman's private life, but there are remarkable similarities between their two lives and works. Goldman had also been influenced by Ibsen, taking from *A Doll's House* the point "'that only perfect freedom and communion made a true bond between man and woman, meeting in the open, without lies, without shame, free from the bondage of duty'" (Goldman, cited in Falk, 1984/1990, 131–132). Falk notes "her insistence that the fulfillment of each person's inner needs was as vital to the general good as the most salutary political events" (Falk, 1984/1990, 131). Goldman even found that many younger men were drawn to her, and she to them, though she could find no conventional bond that would last with any of them, she strove to remain on good terms with them. She complained to one younger man in the very year 1922:

> Don't for a minute think I am blaming you, my Arthur. My brain sees, even if my heart refuses to submit to the verdict of my mind. You are thirty and I am fifty-two. From the ordinary point of view it is natural that your love for me should have died. It is a wonder it should ever have been born. How, then, can it be your fault? Traditions of centuries have created the cruel injustice which grants the man the right to ask and receive love from one much younger than himself and does not grant the same right to the woman. Every day one sees decrepit men of more than 52 with girls of twenty, nor is it true that these girls are with such men only for money. I have known several cases where girls of twenty were passionately devoted to men of sixty. No one saw anything unusual in that. Yet even the most advanced people cannot reconcile themselves to the love of a man of thirty for one much older than her. You certainly could not. . . . (Goldman, cited in Falk, 1984/1990, 200)

It is well for us today to remember how shocking it was for Joyce's audience to have Molly presented as having an affair out of wedlock with Blazes Boylan, Bloom masturbating to the sight of Gerty MacDowell on deliberate display, and to implications that Molly is attracted to the much younger Stephen.

"Sweetness and Light"

Matthew Arnold had envisioned in *Culture and Anarchy* that "man's two great natural forces, Hebraism and Hellenism, will no longer be dissociated and rival, but will be a joint force of right thinking and strong doing to carry him on towards perfection" (Arnold, 1869/1960, 207). As Ellman (1959/1982) suggests (395), Stephen and Bloom may be symbolically uniting in just such a reconciliation of opposites/sameness: "Extremes meet. Jewgreek is greekjew" (Joyce, 1934/1961, 504). By setting his novel in 1904, Joyce can afford to be as optimistic as Arnold, although it would be 45 more long years after *Culture and Anarchy* that the Home Rule act was ratified by Parliament, and 53 years before the Irish Free State was finally established, with many acts of violence erupting, the most prominent being the Easter Uprising of 1916. Joyce's fondness for the political philosophy of anarchy itself underwent a sort of reconciliation of opposites, as well, though his use of Matthew Arnold: he reconciles Arnold's hatred of anarchy with Arnold's notions of Hebraism and Hellenism to come to as utopian a conclusion as Arnold himself:

> For is not this the right crown of the long discipline of Hebraism, and the due fruit of mankind's centuries of painful schooling in self-conquest, and the just reward, above all, of the strenuous energy of our own nation and kindred in dealing honestly with itself and walking steadfastly according to the best light it knows,— that when in the fulness of time it has reason and beauty offered to it, and the law of things as they really are, it should at last walk by this true light with the same staunchness and zeal with which it formerly walked by its imperfect light? . . . we will neither despair on the one hand, nor, on the other, threaten violent revolution and change. (Arnold, 1869/1960, 206–207)

Stephen and Leopold's gentle comradeship, and Molly's final "Yes" imply the (somewhat cloying-sounding, admittedly) Arnoldian idea of "Sweetness and Light," "the view in which all the love of our neighbour, the impulses toward action, help, and beneficence, the desire for removing human error, clearing human confusion, and diminishing human misery, the noble aspiration to leave the world better and happier than we found it" (Arnold, 44) are all a part of what Arnold values as "culture," and these goals partake of "Sweetness and Light." After World War I and the Easter Uprising (followed by the Russian Revolution as well), Joyce was probably even more reluctant to broker in politics than he had been earlier in his writing, and he finally opted for a philosophy that was totally humanitarian, but also one that could be practiced only at the level of the individual. Later, in his own way, perhaps, he would annihilate history, or at least rewrite it, in his *Finnegans Wake*. Indeed, though many critics panned *Finnegans Wake*, Margaret

Schlauch, writing in *Science and Society: A Marxian Quarterly*, while lamenting Joyce's lack of acknowledgment of historicity, admits that "The Chief motive for Joyce's bizarre linguistic technique seems to be a revolt against one of the limitations of language hitherto assumed to be inescapable" (Schlauch, cited in Deming, 1970, 723). Like Emma Goldman, Joyce refused to accept the limitations imposed by society, culture, gender roles, and language (besides numerous pamphlets and a collection of essays, *Anarchism and Other Essays*, Goldman published *The Social Significance of the Modern Drama* in 1914, *My Disillusionment in Russia* in 1923 and her autobiography *Living My Life* in 1931).

That Joyce, even as a writer and not an activist, identified himself as an Anarchist, is indicated by a short "epiphany" he wrote in 1906, shortly after being evicted from an abode in Rome and finding, after some difficulty, two small rooms:

> [Scene: draughty little stone-flagged room, chest of drawers to left, on which are the remains of lunch, in the centre, a small table on which are *writing materials* (*He* never forgot them) and a saltcellar: in the background, small sized bed. A young man with snivelling nose sits at the little table: on the bed sit a madonna and plaintive infant. It is a January day.] Title of above: *The Anarchist*. (Joyce, cited in Ellman, 1959/1982, 228)

Before we dismiss this as merely a self-deprecating and humorous remark by Joyce, we should remember that he kept an ironic distance from all of his autobiographical characters: Gabriel Conroy, Stephen Dedalus, and Leopold Bloom. As noted previously, even as late as 1930, Joyce stressed in his biographical sketch for Gorman the influence that anarchist thinkers had had on him.

References

Arnold, M. (1960). *Culture and anarchy*. Ed. J. D. Wilson. Cambridge: Cambridge University Press. (Original work published 1868).

Barnes, H.E. (1930) World politics in modern civilization: The contributions of nationalism, capitalism, imperialism and militarism to human culture and international anarchy. New York, NY: Knopf.

Bertland, A. (2000). "Habermas and Vico on mythical thought." In L. E. Hahn. (Ed.) *Perspectives on Habermas*. Peru, IL: Open Court Press,. 71-88.

Burns, C. L. Parodic Irishness: Joyce's reconfiguration of the nation in *Finnegans Wake*." *Novel: A Forum on Fiction*. Spring 1998. Retrieved from http://findarticles.com/p/articles/mi_qa3643/is_199804/ai_n8783546/pg_1?tag=artBody;coll/

"Conscience." Def. I. 2. The compact Oxford English dictionary. (1971). (Vols. 1-2). Oxford: Oxford University Press.

Deming, Robert H., ed. (1970). *James Joyce: The critical heritage*. Vol. 2. 1928-1941. New York: Barnes and Noble.

Duffy, E.. (1994). *The subaltern Ulysses*. Minneapolis, MN: University of Minnesota Press,.1-22.

Ellman, R. (1982). *James Joyce. New and revised edition*. New York, NY: Oxford University Press.

_____. (Ed). (1966). *Selected letters of James Joyce*. New York: Viking.

Falk, Candace. (1990). *Love, Anarchy, and Emma Goldman: A biography*. New Brunswick, NY: Rutgers University Press. (Original work published 1984).

Gibson, G. C. (2005). *Wake rites: The ancient rituals of Finnegans Wake*. Gainesville, FL: University Press of Florida.

Gifford, D., with R. J. Seidman. (1988) *Ulysses annotated: Notes for James Joyce's Ulysses*. Berkeley, CA: University of California Press.

Gilbert, S. (1955). *James Joyce's Ulysses: A study*. New York, NY: Vintage.

Gleckner, R. F. (1982) Joyce's Blake: Paths of influence. In R. J. Bertholf and A. S. Levitt (Eds.). *William Blake and the moderns*. . (pp.135-63).Albany, NY: State University of New York.

Huxley, T. H.(1897). Government: Anarchy or regimentation. *Method and results: Essays*. (Vol. 1-12) (Vol 4., pp. 383-430). New York, NY: D. Appleton. (Original essay published 1890).

Joyce, J. *The Dead*. (1994). (Daniel R. Schwarz, Ed.). Case studies in contemporary criticism. Ed. R. C. Murfin. Boston, MA: Bedford Books. (Original work published in 1914).

_____. *Dubliners: Text, criticism, notes*. (A. W. Litz, Ed.). New York, NY: Penguin, 1996. (Original work published 1914).

_____. *Exiles.* (1945). Norfolk, CT: New Directions.(Original work published in 1916).

_____. *A portrait of the artist as a young man*. (2007). (H. W. Gabler with W. Hettche, Text Eds.). Ed. John Paul Riquelme. New York: Norton. (Original work published in 1916).

_____. *Selected letters of James Joyce* (1966). Ed. Richard Ellman New York: Viking,

_____. *Ulysses*. (1990). New York, NY: Modern Library. (Original work published 1922, renewed 1934).

Joyce, S. (1958). *My brother's keeper: James Joyce's early years.* New York, NY: Viking, 1958.

Larissey, E. *Blake and modern literature.* Houndsmills, UK: Palgrave 2006.

Levack, A, P. (1993). Ireland. *Collier's Encyclopedia.* Ed. Bernard Johnson. Vols. 1-24. Vol. 13. 250-8.

Litz, A. W. (Ed.) *Dubliners: Text, criticism and notes.* New York: Penguin 1996.

"Reclus, Jean Jacques Elisée." *The anarchist encyclopedia: A gallery of saints and sinners.* Reprinted from the 1911 Edition of the *Encyclopedia Britannica* pp. 957-8. Retrieved from http://recollectionbooks.com/bleed/Encyclopedia/ReclusElisee.htm/ Updated 7 July 2009.

"Spencer, Herbert." Retrieved from http://en.wikipedia.org/wiki/Herbert_Spencer/

"Stirner, Max."*Wikipedia.* Retrieved from http://en.wikipedia.org/wiki/Max_Stirner

Tucker, B. (Oct. 29 1881). "The Irish Situation in 1881." *Liberty. Anarchist Library.* Retrieved from http://flag.blackened.net/daver/anarchism/tucker/ireland.html

_____. "Relation of the State to the Individual. (Nov. 15 1890). Liberty. http://libertarian-labyrinth.org/liberty/07-15.pdf

Valente, Joseph (2007). "Thrilled by his touch: homosexual panic and the will to artistry in *A portrait of the artist as a young man.* In *A portrait of the artist as a young man.* By James Joyce. John Paul Riquelme, ed. New York: Norton. 422-439. (Reprinted from *James Joyce Quarterly,* 31:3 (Spring 1994) pp. 167-88.

Wilson, J. D. (1960). Preface and Introduction. In M. Arnold *Culture and Anarchy.* 1868. By Matthew Arnold. Cambridge: Cambridge UP, 1960.vii-xl.

Yeats, W. B. (1989). *The collected poems of W. B. Yeats.* (Revised 2nd ed.). (R. J. Finneran, Ed.). New York, NY: Simon and Schuster.

4. Representing Chaos: Spanish Anarchism in Literature

Michael D. Gilliland

This chapter examines the relationship between literature dealing with anarchism and the historical developments of Sp anish anarchism as a social movement. The Spanish anarchist movement was the largest and most advanced example of political anarchism in history. At the time of the outbreak of the Spanish Civil War the *Confederacion Nacional del Trabajo*, the anarchist labor union, counted over a million members in a nation with a total population of less than 25 million (Bookchin 1). It has been described as the most radical militant labor movement in European history (Borkenau 35). As military leaders attempted to overthrow the Second Republic citizens responded in many regions of Spain by revolution, reorganizing and collectivizing agriculture and industry along libertarian lines. Their defeat at the hands of both Communists and Fascists signaled a period of crisis for anarchist thought and organization until its resurgence in the New Left movement of the 1960s.

Today with the growing influence of anarchist activists in such varied examples as the anti-WTO protests in Seattle in 1999, the Greek uprising in 2008, the Occupy movement, the radical ecology movement, and the workers' control and cooperative movements (Milstein 104, 121), it is useful to go back and examine the Spanish anarchists by asking certain questions. Why Spain? How did such a movement develop? What were its aspirations? How did they organize so effectively, and what were the ultimate causes of its failure? The answers to these questions can help explain anarchism's continuing appearance and message on the world scene.

This study looks at Spanish anarchism through its varied representations in 20th century novels[1]. Three works of literature will be discussed; each with Spanish anarchists as characters. The first, Vicente Blasco Ibañez's *La bodega*, was published in 1905. The second, *Baza de Espadas* by Ramón del Valle-Inclán, was published in 1932. Lastly, *Chaos and Night* by Henri de Montherlant was published in 1963. The varied publishing dates allow for an examination of the way anarchism as a social movement was represented at different points in its development. The conclusion highlights the value of literature in adding to knowledge gained from historical study.

Works of art can offer a window into the cultural feelings and attitudes of a given time and place. By examining how the representations of Spanish anarchists in literature are related to the actual historical rise and development of the movement, we can more easily understand the obstacles and influences such a movement faced in the larger culture. Such study provides an important cultural context to the historiography of anarchism while adding value to the works themselves.

Blasco Ibañez's La bodega

Vicente Blasco Ibañez (1867–1928) was an author, journalist, politician and Federalist leader in Spain. Inspired by both the political ideals of the French revolution and the literary examples of French realism as seen in Flaubert, Zola and Hugo, Blasco Ibañez sought through his writing to represent the new historical paradigms which coincided with the expansion of social and political space to those formerly excluded (Caudet 49, 50, 79). The novel in this regard is meant as a tool for the public in understanding the world. As Francisco Caudet explains: "In these ways, the novel functioned as a mechanism that, in a melodramatic serial fashion, awoke the desire to know and resolve the urgent problems that besieged man in his socio-political and economic relations" (19).

Blasco Ibañez started his literary career in Valencia. He was an active leader of the Federalists, producing the periodicals *La Bandera Federal* and *El Pueblo*. Mercilessly condemning the Restoration monarchy for its forcible maintenance of a corrupt and feudal status quo on Spain, his political actions repeatedly won him time in both prison and exile (Caudet 20). Feeling the need to address wider concerns than the affairs of Valencia, the author left to write between 1903 and 1905 what would be considered his four social novels: *La catedral*, *El intruso*, *La bodega*, and *La horda*. Following the example of previous works by Zola, the author sought to attack the social pillars on which he believed the monarchy ruled:

The parallels of Blasco Ibáñez's social novels with this cycle of Zola, therefore, are clear. *La catedral* was written against clericalism. *El intruso* against capitalism and Jesuitism. *La bodega*, against the latifundia system and against the persistence of feudal social relations between owners and peasant workers. *La horda*, against all of these 'plagues'— to say in the terminology of Zola—that impeded the modernization of the country and the emancipation of the 'horde' of the destitute. (Caudet 58–59)

La bodega is the author's attempt to describe the social situation in Andalusia. It is set in Jerez de la Frontera, a center of the Sherry-wine trade in Spain. The time-frame of the book begins roughly around the last years of the 1880s, and the story centers on a number of characters in various roles who are used to convey a general sense of the region as a whole. Most important for the present study is Don Fernando Salvatierra, an aged anarchist revolutionary who, modeled on a real leader of the movement at that time, is the most noble protagonist of the story. Also useful is the presentation of the Dupont family, owners of the winery and the lion's share of land in the valley, who treat the region as their own personal fiefdom. Always in the background are the masses of Jerez: vineyard workers, *braceros*, gypsies.

The story ends with a literary retelling of the failed Jerez uprising in 1892. Murray Bookchin provides a historical overview of what occurred (118–119). Responding to the repression of anarchists and labor leaders, thousands of workers gathered outside the city. Five hundred men eventually entered the city and broke up into small bands, doing little more than accosting late night travelers. The Civil Guard, strategically placed throughout the city, waited for the mob to kill two civilians before they were given orders to respond. The incident gave the authorities whatever pretense they needed to arrest hundreds of workers suspected of labor agitation. A prominent anarchist leader, Fermín Salvochea, was convicted by a military court for incitement even though he had been locked away in a Cadiz prison during the entire affair. Other show trials ended in the garroting of defiant anarchists.

La bodega offers a fascinating glimpse into the lived experience of Andalusia around the turn of the century. As a naturalist work it pays special attention to the social positions, authority, opportunities and desperate conditions of its characters. Through its focus on an anarchist leader it represents a great deal about the libertarian movement in the South. His relationships with the community of workers and their often idolizing opinion of him explain the resiliency of anarchism in spite of periods of violent suppression.

Anarchism's Religious Symbolism

Salvatierra, modeled on the life of Fermín Salvochea, is one of the "apostles of the Idea." He is a student of both medicine and science. His personal commitments require him to walk enormous distances to give what aid and support he can. He never drinks alcohol nor smokes. Living on a meager diet of bread and oil, and giving away whatever money, clothing, or extra food he comes across, Salvatierra is universally respected. The book's opening description of him is full of high praise:

> He was a "lay saint," as even his opponents confessed...Above egotism, there was no action that he considered insignificant if it aided the unfortunate, and yet, his name produced anxiety and fear among the rich. It was enough for him to show himself, in his wandering existence, for some weeks in Andalusia, for the authorities to sound the alarm and assemble the public forces. He went from one place to another as Revolution's wandering Jew, incapable of causing harm himself, hating violence while preaching it to those below as the only means of salvation. (Blasco Ibañez 194–195)

These saint-like qualities are counter posed with the religion-obsessed owner Don Pablo Dupont. Capricious in giving, quick to anger, self-righteous, Don Pablo is feared by everyone. The master of the bodega considers all labor unrest and insurrections to be the result of sin and erosion of the Faith. As such he forces his workers to attend mass at the vineyard's ornate chapel, with each worker recording his attendance to safeguard his job. Dupont's commanding personality comes from his own sense of self-worth:

> For Dupont, every owner was one by divine right, like the ancient kings. God desired the existence of rich and poor, and those below should obey those above, because it was so ordained by a social hierarchy of celestial origin...Sometimes, on meeting in the street a dismissed worker from the winery, he became indignant when the worker did not bow. 'You,' he said imperiously, 'although you are not of my house, your duty is to bow to me always, because I was your owner.' (225–226)

These examples help to demonstrate how anarchism has been regarded as a quasi-religious, essentially millenarian movement. Religious symbolism is used ironically to describe the apostate who looks to science and progress in the place of religious dogma. It coincides with the strict morality invoked by Salvatierra. This deeply emotional and ironic vocabulary was actually a common characteristic of the Andalusian movement (Bookchin 91). Appeals to justice and the cause of the people, experiments with more "natural" practices such as vegetarianism and nudism, and the firm belief in a natural man corrupted by the restraints of society, were all certainly more personal and relationally based than the scientific rationalism of the state socialists and the communist parties.

Although similar in some respects, the values of the new order are meant to change and often substitute for the values presented through religion. Salvatierra denounces charity as the egotism of the rich, to be replaced by justice in the division of resources. Instead of obedience is the call for rebellion and protest. Sympathy is to be replaced by solidarity with the oppressed. Salvatierra describes the social values as the actual fulfillment promised by religion:

> Men had begun again their march towards brotherhood, the ideal of Christ; but detesting gentleness, looking down on begging as debasing and useless. To each his own, without concessions, whose privileges degrade and awaken hatred. The true brotherhood was Social Justice. (392)

Much like the Second Coming of Christ, "modern man" now looks to the time of the Social Revolution for the hope of equality and peace on Earth. This replacement of values is profoundly humanistic; it places people, or more specifically the masses of the oppressed, in the position to enact fundamental change. Gonzalo Sobejano describes it well:

> The terms of the discourse seem to break from Nietzsche, but the corollary remains its own. The socialist apostle sees coming a new redeemer who is not an individual, but rather the 'immense mass of the disinherited, of the miserable, with the name of Revolution." And this mass that goes to redeem itself by itself, walks towards brotherhood, the Christian ideal as well. (Caudet 157)

The practice of these substituted values illustrates the new ideal of the socialist man and woman, rejuvenated and ennobled by the changing paradigms and relationships the modern world offers. These new values are being discovered. They are growing and developing as humanity gains a greater understanding of itself. Blasco Ibañez comments on this development in reference to the educational tool of the social novel:

> Today we live in a period of revolution. The Christianity of our age is socialism: the human application of well-being. We perceive a new atmosphere in our turn, those above, looking with growing interest at those below; no one feels secure in the place they occupy; new rights are recognized, and the great mass shakes off the shroud of shadow and forgetfulness. (Caudet 79)

The difference between Marxist scientific rationalism and the outlook of the peasant anarchists, often described as millenarians, actually had more to do with Nietzsche than with Christ. The Marxist tradition, by explaining social change completely within the context of the materialist dialectic, takes progress out of the hands of the participants. Thus the damaging effects of capitalism are seen as a welcomed and necessary step in the process towards socialism. Socialism can only come when capitalism has created a mass proletariat. Pre-capitalist societies do not have the potential for revolutionary change.

For the anarchist, the determining factor in creating a liberating society is the desire to live those values now, such desire being an example of the Nietzschean "will to power." The possibilities of ever-increasing freedom among humans are only predicated on our desire to live differently. Because the growing authorities of the State and capitalism are not necessary steps, they are only to be fought against and replaced by new social forms. These ideological differences echo the disputes between Marx and Bakunin. They also illuminate Bakunin's insightful reservations about scientific claims replacing religious claims in limiting possibilities for action.

If an individual's will is the true source of change, progress is not dependent on the highly impersonal and abstract theories of materialism. A certain kind of faith—a new humanistic belief that people can choose to become free— has an effect on the direction society takes. The role of possibility, will and faith in Spanish anarchism was noted by Franz Borkenau:

> [The working-class movement] had progressed, against the strong opposition of the authorities, without a clear theory of its own, but when it came into contact with the newly founded International and its anarchist faction in the 'sixties, had at once with passion and enthusiasm accepted Bakunin's faith. The new gospel (for this is what it was, in a literal sense, replacing directly the old Catholic faith of the people) reached Andalusia only through common participation in the popular uprisings of the 'seventies.' (17)

The same observation was made by George Orwell during the Civil War in reference to Catalonia:

> It struck me that the people in this part of Spain must be genuinely without religious feeling—religious feeling, I mean, in the orthodox sense...To the Spanish people, at any rate in Catalonia and Aragon, the Church was a racket pure and simple. And possibly Christian belief was replaced to some extent by Anarchism, whose influence is widely spread and which undoubtedly has a religious tinge. (81)

Certainly anarchism's historical religious symbolism, the focus on morality in its rhetoric, and its sometimes simplistic view of revolution as the end to all forms of oppression, have all encouraged misunderstanding of the essence of the movement. A similarly simplistic naiveté is evidenced in the novel when Salvatierra claims that the Revolution will signal an end to disease (202). Many historians have seen in this and in anarchism's praise of peasant communalism a reactionary, backwards focus that, while voicing the discontent of powerless sections of society harmed by the merciless advance of modernity, was sorely unable to adapt to the changing circumstances and offer an organized resistance. Eric Hobsbawm in *Primitive Rebels* describes anarchism as essentially a millenarian movement whose impractical idealism and illogical aims doomed it to obsolescence as it gave way to more modern forms of labor organization (92). Raymond Carr presents a similarly unfavorable account of anarchism in *Spain: 1808-1975* (443–445). Gerald Brenan compares the movement to the American revivalist periods; its heavy emotionalism causing periodic swelling of the ranks: "And so the Spanish anarchist movement, narrow, ignorant, often terribly ruthless, holding with uncompromising determination and unfailing optimism utterly impractical designs..." (197).

Such a view of anarchism does not adequately take into account the truly revolutionary challenges and experimentation that caused the movement itself to develop over time. Science and rational inquiry were highly respected for providing opportunities for human development; self-education was seen as one of the greatest responsibilities of an individual. The changing ideological currents from early collectivism to a focus on anarcho-syndicalism produced alterations in tactics which by the time of the Civil War had changed the political landscape of Spain. The simplistic views of revolution proclaimed by peasants in the 1880's was to change into the nuanced, practice-based views of revolution illustrated by the CNT's Zaragossa Congress in 1936 or by the writings of the anarchist leader Diego Abad de Santillán (Graham 468–469). Yet the means chosen were dependent on the ideals of anarchism and always related to them. This opinion of the movement can be demonstrated by comparing anarchism to the truly anachronistic, tradition-based movement that was active in Spain at the same time: Carlism. As Bookchin shows, the differences are as stark as possible (109).

In *La bodega* readers are provided a context for religious parallels. The selfless actions and ideals help to explain the use of symbolism in anarchist propaganda as well as its frequency in descriptions of activists. Such language was typical of peasant anarchism; a testament to its obvious appreciation of irony. It is also fitting in the representation of Fermín Salvochea, a man adored by the movement as anarchism's "greatest saint" (Bookchin 126).

Anarchism's Ties

Blasco Ibañez offers a number of other insights into the movement in Andalusia. The first is the spread of the works and ideas of Peter Kropotkin.

Much of the terminology and focus is influenced by his *The Conquest of Bread*: the pressing need of food as both the reason people continue to work in bondage, and as the primary cause of the failure of previous insurrectionary attempts. Kropotkin notes:

> The three great popular movements which we have seen in France during the last hundred years differ from each other in many ways, but they have one common feature...it was always middle-class ideas which prevailed. They discussed various political questions at great length, but forgot to discuss the question of bread. (95)

And again:

> It has always been the middle-class idea to harangue about 'great principles'—great lies rather!...We have the temerity to declare that all have a right to bread, that there is bread enough for all, and that with this watchword of 'Bread for All' the Revolution will triumph. (97)

References to bread as the nagging predicament of the poor is one of the constant themes in the novel. It is also understood that the world is capable of producing bread for all in a more just social system.

Also evident is the growing acceptance of libertarian communism as the ideal social organization. Salvatierra is convinced that communism will bring an end to inequality and human suffering:

> And Salvatierra, before the respectful silence of his friends, praised the revolutionary future, that of the communist society, the generous dream in which men would find material happiness and peace of mind. The evils of the present were a consequence of inequality. The same sicknesses were another consequence. In the future, the hungry would die from the eventual wearing out of their body, without knowing suffering. (201)

The anarchist sees a benefit in the great estates of the *latifundia*, the Spanish plantations prevalent in Andalusia. They will make the revolution easier:

> He did not loathe the great estates. They represented an easy transition to the communal ownership of the land, the generous dream whose realization he believe was approaching. To the degree that the number of the landed properties was reduced, the problem would more easily resolve itself and the protests of the former owners would lessen. (385)

Such statements reflect the dissemination of Kropotkin's ideas and their growing popularity over Bakunin's collectivism. Fermín Salvochea agreed with the value of the Russian's work, himself translating into Spanish Kropotkin's widely read *Fields, Factories and Workshops* (Bookchin 126).

La bodega also reflects the close ties between the anarchist and federalist movements in the South. Salvatierra, as did Salvochea, spent his youth involved in the attempts of the Cantonalist uprising at the time of the First Republic. After the failure of the federalist movement, the revolutionary, like many others, was drawn to the more sweeping anarchist views of the roots of oppression. Blasco Ibañez, himself a federalist leader, maintained relations with various anarchist clubs. While not an anarchist, the author's affinity to the movement caused him to represent it as the point of view of the working poor (Caudet 70, 72, 95).

Perhaps more developed in the story is the overlapping of the temperance movement with the anarchists. Drinking and drunkenness are condemned very forcibly as the vice that robs the strength and will of the working classes:

> Salvatierra spoke of wine as an invisible and omnipotent character who intervened in all the actions of those human machines, blowing into their limited thought and sly as a bird, spurring them on while disheartening them in their gleeful disorder...'Wine,' exclaimed Salvatierra, 'that is the greatest enemy of this country: It kills the energy, creates false hopes, ends with a premature death; it destroys everything: even love.' (387)

Once again this description is contrasted with that of the Duponts as owners of the winery who encourage drunkenness and view the land of wine with great pride.

The Uprising

In spite of his sympathetic portrayal of the landless workers, the author's description of the Jerez uprising at the end of the story is a merciless criticism of the futility and hopelessness of revolt. Lacking any clear direction or plan, the thousands of laborers have still assembled out of a desire to act. Fear and temerity outmatches their zeal, however. The small minority that eventually enters the city wanders aimlessly in broken groups. Provoked into the city by false rumors of support and nervous in the strange surroundings, the workers begin the pointless farce of checking pedestrians' hands for calluses in search of the "bourgeoisie." When such spectacle finally ends in useless murders the police and Civil Guard rush out of hiding to crush the bewildered herd. The exaggerated punishment on the working classes for what came to be a minor event would play out for months.

The purpose of retelling the story of the uprising was not only to demonstrate its failure, but draw attention to the hopeless cycle of similar events as long as the underlying problems are not addressed. As Caudet explains:

In *La bodega* were recounted the events of Jerez in 1892, but as a key to the present, for those tragic events were presented as an example of the inability of the Restoration to find solutions to the social question, so that already at its height in the first years of the new century, between 1901 and 1905, it was again producing, besides strikes in Bilbao and in Barcelona, new peasant revolts in many parts of Andalusia. (62)

The miserable workers are doomed by their isolation and material condition, the author seems to say, until they can be aided by the other regions of Spain. The last statement of Salvatierra, still filled with religious symbolism, looks for hope in the cities where similar dispossessed workers may yet lead the way:

> in them other flocks of the hopeless and the miserable, but those who denied the false comfort of wine, who bathed their rising souls in the brightness of a new day, who felt on their heads the first light of the sun, while the rest of the world remained in shadow. They would be the Elect; and while the peasant remained in the countryside with the resigned seriousness of an ox, the disinherited of the city were waking up and beginning the trek towards the only friend of the wretched... Social Revolution. (540–541)

The overwhelming value to stress concerning *La Bodega* is its ability to convey a sense of what life was like on a daily basis for the people in the South. It expresses the persecution of labor leaders following the Black Hand hysteria, placing it in a relatable context to similar "Red Scares" throughout the world. It demonstrates the relationship of anarchist "believers" to a larger public who considers the radical notions utopian, yet still harbor a deep respect. Perhaps most successfully, the novel puts human faces to the material depravity of the masses in Andalusia. Such forms of knowledge surely supplement the rich historical record available.

Valle-Inclán's Baza de Espadas

Ramón del Valle-Inclán (1866–1936) is considered one of the most outstanding Spanish novelists and playwrights of the 20th century. He had the rather unusual distinction of being sympathetic to both the aristocratic Carlism of his day and also to radical anarchist tendencies. During the course of his life Valle-Inclán produced a prolific amount of works which earned him fame as a major figure of Modernist literature. Born in Galicia of noble lineage in 1866, he was pressed by his father to study law at the University of Compostela. After his father's death he gave up law school in order to pursue his literary interests. As a newspaper reporter Valle-Inclán traveled across Spain and settled for a time in Mexico. After returning to his home country he began to publish literature. Jailed repeatedly for his opposition to the Primo de Rivera dictatorship, Valle-Inclán gained the respect of radical elements in Spain. As a widely-read figure of the Generation of '98 he earned the position of Director of Fine Arts in Rome, but soon was forced by ill-health to return to Galicia where he died of cancer on the eve of civil war in January of 1936. Some of his most well known works are *Sonatas* (1902), his trilogy *The Carlist War* (1908–09), *Tirano Banderas* (1926), and his *El ruedo ibérico* (1927–1932) ("Biografía: Ramón del Valle-Inclán").

El ruedo ibérico is a series of three books: *La corte de los milagros*, *Viva mi dueño*, and *Baza de espadas*, the last of which was never completed. The books are written as semi-historical fiction of the times surrounding the reign and overthrow of Queen Isabel II during the Glorious Revolution of 1868. Valle-Inclán had originally planned on a series of nine books which would carry the story into the 1880s, but he did not have a chance to finish (Schiavo). By writing a story about what he considered to be a starting point of degeneracy and corruption in Spanish history he painted obvious parallels to the current situation of dictatorship in the 1920s.

Baza de espadas was first published as sets of stories in the Madrid daily newspaper *El Sol* between 1930 and 1932. The writing ended before the work was completed so the published book contains five chapters. In writing his narrative history Valle-Inclán chose not to tie the story to any principal protagonist. As such the story is a collection of different characters tied together by the political environment (Vélez García). The revolutionaries in Cadiz are juxtaposed with the weak and lascivious royals. The theatrical egotism of General Prim and the military cadres loyal to the throne are dark opposites of the anarchist leaders who hold on to their idealism. The story ends before the revolutionaries are able to land in Spain and declare the First Republic.

The Three Faces of Anarchism

Mikhail Bakunin deserves credit for the spread of anarchist ideas in the Latin countries. He was the organizer of Giuseppe Fanelli's trip to Barcelona to establish the Spanish chapter of the International Workingmen's Association. He also carried on correspondence with many of its leaders (Purkey 81). His opinions had the effect of causing Fermín Salvochea to embrace anarchism (Bookchin 125). Yet in spite of being so influential in the development of the anarchist movement in Spain, the Russian never traveled there himself. Taking this into account, Valle-Inclán's inclusion of him in the story is directly related to Bakunin's role as a symbol.

The Russian revolutionary is presented in larger-than-life proportions. He is the Slavic giant, the naive giant, and the bearded giant. His movements and actions are depicted as theatrical, and his appetites astound the Spaniards (Valle-Inclán 76). Bakunin is full of contradictions; malice and violence are displayed side by side with his full life and jovial character. When he explains his principles, Bakunin has a powerfully quick mind. Yet it is combined with forgetfulness, childlike innocence and an inability to handle money responsibly. His representation in the novel comes across as less of a human character than as the embodiment of a primeval force. Such is his role as the apostle of universal revolution; Valle-Inclán uses him to exemplify the most radical expression of the movement's developing ideals.

Bakunin has taken anarchy not as merely a political goal but as a philosophical approach to life.[2] There can be no enlightened despotism; the rule of reason is negated by Bakunin's vital principle, which places no limits on the expression of life (123).The Idea is the state of being in which all individuals are completely free to develop in their own way (152). Life itself is a struggle to expand freedom against every force that would limit it, hence "the passion to destroy is also a creative passion" (85). His message of the redeeming qualities of expressions of freedom has a very existentialist tone: "Rebellion is a state of grace" (122). The corrupting influence of authority has kept humanity from reaching its true social potential. His mission is thus to overturn the rule of the bourgeois order: "I begin by damning whatever revolution that is not for destroying all the Institutions of the State. (151).

Whereas Bakunin holds nothing back, Salvochea is the picture of a reserved disciple. Having left his comfortable lifestyle in order to devote himself to the ideals of social revolution, the Spaniard looks to his teacher for guidance. Bakunin chides him for not completely escaping the social prejudices of the bourgeoisie (79). Yet his character again displays the austere, selfless commitment of a lay saint. The over-consumption of the Master is a continual contrast to the abnegating simplicity of Salvochea's life. His quiet demeanor hides the same longings for a revolutionary change as his teacher:

> He spent much time absorbed in his vague revolutionary dreams, his sleepy eyes looking over the distance of the sea, his mood suspended in the apocalyptic vision of uniting men with new bonds of love, freed of all the differences of races, of peoples and of hierarchies: he yearned for a vast avenging revolution, the furies lit by a redeeming terrorism. (70)

Salvochea's immediate concern in the novel is the protection and aid of an abused girl, Sofi. While the other republican revolutionaries endlessly debate on the political events in Spain, Fermín's care for Sofi demonstrates the anti-political message of the new social gospel. The goal of this universalist revolution is to redeem and empower all people to live their own lives. Although he never stops promoting the destruction of the State, Salvochea identifies with the unfortunate woman. His legitimate concern and actions are represented by the author as the most noble and far-reaching standards of social change, highlighting the political opportunism of other groups in the story.

Sergei Nechaev plays a more vilified role in the story. Often called merely "the Boy," Nechaev is based on an actual Russian associate of Bakunin's. A fanatic, Nechaev welcomed all acts of violence as contributing to the disruption and instability of the social order. The political end justified any means. Bakunin's relationship with such a dangerous man was used against him when he was expelled from the International. When he broke off ties, Nechaev stole a number of papers before he fled away (Marshall 283–285).

The fanaticism and dangerous nature of Nechaev are prominently displayed. Neither Bakunin nor Salvochea trust him. He is suspicious and resentful. He defends petty theft as the promotion of disorder, claiming that anyone who fails to act in such a way is a traitor to the cause (119). At the same time he is willing to endure anything himself. He lives a hard life of deprivation and sacrifice for the sake of the revolution. Bakunin provides a telling description:

> He's not a *canaille*, but when he believes he's acting for the good of the cause, nothing stops him. Introduced into your good graces, he would spy on you, slander you, open all your drawers, read all your mail, and when he found a letter that seemed interesting, which is to say compromising, he would not hesitate to steal it from you. If you present him to a friend, he would immediately set out to make you enemies. His primary motivation is always to sow hatred and discord. (69)

Sergei's role is not only as a figurehead for "propaganda of the deed," but as an example of violence divorced from any truly beneficial potential.

Relevance to Republican-Era Anarchism

In the same way that Valle-Inclán uses the negative portrayals of military leaders in 1868 to criticize the Primo de Rivera dictatorship of the 1920s, his representations of anarchists also reflect an awareness of that movement in the first years of the Second Republic. Varied descriptions of Bakunin reflect the increasing prevalence of materials in Spain regarding the anarchist's life and works (Purkey 81). Bakunin's radical message is seen as an ideal or essential attitude that Salvochea, representing anarchism as it has developed in Spain, is still learning to put into practice. There is pride in the depiction of the Spanish anarchist. His accomplishments and solidarity with the oppressed are taken as acknowledged facts.

The addition of Nechaev in the story is meant to provide a note of caution. Anarchism's historic defense of criminals and prisoners stems both from the shared experience of anarchists as outlaws, and as part of the larger claim that criminality is fostered by an unjust and oppressive social system. Calls for the abolishment of the prison system were made by many famous anarchists, including Peter Kropotkin and Alexander Berkman (Baldwin 219, Berkman). The movement's unwillingness to condemn criminality on the part of the lower classes provoked resentment from many citizens.

When the Republic was declared, officials moved quickly from the political rhetoric concerning freedom and autonomy to demands that the citizen's first responsibility be the maintenance of public discipline. As Chris Ealham explains:

> This emphasis on order was evident at the very birth of democracy, when Macià announced: 'Anyone who disturbs the order of the new Catalan Republic will be considered an *agent provocateur* and a traitor to the nation'...These themes were later developed by Companys, Barcelona's first republican civil governor, who emphasized the need for 'discipline' within a 'republic of order', promising 'strong measures' against those who represented 'the negation of authority.' (63)

Such statements reflected the liberal republican opinion that law and order could solve the complicated social questions facing Spain. Citizens were expected to wait patiently for the gradual application of reforms. The uneasy political climate fed into fears that disorder would create a situation whereby power would fall back into the hands of military despots.

Valle-Inclán's work was an attempt to examine the Iberian cycle of military seizures of power followed by abortive attempts at reform. As such, the author alluded to the possibility that the Second Republic could go the way of the First. Nechaev, as a representation of dangerous and criminal elements gathered under the fold of anarchism, is a criticism of the lack of discernment. As Bakunin explains his continued relationship with the fanatic: "...Today nothing weighs on me so much, but we are too united, and we are already unable to break apart..." (69). To Spain's middle classes, this statement echoed anarchists' own ties to dangerous "uncontrollables."

Sympathetic to many of anarchism's ideals, Valle-Inclán nonetheless reflected the worries of an insecure republican position in his novel. Although calls for discernment were justifiable regarding unprincipled individuals, they contradict the inclusive attitude of the movement. For anarchist organizers living among the workers, immigrants, and families of Barcelona's poorest districts, lower class criminality was an inevitability in a society that creates and represses a lower class. They argued that the maintenance of present inequalities fell on the republican state, and thus it was still the role of the dispossessed to revolt against their position and act directly in solidarity with others.

Montherlant's Chaos and Night [Le Chaos et la Nuit]

The French novelist and playwright Henri de Montherlant (1896–1972) provides a deeply contrarian view of an anarchist in his work *Chaos and Night* (1963). Born in Neuilly outside of Paris, Montherlant gained prestige in the 1920s for his early literary works. As a committed anti-humanist writer his novels share themes of nihilism, the absence of Truth, and the psychological penchant for self-deception. Montherlant's childhood was spent in a reactionary household, with his father regularly highlighting their aristocratic lineage. He served in the army during World War I; the experiences in war influenced him later to stress the values of heroism and power, military camaraderie, and manly virtues in his writings. The misogynist portrayals of his characters prompted Simone de Beauvoir to respond in an entire chapter of her book *The Second Sex*. During World War II Montherlant was vilified as a collaborator for his criticisms of France's Third Republic, and for his opinion that the occupation of France was justified by Germany's superior force. Suffering from sickness in his later years, Montherlant committed suicide in 1972 (Indiana vii-viii).

This background allows the reader to appreciate the portrayal of Spanish anarchism from the point of view of a writer unsympathetic to the movement. The time-frame for the writing of the book, published in 1963, corresponds to the period after the Spanish Civil War when anarchists were thrown into exile. The perspective of Montherlant, as a French writer in the country that received the largest amount of refugees from the conflict, provides insights into anarchism's crisis after the fight for Spain was lost. Through it the period of anarchism's crisis can be examined.

Chaos and Night, set in 1959, focuses on the decaying condition of a Spanish anarchist refugee, Celestino Marcilla. Twenty years of exile in France have nurtured his bitterness and resentment towards the direction the world has taken. A vain, self-righteous and vengeful man, Don Celestino has a distinct ability to "never see reality as it really is" (Montherlant 50). He attempts to dominate his small circle of relationships through insults and manipulation. Collecting on a small stipend from his family's aristocratic estates back in Spain rather than attempting to get work, the old man lives with his daughter Pascualita. She resents her father for paying no attention to her future, focusing instead on his petty political obsessions.

Fearing his death Don Celestino struggles to ignore the insignificance of his life, his political opinions, and his activities. When word of his sister's death in Madrid reaches him, it awakens delusions of a heroic end; a dangerous return to his country where police still threaten him for violent acts committed during the war. What he instead discovers on his arrival in Spain is a modern, developing nation that has forgotten him and his kind completely. This fact is too much for Celestino, who shamefully ruins his last remaining relationship with Pascualita in order to hide in indifference. His death from the cumulative weight of perceived betrayals and injustices demonstrates how pride, fear and weakness can be consuming traits.

Defeat and Marginalization

Such a profoundly negative depiction of an anarchist is very much tied to the historic destruction of the movement in Spain. Montherlant explains in the preface that his original idea for the plot was based on a desire to express the weakness and self-loathing exemplified by the final chapters. He notes how he came to represent the protagonist:

> I had some hesitation about the civil status I should give my hero. A Spaniard living in Spain? I do not possess the knowledge of Spanish society that would have been required. Living in France, then? In this case it seemed reasonable to make him a political refugee rather than a supporter of the present régime: it was the feelings natural to an exile belonging to a defeated party which brought him to the situation around which I wrote the book. (11)

Thus the book relies on the fact of exile and its emotional effects to set the stage for the anti-hero. Had the revolution continued and Franco's troops been defeated, such a characterization would have fallen on another group.

The shattering of effective organizations such as the CNT marginalized the libertarian movement as a whole, rendering it unable to speak for itself. While the anarchists continued to provide a unique perspective on world developments, they had little means of sharing such a message with a broader culture. The silence that proceeded, combined with the ascension of antagonistic groups, explains the portrayal of anarchism as a movement of the past. The end of World War II witnessed shifting concentrations of power, the rising role of an anti-colonial world movement, and what seemed to be an explosion of technological progress including nuclear energy and weapons. The perceived absence of an anarchist perspective on these events was taken as proof that the movement had little to offer (Marshall 539).

The presentation of anarchism in *Chaos and Night* is completely based on the appraisal of the movement as a footnote in history. For Celestino the driving force of his obsessions is his desire to prove himself and his political beliefs relevant in a world in which they are increasingly irrelevant. For this reason he devotes his time to newspapers, responding with comically incoherent letters to the editors. He explains to his friend Ruiz:

'One cannot understand the evening papers if one hasn't read the morning ones. It's like a serial: if you miss a single number, you're lost.'

'What if you are?'

'To be unaware of what's happening in our time, what's coming in, what's changing, is to sin against progress, to show that you despise it...'

'...Missiles, pluviometers, Pakistan, yams: everything, I must keep up with everything! Always at the listening post, always on the look-out.' (22)

His attention to world events, however, never translates into a single relevant action. At the end of the day Celestino is still defined by his inability to maintain a human relationship in any form. He is isolated and alone.

The opinion of the other characters in the story confirm the view that anarchism is antiquated. Ruiz argues with Celestino: "Your will aspires towards the future, perhaps, but your innermost being belongs to the past; all anarchists belong to the past, because they only believe in death." And again: "...Your secularism is as antiquated as your anarchism..." Celestino's political beliefs are just another manifestation of his loose grasp on reality: "You have never understood a thing about anything—which is why you became an anarchist..." An almost identical opinion is explained to Pascualita by the family's lawyer in Spain: "Your father, being an anarchist, has a totally unreal view of the world: anarchism is first and foremost an absurdity. His fears are also part of his unreal view of the world" (24, 29, 30, 113).

The inability of anarchists to provide their own defense meant that the movement was swallowed up in caricatures from both sides of the political spectrum. To those on the Right anarchism was the excuse of the criminal classes against law and order, and a political banner for the murderous impulse in people evidenced by church burnings and anti-clerical riots (Ealham xviii). Criticisms on the Left echoed those of Marx, Engels, Trotsky, etc., labeling anarchism as anti-revolutionary, hopelessly ineffective, and mainly as a variant of the bourgeois liberal order. Perhaps more importantly, it placed the blame on anarchists for the victory of Fascist forces in the Civil War by claiming that their independence and focus on social revolution had fatally weakened the Republican war effort. This view is expressed by Ruiz:

If you were capable of compromising anything, you would compromise your own party. What is more, it's because of men like you that we lost our war. You're always going on about Don Quixote. Don Quixote was the first anarchist; he was irrational and pig-headed, which is why he lost his battles nine times out of ten. (30)

Celestino hears the same Communist party narrative when he tries to engage in a dialogue with a leftist French journal. The editor responds,

> referring to 'certain Spaniards of today, out-of-date anarchists, who reveal the same fatal lack of understanding of the laws and the tasks of the revolution as their fathers,' and going on to show these same fathers 'sabotaging the workers' insurrection in 1937 and helping to save the dictatorship of the bourgeoisie, in other words proving themselves, at the most critical moment, counter-revolutionary. (49)

Even Celestino had come to accept that, like it or not, Communism would be the future of the proletariat. Anarchism had no support in either Spain or France: "Detested in Spain, even under the Republic, in France the word anarchist, very nineteenth century, evoked the idea of fanatics hurling bombs into crowds, or criminals using the label as an excuse for indulging in larceny" (97).

The Absence of a Revolution

A related development in the representation of the Spanish Civil War is the blending and disappearance of the social revolution into the narrative of the Second Republic's defense. Republican and Soviet propaganda in the foreign press during the war was united in the denial that a revolution was taking place in Spain. At home, actions not directed by the central government were condemned as the diversion of manpower and resources from the war effort (Orwell 59). The issue was not commitment to the repulsion of Fascist forces, however, but a question of the authority of a slow-to-respond central government.

In reality there was never a question of a lack of support for the war effort in the anarchist-controlled areas. The masses of workers if anything were more likely to take a personal stake in the war when it was a portrayed as a defense of the gains being won by the revolution. This is evidenced by the spontaneous repulsion of military forces by citizens across Spain at the outset of the coup attempt (Orwell 49–52), by the early successes of anarchist militias on the Aragon front, and by the increased productivity attested to by many of the 1,600 collectives established across the country (Guérin 134–135). The later events of the war, including the suppression of dissidents, the formation of the secret police, and other authoritarian policies of the Republican government promoted apathy and disinterest in the war. Yet these actions in Spain were excused by the standard war slogan: first the war, then the revolution. In this way government forces could maintain an ambiguous line with the working classes in Spain, holding out the possibility of a future revolution while at the same time doing its utmost to roll back the collectives and other revolutionary activity (Orwell 55). This deceitful position concerning revolution was only strengthened by the entrance of anarchist groups into the coalition government at the expense of workers' gains (Marshall 465).

The portrayal of history in *Chaos and Night* reflects the "No Revolution" narrative. As such, none of the successes or creative developments of anarchist groups are ever portrayed. The role of the anarchist is always destructive, never constructive. Celestino identified himself the same way: "Let others be constructive, much good might it do them! His job was to destroy. That was simple and uncomplicated, just the thing for an ideological throwback" (144). His actions directly before the coup attempt are similarly violent: "From the beginning of '36 it was nothing but *juerga* in the streets. The decline of the Republic was the last thing he worried about; the aim was to have a good time, and to hell with 'solidarity': he shot at the socialists too" (41). Anarchism is the religion of death and the worship of Nothing, as nothing is the only thing left when a person is against everything (227). In this way anarchy is reduced to the familiarly derisive definition of chaos rather than the promotion of an alternative social model.

The Protagonist as Non-Representative

In spite of the unfavorable depiction of anarchism in the novel, Montherlant makes it clear that the character of Celestino is not meant to typify the Spanish Left:

> The number of anarchists or pseudo-anarchists in Spain in 1936 is usually estimated at two millions, and this without counting those who were never registered. It is more than likely that there existed a Celestino among these two million odd, and Spanish friends, both left-wing and right-wing, to whom I have shown my manuscript confirm this. Moreover, as I have never ceased pointing out, Celestino is an exceptional case, ill at ease even with his own party. (12)

The scarce references to other anarchists leave open the possibility that anarchism is not merely a rationale for violence. Celestino associates with no one from anarchist circles, out of fear of losing the protection of the French state: "...moreover, as might be expected, he had nothing but aversion for anything to do with association, solidarity, mutual aid" (47).

Celestino's values are actually shed of any anarchist meaning except violence and nihilism. They are often a counter-value. The exiled Spaniard is in no way an internationalist; he cares nothing about the condition of the French proletariat (80). It was perhaps the realization of the cheapness of life among the street urchins of his youth that drew him to the working classes in the first place (117). His political beliefs themselves are only skin-deep and carry no real conviction other than a stubborn insistence that he is right. These beliefs easily ignored when he feels it convenient: "In effect, what had been revealed to him was that the State acquires some meaning when it allows you to kill legally those of your compatriots who do not think as you do" (41). The book makes clear that he prefers war and strife to any dreams of social harmony (50). Faced with death, Celestino knows only egotism: "The advent of socialism is more important than the moon...but my death is more important than socialism" (225).

Montherlant is at pains to throw doubt on the very idea of powerful social bonds, at least in the modern world:

> In Paris, and doubtless elsewhere, it is a general rule that twenty years of conversation, of familiarity, of kindness, of intimacy or of what passes for intimacy, with one's wife, one's mistress, one's friends, one's secretary, one's servant, creates nothing and is nothing: one parts for ever in an instant, as though one had never met...Separation without continuous pain mean indifference, no matter in what tender colours this indifference is painted. (35–36)

The ties that do exist between people are portrayed as negative traits: the fear of being considered weak, the perverse joy of petty revenge, the desire to dominate others. Indifference becomes the goal and the highest ideal for Celestino; with it he attempts to shield himself from the pain of human futility (233). It is the reason for his attempt to break all human ties with friends and family.

This imposition of hateful values on anarchist symbols is expressed powerfully as Celestino prepares to return to Spain. Going through his things, the old man finds the red and black anarchist scarf that he had carried with him over the border into France. Wanting to keep a piece for nostalgia, but afraid of being identified as a Republican, Celestino debates which color he should keep. The reason behind his conclusion is given: "He had finally chosen black, because black represented non-hope, which was even more important than blood" (143). Anarchism's symbol for the suffering of the oppressed and the revolutionary cause was given new meaning; a personal meaning that placed itself in direct opposition to the goals of the movement.

Montherlant uses anarchy as a metaphor for the meaninglessness of life. Celestino comes to this self-realization just before the moment of his death:

> Comrades! How foolish you have been to suffer—to suffer for the sake of chaos, which will dissolve into night...there was chaos, which was life, and night, which was whatever exists before life and after

life (Chaos and Night, two characters in the divine comedy of Hesiod, whom Celestino had never read). There was non-sense, which was life, and non-being, which was what exists before life and after it. (239, 242)

By representing anarchism negatively, *Chaos and Night* is silent concerning the value such a movement held as an example to future social experiments. The pessimistic message of the novel also strongly contradicts the humanistic values and social bonds on which the movement has been historically based. Such a relegation of anarchism to the dustbin of history is actually typical of the time-frame of the work, set shortly after the devastating defeat and collapse of anarchist organizations. Montherlant published this work near the end of the post-war disappearance of anarchist thought on the world scene. At the same time, various activists and social leaders were already beginning to re-examine the relevance of anarchist ideals as they applied to their own liberation struggles (Marshall 669).

Conclusion

Historical fiction can be a much more informative source for insight into social problems than academic studies in the social sciences. The reason is that a writer is freed from the restrictions of protocols involved in social science research; he or she can use the full force of imagination to represent both problems and solutions. Artistic works influence the society around them, and are likewise influenced by it. Although not always historically accurate, even the inaccuracies shed light on the cultural feelings and attitudes in evidence at the time. The reader benefits greatly from the additional context provided by the fictional account.

Spanish anarchism is intriguing because of its experiments in alternative social models. Although the strength of this early movement came to an end as the world witnessed the rise of state communism and fascism, its example has been used to challenge oppressive human relations in the present era. As Murray Bookchin concludes in his classic study of the anarchists:

The basic question raised by Spanish Anarchism was whether it is possible for people to gain full, direct, face-to-face control over their everyday lives, to manage society in their own way—not as 'masses' guided by professional leaders, but as thoroughly liberated individuals in a world without leaders or led, without masters or slaves. (8)

Such a question will constantly be played out through a vast network of human relations in which people can choose to behave in libertarian or authoritarian ways. Anarchism represents the ever-present possibility of rebellion, the direct action of an individual for his or her own freedom. It is impossible to say whether the anarchists' beliefs of mutual aid and non-coercive possibilities will eventually win out. Whether they do or not depends on the success of creating and strengthening new social values and bonds (Turcato xxiii).

Notes

1. Translations from Spanish sources are mine.
2. "What I preach then is, to a certain extent, *the revolt of life* against science, or rather against the *government* of science...Science, being called upon to henceforth represent society 's collective consciousness, must really become the property of everybody...The world of scientific abstraction is not revealed; it is inherent in the real world, of which it is only the general or abstract expression and representation. As long as it forms a separate region, specially represented by the *savants* as a body, this ideal world threatens to take the place of a good God to the real world, reserving for its licensed representatives the office of priests..." Bakunin, Mikhail. *"On Science and Authority."* In Graham, Robert, ed. *Anarchism: A Documentary History of Libertarian Ideas, Vol. 1.* New York, NY; Black Rose Books, 2005, pg. 92

References

Baldwin, Roger, ed. Kropotkin's Revolutionary Pamphlets: A Collection of Writings by Peter Kropotkin. New York, NY: Dover Publications, 1970

Bakunin, Mikhail. "On Science and Authority." In Graham, Robert, ed. Anarchism: A Documentary History of Libertarian Ideas, Vol. 1. New York, NY; Black Rose Books, 2005

Berkman, Alexander. *Prison Memoirs of an Anarchist.* New York, NY: New York Review of Books, 1970

"Biographia: Ramón del Valle-Inclán." ElPasajero.com. 21 November 2000. Web. 29 November 2009 ‹http://www.elpasajero.com/Biografia.htm›

Blasco Ibañez, Vicente. La Bodega: Edición de Francisco Caudet. Madrid: Ediciones Cátedra, 1998.

Borkenau, Franz. *The Spanish Cockpit: An Eyewitness Account of the Spanish Civil War.* London; Phoenix Press, 2000.

Bookchin, Murray. *The Spanish Anarchists: The Heroic Years, 1868–1936.* New York, NY: Harper Colophon, 1977.

Brenan, Gerald. *The Spanish Labyrinth.* New York; Cambridge University Press, 1980.

Carr, Raymond. *Spain: 1808–1975*. Oxford, England: Oxford University Press, 1982

Caudet, Francisco. "Introduction." In Vicente Blasco Ibañez. *La bodega:* Edición de Francisco Caudet. Madrid: Ediciones Cátedra, 1998

Ealham, Chris. *Anarchism and the City: Revolution and Counter-Revolution in Barcelona, 1898–1937*. Oakland, CA: AK Press, 2010.

Graham, Robert, ed. *Anarchism: A Documentary History of Libertarian Ideas*, Vol. 1. New York, NY; Black Rose Books, 2005.

Guérin, Daniel. *Anarchism*. New York, NY: Monthly Review Press, 1970.

Hobsbawm, E.J. *Primitive Rebels*. New York, NY: The Norton Library, 1959

Indiana, Gary. "Introduction." In Henri de Montherlant. *Chaos and Night*. New York, NY: New York Review of Books, 2009

Kropotkin, Peter. *The Conquest of Bread*. Oakland, CA: AK Press, 2007

Marshall, Peter. *Demanding the Impossible: A History of Anarchism*. Oakland, CA: PM Press, 2010

Milstein, Cindy. *Anarchism and Its Aspirations*. Oakland, CA: AK Press, 2010

Montherlant, Henri de. *Chaos and Night*. Trans. Terence Kilmartin. New York, NY: New York Review of Books Publishing, 2009.

Orwell, George. *Homage to Catalonia*. New York, NY: Harcourt, Brace & World, Inc., 1952.

Purkey, Lynn. "Anarchists As Ethical Models in Valle-Inclán's El ruedo ibérico." España Contemporánea, Tomo. 20, No. 2, Fall, 2007

Schiavo, Leda. "La génesis de El ruedo ibérico." The Virtual Cervantes Center, University of Illinois. Web. 29 November 2009 ‹http://cvc.cervantes.es/obref/aih/pdf/06/aih_06_1_171.pdf›

Turcato, Davide. "Introduction: Making Sense of Anarchism." In Graham, Robert. *Anarchism: A Documentary History of Libertarian Ideas*, Vol. 2. Montreal: Black Rose Books, 2009

Valle-Inclán, Ramón de. Baza de Espadas. Madrid: Espasa Calpe, 1961.

Vélez Garcia, Juan Ramón. "Configuración de los personajes históricos en El ruedo ibérico de Valle-Inclán." Ogigia: Revista electrónica de estudios hispánicos. No. 2, July 2007 Web. 30 November 2009 ‹http://www.ogigia.es/OGIGIA2_files/OGIGIA2.pdf›

5. The Anarchist Imagination and the Materiality of Cultural Production: Anonymous Authorship in B. Traven

Scott Drake

> "You see it's like this: in your hands your story is worth just one dime. In my hands your story is worth in the neighbourhood of five grand cold cash. I am paying you your dime with full interest. I am honest, you see; I do not steal plots, I pay what they are worth to the owner."
>
> —Fibby in B. Traven's *The Death Ship*

> "It is this ideology which directs attention to the apparent producer, the painter, writer or composer, in short, the 'author', suppressing the question of what authorizes the author, what creates the authority with which authors authorize."
>
> —Pierre Bourdieu, "The Production of Belief"

> "The bush was singing its eternal song of stories, each story beginning with the last line of the story just ended."
>
> —B. Traven, "The Night Visitor"

If there is a "red thread" that runs through B. Traven's literary production it is a brutal indictment of capitalist relations of production. At the heart of this indictment stands the notion of private property and its function as the ground upon which the bourgeoisie perpetuates the exploitation of the working class. From the jungles of Chiapas, to the Mediterranean, from California business offices to the streets of Tampico, Traven's characters find themselves caught up in systems of capitalist production based on private property ownership. They, as individuals, are exploited, marginalized and dispossessed, not only of exchange commodities, but their own identities, except for a faint glimmer of unrealized liberty and freedom. For some critics, Traven's response to the alienation and powerlessness of isolated working class individuals is a retreat into anonymity (or pseudonymity). Donald Chankin (1975), for example, argued that his works are characterized by "an anxiety arising from fear of betrayal, leading to loss of identity and disintegration of self" (14). Taken in this way the theme of anonymity, which pervades the Traven *oeuvre*, appears as a withdrawal into an autonomous self as the last refuge of the individual. Or, put another way a withdrawal into the imagination as protection from a dominant capitalist order.

To perpetuate this division between the imagination and the material conditions of textual production, however, is to reduce the political importance of literary production. This is of particular significance in terms of anarchism because, for much of the nineteenth and twentieth centuries, anarchism was thought primarily as a political movement. Its political content, then, has what Allan Antliff (2001) called a "tenuous affinity" with aesthetics (1). Antliff (2001) claimed the two are intertwined and that the political component of anarchism is central to understanding aesthetic practice in modernism. This essay will push this even further to suggest that aesthetic practice cannot be divorced from the materiality of cultural production. Traven's image, then, as an anonymous author—an extension of his literary aesthetics—is an active engagement with the material relations of literary property. The fictional critique of capitalist property relations is countered within the text through a form of cultural production whose ground is "other" texts and this aesthetic is co-extensive with the production of Traven's own anonymous authorship in order to imagine a form of collective intellectual property. In other words, Traven's flight into anonymity is the flight towards the construction of a collective form of material property relations that would counteract the commodification of literary property through the copyright regime.

A central theoretical claim of this essay is that the aesthetic relations between the work and the author are irrevocably intertwined with the material, or more properly, to cite Michel Foucault (2004/2008) "economic-juridical" (163) relations of authorship and copyright. Martha Woodmansee (1984) chronicled the emergence of the modern author as a professional writer in Germany and she tied this emergence to a philosophic-aesthetic discourse of subjectivity in which the author was no longer an inspired medium or a craftsman who "was master of a body of rules, preserved and handed down to him in rhetoric and poetics, for manipulating traditional materials" (426). This new philosophic-aesthetic discourse, typically referred to as Romanticism, re-conceived the individual author as an active force in the shaping or the aesthetic form of the text. Woodmansee (1984) explained that underlying the relation between the book and the author was a "radically new conception of the book as an imprint or record of the intellection of a unique individual" (447). Seán Burke (1995), likewise, noted a shift in the history of authorship whereby there was a "power newly assigned [...] to individual consciousness in the creation of the world which it had hitherto been assumed to mirror or represent" (xix). I will refer to this new aesthetic as expressive authorship. It is in this sense of the author's literary work as the material expression of a interior depth of the self, and thus in actuality one's own essential being, that Woodmansee (1984) argued legal discourse comes to acknowledge the author's right to protection over their intellectual property. Not only does the juridical order acknowledge authorial property rights, in re-conceptualizing the concept of the work, the aesthetic of expressive authorship came to define what constitutes the material property of the work. Essential to literary property is the notion of "form" as the specific component of a work that is particular to the individual creator. Woodmansee (1984) wrote: "In his central concept of the 'form' taken by a though—that which it is impossible for another person to appropriate—Fichte [...] establishes the grounds upon which the writer could lay claim to ownership of his work—could lay claim, that is, to *authorship*" (445). In essence, her claim is that expressive authorship, as it is articulated in the philosophical-aesthetic discourse of the late eighteenth century, establishes the terms by which subsequent legal and material questions of literary property will be resolved.

The problem with such claims, as David Saunders (1992) warned, is that "it will always be the role of copyright law to support the authorial personality required and enshrined by Romanticism" (216). The conflation of a philosophical-aesthetic discourse and a legal discourse minimizes the function of positive law as a reference to "laws as they actually have been, not normatively to what they might or should have been" (Saunders, 1992, 6). For Saunders (1992), then, the aesthetic and the legal are clearly separate realms whose points of reference are not compatible. In distinction from theories of aesthetic subjectivity, he wrote "the object of the law of copyright has been the regulation of printed books as traded commodities" (Saunders, 1992, 213). What Saunders (1992) critique establishes is that the author, when taken in the context of its legal standing, does not refer to an individual subject, but rather to its role in regulating the book trade. What he fails to recognize is the extent to which the legal sphere that gives rise to copyright is inseparable from a capitalist economy. In other words, his conceptualization of the legal field is problematic in that it makes the assumption that its frame of reference is self-contained. Foucault (2004/2008), on the other hand, points out that "The economy does not purely and simply determine a juridical order that would both serve it and be constrained by it. The juridical gives form to the economic and the economic would not be what it is without the juridical" (162–163). Legal decisions regulate the economic sphere, and so any analysis of the juridical aspects of literary property are intertwined with capitalist relations of production.

Through the field of cultural production Pierre Bourdieu (1993) explores this apparent separation, or independence, as a structural relation. For Bourdieu economic, legal and artistic or literary fields "are structured by their own histories, internal logic, and patterns of recruitment and reward as well as by external demands" (DiMaggio, 1979, 1460). What this means is that this apparent autonomy is not total, it butts up against another field external to its own internal structure. In fact, the field of literary production is a structural relation between two poles whose content is the struggle that occurs between them. DiMaggio (1979) explained that for Bourdieu a field is "both the totality of actors and organizations involved in an arena of social or cultural production and the dynamic relationships among them" (1463). The field of literary production, then, is constituted in the struggle between control over symbolic production. At one pole of the spectrum lies "large-scale cultural production" orientated towards economic profit as a means to dominate the field, while at the other lies "restricted production" geared towards consecrating works and authors whose concerns are immediately invested in the autonomy of art (Bourdieu, 1993, 115). Even though restricted production, that is to say, production meant for other literary producers as opposed to a mass public readership, disavows any economic impetus, its actual material product, the book, is nevertheless connected to commercial enterprise. Bourdieu (1993) explained that "the literary and artistic field is contained within the field of power, while possessing a relative autonomy with respect to it, especially as regards its economic and political principles of hierarchization" (37). The relative autonomy of the field of restricted production stems from the field's own consecration of literary works whose value derives not from the economic capital they produce, but their ability to accrue symbolic capital. But the accrual of symbolic capital, however, is not outside capitalist production. On the contrary, as Bourdieu (1993) argued, symbolic capital converts into economic capital in the long run. Therefore, even at its most autonomous pole, the field of literary production "continues to be affected by the laws of the field which encompasses it, those of economic and political profit" (Bourdieu, 1993, 39). The significance of this vision of the field of literary production in terms of understanding the relation between work and author, is that this relation needs to be thought in two separate, but related, spheres at the same time: its aesthetic and material modes of production.

My attempt to bring together the aesthetic and material relations of textual production is significant for the anarchist literary imagination because their supposed independence highlights a tension within anarchist thought. David Weir (1997) notes that in classical conceptions of anarchism—that is Godwin, Proudhon, Bakunin and Kropotkin—there is a clear delineation between politics and aesthetic production. Art in this delineation, he argued, was subservient to "social concerns" (Weir, 1997, 39). In the context of the nineteenth century, where realism and naturalism were the dominant aesthetic movements, it is not surprising to conceptualize literature as a representation of the actual material conditions in which people lived. If anarchism is fundamentally about social transformation or revolution, then the function of literature in the anarchist imagination would be to conjure this transformation into existence. Rudolf Rocker (1960/1973) argued,

> Where the influence of political power on the creative forces in society is reduced to a minimum, there culture thrives the best, for political rulership always strives for uniformity and tends to subject every aspect of social life to its guardianship. And in this it finds itself in unescapable contradiction to the creative aspiration of cultural development. (15–16)

Rocker (1960/1973) draws an implicit link between artistic practice as a liberatory practice a homogenizing force of the state in order to suggest that cultural production is a key component of constructing an anarchist social organization. An anarchism rooted in materiality takes aim at the way capitalist infrastructure perpetuates exploitation, and so it is at this level, and not at an artistic or aesthetic level, that transformation must occur. It is precisely, however, the independence of the aesthetic from the material, that needs to be re-thought. Weir's (1997) main argument, that as political and material reality of anarchism recedes from the realm of the possible its ideas find a new home in aesthetic production, reproduces the aesthetic/ material tension and casts them as separate fields of reference. In fact, his argument amounts to saying that anarchism's influence has been cultural rather than political or material: "there is no question that a great many anarchists, faced with their obvious isolation from politics at large, were driven toward culture as the only available means of disseminating their ideology" (Weir, 1997, 4). Authorship, as a textual site, links the aesthetic and the material aspects of cultural production. The figure of the author, in particular the construction of self-reflexive anonymous authorship—such as the name B. Traven—becomes an aesthetic site upon which the material struggles for control of production and ownership play out. Traven's anonymity, then, must be thought as a textual relation that enacts anarchist politics through an aesthetic materialism. For Traven an anarchist literary imagination is not confined to the content of the works, rather it includes its own material production within an economic-juridical order of capitalism and in this sense its own aesthetic is a site upon which the struggle for a form of collective production is inscribed.

There is no shortage of critical evaluations associating Traven's work and life with anarchist themes and ideas; in short, with an anarchist literary imagination. What these evaluations attest to, however, is less a cohesive understanding of Traven's anarchism, then the tensions (individual freedom/ cooperative existence) within the concept of anarchy. Traven's anarchism is depicted as an ideology, or philosophy, that shapes the fiction. Michael Baumann (1976), for example, claimed that Traven seeks to abolish the state. His anarchism manifests itself as "opposition to the state and disbelief in institutions and authority. Implicit in Traven's attack on the state is the conviction that in nature man is free" (Baumann, 1976, 60). Robert Goss (1987), on the other hand, in his problematization of the Marut-Traven-Croves convergence of identity, wrote "Traven's writings are from the beginning guided by a quite different kind of 'anarchism,' the communal or communist (Communist with a small 'c') anarchism that we associate with Kropotkin, or (in America) with Alexander Berkman's book *The ABC of Anarchism*" (53). The point is that both Baumann and Goss (and they are only two examples) look beyond the immediacy of the work to a guiding thematic principle which ultimately turns out to be the expression of an author's personality or identity.

Traven's "anarchist vision," in such criticism is merely the ideology at the root of the fiction and thus offers critical work an insight into the man's personality. What remains absent in such criticism is a sense that Traven's fiction is more than a representation of a given materiality. His fiction is also the construction of an anarchist vision to which there is no corresponding materiality because it has yet to be created. His works exhibit an awareness of themselves as cultural texts that are part of the materiality they are attempting to create. Their frame of reference includes a reflection on the role of narrative in producing a dominant bourgeois culture that both lends the texts self-reflexivity and identifies a barrier to working class achievement of revolutionary consciousness. Traven's works derive a certain amount of cultural cachet because of their apparent authenticity, by the way they accurately describe itinerant working class conditions. The source of such claims to authenticity are grounded in Traven's own autographical writings, which emphasize this tension between the work and the personality that creates the work. For example, in a letter to his publisher, *Büchergilde*, he wrote "I think the story [*The Death Ship*] is good and entertaining because I did not pick it out of the seams of my pants, because I did not invent it. If one tells a true story, one cannot think a long time about artistic form" (as cited in Baumann, 1976, 9). Similarly, in a denunciation of biography, he explained: "The creative man should have no other biography than his own works. In his works, he exposes his personality and his life to criticism" (as cited in Guthke, 1987/1991, 18). There are, however, two points that need to be clarified in relation to using "Traven" as an authoritative source. The first is that given Traven's own autographical obfuscation, such statements refer back to a fictional identity, a point to be expanded in the discussion of Traven's authorship. The second point is that in privileging the author's ideas as an expression of personality, critics diminish the aesthetic form of the works.

What often gets understated is that his fiction has its own internal and aesthetic logic, but these aesthetic relations are not exterior to the relations of production that are its content. In order to understand Traven's authorship as an aesthetic practice that functions in the material sphere of the economic-juridical order, we have to move beyond an analysis of the works by means of merely their content. In fact, what needs to be recognized is the interrelation between content and form. Will Wyatt (1980) pointed out, "Those who take at face value Traven's claim that he wrote only of what he had seen do him the disservice of denying him his art" (247). Some critics have identified in Traven's narrative style an artistic sense that seeks to deny itself. Baumann (1976), for example, in a discussion of the many literary references in *The Death Ship*, argued that "the explicit allusions force us to take note of Traven's pose as an illiterate American sailor-workingman" (96). These cracks, or contradictions, expose the extent to which the narrator Gales is an aesthetic construction rather than an authentic person. This may be problematic for the novel's verisimilitude, but it also open new avenues for exploring the work as an object whose signified is fictional or cultural discourse itself. That is to say, Traven's fiction responds, not simply to a material world, but to the way in which that world's representation takes shape in cultural production. Guthke (1987/1991), similarly, takes up the issue of the narrative style in order, once again, to push back analysis to the level of content. He wrote that Traven "had little sense for the aesthetic composition of his epic subject matter; he jarringly interrupts the flow of the narrative with cicerone passages; he handles language carelessly, some claim, to the point of being sloppy—an effect others may view as deliberately unconventional, informal, and antibourgeois" (Guthke, 1987/1991, 210). It is as though Traven's message, the political content, we could say his anarchist critique of property relations in capitalism, permeates the works despite their aesthetics. On the contrary, my claim is that Traven's aesthetics are central to his authorship as co-extensive with the political content of the works. In order to explore how this relationship functions I will explicate the content of *The Treasure of the Sierra Madre*, demonstrate how this content is a central component of its aesthetic and finally how this aesthetic relates to the construction of Traven's anonymous authorship in the economic-juridical order. Having established this, it will be possible to explore how this self-reflexive anonymity not only critiques the incipient dominance of capitalist values in literary production, but also envisions a form of collective cultural production.

Forms of Property

Probably the best known of Traven's works, thanks to John Huston and Humphrey Bogart, *The Treasure of the Sierra Madre* tells the story of three down and out Americans in Mexico after the demise of the oil boom in Tampico who set off in search for gold. Though on its surface the novel is perhaps the least visibly "anarchist," it nevertheless, as the rudimentary genesis of Traven's conflation of indigenous communal property and a revolutionary anarchist vision, serves as a key text for understanding the relations between content-form and the materiality of the book trade. In terms of conceptualizing anarchism I am guided here by Rocker's (1960/1973) explanation "Anarchists desire a federation of free communities which shall be bound to one another by their common economic and social interests and arrange their affairs by mutual agreement and free contract" (7). The novel turns upon the struggles, both external and internal, that Dobbs & Co. (Dobbs, Curtin and Howard) face in attempting to extract hidden riches from the mountains of the Sierra Madre. The novel ends ironically when Dobbs, who robs and attempts to murder one of his companions, is himself robbed and murdered on the outskirts of Durango, only miles from legitimizing his treasure. To add to the irony, however, the mestizos who murder Dobbs, fail to adduce the gold's value and throw it away believing it to be nothing but sand. At the heart of the story is two competing conceptions of property. On the one hand, capitalist ownership of the gold as a commodity legitimized through the institutions of the State, is the object of Dobbs & Co.'s quest. On the other hand, the communal ownership of the indigenous villages where gold is an artistic object whose value lies elsewhere than its commercial value. Inherent in Traven's representation of both these conceptions of property are the social relations involved in their establishment as property.

For Donald Chankin (1975), in *The Treasure of the Sierra Madre* "The center of interest is in the psychological element, not, as some critics maintain, in the social commentary of a proletarian author" (45). In terms of a critical interpretation, Chankin (1975) attempts to "broaden" Traven's audience by appealing less to its revolutionary ideas and more to exploring the human psychology in the characters of *Treasure*. The individual, in this sense, precedes social relations, and the novel's aesthetic centers on the interiority of the individual subject. Despite the psychoanalytic discourse of Chankin's (1975) analysis, he continues to perpetuate the idea that fiction represents an authorial expression of personality In effect, he claimed that "The difficulties which arise in the Sierra Madre, however, originate in the characters of the prospectors themselves" (Chankin, 1975, 44–45). While he acknowledged that in *The Death Ship* social forces contribute to the individual's isolation from "civilization and its restraints," in *Treasure* fear, as the emotion that leads to the disintegration of Dobb's ego, "stems directly from the individual" (Chankin, 1975, 48). I bring up this brief example of how the notion of individual personality pervades Traven scholarship for two reasons. The first is that it returns to the notion of an individual source of production. Traven's fiction—its tensions, its anxieties, its ideas—are grounded in the individual, but more importantly in a discourse of literary property. The second reason I draw attention to the perceived importance of the individual in Traven's work is that a romanticism of this nature, where the individual, "natural" wo/man at its core, stands against any social force, an individuality that condemns any authority beyond the individual, persists in the anarchist imagination. If we are to imagine a form of cultural production, infused with anarchist conceptualizations of property and ownership, then we have to understand the dynamic aspects of power as they play out in cultural production. To suggest that authors such as Traven ignore such relations, or make them subservient to the interiority of the individual is to reduce the impact of the literary imagination to affecting personal change. Indeed, as Murray Bookchin (1995) argued, this brand of individual, or what he called "lifestyle anarchism" relies on an "unmediated, ahistorical, and anticivilizatory 'primality' from which we have 'fallen'" (Evaluating Lifestyle Anarchism section, par.1). By taking as a starting point the notion of an essential authenticity, anarchist discourse and practice can only engage in cultural production as a negative freedom, a desire to escape from rather than a desire to create a form of social organization.

In narrowing the importance of Traven's fiction to the individual, Chankin (1975) makes the social dimension of the novel, which revolves around the privatization of property and the institutional function of the state as a legitimizing force of private property, a secondary issue. Out in the Sierra Madres, away from "civilization," the three prospectors turned entrepreneurs shed their working class status as they attempt to acquire the necessary capital to put themselves into business. The narrator explained:

> The three men, gathered together solely to gain riches, had never been real friends. They had in common only business relations. That they had combined their forces and brains and resources for no other reason than to make high profits was the factor which had prevented them from becoming true friends. (Traven, 1927/1935/1967, 88)

In fact, this entrepreneurial spirit is entirely consistent with Dobbs's motivation at the novel's opening when he thought "How can I get some money right now?" (Traven, 1927/1935/1967, 1). And though his situation as an itinerant working class male leads us to believe that given his poverty, his desire to acquire money is a matter of immediate subsistence, the narrator explained its real function: "If you already have some money, then it is easier to make more, because you can invest the little you have in some sort of business that looks promising" (Traven, 1927/1935/1967, 1). The quest for gold, in this scenario, is not an end in-itself, rather it is the means to create surplus profit, and gold is a form of capital. Gold is acquired in the novel through various means, but one thing that remains constant is that it only transforms into capital when it is removed from the earth, that is to say, when it is abstracted and becomes a property in its own right.

We can, here, draw a distinction between personal and private property. Personal property refers to commodities which are removed from the circulation of capital while private property is property whose function is the creation of surplus value. The later can be equated with the means of production and thus embodies a social relationship. For the explorers, gold is private property because it is capital that will be invested and put in the service of the production of further capital. The narrator explained: "It isn't the gold that changes man, it is the power which gold gives to man that changes the soul of man" (Traven, 1927/1935/1967, 68). Personal property, on the other hand, has a use-value, but is not capital in the sense that its function is not the generation of surplus profit. Pierre-Joseph Proudhon (1840/1994), in his critique of the concept of property, distinguishes property (private) from possession (personal). For him, property equals an absolute dominion over the object, while possession indicates a limited right to one's labor or occupation. He wrote:

> The field which I have cleared, which I cultivate, on which I have built my house, which supports myself, my family, and my livestock I can possess: (1) as the original occupant; (2) as a labourer; (3) by virtue of the social contract which assigns it to me as my share. But none of these titles give me the domain of property. (Proudhon, 1840/1994, 58)

Even this notion of labor, though, does not guarantee individual and permanent ownership. Indeed it individual ownership is what cordons off private property by extracting it from the communal nature of its production. On the contrary, Proudhon (1840/1994) wrote

> this incontestable and uncontested fact of the general participation in every kind of product makes all individual productions common, so that every product made by the producer is mortgaged in advance by society [...] The labourer is not even possessor of his product; scarcely has he finished it when society claims it. (115)

Property only comes into existence when this common production, that which is socially created, is privatized, excluding access by means of proprietorship. Dobbs & Co. are all associated with the creation of private property.

A question that arises in the novel, is how ownership of property is legitimized. Karl Marx (1867/1977) claims that primitive accumulation, "an accumulation which is not the result of the capitalist mode of production but its point of departure" (873), is "the historical process of divorcing the producer from the means of production" (875). It arises as a result of the privatization of commons lands, which has two effects. First, it expropriates the means of production from individual producers, and second, in so doing, it also creates a mass labor force that needs to sell its labor power on the free market for subsistence. According to Marx (1867/1977), this is the historical of the shift from feudalism to capitalism in Europe. Dobbs, Curtin and Howard are, from the outset, associated with this dispossessed laboring class. In fact, it is precisely as an attempt to escape their class position that they go in search of gold:

> It was not exactly the gold alone they desired. They were tired of hanging around waiting for a new job to turn up and of chasing contractors and being forced to smile at them and laugh at their jokes to keep them friendly. A change was what they wanted most. This running after jobs could not go on forever. There must be some way out of this crazy-go-round. (Traven, 1927/1935/1967, 69)

Unlike the situation in Europe, however, Treasure's geo-political landscape signals a colonial rather than industrial context. The world in the novel is not entirely mapped, the wilderness abounds and unowned tracts of land are available for appropriation as private property. Howard explains to his neophyte companions

> "Not so difficult to see, boys, after I've made it clear what is virgin soil and what isn't." Howard went with a pencil over the map he had spread out before him. "We have to go where there is no trail. We have to go where we can be positive that no surveyor or anybody

who knows something about mining has ever been before." (Traven, 1927/1935/1967, 74)

For Marx (1867/1977), this situation is a barrier to capitalist expansion. Unowned land is ripe for appropriation, thus the wage-laborer can set up his/her own means of production without being dependent on others for subsistence. The establishment of independent producers, however, means that there is no surplus labor force to create value for other owners. Marx (1867/1977) wrote:

> The essence of the free colony [...] consists in this, that the bulk of the soil is still public property, and every settler on it can therefore turn part of it into his private property and his individual means of production, without preventing later settlers from performing the same operation. (934)

In the colonial context of early twentieth century Mexico, gold becomes the means, for Dobbs, Curtin and Howard, to establish themselves as independent producers.

While the Dobbs & Co. excursion represents an emerging capitalist interest, the indigenous population represents a form of communal ownership. This form of communal ownership is intriguing because instead of revolving around the production of capital, its sense of value derives from a proximity to social well-being. The clearest expression of communal property occurs in Howard's narrative "about that treasure-burdened woman, the most honorable and distinguished doña Catalina María de Rodríguez" (Traven, 1927/1935/1967, 186). In this story a prominent doctor, don Manuel, gains possession of an indigenous owned gold mine because he cured a chief's son's eyesight and in exchange the chief, Aguila Bravo (who had no money), assured don Manuel the rights to an ancient mine. When don Manuel comes to claim possession of the mine, he exclaimed: "it is rather strange that you, Aguila Bravo, did not exploit the mine yourself. You could easily have earned a hundred thousand gold florins, with which you could have paid me in full for my work and I would have been satisfied" (Traven, 1927/1935/1967, 194). In other words, he doesn't understand why Aguila Bravo didn't use the gold as capital to produce the money required for the service on his son's eyes, that way maintaining possession of the means of production. Bravo responds with laughter, signaling both a comprehension and a disagreement with the white man's assessment. He has all that is required for happiness: family land to provide daily necessities, good standing within the community and peace. Further, he explained

> we were always the masters of our gold, never its slaves. We look at it and enjoy it. Since we cannot eat it, gold is of no real value to us. Our people have fought wars, but never for the possession of gold. We

fought for land, for rivers, for salt deposits, for lakes, and mostly to defend ourselves against savage tribes who tried to rob us of our land and its products. (Traven, 1927/1935/1967, 194–195)

In this subsistence economy gold functions as an object of beauty, rather than capital. Through this representation of indigenous communal culture Traven differentiates social relations of production in terms of property ownership.

While in *Treasure*, Traven merely sketches the idea of communal indigenous property, in the *oeuvre* it becomes more explicitly central to his overall notion of an anarchist society. Heidi Zogbaum (1992) wrote:

> [Traven] was not just fascinated by the exotic qualities of the Indians but discovered something in their way of life, their social organization, and their economic performance that persuaded him even further that Mexico was the country where the fight against world capitalism had taken a tangible form. (34)

In fact, Traven creates a dichotomy between Western and indigenous forms of society. In the untranslated *Land of Springtime* he wrote "in Europe, individual ambition prevails. Here among the Indians, there is communal ambition" (as cited in Zogbaum, 1992, 80). In this sense Traven's "Indian" culture is an aesthetic-ideological representation rather than a reflection of reality. In this representation, Zogbaum (1992) argued "Traven managed skillfully to blend his own anarcho-syndicalist ideas with the ideas of the *indigenistas* to argue that ultimately the working class would win political and economic power" (81). For the indigenous peoples, the value of gold cannot be traded on the market, or it if is traded on the market it loses its value. Against the pre-dominance of gold as capital in Western society there emerges in *Treasure* a non-market based economy. Rather than focusing on the production of capital the indigenous communities exemplified by Bravo base themselves on material needs. They do not exchange gold because it threatens their ability to access land and food. This does not mean that gold as an artistic object is not an important component of the communal fiber. The novel does not make clear break between material necessity and art. On the contrary, material comfort is a requirement for artistic production and artistic production satisfies a communal desire for beauty. Traven develops this theme at greater length in the short story "Assembly Line" (1966/1993). In this story an American tourist, E.L. Winthrop, stumbles upon an indigenous man selling remarkable and unique baskets, which are described in aesthetic terms: "Bast and fibers dyed in dozens of different colors were so cleverly— one must actually say intrinsically—interwoven that those attractive designs appeared on the inner part of the basket as well as on the outside" (Traven, 1966/1993, 74). Winthrop buys the lot (16 in total), sells them to a confectioner in New York (for over triple what he paid) who wants them to package chocolate and then secures a contract to provide ten thousand more. When he returns, the unnamed indigenous producer informs him that he can only provide the requested amount for what appears to be an exorbitant price. He explains to an incredulous Winthrop that if he were to fulfill the order he would have no time to work his land and provide food for his family. Winthrop counters that he could hire friends or relations to look after his fields while he produced the baskets, to which the unnamed man replied:

> They might, patroncito, yes, they might. Possible. But then you see who would take care of their fields and cattle if they work for me? And if they help me with the baskets it turns out the same. No one would any longer work his fields properly. In such a case corn and beans would get up so high in price that none of us could buy and we all would starve to death. Besides, as the price of everything would rise and rise higher still how could I make baskets at forty centavos apiece? A pinch of salt or one green chili would set me back more than I'd collect for one single basket. (Traven, 1966/1993, 85–86)

The economy of the village is founded on use-value, on immediate material needs and to upset the balance between material and artistic production by transforming to a capitalist mode of production would destroy the essential communal nature of the society.

While in "Assembly Line" and *The Treasure of the Sierra Madre*, this communal social organization associated with indigenous culture is central to Traven's anarchist vision, it is important to situate this organization in relation to a pervasive, if not all-encompassing, global capitalism. These communal spaces are never entirely outside the institutional range of the state and its role in producing the necessary conditions for capitalist production. While capitalist exchange appears as something external to the village economy in "Assembly Line," in *Treasure* it is more insidious. The bandits who murder and rob Dobbs as he reaches the margins of civilization are apprehended by Joaquín Escalona, "constitutionally elected alcalde or mayor of this community, elected by all the citizens of this place and its vicinity, and legally recognized by the state legislature" (Traven, 1927/1935/1967, 285). Though he is certainly a democratically elected figure, he receives the legitimacy of his election through the power of the state legislature. What's more he arrests the bandits, not for murder, but theft of property. Thus, though there is a different economy at work on the communal lands, it is not entirely outside the reach of capitalist juridical and political institutions. In fact, as Zogbaum (1992) pointed out, "on the one hand, the indigenous cultures were hailed as anticapitalist, on the other hand, they were understood to be capitalist on a communal scale" (77). Rather than understand these spaces as complicit with, or co-opted by, capitalist production, they stand as sites of struggle where an anarchist social organization can be formed from within the very structure of capitalism. In *Treasure* this takes shape in the indigenous worker revolts after don Manuel gains ownership of the hidden mine in Howard's story. In order to extract the profits, don Manuel requires laborers and these workers are explicitly drawn from surrounding indigenous villages. We are told

> Although the mine gave him great riches, he treated his Indian laborers worse than slaves. He hardly paid them enough to keep them alive, and he made them work so hard that often they broke down. Day and night he was after them, whip in hand, and using his gun whenever he thought it necessary. Indians, particularly those of the North American continent, cannot be treated in this way for long. No wonder that one day there was rebellion in the mind of don Manuel. His wife escaped, but don Manuel was slain and the mine destroyed. The Indian laborers left for their homes. (Traven, 1927/1935/1967, 198)

The vision arising out of such resistance suggests that revolution will begin at these communal spaces when they are confronted with capitalist production. While the possibility of revolution is admittedly only on the horizon in *Treasure* its essential tensions are constructed in the opposition between communal and capitalist ownership. The centrality of the revolutionary potential of such communal spaces emerges in its fullest articulation in Traven's "Jungle Cycle."

In the novel it is clear that the mere extraction of gold is not enough to establish ownership. Howard repeatedly points out that the labor involved in extraction capital from the land is one things, but transporting it back to civil institutions which will confer upon its bearers the status of property owner. He informs his partners "to find gold and lift it out of the earth is not the whole thing. The gold has to be shipped. And shipping it is more precarious than digging and washing it" (Traven, 1927/1935/1967, 210). While Howard's cautionary tales about the difficulties of transporting the gold back to civilization foreshadow Dobbs's eventual attempt to murder and rob his partners, they also mark out the extent to which property is legitimized through capitalist juridical and political institutions, without regard to its origins. Further, once capital is legitimized it confers a status upon the owner regardless of the means of its appropriation. Dobbs recognizes the security which the state and its institutions will confer on him, as he reaches the outskirts of Durango, after having attempted to murder Curtin and stolen Howard's gold:

> He was all jubilation. He sang and whistled and danced. He was now safe. He could see the flares of the oil-fed engine seeping along the railroad tracks, could hear the trains rolling by and the coughing and the bellowing of the engine. These sounds gave him a great

feeling of security. They were the sounds of civilization. He longed for civilization, for law, for justice, which would protect his property and his person with a police force. (Traven, 1927/1935/1967, 260)

The state becomes a force that bestows ownership and whose authority sanctions private property as the means of production. The irony of Traven's narrative at this point cannot go unnoticed, especially given that Dobbs himself is murdered within sight of Durango and the very safety that gives him cause for hope. The more poignant aspect of his critique, however, rests in the way civil institutions of the state function in the service of the economic system, that is to say, they work to legitimize capital regardless of its origins.

Throughout *Treasure* the narrative revolves around the privatization of property that is, at its origin, common. The sense of lawlessness that pervades the Sierra Madre region is, in fact, a direct result of the legal-institutionalization of private property. As private property acts as a means to produce profit, and hence political, economic and social power, it also acts as a catalyst for exploitation and violence. That the world of *Treasure* is replete with violence, theft, and treachery is undeniable. The brutality of this world, however should be contextualized, not as a critique of individual desires, but rather as a structural problematic whose root resides in the division of the commons into private property. Private property, in the novel, is not an inherent right of the individual. It is, instead, a social product that furthers a program designed to concentrate wealth in the hands of the few, who then work to maintain the social relations of production as a means to increase the capacity to accrue capital and power. What underlies the force of Traven's critique, in *Treasure*, is the idea that property is communal, that production should be shared in order to maximize access to material necessities.

Narrative Origins

There is within *The Treasure of the Sierra Madre* a self-reflexivity that turns back on its own relation, as a literary commodity, to capitalist production. Its most explicit formulation in the novel occurs in the distinction between fiction and authentic, or true, stories. Popular fiction is associated with entertainment, with luring or seducing readers into believing the fiction is an accurate representation of reality. The narrator stated:

> The stories told in the pulps seems to them [audience at Orso Negro] right now just so much rot. Who writes these stories, anyhow? Men sitting in an office in a big city. Men who have never been on the spot themselves. What do they know? The real life is quite different.

Here is was, the real life, and the man who had lived the real life and had seen the world, who had been rich, very rich, and who was now so broke that he had to ask a fellow in the street for fifty centavos for a meal. (Traven, 1927/1935/1967, 52)

Howard's story, which the above narrative interjection precedes, is upheld as the truth and this truth is opposed to fiction. That is to say, the truth of the story is set against entertainment and the accrual of profits as a result of tapping into a desire for adventure. More than merely a vehicle for the creation of capital, fiction, in its romanticism, distorts reality. As cultural products, fictional texts perpetuate the social relations of capitalist production. Fiction glamorizes adventure to the extent that individuals are seduced by its promises and search out their own adventures. The reality, for Traven, is that the search for wealth, disconnects them from their communities, which puts them in a position to become slaves of their properties (or would be properties) or exploited labor for the propertied classes. In other words, as cultural artifacts, fictional works also exert an influence on the development of consciousness. It is precisely the change in consciousness, or rather the lack of working class consciousness, that is problematic in the characters of Dobbs, Curtin and Howard. The narrator interceded to inform the reader

With every ounce more of gold possessed by them they left the proletarian class and neared that of the property-holders, the well-to-do middle class. So far they had never had anything of value to protect against thieves. Since they now owned certain riches, their worries about how to protect them had started. The world no longer looked to them as it had a few weeks ago. They had becomes members of the minority of mankind. (Traven, 1927/1935/1967, 86)

As an instrument of capitalist production—the text—becomes literary property, a property that requires protection from theft, plagiarism, piracy and other appropriations. As such the text requires the existence of copyright to institutionalize a limited domain over property and ensure its ability to accrue profits for its creator/owner.

The Statute of Anne (1710), the first copyright law, simultaneously enacted a form of the public domain. The title, "An Act for the Encouragement of Learning," itself recalls the new focus on a form of regulation that benefits the creation and maintenance of civil society. Ronan Deazley (2006) pointed out that as "A purely statutory phenomenon copyright was fundamentally concerned with the reading public, with the encouragement and spread of education, and with the continued production of useful books" (23). In setting a time line for the ownership of copies, Parliament recognized both the importance of authors as producers and hence as individuals who are entitled to remuneration for their labor, and the value of a cultural production that was not grounded in the individual product as an expression of individuality, but in collective cultural products as sources for further production. As such the literary object is not the perpetual property of individuals, but reverts back, as common property, to the culture from whence it emerges. Texts are, so to speak, shared products that can be appropriated at any point after the time limit by anyone for cultural production itself. In other words, their openness to being copied and re-worked is the foundation of cultural production. The Statute of Anne codifies the tension between the individual author as owner and collective cultural production as a central component of civil society.

The apparent opposition between fiction and truth, in *Treasure*, is problematized in the form of the novel. Stories are valued because of their truth. After Dobbs relates the story of the Green Water Mine as told to him by Howard, Curtin curiously responded "I figure this story is a true one" (Traven, 1927/1935/1967, 67). Later Howard inquires whether they have heard the story of Catalina Maria de Rodriguez by which "I mean, of course, the true story" (Traven, 1927/1935/1967, 186). But what distinguishes the story as "true" as opposed to fiction? The story's truth is supported by the lived experience of the narrator. Without this element of truth the story is just one more piece of fiction floating around the capitalist market. In other words, the story's truth is verified in the person of the author. The lived experience of the author shines through the story, it provides the details that signal its veracity. Dobbs in reflecting on Howard's story "had felt that he himself was living the story" (Traven, 1927/1935/1967, 67). In other words, the apparent signified of the "true" narratives are a material reality that differs from the imaginative signified of fiction. But the relation between the novel's representations and its reality blurs this very line. Nowhere is this deconstruction as revealing as in the narrated stories within the novel. Their narration, in fact, as re-told stories, that is appropriated stories, points back to a frame of reference that is fictional or imaginative rather than purely representational. In other words, the narratives within the novel are self-reflexive representations of representations. It is at this textual level that the novel's form asserts its significance.

What is most significant about the three stories which exemplify "true" stories in *The Treasure of the Sierra Madre* is that they are all derived from other narrative sources. For example, the Green Water Mine, while Howard is a participant at the very end, is a story that Howard hears from Harry Tilton "the one who later told the story" (Traven, 1927/1935/1967, 63). The truth of the experience is located in the narrative which he hears and subsequently re-works from his own perspective. Similarly, his second story about Maria de Rodriguez is historical and cannot have been experienced by its "author" because it occurs "At about the time of the American Revolution" (Traven, 1927/1935/1967, 187). Not only is it not the product of experience, it is not even unique as Lacaud complains, "That story is more than a hundred years old" (Traven, 1927/1935/1967, 210) signaling that he'd heard it before. In this sense, Howard circulates previously told stories that are neither original to the "author," nor do they originate outside of narrative. Even Lacaud's story is indebted to textual production. He narrates a particular story about a massacre perpetrated by the banditos who are on their way up to the gold site, in order that the prospectors will know what sort of enemy they are up against. At the story's conclusion he stated: "That is all I know about this train assault and about the rounding up of the bandits [...] Part of it I had from don Genaro, who read it to me from the papers, and part of it I heard on my way down to the village and from villagers who had been to market in town" (Traven, 1927/1935/1967, 153). What is interesting about the relation between stories and their "authors" in this novel, that is to say, the aesthetic relation is that the stories repeatedly turn back towards the author's experience as their guarantee of truthfulness, while at the same time the stories themselves are others stories which the "authors" experience as stories. In terms of cultural production they enact a textual space where stories beget stories, where stories are collectively produced between the telling of multiple authors. This textual aesthetic, where narrative originates in other narratives, envisions the figure of the author as a carrier of other stories rather than an original creator. This form of collective cultural production rebukes the romantic conception of authorship whose ideological foundations perpetuate copyright as a guarantor of capitalist property. This form of narrative production is in line with the critique of private property at the level of the novel's political content.

Signified of Authorship

In this roundabout way, I have described as arising out of *Treasure*, a vision of the author not as an originator and hence producer of stories, but rather as a carrier, or "possessor" of stories. It is this vision of the author, as a self-reflexive anonymity whose existence testifies to the collective nature of literary production, that is co-extensive with the construction of the name B. Traven. The name B. Traven for over a half century stood for mystery because the person to whom the name referred was unidentified. Was he American, was he German? Was he a woman, a collective, a murderer, a plagiarist, proletariat, aristocrat? Jack London, an illegitimate heir to the German Kaiser, Mexican president Calles, Esperanza López Mateos? While the Traven archive has revealed the existence of a man behind the name, a man who, in fact, embodied many names, this discovery did not occur in print until the early nineties, some twenty years after his death. What we need to consider is not the person behind the name, but rather the aesthetic through which the name circulates as a text whose source is steeped in fiction. Even Traven's more conscientious biographer, Karl Guthke (1987/1991), who had unprecedented access to the archive claimed "where in Traven's case does one draw the line between truth and fiction? And what can one conclude from this line, assuming that one could draw it with some degree of certainty?" (12). Traven's absence has always been a key element of scholarship about his works. Most, if not all such scholarship, however, posits some relation between the person and the work. I want to be clear that my engagement with Traven is not as a person, but rather as a textual construction that is co-extensive with the political and social content I have just explored with regards to property. In order to explore Traven's anonymous authorship as an aesthetic, I will look briefly at three variations on the "origins" of his identity/works: Ret Marut, Berrick Traven Torsvan and the "other man" theory.

The name B. Traven first appeared with the 1925 serial publication in German of *The Cotton-Pickers*. *Buchergilde* editor Ernst Preczang began correspondence with the mysterious author whose address was simply a post office box in Mexico, without knowing anything about the man himself. In this early correspondence, Traven refused to provide autobiographical information. He cited as justification for his reticence that his life means nothing in comparison to his works: "'Who is this man? Think of the mystery that surrounds him!' Ask questions like that and the person becomes more important than his work. But I desire that the person be totally unimportant" (as cited in Guthke, 1987/1991, 19). Additionally, he argues that the writer is but one aspect of the production process and so should not be elevated above the various workers involved in publication. "The typesetter who set my book," Traven was quoted as saying in a letter to Manfred Georg, "is just as important to cultural life as I am, and for that reason one should be no more concerned about my personality, about my private personality, than about the personality of the typesetter" (as cited in Guthke, 1987/1991, 24). His refusals, however, often as not, incite the curiosity of journalists and scholars to the extent that by the late nineteen twenties there was rampant speculation that the author was German. After all the texts were published first in German. In order to counter this speculation, Traven revealed that he was American, that he spoke and wrote in English, but had been unable to find an American publisher due to the political situation. In a letter to Charlot Strasser, he wrote "B. Traven is an American, he was born in the

United States; both his parents were Americans and were born in the States" (as cited in Guthke, 1987/1991, 24). Traven further claimed that "His mother tongue is English. Although he writes a great deal in German, he nonetheless writes half, if not more, first in English, since he finds it easier to record difficult chains of reasoning" (as cited in Guthke, 1987/1991, 25). The biographical outline that he began to sketch, however, could not quench the insatiable appetite of an unrelenting public and so a more detailed identity emerged. *BT News*, a newsletter collaboratively published by Traven's agent, Josef Wieder; his translator, Esperanza López Mateos; his wife, Rosa Elena Lujan; and himself, chronicled the "official" biography in 1952:

> Since the age of seven, Traven has lived on his own and has had to make his own living. He has never gone to school. His school is life, harsh and unrelenting life itself. He first came to Mexico at the age of ten, when he got to know the harbors of the Pacific coast as a cabin boy on a Dutch tramp steamer. (as cited in Guthke, 1987/1991, 29)

While this remained the official biography, with the celebratory status conferred upon the author after the screening of Huston's film, there were significant other stories in circulation that problematized this biography.

In 1947, when Hal Croves appeared as a technical advisor on the set of John Huston's film adaptation of B. Traven's novel, *The Treasure of the Sierra Madre*, he sparked what would amount to an industry intent on unmasking the real identity of the mysterious author. Prior to filming, Huston had been in correspondence with Traven and had asked him to collaborate on the script. Traven expressed an interest, but when Huston traveled to Mexico to meet him he was greeted early one morning, not by Traven, but by Croves. Croves brought with him a letter from Traven stating that "Croves could represent him in every way" (Wyatt, 1980, 135). On location in Mexico, it didn't take long for rumors to circulate among the crew that Croves was, in fact, Traven. At the time, Croves neither confirmed nor denied the accusations; instead, he remained an aloof and peripheral figure which only added to the mystery that had begun to swirl about his identity. The Mexican journalist Luis Spota working off the Croves-Traven suspicion encountered a post office box rented to a B. Traven Torsvan with instructions to send correspondence to another Mexico City post office box. The first post office box was paid for by an M.L. Martinez. Subsequently, Spota managed to get his hands on Torsvan's alien registration card from 1930, which stated that Torsvan was "a man with American citizenship, born on March 5, 1890, in Chicago [...] entry in 1914 via Ciudad Juárez" (Guthke, 1987/1991, 336). In addition, this information is repeated on both his identity card and death certificate. He further tracked Torsvan down to the address of one M.L. Martinez in Acapulco. When Spota approached Berrick Traven Torsvan and queried him about being B. Traven, Torsvan denied the claim. He did, however, suggest that B. Traven was his cousin. When pressed he admitted to an involvement with the production of the works. As Guthke (1987/1991) described, "Torsvan was not Traven, but he—and not only he—had given the author some help with his work. 'I am sure that B. Traven did not write his books alone,' Spota quoted Traven as saying. [...] 'Traven has seen very lite of what he wrote about; indeed, I can almost say that the majority of his subjects were told to him by others'" (p. 339). Spota published the conclusion that not only was Croves Torsvan, but Torsvan was also Traven. This exposé helped to solidify Traven's identity as an American who had arrived in Mexico long before the first works published under the name B. Traven.

Around the same time another story about B. Traven's origins began to gain credence. In this version Traven was identified as a German anarchist from the Bavarian revolution: Ret Marut. As far back as 1927, the two figures were connected. Erich Mühsam, former Bavarian comrade, in a search for Marut, stumbled upon Traven's novels and with the assistance of Rudolph Rocker "compared the writings of Ret Marut with the writings of B. Traven and concluded that the two authors were on and the same" (Wyatt 1980, 60). Traven vigorously denied the claims right up until his death. Ret Marut was a minor literary figure and propagandist who self-published a journal, *Die Zeigelbrenner*, several short stories, a novella, and eventually participated in the Bavarian revolution of 1919. Three days after Kurt Eisner, then President of the Republic, was murdered on his way to step down as President after the electoral defeat of his party, Ret Marut was elected to the Central committee of councils (Guthke, 1987/1991, 144). His role as the head of the Press department meant that he was "chief censor of all bourgeois newspapers in Bavaria" (Guthke, 1987/1991, 144) and among other projects, he attempted to socialize the press. The Republic of councils, however, was never stable. Security Troops supported by Johannes Hoffman, president elect of State assembly, who took refuge in Bamberg after the declaration of the Republic of councils, attacked the newly established council. But the councils reconvened less than a month later, as the Second Republic of Councils and called for a general strike. Ultimately a combination of Hoffman forces, white guard and free corps (Kaiser troops) invaded Munich, arrested and murdered the revolutionaries. Marut, unlike many of his comrades—notably Gustav Landauer and Eugen Leviné, escaped. He continued to publish *Der Zeigelbrenner* from various locations across Europe, one of which even chronicled his escape, until December 1921. After that Marut disappeared off the map.

While speculation that Traven was in fact Marut began its circulation with his former comrades, the story didn't take root, in part because there was general consensus that Traven was American, until Rolf Recknagel's research made the link explicit. The existence of this other Traven provided new details that opened the way for further elaborations of the nature of Traven's identity. In 1980 Will Wyatt dug up evidence that would solidify the link between the two writers. Traven attempted to claim American citizenship in London, but the American authorities would not grant him this status. A freedom of information request brought Wyatt some information that was to prove useful in uncovering his identity. Marut had been, in fact, detained in London in 1923 for failing to register as an alien. American officials did not find his story that his birth certificate was burned in San Francisco during the fire of 1906 credible. Eventually he confessed "his real name is HERMAN OTTO ALBERT MAX FEIGE, and that he was born at Schwiebus, in Germany, in 1882" (Wyatt, 1980, 274). Officials apparently checked on the accuracy of his claim only to be told that no such person existed. Wyatt, however, scoured historical records and found a birth registry for an Otto Feige. From here he tracked down Feige's younger brother, Ernst Feige. Ernst reported to Wyatt that "Otto" had left home shortly before World War I and was never seen again. His younger sister, Margarette Henze, added that they had last received a letter from his stating that he was in trouble with the authorities and attempting to flee extradition to Germany (Wyatt, 1980, 335). Later, she claimed "The police had called at the house earlier in the day and asked for Otto. The mother, knowing about Otto's radical politics and that he had been held by the authorities in England, was desperately afraid of bringing trouble on the family. So she told the police that the man they sought was nothing to do with them; she had no son called Otto" (Wyatt, 1980, 336). The mother upon hearing his denied that any Otto Feige had ever lived in the area. Wyatt coupled these reported events with photos of a young Feige and those of Traven/Marut in order to identify not only that Marut was Traven, but that Traven was definitively Otto Feige.

This "discovery," however, has been challenged by other biographers, like Karl Guthke (1987/1991). He claimed that it wouldn't be far-fetched to imagine that Traven, the master of disguise and obfuscation, adopted the name of someone he knew intimately in order to elude identification and still potentially flee his German pursuers. In this sense the Otto Feige confession is one more pseudonym (only this time based on a real person) in a collection. Guthke (1987/1991) suggested, "Is it not more likely that Otto Feige was a borrowed name, the name of another, actual person?" (91). For Wyatt (1980) the details are too convincing, the similarity of the names, the occupation of the parents, the birth date. Guthke (1987/1991), however, noted that if we read these details with care, "Marut's statements did not correspond exactly with those at the Schwiebus registry office" (92). Guthke (1987/1991) further explained that Marut's identification as Feige is not useless. Instead, it informs us that whoever Marut/Traven may have been the most certainly came from East Germany because he was significantly familiar with both the geography and the people. Feige's hometown, like Stanislav's in *The Death Ship*, is a victim to shifting territorial borders. What seals the deal for Guthke (1987/1991), however, is the absence of a thematic connection between the works of Traven and the life of Feige. In other words, he wrote

> A fixation on problems of identity, illegitimacy, official documentation, and proof of one's existence—a fixation bordering on compulsion—clearly runs through the works of Marut/Traven This fixation points toward illegitimate birth and the lack of papers, toward the lack of a homeland, a home, a father, a family. Such was not the case with Otto Feige from Schwiebus. (Guthke, 1987/1991, 96)

Ultimately, what Guthke (1987/1991) does is suggest that there must have been some incident in the (early) life of Traven that created this "fixation" with identity that permeates both his work and life. In other words, we can only understand Traven's anonymity by tracing it to its origins. The problem, however, remains that in this circumstance it is precisely the origins that are inaccessible, that remain always a matter of speculation because it turns out the name "Ret Marut" is always a pseudonym and has no recorded documents prior to 1907. Wyatt (1980) provides a substitute figure, Otto Feige, Guthke (1987/1991) provides a psychological portrait (he says that Traven himself may not have known his origins because of an illegitimate birth and so spent the rest of his life creating fictional identities in order to supplement for this essential lack). What I want to suggest is that the construction of Traven's authorship as an absence forces criticism to engage with his "identity" as a text, and part of that text includes the sense of its own narrative origins. Traven repeatedly makes the claim that there is no writing without a corroborative experience. It is this notion of experience that we must next follow up on and which also gives rise to another interpretation of the Traven mystery.

This interpretation of Traven's absence has been referred to as the "other man" theory. Its basic outline is as follows: a man named B. Traven existed but he was not the author of the works, rather he was sort of a transcriber who either collaborated with another who actually experienced the events described in the novels and stories or he outright stole them and pawned them off as his own. There are many variations of this story and so for brevity I will stick to two main ones. While these stories are taken up mostly by scholars and journalists, it is interesting to note after Guthke (1987/1991) that their origins can be traced to Traven. In the famous interview with Luis

Spota, Torsvan claimed that Traven did not work alone: "I am sure that B. Traven did not write his books alone [...] Traven has seen very little of what he wrote about; indeed I can almost say that the majority of his subjects were told to him by others" (as cited in Guthke, 1987/1991, 339). While Spota declared Torsvan was Traven, others took up Torsvan's claim and gave it life. Max Schmid, for example, argued that:

> Ret Marut gave the B. Traven works their literary form, but the experiences depicted in *The Death Ship, The Cotton-Pickers, The Bridge in the Jungle, The Treasure of the Sierra Madre*, and many of the *Bush* stories derive largely not from his own range of experiences, but rather are based on the manuscripts of another man who had settled in Mexico a full decade before him. (as cited in Guthke, 1987/1991, 54)

For Schmid, though this "other man" is not known, he is the fictional Gerard Gales. Michael Baumann (1976) takes up Schmid's argument in principle, but adds a language question as further evidence. In short, his claim is that there is no way that Marut, having arrived in Mexico sometime in 1923 could have gained all the experience necessary to write the novels set in Mexico that he did, starting in 1925 with the serial publication of *The Cotton-Pickers*. What Baumann (1976) claimed is that Traven is Marut, but Traven/Marut met someone name Torsvan who had originally written the stories, couldn't find publishers, so Marut arranged to write them himself, by translating them into German and adding his own knowledge. For Baumann (1976), this accounts for a philosophical and linguistic differences between Marut and Traven. Yet, Baumann (1976) wrote, Traven/Marut's contributions were not insignificant: "In addition to his having 'rewritten' the *Erlebnisträger*'s manuscripts in German and made them reflect his philosophy, he turned his face toward Europe, and, specifically, toward Germany, as often as he turned it toward America" (34). It is interesting to note, here, that Baumann's speculation insists that the Torsvan stories were written, that is they appear in Baumann's retelling as "manuscripts." What is really at stake, however, in both Schmid and Baumann, (Guthke too, in his rejection of the "other man" theory) is the notion of ownership as derived from personal experience.

The point is that the name B. Traven doesn't signify a determinate relation with a person. On the contrary, it refers to a form of textual production. As a name without a definite reference point, or rather only a reference point that can be reconstructed like a fictional text, it appears as part of an aesthetic. Guthke (1987/1991) pointed out: "The tale of a well-known writer's fantastic disappearance and rebirth in a new identity borders on literature—the art of the possible and of the imaginary become real" (41). It is an aesthetic which highlights the ways the author is not the master of his own creation, but is rather a product of the field of cultural production. Like the fictional works to which the name B. Traven is attached, the construction of authorship in Traven, that is the way the name appears as a fiction, functions to re-conceptualize a vision of authorship as a carrier of stories, as a means of dissemination, rather than as an owner who guards access to property. In this sense, the aesthetic forces us to engage with the author as intertwined with a form of cultural production whose aim is not profit. In this sense, Traven imagines authorship as a site of struggle in which the very conflicts between communal and capitalist ownership are inscribed in the production of his own name. There are two effects of this aesthetic of authorship: i) Traven extends the aesthetic relations (the imagination) of his fiction to the material order through his production of the absent author, and ii) imagines the author as a site in which is becomes possible to put aesthetics into practice at the material level by emphasizing the collective nature of authorship. But further, implicit in this form of authorship is the recognition that authorship is not a benign space that is simply occupied, or even a natural creative relation between individual and their work, but rather a construction that is inseparable from the material economic-juridical order of capitalism. Literary production, in other words, is not an autonomous sphere, a free play of the imagination independent of economic and legal considerations. Authorship immediately locates literary production within an economic-juridical order. To understand this connection is to be able to contextualize Traven's absence as not merely a mask to shelter an identity, but to draw attention to the pervasiveness of the increasing economic pressures faced by writers and publishers in a capitalist market. The significant aspect of Traven's absence is that it undercuts the importance of the individual and privileges instead a form of cultural production whereby stories arise out of stories, thus politicizing cultural production in the context of capitalist production and copyright.

It is instructive, then, to determine the mode of production by which Traven's stories are "created." His autographical statements demonstrate a propensity to persuade readers and editors alike that his fiction is based on lived experience. Both Zogbaum (1992) and Guthke (1987/1991) suggest, however, that in reality the stories are often repetitions of stories that have been told to him. In this sense, the narratives are based on an aesthetic or literary experience. Once again, we are in a textually mediated realm of reality. Zogbaum (1992) explained "Traven went around collecting stories and opinions as he had done since his arrival in Mexico. He chatted with anonymous people who told him about their lives and their environment, and he stored away the information give him" (74). She also recounted how Traven adapted "a true and well-known story that still forms part of local folklore" (Zogbaum, 1992, 125) in his novel *March to the Caobaland*. In addition, Guthke (1987/1991) reported that Traven attended courses at the Universidad Nacional de México in the summers of 1927, 1928 and 1929 "preparing for his future literary production, attempting to acquire the knowledge that would lend his novels authenticity apart from personal experience" (189). There were unfiled accusations of plagiarism specific to *The Treasure of the Sierra Madre*. Zogbaum (1992) reported

> The daughter of Traven's friend in San Cristóbal, Ewald Hess, maintains that the idea of transporting gold in animal hides was plagiarized by Traven from her father. This accusation would certainly fit the timing of the writing of *Der Schatz der Sierra Madre*. In Chiapas, Traven also had heard the story of how several people had spent a miserable night tied by their belts to a mahogany tree. This pitiful position was preferable to "being caressed by the paws of a tiger which they thought stalked nearby." Traven also incorporated this episode into *Der Schatz der Sierra Madre*. (87)

To contextualize this, the charges of plagiarism only arise in a system of property, only when the author is understood as an original producer whose products stems from within the self. None of the charges of plagiarism are based on textual plagiarism so there is no monetary value attached to the claims, which changes the nature of the accusation. That said, there is another context in which such "borrowings," form the basis of cultural production. In this sense, the free circulation of cultural texts (narratives) would be an essential component of an anarchist cultural production, that equates to a holding in common literary objects so that they can be used for further literary production. The imagination is produced, precisely from such cultural texts. And this is one of the main aspects that emerges both Traven's aesthetic, there is no unmediated world, both the fiction and the author refer back to other cultural texts. In discussing in a letter with his German editor Ernst Preczang the conclusion to *The Death Ship*, where the main character floats at sea alone after a shipwreck, Traven wrote:

> I want to give [the reader] the gift of moving him to draw his own conclusion. I wish that after reading the novel the reader will continue to think for himself, continue to experience things for himself, continue to write for himself. I don't want to empty out the reader, I want to inspire him to consider how things go from here. (As cited in Guthke, 1987/1991, 251–252)

Taken in this sense, the text is not an end in itself. Rather it serves as a building block for further cultural production, to be used by the reader as him/herself a cultural producer. That being said, we should not draw the conclusion that B. Traven was an open source name, where anybody could adopt the name. It does, however, open the door to a conceptualization of the multiple people involved in cultural production.

Guthke (1987/1991) pointed out that there are dangers associated with Traven's radical commitment to anonymity. Among these dangers he cited that "others may circulate works under his name hoping to capitalize on his fame" or that he may himself be charged with using someone else's works so that "far from creating the novels that gained fame (and royalties) under his name, he might at best be their translator or editor, a parasite who based his novels on the experiences of someone else" (Guthke, 1987/1991, 43). In the first scenario, Traven was at a great disadvantage because in order to confront pirated editions of his work, he would need to publicly identify himself. Although it seems at first counter-intuitive that someone invested in disseminating works of others to keep tight control over who had access to re-print those works, I think we can make a distinction between publication for artistic and commercial purposes. While there were certainly instances where other "authors" attempted to claim Traven's work as their own, or circulate works under the name Traven, these only become a point of contention if the purpose is the production of capital. Traven himself distinguished between these purposes in a letter to the *Büchergilde*, stating, "With every book offered by a commercial publisher, there is always the suspicion: Does he want to serve literature, or only his bank account?" (as cited in Guthke, 1987/1991, 239). Traven, in this sense, did use his copyright protections to prevent his works from benefiting those whose interests ran counter to his own anarchist ideas. For instance, when the Nazis took over the Berlin office of *Büchergilde* they also took control of his works. Traven responded quickly and decisively, instructing its new management that he had withdrawn publication rights. In a letter to his editor, he wrote

> My goal is not to leave any doubt about my position toward the political buffoons in Germany. I cannot rid myself of the suspicion that these people will take any literature which has achieved any standing in the civilized world and exploit it to their own ends, though not necessarily for financial gain—though I believe they would try that too [...] Losing the profits I might have by leaving the books in circulation means nothing to me. In matters like this I prefer clarity to profit. (as cited in Guthke, 1987/1991, 302–303)

Traven crafted an open letter that denounced the Berlin *Büchergilde* continued publication of his works abroad despite the fact that they had been banned under Nazi rule in Germany. He threatened to publish the open letter if his demands weren't met. Apparently this worked as in 1933 all rights were transferred to his European agent Josef Wieder (Guthke, 1987/1991).

But if Traven wielded copyright to prevent both ideological and capital profiting off his name and reputation, he also granted copyright on the basis of creating a communal interest. His decision to publish with *Büchergilde*, while it was certainly an opportunity he could not pass up financially, also had an ideological component. The *Büchergilde* was a "nonprofit organization" (Zogbaum, 1992, 24) with direct communication with its membership through its newsletter. Its membership "came from the working class" (Guthke, 1987/1991, 225). Between 1925 and 1929 relations between Traven and his publisher were good, but a shift in management that Traven characterized as a move to "become a 'business' instead of a 'democratic institution of the workers'" (as cited in Guthke, 1987/1991, 293) strained and eventually led to the dissipation of the relationship. The publisher was more than an avenue to generate profits for Traven. His affiliation, then, can be noted when in the process of donating a large portion of his collection to the Zurich-*Büchergilde* he does so "with a heart brimming with joy at the thought of serving an institution which I hope will become the largest and most significant cultural community of European workers" (as cited in Guthke, 1987/1991, 295). As relations soured, however, he criticized management for publishing his works "not for their revolutionary content, but for financial reasons" (as cited in Guthke, 1987/1991, 297). Not only was his investment in the publishing house as a communal space, but his distribution of copyrights among different people becomes a mode by which collective ownership takes material form. Copyright to Traven's works fall under the names M.L. Martinez, Esperanza López Mateos, Rosa Elena Lujan, Josef Wieder. In other words, Traven sought to expand the name to include numerous individuals in its production, not merely as a business, but as a form of cultural production that included the various aspects involved in the materiality of publishing. It is in this sense that B. Traven, both as an aesthetic and as a material production is a collective form of cultural production that puts an anarchist form of organization to work.

Scholars such as Antliff (2001) and Weir (1997) have drawn attention to the means by which anarchism as a political movement influenced early twentieth century artistic movements at the aesthetic level. In this sense anarchism functions as the ideological background against which, or within which, the literary imagination takes shape. Its reach, however, remains within the imagination or within aesthetics as a realm relatively independent of the materiality of cultural production. Anarchism is first and foremost a practice whose goal is revolutionary social and material transformation. My contention throughout this paper has been that the absence of a definitive person behind the name "B. Traven" enables us to engage with the name as an aesthetic form of cultural production that emphasizes its collective nature. In this sense, the obvious anarchist content within Traven's fiction combined with the representation of cultural production as a shared venture as the aesthetic content of his works, cannot be separated from the construction of B. Traven's authorship. This form of authorship makes us aware that as a material site, that is one signals both a creative relation with the fiction and a economic and legal relation to the work, is not a natural relation, that, in fact, the current dominance of the copyright regime primarily serves the interests of a capitalist order. In part B. Traven's authorship allows us to re-think the relations between content and form, but also between form and materiality and the ways in which the imaginative aspects of cultural production are already within a material order. Traven's absence, then, signals only the absence of an individual. This absence is immediately filled by the actual relations of cultural production which are collective. Authorship, in B. Traven, is a site that connects an anarchist aesthetic with the materiality of cultural production.

Note

1. There are very real problems with such aesthetic representations, not the least of which include a glossing over of cultural heterogeneity among indigenous groups which ultimately pervade colonial/postcolonial discourses of resistance. But for the current context, that is attempting to understand how anarchist aesthetics can function with the material sphere of the economic-juridical order of capitalism, such problems need to be bracketed—but not forgotten.

References

Antliff, A. (2001) *Anarchist modernism: Art, politics, and the first American avant-garde*. Chicago, Il: U of Chicago P.

Baumann, M. L. (1976) *B. Traven: An introduction*. Albuquerque, NM: U of New Mexico P.

Bookchin, M. (1995) Social anarchism or lifestyle anarchism—an unbridgeable chasm. Retrieved from http://libcom.org/library/socanlife8

Bourdieu, P. (1993) *The field of cultural production: Essays on art and literature* Randal Johnson, Ed. (Richard Nice and R. Swyer, Trans.) New York, NY: Columbia UP.

Burke, S. (1995). *Authorship: From Plato to the postmodern: A reader*. Edinburgh: Edinburgh UP.

Chankin, D. O. (1975). *Anonymity and death: The fiction of B. Traven*. University Park, PN: Pennsylvania State UP.

Deazley, R. (2006). *Rethinking copyright: History, theory, language.* Cheltenham, UK: Edward Elgar.

DiMaggio, P. (1979). Review essay: On Pierre Bourdieu. *The American Journal of Sociology,* 84 (6), 1460-1474.

Foucault, M. (2008). *The birth of biopolitics: Lectures at the Collège de France, 1978-1979.* Michel Senellart, Ed. (Graham Burchell, Trans.) New York, NY: Palgrave MacMillan. (Original work published 2004).

Goss, R.T. (1987). From Ret Marut to B. Traven: More than a change in disguise. In Ernst Schürer & Philip Jenkins (Eds), *B. Traven: Life and work* (pp. 44-55). University Park, PN: The Pennsylvania State UP.

Guthke, K.S. (1991). *B. Traven: The life behind the legends.* (Robert C. Sprung, Trans.). Brooklyn, NY: Lawrence Hill Books. (Original work published 1987).

Marx, K. (1977). *Capital: A critique of political economy. Volume one.* (Ben Fowkes, Trans.) New York, NY: Vintage Books. (Original work published 1867).

Proudhon, P.J. (1994). *What is property?* Donald R. Kelley & Bonnie G. Smith (Eds.) (Donald R. Kelley and Bonnie G. Smith, Trans.) Cambridge: Cambridge UP. (Original work published 1840).

Rocker, R. (1973). *Anarchism and anarcho-syndicalism.* London: Freedom Press. (Original work published 1960).

Saunders, D. (1992). *Authorship and Copyright.* London: Routledge.

Traven, B. (1967). The *Treasure of the Sierra Madre.* New York, NY: Hill and Wang. (Original work published in German 1927, in English 1935).

Traven, B. (1993). *The night visitor and other stories.* Chicago, IL: Ivan Dee Publishers. (Original work published 1966).

Weir, D. (1997). *Anarchy and culture: The aesthetic politics of modernism.* Amherst, MA: U of Massachusetts P.

Woodmansee, M. (1984). The genius and the copyright: Economic and legal conditions of the emergence of the "author." *Eighteenth Century Studies,* 17 (4), 425-448.

Wyatt, W. (1980) *The secret of the sierra madre: The man who was B. Traven.* Garden City, NY: Doubleday & Company, Inc.

Zogbaum, H. (1992). *B. Traven: A vision of Mexico.* Wilmington, DE: Scholarly Resources Inc.

6. "The Freedom that Allows Other Freedoms to Exist": Anarchistic Influence in *The French Lieutenant's Woman*

Bryan L. Jones

Although scholars usually describe the narrative technique of *The French Lieutenant's Woman* as marking the transition from modernism to post-modernism, John Fowles' post-modernist narration is better understood as a political maneuver that subverts the abuse of authority inherent in Marxist thought. Criticism of the novel usually deals with its narrative form while the novel's economi c and political aspects receive short shrift. The novel's complex structure lead many to consider it unfilmable, so comparisons between Harold Pinter's screenplay and Fowles's novel make up a good portion of the remaining criticism. Among the best papers dealing with the novel's social and economic themes is David W. Landrum's article "Rewriting Marx: Emancipation and Restoration in The French Lieutenant's Woman." According to Landrum the use of Marxist epigraphs in the novel show that "the meta-narrative of Marxism is affirmed in its recognition of the need for emancipation and restoration; but it is also subverted in relation to the substance and nature of the emancipations required to truly restore human relationships" (103). The novel subverts Marxist thought in a very specific way; one that reflects the culture's growing distrust of the authoritarian thrust of Marxism. In doing so Fowles constructs a narrator whose techniques highlight the basic framework of anarchistic thought.

Fowles did not come to construct such a narrator by accident. According to James R. Aubrey's research, when Fowles left the military he reflected that "I ... began to hate what I was becoming in life—a British Establishment young hopeful. I decided instead to become a sort of anarchist" (13–14). John Fowles' novel reflects anarchism on two fronts: its narrative techniques, which remove the authority from the typical Victorian authorial voice, and its use of Sartreian Existentialism, which promoted human agency. The 1960s were a time marked by several anti-authoritarian uprisings. The time is also marked by a change in Marxist thought. Several key theorists were beginning to break away from dogmatic conceptions of Marxism, which later became known as vulgar Marxism, and develop new conceptions. Several scholarly articles demonstrate how the novel's narrative techniques reflect the change between modernism and postmodernism with many seeing his work on the threshold between the two (Salami 23–25). These narrative techniques also reflect underlying anarchist principles dating back as far as the time of the novel's setting.

Anarchism and the New Left of the 1960s

Fowles' novel offers a critique on two cultures, the Victorian age and the culture that exists in the same country one hundred years later. Landrum is right to point out that: "It is the parallel plot,...dealing with...Sam and Mary, that more closely focuses on class conflict and illustrates the tensions that arise from social stratification" (104). What is missing from his critique is a mentioning of the way the novel reflects the 1960s view of how these *tensions* are best dealt with. From today's perspective we can begin to see the creation of this novel as a symptom of the emergence of anarchistic ideas into the left-wing political movements of the 1960s. According to the entry for "Anarchism" in *The Blackwell Dictionary of Twentieth Century Social Thought*,

> anarchist ideas reemerged, sometimes spectacularly, in the context of the New Left movements of the 1960s. Their influence is still discernible today, notably in movements for peace, feminism, lesbian and gay liberation, radical social ecology, animal liberation and workers' self-management. Direct action, the classical anarchist alternative to conventional political action, has also become popular. (15)

The problem with Marxism—at least what the 1960s counter culture believed was the problem—is that it rests to heavily on Authority. In the 1860s it was debated that Marx's dictatorship of the proletariat would only lead to the same end to which any other dictatorship has lead. In "Statism and Anarchy," Bakunin writes "from whatever angle you look at this question you come to the same sad conclusion: government of the vast majority of the masses by a privileged minority" (162–163). If Pol Pot, Stalin, and Mao were the examples of that dictatorship, then its looks as though the anarchists were right to oppose Marx on that point. Marx was still considered to have sound theories about economics and culture in the 1960s. Because of that recognition, the two sides of the great debate about the State's responsibility to its people began to blend a bit. The result was a growing mistrust of authority and a belief that people could better govern themselves.

In "Marxism and the New Left," an essay on the distinctions in the approach to Marxian theory between the Old Left's dogmatic view and the approach taken by the New Left, Howard Zinn writes:

> The New Left is anti-authoritarian...It is anarchistic not merely in the Marxist sense of the ultimate abolition of the state but in demanding its abolition as an immediate requirement. Authority and coercion, moreover, must be abolished in every sphere of existence, and, from the outset, ends must be represented in the means. Marx and Bakunin disagreed on this point, but the New Left has the advantage over Marx in having seen how a dictatorship of the proletariat can easily become a dictatorship over the proletariat (365).

It is precisely this perspective on Marx that is expressed in the pages of Fowles' novel in the way that authority is presented. The character that is the chef example of authority is Mrs. Poulteney. Fowles writes, "She acknowledged no bounds to her Authority" (20). Landrum points out that "Some class considerations are seen in the development of the main plot [such as the fact that] Sarah Woodruff must compromise her personal freedom by working, out of economic necessity, for the tyrannical Mrs. Poulteney" (104). However, he neglects to remark on the importance of that tyranny to the political concerns of the novel. The narrator comments that "there would have been a place in the Gestapo for the lady; she had a way of interrogation that would reduce the sturdiest girls to tears in the first five minutes" (Fowles 20). The Gestapo was an acronym used for the secret state police in Nazi Germany. But, lest we be confused and mistake Fowles' metaphor to mean that Mrs. Poulteney is comparable to a storm trooper and not the dictator himself, Fowles adds the following as a means of clarification: "Her only notion of government was an angry bombardment of the impertinent populace" (20). It should be pointed out that the communists were one enemy of the Gestapo in Nazi Germany, but it would be hard not to note that Stalin's dictatorship utilized similar techniques. Some examples being the Great Purge and Gulag labor camps.

That the above example comes from a subjective comment made by the novel's narrator is also of note because the novel's narrative techniques are anarchic in nature as well. As Fowles writes: "the novelist is still a god, since he creates . . . what has changed is that we are no longer the gods of the Victorian image, omniscient and decreeing; but in the new theological image, with freedom our first principle, not authority" (97). The freedom expressed in the characters he creates and the freedom he allows his readers stem from the same political stance. In The French Lieutenant's Woman, the narrator preaches about "the freedom characters must be given" (Fowles 405). This procedure demonstrates, at the textual level, that the novel is an artifice and that authority is merely a social construct. Here, authority is seen along the same lines as Louis Althusser sees ideology. Althusser writes "what is represented in ideology is therefore not the system of the real relations which govern the existence of individuals, but the imaginary relation of those individuals to the real relations in which the live" (162). The authority bestowed upon the author is only imaginary because it is due to "a convention universally accepted at the time of my story: that the novelist stands next to god" (95). The same can be said of the authority bestowed upon every tyrant of the world.

In an essay titled "Freedoms in the French Lieutenant's Woman," Richard P. Lynch writes: "Fowles is dealing in particular here with three different kinds of freedom: social, existential, and narrative, though in his statements outside the novel, he does not appear to distinguish between the first two... In Fowles's thinking, existentialism is primarily a response to social and political pressures on the individual to conform" (50–51). If the novel is examined in terms of its anarchistic influence, then the possibility arises that Fowles may not distinguish much between all three kinds of freedom. Lynch goes on to point out that "Narrative freedom, the "freedom" of fictional characters (or the illusion of it) from their authors, is a metaphor for freedom from God, a precondition for existential freedom in Fowles and Sartre" (51). Freedom in the novel must first be understood in terms of existentialist thinkers like Sartre, but conceptions of freedom in the novel are better understood as anarchistic. While at college at Oxford, Fowles was introduced to the existentialism of Sartre and became a writer himself (Aubrey 14). It is worth mentioning here that in Fredric Jameson's view Marxism and Existentialism have always existed in tandem for Sartre (Jameson 207). In fact, there is talk of a lost constitution written by Sartre "mixing economics with a utopian vision freely adapted from the writings of Marx and Proudhon...[that] provides evidence that Sartre's vision of a non-authoritarian socialism precedes the postwar period" (Ungar 5). Just as Fowles' narrator understands that god has come to be defined as "the freedom that allows other freedoms to exist;" given the way that authority is presented in the novel, we can conclude that author must also "conform to that definition" (97). Fowles reached the conclusion that "[t]he novelist is still a god, since he creates (and not even the most aleatory avant-garde modern novel has managed to extirpate its author completely)" (97). A similar conclusion is reached with anarchists concerning the relationship of authority to society; that it can never be fully erased but it can be equally distributed among citizens. Fowles mirrors this current anarchist conception when he writes "I do not fully control these creatures of my mind, any more than you control—however hard you try, however much of a latterday Mrs. Poulteney you may be—your children, colleagues, friends, or even yourself" (97).

Fowles' Narrator as Anarchist God

Much has been written about the ways in which Fowles' novel demonstrates both modernist and postmodernist techniques. According to Katherine Tarbox:

> Disorienting work like The French Lieutenant's Woman...[has] produced a generation of evolved readers-turned-writers, a generation of young British (and other English-speaking) writers who have been inspired to push the limits in their own narrative practices. Fowles has participated in the ongoing metamorphosis of the novel, helping to bring into being the brilliant postmodern narrative experiments of writers like Peter Ackroyd, Martin Amis, Julian Barnes, Fay Weldon, Peter Benson, Angela Carter, Will Self, and Graham Swift: experiments that have powerful political and existential significance. (101–102)

The novel gives three different endings and its narrator makes an appearance in the story to name just two of the novel's *disorienting experiments*. In addition, the narrator makes several comments on the action and characters in the novel, and provides the reader with many musings on Victorian life along the way. It was around the 1960s that the novel began to utilize less authoritative techniques more frequently. Just why these techniques are present has to do with the emergence of anarchism, into the political make up of "the Left," during the 1960s. Anarchism, contrary to popular belief, is not chaos but the negation of authority. It is through this negation of authority that anarchism and post-modernity are linked because each seeks to topple authority. The word author derives from the same word that authority does and, because in post-modernity the author is "dead," the postmodern novelist seeks to topple the authority of the author. As Fowles' narrator point out, "I live in the time of...Roland Barthes; if this is a novel, it cannot be a novel in the modern sense of the word" (95). In this way, the use of many postmodern narrative techniques can be shown share basic aspects of anarchism. One such technique is way the role of the narrator is often diminished. In many postmodern narratives, the narrator becomes just one aspect of the novel and not its sole figure of determining plot.

Jonathan Culler explains the authority created by a given novel's narrator in the following way:

> To tell a story is to claim a certain authority, which listeners grant. When the narrator of Jane Austen's *Emma* begins, "Emma

Woodhouse, handsome, clever, and rich, with a comfortable home and happy disposition,..." we don't skeptically wonder whether she really was handsome and clever. We accept this statement until we are given reason to think otherwise. Narrators are sometimes termed *unreliable* when they provide enough information about situations and clues about their own biases to make us doubt their interpretations of events, or when we find reasons to doubt that the narrator shares the same values as the author. Theorists speak of *self-conscious narration* when narrators discuss the fact that they are telling a story, hesitate about how to tell it, or even flaunt the fact that they can determine how the story will turn out. Self-conscious narration highlights the problem of narrative authority (87–88).

The narrative techniques utilized by Fowles do not fit perfectly into the framework provided by Culler. His narrator does not give subjective descriptions of characters that the reader is expected to accept passively, nor can it be said that the narrator's subjective comments are unreliable. Self-conscious narration fits best, but that fit is not exactly a snug one. As Katherine Tarbox points out, "The narrator acknowledges his own participation in this cycle of reading and "writing" through his use of epigraphs and footnotes,...in effect, his authorship is transindividual; and because the epigraphs parallel exactly what is going on within the chapter,... he shows that all telling and writing is first a listening—to the voices of others' stories" (93–94). Fowles' narrative technique highlights the problem of narrative authority, but not in the way that is expected of most self-conscious narrators. Fowles' technique allows for equal distribution of authority between both reader and storyteller.

That Culler uses a Victorian writer to exemplify his point is a happy coincidence because not only is Fowles' novel set in the Victorian age, but also Austen's authoritative narrator is precisely the type subverted by Fowles. Austen begins with a subjective description of her character that the reader is expect to take agree with merely because the information comes from the author. Fowles subverts this expectation in a way that equally distributes authority between reader and writer when he comments on the attractiveness his character, Mary. Fowles does this by expertly avoiding all three of Culler's possible narrative categories by writing, "Of the three young women who pass though these pages Mary was, in my opinion, by far the prettiest" (75). His opinion is just that, an opinion. The reader is free to decide which young woman is the prettiest according to his/her own. The statement is not to be taken of faith, nor can it be said that the narrator is unreliable. The state is in fact very reliable due to its admittance of being a mere opinion—one that the reader is then free to accept or reject.

Another way anarchism is demonstrated in the postmodern novel is the method inserting the narrator into the story, just as Fowles inserts his narrator. By inserting the writer into the story the authority of the writer buckles. The writer becomes just another character in the novel, most often a very minor charter, usually "just passing through" with no real bearing on the plot. To cite just one example from another novel, the reader is able to catch a glimpse of Kurt Vonnegut in a scene near the end of *Slaughter House Five*. Fowles' narrator is described as looking quite a lot like Fowles himself. Unlike Vonnegut, Fowles does more that merely "pass though" the story. Fowles actually defies the laws of time and space. This, however, is not the move of a being seeking dominance. Fowles is not the Victorian God, which Bakunin saw as a tyrant that made humans into slave. With his twisting of time, Fowles becomes "the freedom which allows other freedoms to exist" (97).

The conclusion reached by Landrum is:

> Fowles critiques Marxism by juxtaposing, as epigraphs, some apparently contradictory statements Marx made. Simultaneously, however, he "opens up" these texts and, by illustrating them with a dramatic framework (the Sam/Charles plot of the novel), is able strongly to assert the truths they contain. So it is that the epigraphs at first bear on the text of the novel, but soon the text of the novel begins to have some bearing upon how the epigraphs are understood. In *The French Lieutenant's Woman*, human emancipation is accomplished not by any authoritative impositions, but by the uncovering of possibility and by a dissolution of certainties that permits genuine liberation to come about. (113)

The truths within these epigraphs that are *opened up* is that Marx was, after all, only human and that his theories were just that, theories. Like all theories they need to be tested, added to, negated, and so on, until a true conception can be developed. As Howard Zinn writes, "the new radicalism, I believe, should [strive to] be anti-ideological,...but it should also be—and has not sufficiently been—concerned with theory. It needs a vision of what it is working toward" (363). He goes on to write that "[i]n the first requirement of this theory, the vision of the future, the Marxian vision is useful. (Of course it is vague, but what better guard against dogmatism?) (363).

Conclusion

Often the form and function of a narrator is understood as meeting a certain aesthetic requirement that has no bearing on the politics of a given time period or novel. Critics often start with a set of categories then try to drop the narrator into the correct slot, leaving political concerns to historical analysts or those more concerned with the ways in which economics are presented. Those who analyze the techniques utilized by a narrator to often merely try to pin point the right time period with which to place a given narrator. Is author A, writing in time period X, a precursor for the types of narrators found in time period Y? This view is reductive because the ways in which a narrator presents a story can say as much about power relations as the maneuvering of characters can. By analyzing the political consciousness of a given time period, one can come to understand why certain narrative techniques "catch on" in certain time periods. According to Christopher Butler, "the novel [as a mode of production] has borne a disproportionate amount of the burden of being 'postmodern,' because its hitherto usual 'discourses'—in the relationship of author to the text...—lay it at so many points open to a postmodernist critique" (73). The novel also opens itself up to an anarchistic critique by way of the very same relationship. For Butler the movement from modernism to postmodernism is marked by the movement, "[f]rom modernist mastery and formal control...towards a playful...account of characters" (73). This movement also marks the difference between Marxism and anarchism.

Herbert Read was a popular anarchist writer in England who died near the time Fowles published *The French Lieutenant's Woman*. Read's writings focus on the anarchist conception of freedom. According to Read, Marxism is too myopic in its focus on work. Read writes:

> If man had created himself merely by his work, he would have remained within a sensational and instinctual world, like an ant. The development of consciousness, which I agree with Marxists in treating as an existential, historic event, means that subjective factors, essences, entered into the dialectical process; and only that fact can explain the evolution of man to his present moral and intellectual stature. And, of course, it is quite ridiculous to confine the evolutionary factors to work. (530).

Read continues by adding, "it was *play* rather than *work* which enabled man to evolve his higher faculties—everything we mean by the word 'culture'... it is the theory of all work and know play that has made the Marxist a very dull boy" (530–531). Herbert Read concludes that, "anarchism is the *only* political theory that combines an essentially revolutionary and contingent attitude with a philosophy of freedom" (538). John Fowles' narrator is both the modernist author and the Victorian god writing in the postmodern age: dead. The death of this author-god grants freedom to both reader and character alike.

References

Althusser, Louis. *Lenin and Philosophy and Other Essays*. New York: Monthly Review Press, 1971.

Aubrey, James R. *John Fowles: A Reference Companion*. New York: Greenwood Press, 1991.

Bakunin, Michael. "God and the State." *The Essential Works of Anarchism*. Ed. Marshall S. Shatz. New York: Bantam, 1971. 126–154.

_____. "Statism and Anarchy." *The Essential Works of Anarchism*. Ed. Marshall S. Shatz. New York: Bantam, 1971. 155–183.

Blackwell Dictionary of Twentieth Century Social Thought, The. "Anarchism." Oxford: Blackwell Publishers, 1994.

Culler, Jonathan. *Literary Theory: A Very Short Introduction*. Very Short Introductions. Ser. 4. New York: Oxford University Press, 1997.

Fowles, John. *The French Lieutenant's Woman*. New York: Little Brown, 1998.

Higdon, David Leon. "Endgames in John Fowles's *The French Lieutenant's Woman*." *English Studies: A Journal of English Language and Literature* 65(4) (Aug. 1984): 350–361. *MLA International Bibliography*. EBSCO. JVL, Tahlequah, OK. 13 May 2009.

Jameson, Fredric. *Marxism and Form*. Princeton: Princeton University Press, 1971.

Landrum, David W. "Rewriting Marx: Emancipation and Restoration in *The French Lieutenant's Woman*." *Twentieth Century Literature: A Scholarly and Critical Journal* 42(1) (Spring 1996): 103–113. *MLA International Bibliography*. EBSCO. JVL, Tahlequah, OK. 13 May 2009.

Lynch, Richard P. "Freedoms in *The French Lieutenant's Woman*." *Twentieth Century Literature: A Scholarly and Critical Journal* 48(1) (Spring 2002): 50–76. *MLA International Bibliography*. EBSCO. JVL, Tahlequah, OK. 13 May 2009.

Salami, Mahmoud. *John Fowles's Fiction and the Poetics of Postmodernism*. Rutherford: Fairleigh Dickinson University Press, 1992.

Tarbox, Katherine. "*The French Lieutenant's Woman* and the Evolution of Narrative." *Twentieth Century Literature: A Scholarly and Critical Journal* 42(1) (Spring 1996): 88–102. *MLA International Bibliography*. EBSCO. JVL, Tahlequah, OK. 13 May 2009.

Ungar, Steven. "Introduction." *What is Literature? and Other Essays*. Jean-Paul Sartre. Cambridge: Harvard University Press, 1988. 1–20.

Vonnegut, Kurt. *Slaughterhouse-Five*. New York: Dell, 1974.

Zinn, Howard. "Marxism and the New Left." *Dissent: Explorations in the History of American Radicalism*. Ed. Alfred F. Young. Dekalb, IL: Northern Illinois University Press, 1969. 357–372.

7. "One Who, Choosing, Accepts the Responsibility of Choice": Ursula K. Le Guin, Anarchism, and Authority

Max Haiven

Towards a Prefigurative Fiction

There is, of course, no single authority on what anarchism is, and defining anarchism is not a challenge I would dare attempt. But whatever it is, it is marked by the presence of an imagination beyond authority.

I mean authority here in the broadest possible sense. Anarchism dreams of the possibilities of a life beyond the sorts of power that locks people into brutal and coercive relationships, whether they be economic, political, social, sexual, cultural or ideological. This rejection of authority, then, implies a rejection of capitalism, state bureaucracy, class stratification, religious doctrine, militarism, nationalism, ethnic exclusivism and a strict and compulsory social division of labor. It ought to extend to the refusal of patriarchy, racism, ablism, homophobia, trans-phobia and other forms of oppression, but it has not always done so (although the anarchist record on this theme is perhaps better most modern forms of political thought and action). Anarchism's challenge not only to concrete institutions of authority but also to the very *idea* of authority also implies a rethinking of personal responsibility and vision, one that would allow us to coexist and cooperate without recourse to some sort of authoritarian or bureaucratic framework, or some sort of cosmic authority or the myth of biological necessity.

In other words, at least one strong, deep root of the gnarled tree of anarchism is the drive to reveal, question, undermine and sabotage authority, both in its obvious institutionalized forms (capital, the state, the police, the division of labor, the school system, etc.) and in all its many intimate disguises and inter-subjective subtleties, such as the way we many anarchist and non-anarchist men treat women in conversation, or the way we assume the authority to kill and eat animals purely for our own pleasure.

Such a commitment to anti-authority means, at one level, a deep and often painful honesty with ourselves, a will to self-question, an overcoming of capitalist/Eurocentric/patriarchal individualism and a personal commitment towards dialogue, community and change. It means the collective cultivation of a profound *responsibility* to one another, to our communities, and to people we have not met and may never meet. In this sense, anarchism is an extremely radical form of *humanism*, not in the sense of an anthropocentric celebration of human beings as the lords and masters of the earth and universe but, rather, an approach to politics, cooperation and life that highlights the open-ended and unsettling question of the *responsibility* of being "human" in this world. That is, the radical courage and tireless curiosity to experiment with what being human might mean, and a deep and abiding respect and love for other human beings and (what eco-critics have taught us to think of as) "more-than-human" beings.

I hasten to make clear that by tarrying and playing with the idea of "humanism" I am not trying to solidify a notion of what the human "is" but to suggest that "humanism" means a complex and never-finished attention-to and dwelling-with the particular *problem* of "being human," which also includes comprehending and being open to all those ways those things we though made us "human" (and separated us from the more-than-human world) are, in fact, troubled and unstable—for instance, recognizing that our bodies are the product of the collaboration of thousands of distinct (if miniscule) life-forms and a vast, interconnected web of worldly processes; or recognizing other animals' capacity for empathy, imagination and technology.

Perhaps anarchism is what humanism (as a bourgeois philosophy) strives to become but cannot. Where bourgeois humanism finds its limits at its need to perpetuate certain (often cryptic) forms of authority like colonialism, racism, patriarchy, intellectualism, the domination and exploitation of the more-than-human world, anarchism is an *approach* (not a goal or an ideology, but a *process*) that stresses going beyond these limits. Indeed, anarchism-as-humanism would be based on the idea that *we can never be human enough*, that the work of realizing what it *might* mean to be human, and to therefore exist in human community, is always on the horizon, and that we approach this horizon on a path of radical equality, militant democracy, staunch anti-oppression and, indeed, a furious love. Already I'm sure I've pissed off a few readers who perhaps envision an anarchism that embraces our ostensibly more animalistic nature, or which seeks to extend or demolish the idea of "the human" once and for all.

While it might be argued that anarchism can be traced to the most ancient roots of human civilization and that it has existed in all cultures in one form or another, this essay focuses on its career in Western modernity and the rise of capitalism where it became known as "anarchism" as such. I want to trace the intermingling of an anarchist critique of authority with the rise (and fall) of another product of Western modernity: the concept of the author.

My basic argument is this:

1. That along with the rise of modern, Western (capitalist/imperialist/colonialist/patriarchal/ecocidal/etc./) forms of authority there arose a modern notion of the author as the "authoritative voice" of a text. Indeed, capitalist-modern forms of political and social authority and the figure of the unique author have supported one another ideologically. As anarchists have built various historically-specific movements challenging authority, they have also struggled with the figure of the author.

2. While many anarchist(ic) thinkers have challenged and even rejected this figure, matters have been complicated in part because it has been necessary to mobilize the idea(l) of the author in order to communicate anarchistic ideas as one aspect of anarchist struggle.

3. I suggest that Ursula K. Le Guin, renowned American novelist and essayist, living legend of science-fiction, Taoist and anarchist, has done some very powerful work in her writing that can help us think with the problem of anarchism and authority. Le Guin has never succumbed to more post-modern impulses to shatter what I'll call "authoriality" or the presence of the "authoritative voice" within her writing (attempts which, more often than not, create works that can only be "enjoyed" by bourgeois audiences who can afford to share their educated time and cynicism with these nigh-unreadable experimental texts). Instead she has, throughout her career, worked with an inspirational subtlety and grace to both infuse her work with complex anarchist themes and to walk a fine line with regards to authoriality.

4. In this sense, I want to identify Le Guin's project as one of authoring "prefigurative fiction," drawing on the anarchistic (or maybe more accurately feminist) idea of "prefigurative politics" or a politics that stresses acting out and creating the world we would like to see in the present. In movement organizing praxis this means that activists do not wait until "after the revolution" to challenge sexism, racism, ablism and other forms of oppression or to build alternative institutions and forms of collectivity; we do it here and

now, within the broader structures of oppression and exploitation, seeking to capsize them from within and stitching together and experimenting with those forms of radical humanity that would make any decent revolution possible.

By prefigurative fiction I mean a form of writing that does not merely map out radical tomorrows in advance. Instead, it is fiction that opens up futures in the present as spaces of reflection and growth, of hope and possibility and, most importantly, as spaces where "the human" might be otherwise, spaces of the radical imagination. It is distinct from other forms of science fiction or utopian literature in its modesty and its modeling of a radical form of authoriality, one that does not seek to impress the egoistic stamp of the author upon the future but, instead, rejects author-ity even as it exists within a form (the novel) where authoriality is (seemingly) compulsory. Just as prefigurative movements plant and tend the seeds of a better tomorrow in the poisoned soil of today, so too does prefigurative fiction hint towards another, post-revolutionary form of culture from within the authoritarian form of the novel. Like prefigurative politics, prefigurative fiction isn't perfect and is always muddy, confused, learning, making mistakes, and "getting called on it." But both are built on a radical unending "humanism" and a profound but never simple love and optimism. It is this critical optimism that marks prefigurative fiction from other acts of speculative fiction, even when it is avowedly dystopian.

Of course, it will be impossible here to give a full picture of Le Guin's life's work which includes over 20 novels, and scores of stories, poems and essays. Instead, I have selected a few texts that I think are particularly revealing and allow us to see the general contours of her development over her phenomenal 45 year career. I should also note at the outset that, other than my discussion above, I don't intend to engage with the wealth of anarchist theory that has emerged over the past 30 years, nor am I going to delve too deeply into the debates surrounding the nature and history of the idea of "the author" which have occupied literary theorists and cultural historians since the 1960s (and before).

Authority, the Author and "Authoriality"

One of the unique products of Western capitalist modernity was the emergence of the idea of the author (Woodmansee and Jaszi 1994). Before the emergence of modern European possessive individualism, the figure of the author (or the more broad character of the imaginative, creative artist) did not exist in any concrete way. Early literary figures like Chaucer or Shakespeare, while admired as writers in their day, were not lauded for their creativity or innovation. Indeed, such writers saw themselves as largely re-tellers of established stories and prided themselves on craft and form, rather than innovative imagination. But with the rise of Western patriarchal masculinity and of a new, literate ruling-class reading public, the figure of the unique author, the individual genius, began to take hold as someone who "owned" or "originated" certain ideas, stories or other elements of culture (see Haiven and Khasnabish 2011).

The emergence of the author was intimately tied-in with the emergence of copyright and other forms of intellectual property and these laws were a sort of "test case" for new legal and philosophical paradigms of individualistic ownership in general (Rose 1993). Much of today's property law (the authority over land, over the means of production, over private property) borrowed from early notions of authorial rights. Further, the idea of the author was critical to emerging understandings (and executions) of authority. The state was to "author" social life in the way the author had authority over a text: the governor was supposed to be able to "read" society and people's motivations and desires like a book; social life was supposed to flow like a story or a musical composition from the legal pen; and, of course, control over the story (of the origins of the nation, of who belonged and who did not, of what happened in the past, of who the heroes and the villains were) was and continues to be a key aspect of social power. Similarly, early capitalists understood themselves as the authors of social productivity, growth and industry, orchestrating the labor of their drone-like (uncreative, unimaginative) workers. The idea of the author was both the creation and the icon of a new order of individualist authority that imagined the world was made up of isolated, self-sufficient (white, male, European) personages, authors of their own fate unbeholden to community. This image, of course, failed to recognize the material fact that these great white men, with their myths of Robinson Crusoe and Economic Man, relied upon the invisiblized, devalued and compulsory work of wives, servants, slaves and colonized laborers, not to mention, later, the working class.

What began as an elite figure of cultural singularity quickly came to take on a critical place in Western and global culture. As new communication and entertainment media emerged, and as literacy grew, the cultural of literary celebrity emerged as a key common touchstone for people alienated from community and who increasingly came to mediate their cultural time through commodities. The emergence of great authors and artists allowed colonial powers to point to their refinements as evidence of European superiority and trace a narrative that located so-called "primitive" collective cultures as inferior and immature in the face of Western individual genius. Similarly, the growing upper-middle class and lower aristocracy of the 18th and 19th centuries (the managers and owners of new forms of authority) were to demand forms of "high" art and culture so as to define themselves as distinct from the working and even middling-classes and their typically more "crude" forms of popular entertainment. Indeed, ironically, it was precisely the *commodification* of "popular culture (like music halls, vaudeville, comic books, sensation fiction and street performers), the way these popular, working class cultural forms seemed to answer only to the dictates of the markets, that made them "low culture" while "high culture" (ostensibly) answered to the higher calling of art, beauty and the expression of the individual will of the artist. While many authors and artists were to disparage and contrast their own independence and romantic imagination against the rising bourgeoisie, industrialists and imperial bureaucrats, both the figure of the creative genius and the figure of the Economic Man came to mutually reinforce one another's cultural authority. The mastery of the author over narrative or language, the mastery of the boss over his legion of workers, and the mastery of the state and the bureaucrat over the population, all resonated with one another. They were to be brought together most disastrously in the form of fascism where control over workers and over whole populations was orchestrated as an act of depraved art, a *totalwerk* where fascists and their charismatic leaders came to impose their authority utterly on society as a whole. This could only occur, however, within a European cultural, social and political context already conditioned to accept and, indeed, celebrate and love authority and already conditioned by a century or more of *economic and sex/gender fascism*, and the inherent fascism of European colonial regimes.

It is no surprise that anarchism's engagement with the form of the author has always been ambivalent. On the one hand, the idea of the author emerges from the dense mire of interdependent myths that shore up capital, patriarchy, colonialism and the state. On the other, however, the figure of the author can offer the an important freedom to think, act and share and a forum for political intervention that is necessary for revolution. From one angle, the author is always positing their authority over the text, the narrative, the reader (in the sense that the author speaks and the reader listens). From another angle, in modern, capitalist times, what forum more than the book, the pamphlet or the letter allows for the sharing of anti-authoritarian ideas and propaganda? Indeed, anarchism would likely not exist as a (relatively) coherent (if deeply conflicted) socio-political radicalism if it were not for the writings of key authors. And anarchists do love books. Indeed, a great many anarchists have arrived at anti-authoritarian politics through particular authors and have overcome political isolation, depression and hopelessness with the help of beloved anarchist(ic) writers of both fiction and non-fiction. It's no accident that the key form that anarchist gatherings have taken over the past three decades has been the "book fair" which, while they are marked by a lot more than books and reading, still do reference and circulate around the (co-)authored text. While every good anarchist knows that books alone can't change the world, all good anarchists also know the world can't be changed without them!

The Problem of Authoriality and Anarchist(ic) Politics

Revolutionary thinkers have tried many strategies for overcoming this conundrum. One of the most basic is to write as a collective and anarchist writers have been doing this for centuries both to reject the egoism of the single author, to glean the benefits of multiple perspectives, or to avoid detection by authorities. But most have found that, without the figure of the author, without a writer on "the other side of the page," many readers are not compelled. Some might argue this response is habituated by an individualistic capitalist culture. Others might suggest that the dependence on the author speaks to people's need for human connection that is lost to a consumerist society dominated by the indifferent commodity and alienating forms of rank and authority—art and literature's power (and, ironically, commercial success) come from their promise of a human connection in a world of loneliness and division. There are also always worries about authenticity, plagiarism and unauthorized editing.

On the flip side, earlier radical movements like the 19th century Romantics saw the figure of the author become a hero, one who might both reject the conservatism of the day and point to new futures beyond industrial misery and endemic poverty and unfreedom. Indeed, the author, in many ways and for many people, became the icon of the empowered, free(-thinking) individual as an anarchist ideal. But others were to criticize the Romantics for valorizing the same individual and individualism as their establishmentarian rivals (Lee 2002). Some revolutionary writers have seized the figure of the author directly and constructed elaborate writerly personas as a means towards political leadership. Perhaps most successful was Lenin (but also Marx, Trotsky, Stalin and Mao—and maybe Bakunin) who used his authoriality to build himself up as a revolutionary leader (and vice versa). Many radicals, however, identify this tendency in Lenin as a key source of the woes of the Russian Revolution and after where new and deadly forms of Soviet authoritarianism took hold under the relentless capitalist attack on the Revolution. Still today many anarchists and others have criticized the cults of personality and attribution which circulate around certain anarchist and radical authors from Noam Chomsky to Derek Jensen to Subcomandante Marcos (even though most of these authors often reject their lionization). In contrast, many artists and authors reject their privileged persona and seek to "disappear" into communities, engaging in art and writing with children and adults as a means towards liberation or using art or text as direct action through graffiti, culture jamming or other anonymous, public acts. It certainly is true that declaring authority is almost completely necessary for the commercial success that could lead to an author's economic survival in a capitalist economy: collectives really don't sell books.

The choice between embracing or avoiding the authority of the author is bisected by another debate over the form of the text itself. On the one hand, there are those anarchist(ic) authors who believe that writing, especially "creative writing," should be geared towards awakening an awareness of the necessity of revolution. For these authors, the power of the author should be used to create narratives that show people how awful the capitalist, colonialist, patriarchal system of authority are and why change is possible, necessary and immanent. On the other hand, some writers link the problems of authority in capitalist society to the problem of the form of writing, not just the content. They point out that there is a sort of invisible authority that shapes the way we write and the way we expect to encounter creative writing and that this form (for instance, the typical story line which privileges linearity, a hero and villain, an individualist focus, an author who can get inside people's heads, etc.) needs to be challenged too. They argue the way we write and create is guided by unquestioned forms of literary authority and that this authority is tied to other, broader systems of domination. Anarchist(ic) authors have long been at the forefront of challenging the reigning aesthetic forms of the day (see Antliff 2007). Indeed, there is a strong connection between anarchism (of various stripes) and the "avant-garde," that nebulous term for *fin de siècle* artists, poets, musicians and playwrights who took as their social and political task to test and break the limits of what art might be and do. The problem, however, is that, all too typically, one of these strategies comes at the expense of the other: either one stresses educating and communicating clearly and risks reproducing authoritarian or propagandistic forms, or one stresses experimentalism and freedom and risks being unreadable to people outside the "affinity group."

To make matters worse, both strategies risk cooptation. For more "accessible" texts written in the dominant forms of the day, the risk is of being taken as merely one more commodified option, just another book on the shelf at the bookstore or in the homes of the more daring bourgeoisie who like to titillate themselves and their dinner guests with dangerous books. On the other hand, anarchist(ic) avant-gardes have a long history of being unwitting pioneers of what will soon become mainstream. For instance, French anarchist Gustave Courbet's radical realism was, not 30 years later, to become the norm. Similarly, the Surrealist and Dadaist movements of the early 20th century were brought within the official "cannon" well within their artists' lifetimes. This problem has been even more profound for indigenous and anti-colonial activists who must both pioneer new forms and revivify stolen or subdued cultural forms at the same time under the shadow of Western appropriation and cooptation.

In this sense, the anarchist literary imagination has always been vexed by the relationship of authoriality to authority.

Le Guin's Earlier Works

It is within this set of problems I want to locate the work of Ursula K. Le Guin and bring her work into dialogue with new social movements of a decidedly anarchist(ic) nature. In this section and the next we'll take a chronological look at a selection of Le Guin's novels and short stories which offer a sample of her development as an author. We'll focus in specific on her work in science fiction, rather than her also impressive work in fantasy, poetry, contemporary and historical fiction and letters.

Le Guin's career has spanned about 40 years and during this time new cultural and political problems, movements and tendencies have arisen. It is important to note that Le Guin's emergence onto the public stage was during the mid 1960s and came at the time of a general upsurge of radical and revolutionary thought and action in North America and Europe. Amidst the continuing imperialist tragedy of the Vietnam War and widespread discontent on the left with the failure of the Soviet Union to live up to its revolutionary promises, young activists were searching for new political visions in ways that are now the stuff of legend and nostalgia. The white "baby-boom" generation was to come of age and reject the simulacrum of peace, happiness and free enterprise that was supposed to have followed the Second World War, angered by both the social and sexual conservatism of "first world" culture as well as the forms of authority, social violence, imperialism and class stratification necessary to maintain that system. It was also a moment where activists were distrustful of older modes of (Marxist-Leninist) radical politics that stressed obedience to the Party Line and rigid party discipline, recognizing that this tended to reproduce internal forms of authority and authoritarianism. So too was it a moment when the interconnected narratives or discourses of oppression noted above were becoming increasingly clear, when awareness of the intersections of different forms of oppression was beginning to awaken. Distrust of leadership, hierarchy, and schematic utopias, of science, of democracy and of politics as it had formerly been known was at an all time high (see Katsiaficas 1987).

The time, then, was fortuitous for Le Guin's early interventions. Le Guin herself was never primarily an activist and was slightly older than the baby-boom generation that were to become her avid readers. But a number of features of her background were key to the rise of her political consciousness and later writing. She was the daughter of Arthur Kroeber, one of the most famous anthropologists of his generation and Dorothea Kroeber, an anthropologist and writer, and grew up in a middle-class family that encouraged reading, thinking critically and women's initiative (Le Guin 2007). Notable is her father's role as a leading American anthropologist of the first half of the 20th century. Anthropology has a dark history as a discourse of imperialism and colonialism, offering an "authoritative" interpretation of "primitive" cultures to justify and enable imperial authority and colonial management. But as anarchist anthropologist David Graeber (2004) has noted, more radical anthropology has a strong affinity to anarchist(ic) ideas because the field stresses that the power structures of any society (including most importantly, "our own" Western, colonial, capitalist society) are, effectively, arbitrary and can be changed. More radical anthropology stresses that power relations are always present in all human societies but that these can take a near infinite number of forms and are often much more fair, just, peaceful and transparent that they are in "our" hegemonic imperial capitalist patriarchal culture. Le Guin's father was among those mid-century anthropologists who encouraged this more broad and critical thinking about his own society (and others).

Another early influence on Le Guin was Taoism, the ancient philosophy that originated in China that many anarchists draw inspiration from (see Williams 1994). Taoism stresses the constant flux of the universe and challenges its adherents to be prepared to constantly critique themselves and embrace change, as well as to see the interconnection of all things and the cyclical and reciprocal nature of causality and fate. This approach implies a personal politics of deep freedom, openness and responsibility, of gentleness and compassion, as well as a libertarian sense of letting others alone and building a life without authority. Taoist philosophers, writing in the heart of Imperial China, also stressed a politics of mutual aid and community. Le Guin was also influenced by more formal anarchist authors including Kropotkin, Godwin, Thoreau, Goldman, and George Woodcock and she developed an early and abiding interest in anarchist ideas that was to come to a head in her 1974 *The Dispossessed* (see Jaeckle 2009).

Le Guin's earliest published science-fiction work was the 1966 *Rocannon's World* (RW) which, while it tends to follow the conventions of science-fiction/fantasy of the day, demonstrated several notable anarchistic characteristics. The story follows an interstellar anthropologist, Rocannon, who leads a research mission to a marginal planet with several bronze-age human-esque life forms on behalf of an interstellar alliance (which, in later books, comes to be known as the Ekumen—these books are collectively known as the "Hainish Cycle"). His mission is disrupted when his team is murdered by a rebel faction of the alliance who have set up their military base on the obscure planet. Swearing vengeance, Rocannon and his inter-racial indigenous companions journey to destroy the enemy base, overcoming their prejudices and differences along the way. While RW is among Le Guin's most "fantastic" works (it features different humanoid alien "races," swords and sorcery and is an almost entirely masculine adventure story), it demonstrates many anarchistic themes. For one, it is an early articulation of theme of critical anthropology that recurs in a great many of Le Guin's works: Rocannon effectively "goes native" and adopts the little planet as his own (the Alliance later names the planet for him). He comes to appreciate the unique cultures of the "native" humanoids and seeks to defend them from the interstellar exploitation and disruption of his own people. Along the same lines, RW is an early example of Le Guin's curiosity and creativity of several different possibilities of "human" community, social order, power structures and hierarchies. In so doing, she broke, in many key ways, with the vast majority of her contemporary science-fiction writers who tended to represent human futures as merely the natural and necessary unfolding of whatever they understood to be "human nature" or humanity's present-day technological trajectories. Here Le Guin foreshadowed the theme of human possibility that has occupied her career, a sort of possibility that reflects a deep anarchist humanism, a faith in the diversity of human potential. But this is not a naïve optimism: for Le Guin, while hierarchy and power relations are fluid, mutable, unnecessary and always specific to their own world, they are never absent. Rocannon's world is no utopia. All of the "alien" races depicted (even the very human Alliance) have severe social problems, entrenched power relations and tenacious hierarchies, classes and castes. The humanism here is not one of perfectibility but of diversity, possibility, flux, one built on a revolutionary pragmatic optimism based on a careful and compassionate observation of human life.

This idiom is continued in one her most popular and influential early works The Left Hand of Darkness (LHD) where an ambassador of the Ekumen (now more fully mapped as a non-interventionist, non-coercive alliance of autonomous planets based on the principle of mutual aid who share a common "human" ancestry) Gently Ai arrives to recruit the planet Gethen, whose inhabitants are without permanent gender, being uniformly neutral except when they mate once per month. LHD was to create massive waves within and beyond the science fiction community at the time of its 1969 release, quickly capturing the prestige of both the Hugo and the Nebula awards and in many ways defining a sub-genre of what was to later to be called "soft" science fiction which, in contrast to "hard" or more scientistically oriented works, stresses societies and relationships. As this very distinction makes clear, science fiction had, to this moment (and still, largely) tended to be a masculinized genre (if one that, in the patriarchal literary cannon, occupied a marginalized, feminized status). Le Guin's achievement in *LHD* was to attack the necessity of gender binaries head-on by imagining the human beyond gender, and by encouraging readers to imagine a planet without the form of patriarchal gender relations that define our contemporary world (and were, in most ways, much more stark in 1969). Readers today continue to find themselves trying to map traits and actions of the Gethens onto gendered norms and find themselves challenged and confounded. In reading LHD, the reader feels one leg of a structure of authority has been removed and the whole edifice of inter-supporting forms of modern-capitalist authority teeters. For Lewis Call (2007), LHD, like all Le Guin's work, does the anarchist work of challenging our basic assumptions not only about how society works, and could work, but also the regimes of scientific, biological and technological understanding that make social authority appear necessary. He notes the way that, in a "post-modern" fashion, Le Guin (here as elsewhere) plays with narrative voice to unsettle the idea of the author and the narrative itself: LHD fluctuates between the perspectives of different characters, draws from Gethenian religious texts, or delves into Ekumen reports, intimating to the reader that all perspectives (including that of the author's herself) are partial (7). For Call, this is evidence of the "post-modern" character of Le Guin's anarchism: it is not simply satisfied to inherit the traditional cannon of anti-authoritarian works but also seeks to trouble, undermine and demolish a much broader set of power relations: the hubris of science, the construction of gender norms, the classical form of the novel itself, and, in some ways, the privileged figure of the author.

Despite the absence of gender divisions, the planet Gethen remains bound up in power and hierarchy and is marked by an ongoing cold-war between two empires, one that is a rigid aristocracy and the other a massive bureaucracy. Le Guin, through her "alien" protagonist, is a dispassionate witness to these systems. And while a lesser anarchistic author might spend their time berating these structures of authority, Le Guin is careful to show how humanity, as an indeterminate and mutable category, persists in these flawed and unjust societies. These forms of power, hierarchy and inequality, she shows, are created and perpetuated by human beings, by feeling and acting social agents. They are concrete and deadly forms of power, but they are also patterns of behavior, they are coded into relationships, and they are reproduced by the way people act. While there is no direct radical critique of these societies, like her implicit critique of patriarchy Le Guin demonstrates how power is always a matter of human creation and agency, rather than necessity or inevitability. Indeed, what perhaps makes Le Guin's novels such a joy to read is that they are based in a profound and radical love, curiosity and compassion for both her characters and their societies, regardless of their flaws. There is a patient honesty to the way she depicts even some of the most odious figures and social systems (there are exceptions to this). But this compassion should not be mistaken for a lack of revolutionary anger or a quietist liberalism—it is, rather, a seeking-out of a richer understanding of human society, sociality, personality and possibility through characters who are neither saints nor devils but the products and producers of their own times and places.

Anarchist themes recur in another of Le Guin's most popular early novels, *The Lathe of Heaven (LH)*. This story is based in the near future on the West Coast of the United States where government and corporate power have instituted a highly plausible intensification of social normativity, bureaucracy, state power and consumerism such that the world feels somewhat dreary and deadened. George Orr (widely speculated to be an *homage* to fellow anarchist George Orwell), a mild-mannered bureaucrat, is assigned to a psychiatrist, William Haber because he fears his dreams are changing reality. The psychiatrist, at first unbelieving, paternalistically subjects Orr to his experimental technique of augmenting hypnotic suggestion with special technology, allowing Haber to guide Orr's dreams. Recognizing Orr's unique abilities, Haber soon begins to use his patient to change reality, ostensibly in the interests of the greater good, which lead to the intensification of the bureaucratic administration of life and Haber's own power within the system. Eventually, Orr refuses to be used by Haber and flees and, with the help of a lawyer, Heather, whom he befriends and falls in love with, seeks to dream away the world Haber has created through him. But he finds that, though he wants, consciously, to erase human discord and war, his dreams have dramatically unexpected effects, erasing, for instance, skin color and summoning hostile aliens in the face of whom humanity must unify. Meanwhile, Haber has discovered a way to manipulate reality through his own mind without the assistance of Orr and plugs himself into his own machine. But Haber's mind, filled with ego, cannot dream with the integrity, honesty and compassion of Orr and imposes a chaotic, entropic nightmare on reality. Orr and Heather finally manage to stop Haber and re-dream the world but at the cost of their own relationship which is lost to another reality. Importantly, Orr, in his efforts to return reality to equilibrium, does not dream a utopia but a world full of problems, implying an anarchistic distrust of grand authored solutions to human problems.

The *Lathe of Heaven* is a powerful metaphor for the way society is co-created. Haber's nightmare is the product of his individualistic egoism, Le Guin is clear that the ability to create the world is a creative, collaborative process and that, when left to an ostensibly benevolent individual, descends into fascism, violence and chaos. While this is a condemnation of individualism, it is also a warning about arguments "for the greater good" in general, evincing anarchistic distrust of the state and of overarching coercive authority even (especially) when it claims to be in the people's best interests. It is also a strong model for imagining our social agency and responsibility as compassionate and autonomous subjects, for the way we shape our society and the way our society shapes us.

For Le Guin, the differences of human potential is both the reason such large, patriarchal plans are so dangerous and, paradoxically, the reason they always fail (although not before doing terrible damage to the world and perpetuating heartbreaking injustices). Among the key recurring themes of all Le Guin's corpus, and one of the key reasons she mobilizes the science fiction genre so effectively, is her imaginative work to politicize difference, and the mobilization of a deep humanist (and, I would argue, anarchistic) compassion to map both what is common across differences and to find the uncommon, the singular and the specific in the relationships between characters and worlds.

The danger that authority poses to difference is explicitly addressed in Le Guin's Hugo-winning allegory for colonialism *The Word for World is Forest* (TWWF) in which human settlers come to a planet, Athshe, which they call "New Tahiti," in order to harvest its abundant forests, enslaving the local population of green humanoids whom the Terrans consider sub-human, docile and stupid. The Athsheans, whom the Terrans pejoratively call "Creechies," however, stage a violent revolution much thanks to the leadership of Selver, an Athshean who lived in the main Terran "city" and befriended a Terran anthropologist Raj Lyubov. After the vicious and patriarchal, John Wayne-esque Captain Davidson rapes and kills his wife, Selver uses his knowledge of Terran affairs to mobilize the Athsheans to destroy the human encampments and city. Selver's people live in a hybrid world, where life and society are thoroughly enmeshed in the dream world. Since time immemorial, the Athsheans have used their lucid dreaming to craft a society almost completely free of violence and coercion, making them seemingly passive and stupid slaves, unworthy, in human estimation, of rights or respect. In order for Selver to lead the rebellion he must first dream a new set of images and ideas. Here, once again, Le Guin highlights the revolutionary power of the imagination. But for Selver and the Athsheans, the victory is Pyrrhic: Lyubov dies, unable to renounce his Terran community or to believe Selver's warnings. And the Athsheans are forever changed: a culture which had developed complex ways of avoiding violence and murder is tainted by the act of rebellion and we, the reader, are left to wonder if the Athsheans will ever be able to rekindle their complex and purposeful peace and equality.

TWWF stands today as among the best fictional works that addresses the intersection of patriarchy, capitalism, colonialism and ecocide. And while it is written with a passion and anger borne of bearing witness to both the American genocide of indigenous people and the contemporary war in the jungles of Vietnam (and accompanying jingoism, racism, and corporate-government collusion), it also has several thoughtful and important warnings for struggle. Notable, of course, is the high price the Athsheans pay for their freedom: the seeds of death and murder are planted in their culture, the dynamic equilibrium with their forest world is disturbed and off-balanced, and leaders and alliances emerge out of an otherwise egalitarian and localist culture. And Lyubov, a bureaucrat and academic, finds the limits of his own solidarity. He is satisfied with what he knows to be useless appeals to Terran authorities some 27 light years away and to the incipient *Ekumen*. Despite their rapport Lyubov is unwilling to fully accept the Selver as a fully mature being and fails to heed Selver's warnings, and so is and accidently killed in the final Athshean uprising.

Le Guin's engagement with anarchism came about most completely in her 1974 *The Dispossessed: An Ambiguous Utopia* which today stands as an anarchist classic and among the most famous books in the history of science fiction. The novel revolves around the life of an experimental physicist, Shevek, from Annares, a planet of anarchists whose ancestors broke away from their "parent" planet, Urras, some 150 years previous. But Le Guin subtitled her novel "an ambiguous utopia" for a reason: the novel follows Shevek's intellectual career and his growing realization that, though their society has no rulers at all and does not tolerate any forms of ownership or authority, it is nonetheless the victim of a creeping social and cultural conservatism and more subtle, interpersonal forms of possessiveness and bad individualism. For instance, he discovers his own mentor has been plagiarizing his work and eventually he reaches a dead-end in his research because there aren't enough other high caliber physicists on Annares, and the practical and community-focused Annaresti do not see the value of this sort of abstract thought.

For these reasons, Shevek chooses to leave his partner and daughter and do what no Annaresti has ever done: travel (back) to Urras both in order to pursue his research at their universities and to stir things up on Annares (this research will eventually lead to the development of the Ansible, an important technology in Le Guin's "Hainish Cycle" which allows for instant interstellar communication). Condemned as a traitor, he leaves his planet in shame only to be welcomed in Urras as evidence of his home planet's poverty and backwardness. His hosts try and ensure that Shevek sees only the image of their planet they want him to see (the cultural and scientific refinement, the wealth and beauty), but through the novel Shevek comes to see that Urras (which mirrors our own world of patriarchal consumer capitalism) is built on inequality, oppression and violent repression and, escaping the university they sought to confine him to, he flees back to his own planet in the hopes of bringing a positive form of change with him. The novel ends as Shevek approaches his home planet and we are left to wonder at his success.

Lewis Call suggests that, in addition to the evident influence of key anarchist thinkers, *The Dispossessed* offers up an anarchist critique of both language and science which move it into what he sees as a post-modern anarchist register: Le Guin's "ambiguous utopia" not only imagines a world without formal structures of authority, it also suggests a society where language itself has been transformed. The Annaresti language, *Previc*, has been invented to highlight and support the collectivist and anti-individualist and anti-possessivist elements of Annaresti culture and its verbs and inflections break down the subject-object dualism which allows individuals to claim ownership, externalize objects and objectify people. It is a language without shame or guilt and, as a result, has very few curse words (except "proprietarian," which is considered to be the worst insult). This is contrasted to the language of Urras, which, like our own English or other Romance languages, is based around concepts of ownership and power. Here Call draws our attention to the way power and authority operate on the subtler registers of language and suggests that Le Guin's approach goes far beyond the "classical" anarchist cannon which sought to use conventional language, rhetoric and narrative to argue for formal freedom from concrete power relations (15). Instead, she demonstrates a "post-modern" desire to see and challenge power even within her own text and authority.

The Dispossessed is a phenomenal anarchist text because it not only presents us with a possible (even plausible) anarchist world and challenges us to imagine how our own could be different, not only because it provides a cogent and moving critique of our own society as it is mirrored by Urras, but because it shows us how an anarchist society can, despite its best efforts, succumb to its own forms of conservatism, stagnancy and repression. The novel is, of course, a prolonged meditation on the politics of the Cold War between American and Soviet superpowers and the anarchist response of "neither/nor." But it emerged amidst a generation that was beginning to challenge the forms of ideology that had lead to both capitalist and Soviet state-capitalist systems, one that sought to look more deeply at human relationships and the possibilities of freedom. Where both American capitalism and state socialism insisted that social order and freedom were effectively economic and structural Le Guin's work spoke to activists trying to think through what a new revolutionary politics might look like on the level of everyday life and relationships. She also mapped out a politics of doubt, indeterminacy, freedom and responsibility.

Le Guin's Later Works

As I suggested above, Le Guin's early work emerged along with and was inspired by, by the social movements of the late 60s and early 70s. These movements were marked by a distrust of older socialist and communist narratives of centralized authority and revolutionary asceticism and Marxist science. They were also movements inspired increasingly from the "third world" and anti-colonial resistance, as well as anti-racist struggles within the United States that would solidify on the issue of civil rights and Black Power.

Especially notable, both historically and in terms of the arc of Le Guin's work, is the rise of feminism both as part of and as a response to the New Left. Tired of the marginalization of women's issues and women's voices within radical social movements, women, beginning in the 60s and accelerating through the 70s, developed new modes and narratives of struggle both within and separate from the largely masculinized student and peace movements. Critical to this shift was a growing awareness that women formed a distinct class or group in society with their own forms of labor and exploitation and their own interests that were significantly different from men. Movements for reproductive rights, women's health, economic and social justice as well as for broader "feminist" issues like war, capitalism and patriarchal culture at large developed unique forms and strategies of protest including, notably, feminist consciousness raising or education, the creation of women's-only spaces and cultures, new protest tactics that engaged and challenged gender norms and direct action against icons of patriarchal domination like the newly emerging video pornographic industry and the "outing" of abusive men (Rebick 2005).

Le Guin herself notes her own relationship to the feminist movement was always relatively peripheral. She notes the way feminism influenced her work (see Killjoy 2009, 10-11). She was criticized, for instance, for early novels like *Rocannon's World*, *Planet of Exile*, *City of Illusion*, *The Lathe of Heaven* and even

The Dispossessed for rehearsing science-fiction's almost exclusive focus on men and rendering female characters as largely one-dimensional supports to male heroism (this was especially the case in the first three books of her best-selling Earthsea fantasy series for children and young-adults). Le Guin's early works, while they do rehearse a patriarchal form, were still radical (proto-) feminist challenges to the genre. And while her early writing does focus almost exclusively on male characters to the exclusion of female ones, her work is possessed of a deep and unflinching honesty which shows just how much trouble boys get into thanks to patriarchal cultures. For instance, in a novel like *Planet of Exile*, patriarchal machismo and male-dominated cultures almost sunder the alliance that will save the two cultures. Similarly, in several early novels Le Guin hints at a nascent post-patriarchal masculinity through several of her early male protagonists who display little or none of the bravado, imperiousness, sexual triumphalism and conquistador-esque triumph of the will so characteristic of the science fiction genre.

In any case, through the 70s Le Guin's work took on a more feminist approach. While novels like *The Word for World is Forest* had already begun to map the relationship of patriarchy to colonialism, capitalism, authoritarianism, and militarism, a young-adult novel like *The Eye of the Herron* (*EH*) (1978) was far more direct. A non-Ekumen story, *EH* imagines a former prison-colony world, Victoria, settled by two groups of refugees from earth: the descendents of prisoners and prison guards (who live in The City), who now form a small, urban elite (called The Bosses), and the descendents of a non-violent resistance movement of the Earth's poor (The Shantih Towners) who are sent into exile only to find themselves the subordinated, rural farmers in their new home. The novel addresses different forms of resistance. First, the Shantih Towners attempt to echo their forbearers' non-violent rebellion on Earth, refusing to work until their conditions are improved and they are allowed to found new towns outside the orbit of the Boss's city. After violent repression, the Shantih Towners opt for exodus, simply walking away from the power of their oppressors and exploring the new planet on their own. This novel, written with young adults in mind, features much stronger female characters including Luz, the daughter of one of the Bosses, who defies her father's will and leaves her life of privilege to join the Shantih Towners, and Vera, a radical matriarch of the resistance. Le Guin shows how patriarchal attitudes of both power and resistance lead ultimately to ruin. Luz's father, desperate to prove his authority to his subordinates fails to make crucial strategic compromises and Lev, a charismatic male leader of the resistance, in his enthusiasm for a direct (though non-violent) confrontation with The Boss's power, is slain near the middle of the book.

Another key component of post-New Left moment, and of radical and new anarchist(ic) politics, has been the growing recognition of the politics of indigenous resistance to genocide and colonialism. Having survived a brutal array of repressive apartheid laws including genocidal residential schools, groups like the American Indian Movement were to surprise North Americans with the depth of righteous anger and the severity of the continuing guilt of their ancestors and government (see Dunbar-Ortiz 2002, Churchill 2002). Le Guin had already been addressing many of these themes in books like *Planet of Exile* and *The Word for World is Forest*, much thanks to her parents' deep sympathy for and writing about the indigenous genocide (especially in California) and her father's famous friendship with Ishi, "the last Yahi." Ishi appeared in the corral of a Northern Californian slaughter house in 1911 and was delivered to Kroeber and his colleagues at the Berkeley anthropology department where he lived and worked until his death five years later (Krober 1961).

Similarly, ecological concerns were to take on much more importance as the consequences of 150 years of industrial capitalist modernity became more glaringly evident in the form of concerns about global warming, mass extinctions, desertification, oceanic dead zones, ecosystem collapse and their more human causes and effects like the epidemic of cancer, diminishing food sovereignty, urban sprawl, toxic environments and peak oil. These too had long been key of Le Guin's writing, explicitly in *The Word for World is Forest* and more implicitly in the ecological decay of the world in *The Lathe of Heaven*. But so too, in books like *The Dispossessed* is Le Guin attentive to the deep and abiding relationships between people and land and the way *terroire*, community, subjectivity, politics and love are all ecological. The Anaresti are a product and producers of their unforgiving planetary ecology—it shapes them and they shape it. In this sense, while Le Guin's work has always been deeply humanistic, it has never abided the human triumphalism that has marked humanism or some of the more "promethean" or technologically utopian strands of anarchist thought.

One of the more profound, if difficult to explain shifts from the movements of the 1960s and 70s to the present has been a general humbling. This is not to say that activists and anarchists have forgotten the tasks of revolutionizing all of society but that, in contrast to the more hyperbolic language and strategies of the New Left, many radical organizers have come to recognize that revolution needs a firm base and have eschewed mass mobilization in favor of community level organizing. More accurately, perhaps, many organizers have understood that mass mobilizations and demonstrations ought to be manifestations of a broad-based movement, the proverbial tip of an iceberg, rather than ends unto themselves (see, for instance, Federici 2012). So too have many organizers (inspired by feminist and anarchist ideas) left off the building of radical and anarchist parties of ideological engines and moved towards attempts to build revolutionary and radical communities and practices within localized spaces based less on convincing people of the necessity of revolution but meeting people's needs and desires in ways that seek to escape the authority o the state and capital. While it is debatable how "new" this tendency is, and how effective it might be in the long term, critics like Richard Day (20005) speak of a shift away from strategies of "hegemony" (trying to "take power" through mastery of the war of ideas) and towards a "prefigurative" politics which builds tomorrow from within today.

Prefigurative politics, in this sense, has been prefigured in Le Guin's work. In books like *The Word for World is Forest* and *Planet of Exile*, she has meditated long and hard about the consequences of more dramatic forms of resistance and the damage they can do to people and civilizations, even when there is no other choice. Books like *The Lathe of Heaven* are damning indictments of forms of social intervention or engineering aimed at "power over" others, even when seemingly benevolent. And novels like *The Dispossessed* and *The Eye of the Heron* tease out the difficulties of resistance and propose "exodus" (as Autonomist Marxists like Paolo Virno, 1996) put it as a form of resistance: the flight from power to create other alternatives, rather than a direct, head on, usually violent confrontation of power.

So by the time the children of the New Left came of age, the terrain of radical politics was quite different. Inspired by these movements there was a resurgence of anarchistic thought reflected in new organizing and protest tactics that surprised the world in their success in Seattle during the protests against the World Trade Organization in 1999 (see Juris 2008, Khasnabish 2008). For the purposes of this argument, I want to suggest that the shift towards a new anarchistic politics reveals a growing awareness of the complexities, subtleties and pervasiveness of authority, an emerging recognition, borne for the most part out of anti-oppression politics, that authority is not merely a *political relationship* but a *politics of relationships* much more broadly and generally. This new anarchistic moment is characterized by a sense that any meaningful revolution starts from a politics of profound responsibility to confront, and work together to overcome, authority in ourselves, in our movements and in our societies as a whole.

In this final section, then, I am going to focus on two collections of short stories written throughout the 90s up to the turn of the millennium and published originally in a variety of magazines and collections: *A Fisherman of the Inland Sea* (1994) and *Birthday of the World* (2002). While these stories do not explicitly address anarchism or even touch on obviously anarchist themes, it is my argument that they are possessed of a distinctly anarchistic tenor and that they stand as anarchist interventions. This, to the extent that they offer sites of reflection, provocation and meditation for anarchists and non-anarchists alike that challenge us to think and rethink resistance, gender, relationships, ideas and, perhaps most importantly, authority. As I shall suggest, each story poses its own, complicated and never easy challenge to authority, both overt and covert, naked and hidden.

Of particular interest are a trio of stories in *A Fisherman of the Inland Sea* which represent Le Guin's cautious speculation on instant interstellar travel within the Ekumen through what she calls "Churten" technology. In her idiosyncratic style, Le Guin leaves the actual "hard scientific" nature of this technology a mystery, even to the fictional scientists who are developing it. The technology is primarily philosophical rather than scientistic—indeed, there are numerous "translation errors" between scientists from different planets with their very different ways of thinking. This is because in essence Churten technology allows human travelers simultaneously mentally project their destination and arrive their physically. For Le Guin, near-instant space travel within the Ekumen had been a "reality" since *Rocannon's World* , but only for non-sentient things. In "The Shobies' Story" (originally published in 1990), the first in the trio of Churten stories, we find an group of explorers from the Ekumen, children and elders, men and women, who have gathered at Hain and are preparing to take the first "manned" Churten mission on a ship called The Shobie (hence the crea are known as "The Shobies"), a dangerous mission they have undertaken for different reasons. Startling here is the profoundly non-militarized aspect of this "test-flight" where our heroes are selected precisely because they are so normal, such a "democratic" cross section or sample of Ekumenical life: children, an elder, a Gethenian, an Annaresti, several Terrans and so on. Indeed, too much knowledge about how Churten works is an impediment to its use because it clouds the imagination of the traveler and, thus, navigation of the vessel.

The Shobie and its crew appear to make a successful jump to a planet only to discover that their experience and memories of the planet are radically different. The dissonance between their perceptions of the planets creates massive existential rifts in the fabric of space and time. It appears that Churten technology "works" by partially actualizing its passenger's expectations and perceptions. But unlike the machine in *The Lathe of Heaven*, Churten technology does not privilege the perceptions of one individual. Rather, because it factors in the imaginations of all the travelers it creates multiple overlapping and conflicting realities. The Shobies can only escape the chaos of their situation by Churtening back to Hain, but this is more than a scientific maneuver—they must synchronize their stories and perceptions in order to arrive back at a Hain that was not merely a chaos. The story ends with the moving images of the Shobies sitting together and telling each other an interwoven story about who they are and where they are going, bringing their perceptions, narratives and imaginations into synchronicity. In order for the Shobies to return home, to escape chaos, they must find a way, through narrative, of *sharing authority*, of becoming authors of a shared fate and purpose.

In the second Churten story, "Dancing to Ganam" (originally published in 1993), two of the Terran Shobies are star struck at the arrival of Dalzul, a planetary hero known for his superhuman charisma and diplomatic mastery. He reveals that he, alone, has Churtened to a new planet of humans, who, though they have not developed spaceflight, are to be invited to join the Ekumen. He explains that he was able to Churten there without the "distortions" of reality experienced by the Shobies because he was alone and because of has absolute confidence in himself, which did not introduce the sorts of confusions and ambiguities the Shobies experienced. He boasts of his popularity on the planet, Ganam, and invites the Terran Shobies to accompany him on the triumphant Churten voyage back to consolidate the planet's membership in the Ekumen. In order to avoid Shobie-like distortion, Dalzul suggests that he and the two Terrans synchronize their perceptions by singing together as they Churten and, sure enough, they reach Ganam he has described where, as per has description, they are treated as guests of honour and Dalzul is treated as a god-king. But the longer they spend on Ganam, the more the two Shobies find dissonances between the planetary society and Dalzul's descriptions and things grow confusing and uncertain. But because of the language barrier between the Terrans and the Ganam's inhabitants, they cannot be sure to what extent this has been caused by the Churten technology. Meanwhile Dalzul, enjoying the Godhead bestowed upon him proceeds towards a ceremony he perceives to be his coronation or apotheosis, but one which ends up killing him as a sacrifice. It becomes clear that while the Terrans were able to successfully Churten together, their success was based on their subordination to Dalzul's ego, an ego which had also shaped their perception of Ganam and its culture and borne of an arrogance that eventually got Dalzul killed. Here is another tale of the tragedy of authority that reveals the way social authority is intimately grounded in the ability to shape narrative.

In the final story, titled "Another Story" or "A Fisherman of the Inland Sea" (originally published in 1994), we follow a scientist born on O, a planet whose social norms and caste system see marriages between four adults (a man and a woman from each of two moieties, called a "Sedoretu") who turns his back on his quiet rural life to join in the development of Churten technology on a distant planet (the story "predates" our previous two but appears last in the collection by Le Guin's conscious choice), a journey which takes years, meaning that he will never return to his home planet (or if he does, most of his family will be aged or dead, though he himself has not aged during the journey). When he arrives at the research station near Hain he receives a garbled message from his own planet (recall, in the Ekumen the "ansible" technology makes interstellar communication instant), but quickly forgets about it. Stirred by a regret he cannot name and a melancholy based on the family and the love he gave up on O, he plunges into his research only to make a massive breakthrough, but one which transports him back in time and place to the moment he left O so many years before. There he rekindles the relationships he once renounced and, many years into the future, at the date he was to have arrived at the research station after his long interstellar journey, he sends his biography (which is the substance of the short story we are reading itself), the garbled message he himself received so many years ago. This is one of Le Guin's only experiments with the theme of time travel and, while it deals with major themes in that subgenre (the nature of causality, the possibility of simultaneous parallel realities, the question of agency and predestiny) these are, as always in Le Guin's work, secondary to a broader human narrative which is one of her most moving, intimate and lyrical.

There are a few anarchist themes in these stories. In "The Shobies Story" we are treated to a vision of a sort of anarchistic form of science and technology, one relatively free of the sorts of hypermasculinized scientism and militarism that characterizes our current scene of "research and development." The Shobies are men and women, from a wide diversity of backgrounds, including children, who volunteer out of a variety of senses of adventure, obligation, professional pride and wonder. They even have along with them an Anarresti physicist who constantly teases her crewmates about their "proprietarian" tendencies. But more importantly, Le Guin gives us a powerful allegory for the critical importance of shared narrative. Not even the most advanced technology of ancient interstellar civilizations can trump the power of common feeling and common potentiality—indeed, Churten technology relies on or merely amplifies something deeply human: the ability to *share futurity* through dialogue and culture. Indeed, as Le Guin herself suggests (1994b, 8–10), the Churten is an allegory for narrative itself, the profound capacity of stories to transport us beyond ourselves and, importantly, to both bring us together, to tear us apart, and to get us into (or out of) a right muddle. Le Guin's Churten stories are allegories about the powers, the dangers and the responsibility of the imagination as a personal and a collective force.

This theme is confirmed by contrast in "Dancing to Ganam" where this power to create and see to fruition shared narrative comes to be subordinated to the charismatic authority of Dalzul. Indeed, his fantasy is remarkably similar to that of Western "Explorers" who "discovered" the New World and who lived in their own fantasy world of indigenous people's being innocent and awestruck, and who proceeded to violently impose their fantasy on the peoples and landscapes of Turtle Island. In this sense, Churten technology is an allegory for all technology in general: technologies are tools for the social imagination to come into being. This is a vitally important theme that has been reflected in recent anarchistic social movement practices that seek not merely to win a different society sometime in the future but to build it in the present and who do not wish to impose their own authoritative script on history and the future but instead seek to create spaces and "technologies" (in the broadest sense of the word) for people to come together and create their own possibilities and narratives. It also speaks to the pleasures and dangers of charismatic authority: Dalzul is not a fascist and his reputation comes from fulfilling the relatively anarchistic values of the Ekumen (diplomacy, peace, negotiation, non-interference, etc.). Yet his impulsive masculine personal magnetism, and the way others cede authority to it, will be familiar to any seasoned activist as a recurring problem in social movements where, in the absence of official hierarchies, unofficial (and often unspoken) politics and authority can accrue around certain (often male) personalities.

Finally, in "A Fisherman of the Inland Sea", Le Guin takes up the possibility of the future "coming back to us" in a similar fashion to fellow feminist science-fiction writer Marge Peircy's famous 1976 *Woman on the Edge of Time*. In that novel, a feminist and anarchistic utopian community projects a messenger back in time to convince a marginalized woman in New York to champion their future, to ensure their particular future comes into being, rather than other, dystopian futures. In "A fisherman", Le Guin plays with this trope: Churten technology can only come into being by a message from a past that was, ironically, created by the use of Churten technology. While this sort of "feedback loop" problem is common stock for time-travel speculative fiction (and, increasingly, Hollywood film), Le Guin's approach is particularly critical because, rather than highlighting the intellectual adventure this paradox invites, she focuses with an almost melancholy tone on the personal relationships and mental life that makes up the existential experience of time and temporality. The anarchistic politics of this story are less in its content and more in its form: an excellent example of Le Guin's deep attention to the relationship between our social worlds, our forms of technology and our personal choices and relationships. Perhaps most radically, Le Guin here enlightens us to the truth that most technological and scientific innovations are, essentially, accidents. But more profoundly: though we may not wish to admit it, the "progress" of human science and technology is deeply rooted in human relationships and emotions. Churten technology, in a very real sense, does not emerge from a laboratory but out of the tremendous angst and melancholy of the story's main character. His nostalgia and regret, and the human relations on which those are based, create the conditions in which Churten technology can emerge. Once again, Le Guin reminds us of the profound, transformative and constitutive power of relationality.

Several stories in *The Birthday of the World* also display critical anarchist themes. In "The Matter of Seggri" (originally published in 1994) Le Guin paints a world where, in her words "a society where men have extreme privilege but no power" (31) a matriarchal world where boy-children are celebrated but grow up to be gladiators and breeding "studs," confined to punitive and fascistic "castles." Meanwhile women enjoy full citizenship and participation in broader society which, while seemingly defined by monetized commerce and ranks, seems generally egalitarian. As with many of her works, Le Guin here jumps around between narrative styles: the short story is to appear to us as a "dossier" compiled by the Hainish and others of the Ekumen regarding the history of Seggri. The first is a brief report of an early Hainish explorer who, with masculine bravado, fundamentally misreads Seggrian society because he only speaks with the men, who boast of their social position and explain that women do all the real work. Rather than seeing a society where men are fundamentally limited in social roles, these explorers admire what they perceive as a perfect patriarchy. Years later, the *Ekumen* sends rapporteurs back to Seggri with an eye to including them. These emissaries (who try and remain covert) discover that, thanks to ancient Hainish genetic engineering, Seggri's male birth-rate is extremely low (a ratio of 1:10), helping to explain how men are both highly esteemed but also denied any civil rights. They discover that, at puberty, boys are taken from their doting matriarchal households and delivered to "Castles" where they will live and die, which are ruled by elder men where they are shaped into athletes, warriors and breeding studs. The visitors from the Ekumen must decide if membership in the egalitarian league, and exposure to the societies of other worlds (and, hence, the revelation that Seggrian society is abnormal) would be ethically acceptable. Other narratives in the suit include a reflection of a Seggrian woman about her childhood and life in the lead-up to the eventual referendum which will see Seggri join the Ekumen. Still another is a "classic" Seggrian short-story which tells of a man's attempt to escape a castle to join a woman he loves. Another is the narrative of a man who is part of a rebellion within a Castle against a sadistic warlord who rules there, a mutiny which (along with the disruptive presence of the Ekumen) spurns a global shift where the gates of the castles are opened, but where men find themselves lost in prejudiced society with no use for them.

In addition to being a moving suite of stories of love within and in the face of hyperbolic oppression, these stories once again illustrate the vast possible diversity of human power relations, but also the way those power relations become culturally normalized. They help to break us out of our normalized assumptions in a patriarchal society by hyperbolizing and rendering stark the inequalities of a matriarchal society. Le Guin is careful to focus on the human relationships of oppression here and her painting of an unequal and deeply prejudiced and oppressive society is not anti-feminist. While women hold all the social power in this society it is not based on any stable notion of human/masculine/feminine nature. Rather, her stories in this cycle focus on the way power relations are nearly infinitely mutable and malleable, and that real people (often good, loving people) participate in, defend, rebel against and pretend not to see the forms of authority they wield or have wielded against them. In other words, these stories both renew our faith in humanity and its anarchistic potentials at the same time as they afford us deep, nuanced and compassionate lessons in the ways this potential is repressed or perverted by authority.

In "Mountain Ways" (1996) we return to O and the "Sedoretu" or four-way marriage compact outlined in "A Fisherman." Here two women form opposite Moieties are in love but cannot find two men to marry. Instead, they deceive a man and a woman into marrying them. Returning to themes of gender ambiguity most explicitly addressed in *The Left Hand of Darkness* this story is a compassionate reflection on the difficulties of gendered norms and performativity within conservative society, as well as an optimistic tale of the ability of love to transcend differences and social barriers, a theme very much at the heart of an anarchist ethos, if one that has suffered from its appropriation by disingenuous "post-modern" narratives that assume that "love is all we need" to the exclusion of economic justice and structural transformation. Le Guin's intervention, here as elsewhere, might equally be noted as an anarcho-queer politics which sees systems of domination expressed through and supported by (often violent) limits on what bodies "matter" and who may love whom (see Davis 2011, Heckert 2010)

"Old Music and the Slave Women" (1999) this story is a sequel to the phenomenal quartet of novellas published as *Four Pathways to Forgiveness* which follows the interconnected stories of four characters during the massive slave uprising on the twin planets of Werel and Yeowe. Here, the dark-skinned Werelites have enslaved the lighter skinned, not only on their home planet but on a harsh but resource rich moon. The arrival of the Ekumen and, particularly the Ekumenical envoy, Old Music, spurs a slave revolution on the moon which leads to the liberation of the slaves but then to a host of social problems now recognizable from the tragedy of postcolonialism and neocolonialism: corruption, internecine violence, new post-colonial forms of patriarchy and internal forms of oppression. In this short story, the revolution has reached the home-planet of Werel and Old Music, who had been secretly helping the liberation struggle, finds himself the prisoner of a brutal, die-hard splinter the save-holding class who refuse to surrender. Taken to what was once the "model" plantation Old Music is tortured when he refuses to be a pawn of the reactionaries. He comes to befriend the handful of slaves who remain with their brutal masters, despite the fact that many others have run away and joined the rebellion. As both slave-holder and revolutionary groups splinter and fight each other, Old Music and the slaves who remain at the compound are caught in the middle of a violent political chaos no-one can fully grasp. Old Music himself is a wry, coy career diplomat whose canny generosity and sharp eye for power offers us a sympathetic and insightful character to work with. While Le Guin here is remorseful about the horrors that follow revolution she does not descend into the sort of liberal hand-wringing we might expect of many authors. Instead, she offers us yet another vision of what can go wrong with struggles to make the world better, a vision that, in spite of the darkness remains oddly optimistic. The story is also a curious meditation on the politics of solidarity as Old Music tries to find common ground with the Slave Women who have chosen to remain at the plantation in spite of their hatred for their masters, whether out of fear, out of personal relationships or because of age or immobility. This solidarity is never easy or given and as sympathetic as Old Music is, we gain here a sobering glimpse of the time and sacrifice necessary for true common cause.

The final story in this collection, and the final story I will address here, is the now quite famous "Paradises Lost" (2002). Not based in the Ekumenical universe, this story follows the five-generation-long mission of a ship sent from a near-future earth (rife with the social and environmental problems we might expect in the coming century) to settle a new planet. While the original crew of the ship (numbering a few thousand) were volunteers, mostly atheistic and egalitarian scientists committed to the project, their children, grandchildren and great-grandchildren begin to grow distant from Earth and from the spirit of the mission itself. The ship is a completely enclosed and risk-free ecosystem that infinitely recycles everything to create an static eternal ecology. The middle generations of travelers, those who neither experienced earth and do not expect to experience the new planet begin to divide between those who wish to continue on course and those who found a new form of patriarchal spirituality and argue that their starship is heaven and that they have transcended the terrestrial hell of an over-polluted earth. This new unofficial religion (which understands itself as merely the "truth" and decidedly non-mystical) begins to consolidate its power throughout the ship's egalitarian culture, stacking committees and establishing connections between influential people. But when the ship finds itself several generations ahead of schedule and destined to reach the new planet in only a few years, these division become stark. While some of the people on board fulfill the mission and land on the planet, the adherents to Bliss depart in the paradise of their risk-free ship, headed for oblivion.

This story is a grim and timely warning about fundamentalist religion and its power over social narrative and our perception of futurity. But is also a telling narrative that focuses on the way unofficial power structures can emerge from even the best planned communities. It also demonstrates that people need forms of myth and spirituality to survive and lead rewarding lives. The mistake of the original travelers was to assume they could create a totally rational society and that the distant promise of a future planet would be enough for several generations to live and die for. The story demonstrates, however, how the emergent forms of religion and spirituality can carry with them forms of coercive power and patriarchal norms. In the same way as we saw in *The Dispossessed*, here we see a glimpse of an anarchist society turning upon itself, struggling against its own freedom, wracked by its own possibility. Once again we receive from Le Guin a chastening lesson in both the potential and the perils of freedom, the secret life of authority, and, behind and through it all, the human relationships, characters, loves and agonies that are the real stuff of society.

The Responsibility of Choice

In these later stories by Le Guin we see something of a shift towards away from more obviously anarchistic themes (such as those evinced in *The Dispossessed*) and towards what I would term "anarchist prefigurative fiction." By this I mean neither fiction that merely makes an argument for anarchism nor fiction that merely offers an obviously anarchist critique of society. While excluding neither of these approaches, prefigurative fiction assumes anarchist principles and speculates on them. In Le Guin's work we are treated to a detailed if non-linear and non-comprehensive guide to the subtleties of human power relations, of the power of social narrative, of the dangers of revolution, of the antinomies of freedom, of the possibilities and perils of democracy, of the unquenchable fire of diversity and difference, of the eternal struggle for justice and of that form of humanism that never rests.

In particular, we are treated to a rich and complicated education in authority and the myriad ways it manifests itself in social relations.

One of Le Guin's most famous lines from *The Dispossessed* offers a particularly cogent articulation of her sophisticated anarchistic authorialism, defining an anarchist as "one who, choosing, accepts the responsibility of choice." For Le Guin, personal integrity and responsibility is, ultimately a choice. This should not be mistaken for a masculinist and bourgeois humanist celebration of the individual will. As Le Guin's writing shows, she is deeply aware of and compassionate towards the way our choices are constrained and the way our social location influences what we believe to be our choices. Rather, choosing here is already a prefiguration of revolutionary optimism and political possibility. We must chose to act towards social justice and equality because we must make a commitment without knowing exactly where that commitment will take us. In doing so we "accept the responsibility" not only of the choices we have made, in the Taoist/anarchist mode of personal integrity and authority, we also accept "the responsibility of choice" itself, of the principle of choice writ-large. As anarchists, we are not simply champions of choice for choice's sake, not just radicals for liberal freedom. Anarchism for Le Guin is about accepting the responsibilities that come with freedom, responsibilities to never fail to struggle against oppression, struggle to come to a better, bigger awareness of our world and the power relations that cross-cut it. And, indeed, to take responsibility for being human.

In the end, this is the form of responsibility that occupies Le Guin as an author. While much science fiction is content to play in the possibilities of the future and, in a libertarian mode, celebrates the genius of the author, Le Guin's work dwells on, with and through the responsibility of the author. She does not seek to escape authority, nor does she simply try and use the "master's tools" of authorial power for "good ends." Rather, she rather courageously mobilizes her authority as an author to, always in an incomplete and humble way, mobilize visions of the future that make us more human, that exhort us to human possibility and responsibility. In this sense, this is Le Guin's prefigurative fictional method, a method takes responsibility, but gives it as well.

Prefigurative fiction, then, is an experiment in an authoriality or responsibility. By doing so itself it invites us to both imagine, cultivate and critique the dynamic tension between authority and responsibility as it exists in our own hearts, our communities, our struggles and our movements. In this sense, anarchistic prefigurative fiction is not a genre into which we can divide certain works or authors. It is an orientation, present to different extents and in different ways in many writers and works, both avowedly anarchist and not. Le Guin is a pioneer of this orientation and one whose contributions to the 20th and 21st century anarchist imagination should be recognized.

References

Antliff, Allan. 2007. *Anarchy and art: from the Paris Commune to the fall of the Berlin Wall*. Vancouver: Arsenal Pulp Press.

Call, Lewis. 2002. *Postmodern Anarchism*. Lanham, MD: Lexington Books.

_____. 2007. "Postmodern Anarchism in the Novels of Ursula K. Le Guin." *SubStance* 36(2).

Churchill, Ward. 2002. *Acts of Rebellion: a Ward Churchill Reader*. London and New York: Routledge.

Davis, Lawrence, and Peter Stillman, eds. 2005. *The New Utopian Politics of Ursula K. Le Guin's The Dispossessed*. Lanham, MD: Lexington Books.

_____. 2011. "Love and Revolution in Le Guin's Four Ways to Forgiveness." In *Anarchism and Sexuality: Ethics, Relationships and Power*, eds. Jamie Heckert and Richard Cleminson. London and new York: Routledge, pp. 103–129.

Day, Richard. 2005. *Gramsci is Dead: Anarchist Currents in the Newest Social Movements*. London and Ann Arbour, MI: Pluto.

Dunbar-Ortiz, Roxanne. 2002. *Outlaw Woman: A Memoir of the War Years 1960-1975*. Oakland, CA: City Lights Books.

Federici, Silvia. 2012. *Revolution at Point Zero: Housework, Reproduction, and Feminist Struggle*. Brooklyn, NY and Oakland, CA: Common Notions (PM Press).

Fekete, John. 1979. ""The Dispossessed" and "Triton": Act and System in Utopian Science Fiction." *Science Fiction Studies* 6(2): 129–143.

Graber, David. 2004. *Fragments of an Anarchist Anthropology*. Chicago: Prickly Paradigm.

Haiven, Max, and Alex Khasnabish. 2011. "What is the Radical Imagination: A Special Issue." *Affinities* 4(2): i–xxxvii.

Heckert, Jamie. 2010. "Queerly Erotic: An open love letter to Ursula Le Guin." *The Anarchist Library*. http://theanarchistlibrary.org/library/jamie-heckert-queerly-erotic-an-open-love-letter-to-ursula-le-guin (August 8, 2012).

Jaeckle, Daniel P. 2009. "Embodied Anarchy in Ursula K. Le Guin's The Dispossessed." *Utopian Studies* 21(1): 75–95. http://www.jstor.org/stable/20719930.

Jose, Jim. 1991. "Reflections on the Politics of Le Guin's Narrative Shifts." *Science Fiction Studies* 18(2): 180–197.

Juris, Jeffrey. 2008. *Networking Futures: The Movements against Corporate Globalization*. Durham, NC: Duke University Press.

Katsiaficas, George. 1987. *The imagination of the New Left: a global analysis of 1968*. Boston, MA: South End Press.

Khasnabish, Alex. 2008. *Zapatismo Beyond Borders: New Imaginations of Political Possibility*. Toronto: University of Toronto Press.

Killjoy, Margaret, ed. 2009. *Mythmakers and lawbreakers: anarchist writers on fiction*. Oakland, CA: AKPress.

Kroeber, Theodora. 1961. *Ishi in Two Worlds*. Berkeley and Los Angelis, CA: University of California Press.

Lee, Debbie. 2002. *Slavery and the Romantic imagiantion*. Philadelphia: Universty of Pennsylvania Press.

Le Guin, Ursula K. 1966a. *Planet of Exile*. Ace.

_____. 1966b. *Rocannon's World*. New York: ACE.

_____. 1967. *City of Illusions*. New York: Ace.

_____. 1978. *The Eye of the Herron*. New York: Delacorte.

_____. 1994a. *A Fisherman of the Inland Sea*. New York: Harper Perennial.

_____. 1994b. *The Dispossessed*. New York: Harper Voyager.

_____. 1995. *Four Ways to Forgiveness*. New York: HarperCollins.

_____. 2003. *The Left Hand of Darkness*. New York: Ace.

_____. 2004. Concerning Ishi. {http://www.ursulakLe Guin.com/Note-Ishi.html}.

_____. 2007. "Frequently Asked Questions." Writer's Website. http://www.ursulakLe Guin.com/FAQ.html (August 8, 2012).

_____. 2008. *The Lathe of Heaven : A Novel*. Scribner trade pbk. ed. New York: Scribner.

_____. 2010a. *Chronicles of Earthsea*.

_____. 2010b. *The Word for World is Forest*. Second Edition. New York: TOR.

Porter, David L. 1975. "The Politics of Le Guin's Opus." *Science Fiction Studies* 2(3): 243–248.

Rebick, Judy. 2005. *Ten thousand roses : the making of a feminist revolution*. Toronto: Penguin Canada.

Rose, Mark. 1993. *Authors and owners : the invention of copyright*. Cambridge, Mass.: Harvard University Press.

Suvin, Darko. 1975. "Parables of De-Alienation: Le Guin's Widdershins Dance." *Science Fiction Studies* 2(3): 265–274.

Virno, Paolo. 1996. "Virtuosity and Revolution: The Political Theory of Exodus." In *Radical Thought in Italy: A Potential Politics*, eds. Paolo Virno and Michael Hardt. Minneapolis, MN: University of Minnesota Press, pp. 189–212.

White, Jonathan. 1995. "Coming back from the silence." Whole Earth Review 85. http://www.writingyourselfhome.net/sciencefiction/ursula_le_guin.htm.

Williams, Donna Glee. 1994. "The moons of Le Guin and Heinlein." *Science Fiction Studies* 21(2): 164–172.

Woodmansee, Martha, and Peter Jaszi. 1994. *The Construction of Authorship: Textual Appropriation in Law and Literature*. Durham and London: Duke University Press.

8. Anarchy in Critical Dystopias: An Anatomy of Rebellion

Taylor Andrew Loy

Foreword: Understanding Anarchy

> The fact that the Anarchist movement for which I have striven
> so long is to a certain extent in abeyance and overshadowed by
> philos ophies of authority and coercion affects me with concern,
> but not with despair. It seems to me a point of special significance
> that many countries decline to admit Anarchists. All governments
> hold the view that while parties of the right and left may advo-
> cate social changes, still they cling to the idea of government and
> authority. Anarchism alone breaks with both and propagates un-
> compromising rebellion. In the long run, therefore, it is Anarchism
> which is considered deadlier to the present regime than all other
> social theories that are now clamoring for power.
>
> —Emma Goldman from "Was My Life Worth Living?" (1934)

> Anarchism is like Christianity; it's never really been prac-
> ticed...[but] it is a necessary idea.
>
> —Ursula K. Le Guin from "An Interview" (1990)

While researching and writing this chapter, I began paying more attention to
how my colleagues *used* the concept of Anarchy in discussions. After witnessing
consistent misappropriations and abuses of the term, I came to realize that I

---

needed to do more than offer an introduction to Anarchy; what I needed was a brief archaeology of these misconceptions.

Too easily Anarchy and, by implication, Anarchism are associated with mindless violence, random acts of destruction, and utter chaos. For a key example of this sort of automatic association, one needs to look only as far back in recent memory as the Centennial Olympic Park bombing in 1996 when the term "pipe bomb" entered the national vocabulary. As a result, *The Anarchist Cookbook* (1971) received a great deal of media attention because it contained instructions for building a pipe bomb. Since then, those who did not already have pre-judged notions were offered a simple equation: Anarchy=terrorism.

Two decades before, in 1976, Anarchy gained cultural currency in the burgeoning counter-culture of punk rock. In large part, this was due to the Sex Pistols' international hit song, "Anarchy in the U.K."[1] Therefore, instead of terrorism and bomb planting, Anarchy carried the cultural baggage of disaffected youth engaged in rampant property destruction and self-destructive behavior. This was certainly not the heart of the punk rock movement, but, for many, it was its face.

Prejudiced and distorted conceptualizations of Anarchy are not recent phenomena. Nearly a century ago, Emma Goldman bemoaned this same tendency: "as the most revolutionary and uncompromising innovator, Anarchism must needs meet with the combined ignorance and venom of the world it aims to reconstruct" (48).[2] The simple act of invoking Anarchism as a possible solution for social problems baffles many people because it is understood as a paradox: Anarchy is seen as an inherently flawed social state, not as a way of solving social problems. How many times have you heard some variation of derisive statements such as: "that couldn't work; it would be complete *anarchy*"?

So, then, if it is not a philosophy of chaos, what is Anarchism? Peter Kropotkin,[3] a prominent Russian Anarchist who lived from 1842 to 1921, writes in *The Encyclopaedia Britannica* (1910):

1 In his film *Sid and Nancy*, Alex Cox laments this reckless corruption of Anarchy through the words of a methadone clinic worker (addressing the character of Sid Vicious as played by Gary Oldham): "Smack is the great controller, keeps people stupid when they could be smart. You guys got no right to be strung out on that stuff. You could be selling healthy anarchy. Long as you addicts, you be full of shit."

2 In fact, Goldman was drawn to Anarchism because she felt that the Anarchists prosecuted for the Haymarket Riot bombing were unjustly accused ("Was My Life Worth Living?"). Her own affiliation with Anarchism began as a response to what she believed to be an unjust profiling of the Haymarket Anarchists.

3 Stephen Jay Gould writes in a parenthetical note in "Kropotkin Was No Crackpot," "We must shed the old stereotype of anarchists as bearded bomb throwers furtively stalking about city streets at night. Kropotkin was a genial man, almost saintly according to some, who promoted a vision of small

Anarchism [is] the name given to a principle or theory of life and conduct under which society is conceived without government—harmony in such a society being obtained, not by submission to law, or by obedience to any authority, but by free agreements concluded between the various groups, territorial and professional, freely constituted for the sake of production and consumption, as also for the satisfaction of the infinite variety of needs and aspirations of a civilized being. In a society developed on these lines, the voluntary associations which already now begin to cover all the fields of human activity would take a still greater extension so as to substitute themselves for the state in all its functions. (*Anarchy Archives*)

A state of Anarchy, then, would not be chaos. On the contrary, it would require a thoroughly articulated network of social and political relationships in order to effectively provide services and protections currently rendered by state governments. Whereas Kropotkin defines Anarchism in terms of an Anarchistic society, my focus in this paper will be the role of individual Anarchists attempting to generate and sustain such a society.

Another difficulty I have faced in appealing to and understanding Anarchy is that ideologues of democracy have hijacked its most alluring features. For instance, Lewis Mumford asserts that "democracy consists in giving final authority to the whole, rather than the part; *and only living human beings, as such, are an authentic expression of the whole, whether acting alone or with the help of others.*" (emphasis added, 1).[1] Here, Mumford claims for democracy what Paul Goodman or Emma Goldman may have just as easily attributed to an Anarchistic system.[2] Proponents of democracy will claim that the large democratic governments as we know them are natural extensions of groups of individuals—endowed with final authority—"acting alone or with the help of others." I would argue that Mumford's equivocation on "the whole" indicates a cognitive dissonance characteristic of some "liberal" Cold War rhetoric; one can get away with invoking the ideas of socialism, communitarianism, or even Anarchism if one calls it, or subordinates it to, "democracy." However, this ideological turf war is a topic for another (much longer) paper. My present aim is to offer a brief introduction to the difficulties of engaging Anarchism as a serious and legitimate ideology—one

communities setting their own standards by consensus for the benefit of all, thereby eliminating the need for most functions of a central government."

1 That I am using this piece as an example of how democracy has appropriated the virtues of Anarchism is ironic because Mumford begins it with an attempt to clarify what "democracy" means. Mumford claims "democracy" is "now confused and sophisticated by indiscriminate use, and often treated with patronizing contempt" (1). This is precisely my concern for "Anarchy."

2 For instance, Emma Goldman writes in the same article quoted above: "my faith is in the individual and in the capacity of free individuals for united endeavor."

that is at least, as Le Guin suggests in the above quotation, as serious and legitimate as Christianity.[1]

Though my objects of inquiry are literary (and, in one case, cinematic), I want to be clear that I am reading and analyzing them as thought experiments for a world not generally receptive to the implementation of Anarchistic ideals. This is the secondary objective of this paper: to reclaim and validate Anarchism. However, the primary objective is to map the emergence and evolution of Anarchy in the specific contexts and genres characteristic to each text.

The first major hurdle in this analysis is that both *V for Vendetta* (the graphic novel) and *The Matrix* resonate with some of the prejudiced expectations of Anarchism associated with terrorism and punk rock. To refer to V as anything other than a terrorist would be intellectually dishonest and extremely difficult to defend. Alex P. Schmid, in his essay in *Political Terrorism: A New Guide to Actors, Authors, Concepts, Data Bases, Theories, and Literature*, an often-cited reference, defines terrorism as:

> an anxiety-inspiring method of repeated violent action, employed by (semi-)clandestine individual, group, or state actors, for idiosyncratic, criminal, or political reasons, whereby—in contrast to assassination— the direct targets of violence are not the main targets. The immediate human victims of violence are generally chosen randomly (targets of opportunity) or selectively (representative or symbolic targets) from a target population, and serve as message generators. Threat- and violence-based communication processes between terrorist (organization), (imperiled) victims, and main targets are used to manipulate the main target (audience(s)), turning it into a target of terror, a target of demands, or a target of attention, depending on whether intimidation, coercion, or propaganda is primarily sought. (28)

V's activities match this definition exactly. I would hope that it *goes without saying*, but it should be noted that acts of "terrorism" and even the "terrorist" label are much more morally ambiguous than recent use, in America at least, would suggest. In fact, it would not be a semantic stretch to define many of the acts instrumental in liberating colonial America from British rule, such as The Gaspée Affair,[2] as "terrorist acts" and the so-called Sons of Liberty as "terrorist." Therefore, it would seem that any moral significance of "terrorism," and by extension any moral judgment made on "terrorists" themselves, depends a great deal on the context of the "terrorist" acts. By mapping out V's Anarchism as embodied in his terrorist acts, I hope

---

1 Of course, there are Anarchists, such as Jacques Ellul, whose political philosophy is rooted in Christian theology.
2 For more information on the 1772 burning of the HMS Gaspée, visit gaspee.org.

to make this indispensable context evident. At first glance, the Wachowski Brothers seem to have created *The Matrix* as a cyberpunk artifact. How well this label fits the movie is arguable. In the very least, it does manifest some of the broader characteristics of the genre. Cyberpunk is an independent and idiosyncratic manifestation of punk counter-culture marked by actors/ actresses who are alienated by the "system" and engaged in technologized rebellion and cybernetic self-redefinition. As such, *The Matrix* carries the burden of punk's destructive, anti-social reputation. Early in the movie, Neo, played by Keanu Reeves, exhibits a propensity for reactionary anti-authoritarianism, but throughout the movie he develops a more sophisticated and intentional anti-authoritarian attitude. While punk ideology is a broad enough cultural movement to embrace both extremes, Anarchism, I would argue, is not. Neo may begin *The Matrix* as "just" a cyberpunk, but by the end he has also become a self-governed Anarchist. These, of course, are not mutually exclusive labels: Anarchists can be punk, but not all punks are Anarchists.

The other literary text included in my analysis is Ursula K. Le Guin's *The Dispossessed*. Instead of resonating with common misconceptions of Anarchism, it invokes a mode of Anarchy founded on non-violence, social responsibility, and mutual aid. The Anarchism of the central protagonist, Shevek, is more recognizable as such to the readers of Peter Kropotkin, Emma Goldman, and Paul Goodman than to readers whose sense of Anarchy stems from its current cultural currency.

By invoking Anarchy and Anarchism, the authors and protagonists in these works are fighting a war on two fronts. Just as Shevek struggles to reconnect Anarres to a vital Anarchistic struggle of inter-planetary proportions, Le Guin engages the general ignorance of authentic Anarchism by challenging her readers' pre-judged conceptions. In *V for Vendetta*, Alan Moore and David Lloyd have to contend with what has become a major hot-button issue, terrorism. That is not to say that terrorism had not been a significant issue prior to the September 11th terrorist attacks in 2001, but that discussing terrorism, at least in America, has become increasingly difficult.[1] An American reading *V for Vendetta* in the eighties would have had a qualitatively different experience than a reader from our current post-September 11th era. Also, by *playing into* the misconception that Anarchy=terrorism, a general reader may find it difficult to imagine how Evey's role as V, whose identity she adopts at the end of the novel, could be anything other than a terrorist.

---

1 One disappointing feature of the *V for Vendetta* film adaptation is that it failed to effectively confront the obfuscation of "terrorism," in American political discourse.

The conceptual burden of *The Matrix* is much lighter. The "punk rock" label was a commercial success throughout the 1980s and 1990s. As a result of punk rock's commodification, its counter-cultural tensions have relaxed into little more than a counter-cultural image, a mere façade of a counter-cultural movement. Punk has effectively become a phase of adolescence rather than a mode of social (dis)engagement.[1] Because punk has been divested of its more dangerous elements, an audience is, perhaps, more likely to identify with or consider a punk character's point-of-view; however, an agent of terrorism, such as V, may come across as more suspect. *The Matrix* franchise has capitalized heavily on cyberpunk's counter-cultural image. Therefore, it is unclear how seriously, or sincerely, we should take Neo's closing promise of liberation, and, as some have noted, the credits' track, "Wake Up" by Rage Against the Machine.

The aim of this paper is not to conclude definitely what Anarchism *is* but what it *does*, how it works within the boundaries of each thought experiment. Ultimately, each of these texts is a performance, an acting out of Anarchistic ideals embodied in each character's response to the demands of their environment. Through the charting of these violent and non-violent rebellions, we will see how successful our Anarchists are at "[propagating] uncompromising rebellion."

Introduction: An Anatomy of a Thesis

> The planner, the builder of castles in the air, the novelist, the author of social and technological utopias is experiment-ing with thoughts; so too is the hardheaded merchant, the serious inventor and the enquirer. All of them imagine condi-tions, and connect with them their expectations and surmise of consequences: they gain a thought experience.
>
> —Ernst Mach (136)
>
> There is something inherently puzzling about milking real knowledge from unreal cows, and this something is the principal explanatory challenge for any account of literature as an instrument of inquiry.
>
> —Peter Swirski (6)

I would include in Mach's "[builders] of castles in the air" both screenwriters and movie directors, and I would expand their products to

---

1 If you have gone to a number of punk rock shows in the past decade, you may have noticed that the average age of the crowds have been slowly converging to thirteen.

include dystopias as well. My primary focal points of analysis will be Ursula K. Le Guin's novel *The Dispossessed*, the graphic novel *V for Vendetta*, created by Alan Moore and David Lloyd, and the film *The Matrix*, written and directed by the Wachowski Brothers. These texts have been selected for this project because they each present disparate versions of anarchistic rebellions. The narratives are substantively different in two important ways: (1) the settings are distinct: in *The Dispossessed*,[1] dystopia is difficult to locate because it exists in suspension between the planets of Anarres and Urras; in Alan Moore's *V for Vendetta*, the dystopic setting is a post-nuclear war London that has fallen under fascist control;[2] dystopia in *The Matrix* exists on the virtual level of the Matrix itself and the level of bleak reality that is outside it. (2) The narratives themselves are embodied in inherently different mediums: a novel, a comic book, and a film.[3] Another interesting difference between these texts is that they were published/released in three different time periods: *The Dispossessed* was published in 1974; *V for Vendetta* was published as a ten-part series from 1982–1988; *The Matrix* was released in 1999.[4]

This chapter is a cross-genre pilot study in Anarchist thought experiments. It is not an attempt to produce an encyclopedic review of the emergence or function of anarchism in critical dystopias. My objective is not so ambitious; my aim is to plot the evolution of each rebellion within its own context. In the end, I hope to broaden an understanding of Anarchy and Anarchism: not an understanding that congeals and grows more rigid, but rather an understanding that expands and flows, nearing a point of superfluidity. At this point I will explicate two key concepts in my analysis: thought experiment and critical dystopia.

Peter Swirski's opening quotation for this section is drawn from his recent work *Of Literature and Knowledge*. In it he investigates how "time and again narrative fantasies dramatically prove their power to encroach on our real-life existence" (4). He refers to some of the more speculative and hypothetical "narrative fantasies" as "thought experiments." The *Stanford Encyclopedia of Philosophy* defines thought experiments as "devices of the imagination used to investigate the nature of things." However, the encyclopedia entry focuses almost entirely on thought experiments in science and philosophy dealing with inquiries into physics, quantum mechanics, and cosmology. Little

---

1 Some editions of Le Guin's text include the subtitle *An Ambiguous Utopia*. While *The Dispossessed* certainly defies any clean categorization, another ambiguity lies in the term "utopia" itself. As such, I have chosen to classify these works as "critical dystopias," a term in which this ambiguity is made more explicit.

2 Moore speculated that nuclear disarmament in England would protect the island nation from attack in a nuclear war.

3 Alan Moore believes the term "graphic novel" is a contrivance of DC Comics that serves as a marketable euphemism for "big expensive comic books."

4 The second and third installments, *The Matrix: Reloaded* and *The Matrix: Revolutions*, were both released in 2003.

attention is given to Swirski's conception of literary thought experiments, which inquire more intimately and directly into *human* nature, that of human beings who are storytellers and as receivers of stories, than into the nature of *things*.

In an attempt to assay "the cognitive purity" of thought experiments as separate from a general class of literary fictions, Swirski outlines five criteria: clarity, coherence, relevance, informativeness, and projectability (108–109). Clarity is gauged by how cleanly the dependent and independent variables are defined in the fictional work. For the purposes of this paper, dependent variables are system components directly affected by a protagonist's actions, and independent variables are system components that function beyond the range of a protagonist's free agency. In an effective thought experiment protagonists follow clearly laid out decision trees in which most of their choices have definite consequences. Coherence is, roughly, a measure of believability. We have all read books or watched movies in which the characters, the settings, or the scenarios were not believable. We accept the *trueness* of the fiction when our experience of the narrative flows seamlessly from its premises. Relevance is a measure of how closely the fictional world resembles what its audience identifies as reality. Informativeness, however, goes beyond mere correspondence; it is a measure of the contemporaneous vitality of a work's theoretical presuppositions. To draw an example from *The Dispossessed*, informativeness would be derived from how accurately Shevek's scientific reasoning resonated with the state of theoretical physics and the philosophy of time in 1976.[1] And finally, the criterion of projectability turns the thought experiment on its head in order to critically examine features of the audience's reality rather than the fictionally constructed reality of the work. In Swirski's words, "projecting themselves into the lives and motives of narrative agents, readers can fathom their own *hypothetical* beliefs and desires, and project them back to better understand the fiction" (118). I will draw from the framework of critical dystopias, because these criteria, outlined above, are to some extent already intrinsic to the genre. The exceptions to this are clarity and informativeness. For this study, little attention is paid to informativeness because it is peripheral to my present aims. However, the criterion of clarity is more useful; in outlining variables and establishing cause and effect relationships, the *experimental* structure becomes more evident.

My working definition for "critical dystopia" is drawn from the work of Lyman Tower Sargent:

---

1 Laurence Davis argues in "The Dynamic and Revolutionary Utopia of Ursula K. Le Guin" that Shevek's temporal inquiry echoes Friedrich Kümmel's "Time as Succession and the Problem of Duration," published in 1968.

a non-existent society described in considerable detail and normally located in time and space that the author intended a contemporaneous reader to view as worse than contemporary society but that normally includes at least one eutopian [sic] enclave or holds out hope that the dystopia can be overcome and replaced by eutopia [sic]. ("US Eutopias" 222)

Where a character locates this utopian enclave can be particularly significant. In the case of *The Dispossessed*, rebels on Urras might consider Anarres to be such an enclave. However, there are others on Urras who view Anarres as a wholly undesirable place. For many Anarresti, the critical dystopian map is turned on its head, and Urras is perceived as a dystopian world inhabited by greedy propertarians and profiteers. The utopian enclave in *V for Vendetta* is almost hermitic; V and Evey are the sole inhabitants of The Shadow Gallery for almost the entirety of the graphic novel. In *The Matrix*, the utopian enclave appears to be the underground rebel hideout of Zion; however, from the point of view of the character Cypher, true utopia is found in a prelapsarian state of "ignorance" *inside* the Matrix.[1] Another distinguishing feature of a critical dystopia, according to David Seed, is that the "text includes a dimension of debate, by characters and within the narrative structure itself, about the values and directions of its future society" (*Dark Horizons*, 69). This is true to varying degrees of each work in this analysis.[2]

An important key to understanding a critical dystopia is in its appeal to contemporaneous readers. This appeal is roughly congruent with Swirski's criteria of coherence, relevance, and projectability. In order for readers to view a society as "worse" than their own, there must be points of contact. It is at these points of contact that the classification of these works as thought experiments gains traction. The brute facts of human existence such as eating, working, copulating, etc., along with higher-level sociopolitical realities such as police, war, law, technology, etc., all get filtered through an ideological matrix of dystopian/utopian thought. At the same time readers identify the dystopian elements that are "worse" than contemporary life, they also acknowledge the "better" features of the utopian enclave. In other words, the utopian and dystopian elements of the narrative form a triad with a reader's own world. Because critical dystopias provide a continuum of possibility—from utopia to dystopia—they serve as thought experiments, a testing grounds for potentially revolutionary ideas. If the narratives resonate

---

1 At one point in the movie, Cypher agrees to betray his companions on the *Nebuchadnezzar* if Agent Smith will plug him back into the Matrix and wipe any memory of the world of Zion.

2 *The Dispossessed* has the most sophisticated internal debate of the three, followed by *V for Vendetta*, and then *The Matrix*. I think a good deal of this difference can be chalked up to the virtues and vices of their mediums.

strongly with our reality as readers, then they may affect how we choose to live our lives.

Another marker of the critical dystopia genre is that it leaves both the protagonist and the reader with an open-ended conclusion. This is in stark contrast to the bleak endings of other dystopian works such as Terry Gilliam's *Brazil*, Aldous Huxley's *Brave New World*, George Orwell's *1984*, and many others. As a result of this open-endedness, the internal debates in critical dystopias are left unresolved. Instead of functioning as cautionary tales, critical dystopias allow for the possibility of hope.[1] By leaving inquiry open, both to their characters and their audience, they function as thought experiments par excellence. In this way, the audience of critical dystopias are invited into the laboratory and encouraged to fiddle with the experimental apparatus.

The paper is divided into three main sections: (1) The Anarchist, (2) The Infrastructure, and (3) The Rebellion. The first section serves as an introduction to the protagonists: Shevek, V, and Neo. The second section is a characterization of the technological infrastructures that perpetuate dystopian power relations in their respective worlds. Also in this section, I introduce my primary analytical framework derived from Thomas P. Hughes's analysis of the evolution of large technological systems. In the third and final section, I discuss how the protagonists resist these deeply entrenched technological infrastructures.

The Anarchist:

Perhaps due to a common tendency to misunderstand Anarchism as outlined in my foreword, both *V for Vendetta* and *The Dispossessed* contain explicit explorations of Anarchism's many faces—even its false ones. Even though there is no explicit invocation of Anarchism in *The Matrix*, Neo's anti-authoritarian behaviors and attitudes coupled with his closing speech touting "a world without rules or controls" suggests an Anarchistic interpretation of the film. As such, I intend to let the texts and the film—or, more specifically, their characters—speak for themselves. Also, throughout the paper, I will draw from a number of Anarchist theorists—including Jacques Ellul, Peter Kropotkin, Paul Goodman, and Emma Goldman—who were definite influences on Ursula K. Le Guin's "new utopian politics."[2] Even

1 For a deeper look at the "critical dystopia" genre, read Raffaella Baccolini and Tom Moylan's introduction to *Dark Horizons: Science Fiction and the Dystopian Imagination*.
2 Whether Alan Moore or the Wachowski brothers are familiar with the primary works of these Anarchists I do not know for certain. However, the influence of these thinkers on the development of Anarchistic ideals is certainly enough to justify their use.

though I stress the unique engagement of Shevek, V, and Neo within their distinct environments, I think there are important points of resonance and contact between them.

Shevek

In *The Dispossessed*, Anarchism is contained in the tenets of Odonianism, the world religion of Anarres.[1] As do most Anarresti, Shevek devotes himself to a way of life inspired by Odo's writings. Much of the internal debates, characteristic of a critical dystopia, are framed around discussing these texts.

Despite having been dead for over 200 years, Odo is a surprisingly active character in *The Dispossessed*. Shevek first *meets* her when he arrives in the Anarresti center, Abbenay, and visits a park cultivated with trees from Urras. The encounter is described so vividly that upon my first reading I was confused momentarily before I realized that Odo was simply a *statue*:

> Some ways before him, down the darkening path, a person sat reading on a stone bench. Shevek went forward slowly. He came to the bench and stood looking at the figure who sat with head bowed over the book in the green-gold dusk under the trees. It was a woman of fifty or sixty, strangely dressed, her hair pulled back in a knot. Her left hand on her chin nearly hid the stern mouth, her right held the papers on her knee. They were heavy, those papers; the cold hand on them was heavy. The light was dying fast but she never looked up. She went on reading the proof sheets of *The Social Organism*. Shevek looked at Odo for a while, and then he sat down on the bench beside her. (101)

Clearly, Le Guin intentionally gives life to Odo's statue. At the risk of taking the episode too literally, I understand it in two ways: (1) Odo is a *living* part of Anarresti society, and (2) Shevek's response to the statue signifies his intimate relationship with Odonian Anarchism. While there may be other, deeper readings of this passage, this simple interpretation provides a salient touchstone in understanding Anarresti society, in general, and Shevek, in particular.

Odo's extant works, as referenced in the novel, include *Analogy*, *Prison Letters*, and *The Social Organism*. Occasionally these works are quoted directly, but, more often, they are only paraphrased or briefly referenced. Odo did not intend for her words to be "[parroted]...as if they were laws," but, as

---

1 To better understand Odonianism, I offer a brief gloss on Anarresti history: approximately 200 years before the events in the novel take place, there was a rebellion on Urras orchestrated by the followers of Odo. To satisfy the revolutionaries, the authorities on Urras agreed to facilitate the colonization of their sister planet, Anarres, by the rebellious faction. Although Odo herself never reached Anarres, her anarchistic writings served as the foundation for the new Anarresti civilization.

Shevek's friend Bedap argues, that is what Odonian education has become (168). Because Odonianism is the cornerstone of the social technologies that maintain the Anarresti way of life, it will be explored more in depth in the following sections on the technological infrastructure and the rebellion. While Shevek shares a common Odonian education with all other Anarresti, he possesses a singular intellectual prowess—surpassing some of the greatest minds on Anarres, Urras, and beyond. Even at a young age, Shevek stands out from his peers as having a keen scientific mind for physics and math. Early on in his intellectual development, he sets his mind to developing a "theory of the General Field in temporal physics," or, in short, "the Theory of Simultaneity."[1] However, his ultimate goal of sharing his theory freely and equally among all the worlds is not made evident until the end of the novel.

Life on Anarres does not remotely resemble the easy-going existence in more traditional utopias. Even though Shevek has a brilliant mind for math and physics, he has done his share of hard, physical labor. During a particularly arduous "afforestation project,"[2] he resents the work because "people who had chosen to work in centrally functional fields such as physics should not be called upon for these projects and special levies. Wasn't it immoral to do work you didn't enjoy?" (*The Dispossessed*, 48). However, he volunteers simply because "[it] needed doing" and no one else was taking up the responsibility (48). During ordinary work rotations every tenth day, as opposed to special long-term large-scale projects, Shevek had "always volunteered for the 'heavies,'" because he was "proud of his strength" (48). Doing what is necessary—that is, responding to exigencies—is for Shevek his social responsibility.

V

V is an enigmatic, shadowy figure. His home, which turns out to be part of an underground complex of the abandoned subway system, is literally called "The Shadow Gallery" (18). The reader discovers early on that he does not even "*have*" a name, but he requests that Evey "call" him "V" (26). His most distinguishing *feature* is a Guy Fawkes mask, which he is never seen without.[3] The significance of the mask cannot be understated. Guy Fawkes's claim to infamy was the Gunpowder Treason, which ended in his capture moments before he was able to set off the explosives to destroy the British Parliament building on November 5, 1605. In England, he is perhaps the most

---

1 This is Le Guin's Anarresti version of a *Theory of Everything*.
2 "The afforestation of the West Temaenian Littoral was one of the great undertakings of the fifteenth decad of the Settlement of Anarres, employing nearly eighteen thousand people over a period of two years" (*The Dispossessed*, 46).
3 Although twice in the novel other characters "see" him without his mask.

infamous terrorist in history—so infamous, in fact, that the British celebrate Guy Fawkes Night every 5th of November. The celebrations include not only mirth and revelry, but also large bonfires built around the Guy Fawkes effigies that were the inspiration for V's character design. Moore's British audience would be extremely familiar with this iconography.

Another mysterious feature of V's modus operandi is that he communicates almost exclusively in quotations, literary allusions, theatrics, and allegory. He also sings and plays music, which serves as a kind of soundtrack for the graphic novel. Many of his allusions and references are idiosyncratically British, and have a good deal more resonance within their national context, such as the hymn "Jerusalem," which was derived from a William Blake poem (48). Other references have a more pop culture appeal such as "Sympathy for the Devil" by The Rolling Stones (54). Many of his references and allusions throughout the novel are unrecognizable to most other characters in the comic because the sources of such information have been declared contraband by the fascist state government, "Norsefire."

The reader of the comic is led to believe that V's vast repertoire is entirely self-taught. However, we are offered fleeting glimpses into V's autodidactic regimen via David Lloyd's illustrations. In a couple of panels (on pages 9 and 18) the titles of some of the many books on V's shelves are clearly visible: *Utopia, Uncle Tom's Cabin, Capital, Mein Kampf, Gulliver's Travels, Decline and Fall of the Roman Empire, Essays of Elia, Don Quixote, Hard Times, French Revolution, Arabian Nights, Faust, The Odyssey, V¹* (Thomas Pynchon), *Iliad, From Russia with Love, Ivanhoe, Shakespeare* (two volumes), *Golden Bough, Divine Comedy*, and *I Am Legend*. While there are a few non-fiction political works and histories, it is interesting to note that no texts specifically relate to Anarchism. Because V continually refers to Anarchy throughout the comics, it seems Alan Moore may have wanted to paint him as a first-generation Anarchist, inspired more by literature and a general political education than by any specific theory of Anarchism.

All the reader is allowed to know about V's past is that he was created by medical experiments at Larkhill concentration camp. As an effect of his treatments, he develops superhuman strength, speed, and intelligence.[2] These abilities effectively grant him immunity from state-enforced violence. He uses his freedom to set into motion a meticulously crafted plan to enact vengeance on his captors from Larkhill and to destabilize the authoritarian regime that created it.

---

1 Later in the series (64) V is reading Thomas Pynchon's V when Evey confronts him about killing the Archbishop. He then quotes the novel: "There is more behind and inside V than any of us had suspected. Not who, but what: what is she?"
2 It is unclear what his capabilities were before Larkhill.

There seems to be no limit to V's capabilities. He is an expert demolitionist, an electrical engineer, a chemist, an illusionist, and a computer hacker, with an uncanny gardening prowess. In fact, his green-thumb makes possible his escape from Larkhill. V receives special privileges because his skillful cultivation of the garden allows the camp to be self-sustaining. He exploits his access to fertilizer to make the explosives that he uses to flee the camp. In a sense, V is the apotheosis of the anarchistic struggle against the state and state-orchestrated violence because he has the capability to readily adapt and respond to virtually any exigency. However, he is limited in one very important way: he has chosen to become an agent of violent rebellion and, as such, he cannot adapt beyond this apparent need. Near the end of the novel, V orchestrates his own demise in order to pass the torch to Evey, who has little appetite for death and destruction. This seems to be a tacit acknowledgement in the novel that not only is a state of violence unsustainable, but also the agents thereof run the risk that their expertise at destruction will no longer be necessary.

Neo

In *The Matrix*, Neo, the central protagonist played by Keanu Reeves, is a computer hacker.[1] Presumably, his hacking abilities have drawn the attention of Morpheus and his cadre. They have been watching him and waiting for the right moment to *free his mind*. However, Morpheus considers him to be much more than simply a valuable ally in the war against the machines. He believes Neo to be the "One" foretold by the Oracle: the prophesied savior of Zion.

From early on in the film, Neo exhibits the knee-jerk anti-authoritarianism of cyberpunk counter-culture. By day, he is a computer programmer for a large technology firm, slaving away on the cubicle farm; by night, he engages in illicit dealings, hacking computer systems and selling viruses. Since he does not seem to want or need the money and his character seems to be generally apathetic about life,[2] it appears that he does illegal things simply because he can. Later on in the film, when Morpheus tells him he's the "One," he refuses to accept it. And then, when the Oracle tells him that he is, in fact, not the "One," he ultimately rejects her ruling as well. It is not until Neo chooses to be the "One," near the end of the movie, that he exhibits

---

1 This, of course, is not Mr. Reeves's first foray into a role of a computer hacker. In 1995, he played the central role in *Johnny Mnemonic*, directed by Robert Longo and written by William Gibson, who is considered one of the progenitors of cyberpunk.
2 How much of this is the "character" of Neo or an artifact of Keanu's Reeves's acting is unclear.

the qualities of a convinced Anarchist sophisticated enough to deliver his closing lines:

I know you're out there. I can feel you now. I know that you're afraid. You're afraid of us. You're afraid of change. I don't know the future. I didn't come here to tell you how this is going to end. I came here to tell you how it's going to begin. I'm going to hang up this phone, and then I'm going to show these people what you don't want them to see. I'm going to show them a world... without you. A world without rules and controls. Without borders or boundaries. A world where anything is possible. Where we go from there is a choice I leave to you.

These lines are delivered as a voice-over addressing an ambiguous audience. It can be understood as a message to the AI controlling the Matrix, the people still trapped within, and, on a meta-level, as a direct address to the movie audience. Not only does this statement clearly refer to an Anarchistic world, it is also a useful general description of the telos of Anarchistic rebellion: the perpetual generation of change and revolution without constraints.

The fact that Neo, Shevek, and V embody Anarchy so disparately should be no surprise. Anarchistic methods depend on the context within which they emerge and the individual characteristics of the agents who wield them. What these characters share is an ability to identify exigency and a passion for responding to it. This awareness and flexibility is part and parcel of the truly adaptive Anarchist.

Due to their aptitudes for technical work, they are each able to respond to the exigencies of their environments and intervene in the technological infrastructures of their worlds. Just as these technological systems are contingent creations, bound to the social and material conditions from which they emerge, so too is the Anarchist's response. In the next section, I look more directly at the unique characteristics of these infrastructures. Then, in the final section, I discuss how our Anarchists challenge them.

The Infrastructure:

> Anarchism does not stand for military drill and uniformity; it does, however, stand for the spirit of revolt, in whatever form, against everything that hinders human growth.
>
> — Emma Goldman (63)

Political power is legitimized and reified through many channels. In highly structured utopian and dystopian worlds, these pathways of power are often intrinsically bound within a technological infrastructure. By necessity, the physical artifacts that are traditionally thought of as "technology" constitute the core of any such infrastructure. However, I will use technology in a much broader sense. Technology is not limited to materiality and is not simply what people *do*; it is a generative doing, a working at, working on, working with, and so on. Also, as in the case of *The Matrix*, technology can function with apparent autonomy from human agency. But, even in this extreme scenario the "machines" still depend on humanity to supply their energy needs. The object of this stage of analysis is to locate and identify specific technologies— both material and social—which are institutionalized or co-opted into the governing apparatus. This dissection will be of crucial importance in evaluating the infrastructural repercussions of acts of rebellion. In knowing how something is put together, one better understands how to dismantle it—and, ultimately, how it ought to be rebuilt.

The stability of these societies is contingent on the perpetuation and maintenance of a technological infrastructure. It is only when protagonist actors are aware of the contingent and fragmentary cohesion of an infrastructure's apparent 'whole' that they are able to challenge that system. However, all rebellions are not created equal; only those actors with a broad awareness of the technological forces at work—and the technical competence to intervene—can ever hope to overthrow a thoroughly reified regime. Because of the high level of integration and redundancy of large technological infrastructures, they can be extremely difficult to topple without a sophisticated understanding of how the components are integrated. Otherwise, these rebellions are in vain.

As stated above, the worlds our Anarchists inhabit differ wildly. Even though *The Matrix* suggests deep philosophical tensions between reality and perception, its technological infrastructure is perhaps the easiest to characterize.[1] The infrastructure in *V for Vendetta*, on the other hand, is more multi-faceted. The setting in the graphic novel is a future version of London controlled by a fascist regime that maintains order through a veritable panopticon of surveillance systems. Outlining the governmental structure and the various ministries is a simple matter, but mapping how they interact and respond to the disruptions perpetrated by V is much more complex. Finally, because *The Dispossessed* spans two worlds, each with its own nuanced techno-political systems, I will focus most of my energies, as does Le Guin, describing the systems in place on Anarres.

As an analytical framework, I appeal to "The Evolution of Large Technological Systems" by Thomas P. Hughes. It is particularly well suited for the purposes of the paper because Hughes incorporates both material

---

1 Again, this analysis largely disregards the convolutions of *Reloaded and Revolutions*.

and immaterial artifacts in his characterization of technological systems. By way of defining technological systems, he writes:

> Technological systems contain messy, complex, problem-solving components. They are both socially constructed and society shaping. Among the components in technological systems are physical artifacts, such as the turbogenerators, transformers, and transmission lines in electric light and power systems. Technological systems also include organizations, such as manufacturing firms, utility companies, and investment banks, and they incorporate components usually labeled scientific, such as books, articles, and university teaching and research programs. Legislative artifacts, such as regulatory laws, can also be part of technological systems. Because they are socially constructed and adapted in order to function in systems, natural resources, such as coal mines, also qualify as system artifacts. (51)

He continues, outlining the interconnectedness and interdependence of a system's components:

> An artifact—either physical or nonphysical—functioning as a component in a system interacts with other artifacts, all of which contribute directly or through other components to the *common system goal*. If a component is removed from a system or if its characteristics change, the other artifacts in the system will alter characteristics accordingly. (Emphasis added, 51)

The "common system goal" is what makes a system *systematic*. Defining this goal is key to understanding how the various components of the following technological infrastructures interact. In order to better understand Hughes's characterization of large technological systems, I will briefly discuss how such systems *move*.

In the history of technology, Hughes is noted for cultivating the term "technological momentum" as a response to notions of technological determinism. Instead of jumping on the train of technological progress, he decides to investigate technological systems as if they were trains—generally speaking, the faster they move and the heavier they are, the harder they are to stop. Hence, a high level of technological momentum "often causes observers to assume that a technological system has become autonomous" (Hughes 76). This gives rise to the illusion of technological determinism. Elsewhere, Hughes concedes that high momentum systems exhibit a "soft determinism," which may be exceedingly difficult to challenge, but is ultimately not irresistible.

Another important feature of Hughes's analytical framework is his consideration of *reverse salients*, which he defines as "components in the system that have fallen behind or are out of phase with the others" (73). Furthermore, the reverse salient metaphor is significant because "it suggests uneven and complex change" (73). Therefore, identifying reverse salients is of the utmost importance because they are, most likely, a system's weakest components, its greatest liability.

The Anarchists in these stories play the part of what Hughes refers to as the "independent inventor." "Psychologically they [have] an outsider's mentality," writes Hughes, "they also [seek] the thrill of a major technological transformation. They often [achieve] dramatic breakthroughs, not incremental improvements" (59). By operating outside the reified technological systems, these inventors have a unique ability to create not only alternate systems, but also radically different components that may revolutionize systems that are already entrenched.[1] These texts suggest that radical innovation is impossible without "an outsider's mentality." As Morpheus tells Neo, "unfortunately, no one can be told about the Matrix. You have to see it for yourself"—and you can only see the Matrix for what it is from the outside. Independent inventors swallow the red pill.

The Dispossessed

> You can't crush ideas by suppressing them. You can only crush them by ignoring them. By refusing to think, refusing to change. And that's precisely what our society is doing!... Change is freedom, change is life—is anything more basic to Odonian thought than that?
>
> — Bedap discussing Anarresti society with Shevek (165)

The setting of the novel spans spatially from the planet Anarres to the planet Urras and temporally from Shevek's earliest memories to his return voyage to Anarres much later in life. A reader's first encounter with the planets of Anarres and Urras are black line drawings of the planets on pages sandwiched between the dedication and the title page. Immediately, it is clear that the planets are inversely related; the surface of Urras is predominantly covered with water, much like Earth;[2] whereas Anarres is covered mostly by land. Another noticeable difference is that there are no state boundaries, marked by dotted lines, on Anarres; Urras has about a dozen. The most

---

1 Hughes goes much farther in characterizing "independent inventors" than would apply to our Anarchists. Much of his discussion of these unique figures is couched within economic terms. While, on an abstract level, Shevek, V, or Neo might be classified as "inventor-entrepreneurs," who are the key inventors in directing the evolution of large systems, the profiteering sense of *entrepreneur* would be antithetical to their respective projects.
2 Urras is, in fact, "five-sixths water" (64).

notable countries on Urras are A-Io, a capitalist society and the seat of the Council of World Governments, and Thu, a socialist state.[1]

Perhaps the most striking feature of Anarresti society is the absence of personal property; in fact, in Pravic, the Anarresti language, the singular genitive case is used rarely and only for emphasis.[2] "Little children might say 'my mother,' but very soon they learned to say 'the mother'... to say 'this one is mine and that's yours' in Pravic, one said, 'I use this one and you use that'" (58). In this way, the Anarresti language establishes the primacy of function and use over personal possession. The only privacy generally afforded to an Anarresti is during copulation;[3] otherwise, there are no locked doors unless the lock serves a purely utilitarian function, i.e., a lock on a moving truck to keep someone from falling out (34).

Every commodity is *distributed* as needed, but much is still left up to individual agency. For food, whether he or she worked or not, an Anarresti could still stop by a local commons each day. Even during a famine one could, as Shevek does in one particular instance, take a "double helping" (261). He arrives at the commons in Abbenay after being stranded without proper rations when the transport train he was on broke down:

> Ravenous still from the journey, he took a double helping of both porridge and bread. The boy behind the serving tables looked at him frowning. These days nobody took double helpings. Shevek stared frowning back and said nothing. He had gone eighty-odd hours now on two bowls of soup and one kilo of bread, and he had a right to make up for what he had missed, but he was damned if he would explain. Existence is its own justification, need is right. He was an Odonian, he left guilt to profiteers. (261)

Just as the serving boy is free to disapprove, Shevek is free to meet his needs as he sees fit.

Only in rare cases, when an individual's actions are *perceived* to be pathologically dysfunctional and incongruent with the greater social welfare, will a local group of Anarresti band together to shame the offender. This

---

1 Chifoilisk, a Thuvian, goes so far to suggest to Shevek that Thu and Anarres have much in common (135–136).
2 Le Guin deploys the singular genitive case as an important component of character development. The beginning of Chapter 2 shows an infant Shevek pushing another baby out of the way to claim a square of sunlight streaming into the nursery as "Mine sun!" (27). Later, in the same chapter, Shevek's professor, Mitis, prepares him for his academic transfer to Abbenay under the tutelage of Sabul by telling him that "he will be *his* man" (58). Finally, in the debates surrounding Shevek's radio communication with the Urrasti, Rulag begins her accusations against him by invoking the first person genitive: "*Your* Syndicate of Initiative" (Emphasis marked) (355).
3 This social arrangement resonates with another critical dystopia, *We*, by Yevgeny Zamyatin (1924). However, this resemblance is merely superficial; the socio-political frameworks in these novels are otherwise diametrically opposed.

shaming comes in the form of a "public reprimand," where "everybody comes to your syndicate meeting and tells you off" (169). Even on Anarres the *many* can still wield authority over the *few*. This fact, as Bedap argues and Shevek comes to understand, is the primary component of the social mechanism that is out of phase. This "government by the majority" exists as a reverse salient for a technological system founded on Odonianism.

Ursula K. Le Guin depicts Anarres as a society struggling for survival under the burden of self-sacrifice and shared labor. Efficiently coordinating their shared labor is paramount. During the initial settlement of Anarres, the early settlers established a worldwide-networked computer system that is primarily responsible for the distribution of labor assignments and other logistical matters. However, Divlab, as it is called, has a distinct advantage over the super-computer in *V for Vendetta*, called Fate; Divlab offers a choice.

In one particular instance, Shevek's partner Takver has been assigned to work at an isolated marine research station, but Divlab has no job openings for Shevek in the same area. He has to make a judgment call: "[The clerk] awaited his decision. It was his to make; and the options were endless. He could stay in Abbenay and organize classes in physics if he could find volunteer students. He could go to Rolny Peninsula and live with Takver though without any place in the research station. He could live anywhere and do nothing but get up twice a day and go to the nearest commons to be fed. He could do what he pleased" (Le Guin, 269). "But the choices of the social being are never made alone," and Shevek decides to take a job assignment where his help is most needed.

Shevek's sense of duty is established in Chapter 2. This chapter consists of eight episodes from Shevek's life presented in rapid succession, beginning with his infancy and ending in his late teens the night before he leaves to study in Abbenay. That night at his going away party, after most of the party-goers have gone off to copulate or to sleep, Shevek kicks off what some might call a bull session: "Suffering is a misunderstanding... We can't prevent suffering. This pain and that pain, yes, but not Pain. A society can only relieve social suffering, unnecessary suffering. The rest remains. The root, the reality" (60). What follows is a meandering discussion of love, pain, brotherhood, and mutual aid. In the end, Shevek concludes that brotherhood "begins in shared pain" (60). By sharing *necessary* pain and reducing *unnecessary* pain, individuals in a society can approach the Odonian ideal of brotherhood. The trouble is, as Shevek discovers through his contact with the Urrasti, the Hainish, the Terrans, Anarres does not have the market cornered on necessary pain. In other words, Anarres's isolation is maintained only by denying its responsibility to an inter-planetary brotherhood, to the Council of World Governments, and, most importantly, to its own past, embodied in the planet Urras.

Anarres is a world ill-suited for colonization. Despite 200 years of intensive cultivation and work, it remains a difficult place to live:

> On arid Anarres, the communities had to scatter widely in search of resources, and few of them could be self-supporting, no matter how they cut back their notions of what is needed for support. They cut back very hard indeed, but to a minimum beneath which they would not go; they would not regress to pre-urban, pre-technological tribalism. They knew that their anarchism was the product of a very high civilization, of a complex diversified culture, of a stable economy and a highly industrialized technology that could maintain high production and rapid transportation of goods. (Le Guin 95)

The Anarresti people understand that their freedom, their anarchistic way of life, depends on maintaining their infrastructure. This maintenance can also be understood as the common system goal: the perpetuation of conditions required for the survival of "a very high civilization," on an inhospitable planet. A new township that is not connected to the Divlab network cannot let others know what help is needed or what help they have to offer to others. Survival on Anarres depends on cooperation and integration. This fact has been known since the earliest stages of colonization. In order to maintain "high civilization" there are necessary evils. The first city of Anarres is named "Abbenay," which means "mind" in Pravic, the native tongue:

> There had to be a center. The computers that coordinated the administration of things, the division of labor, and the distribution of goods, and the central federatives of most of the work syndicates, were in Abbenay, right from the start. And from the start the Settlers were aware that that unavoidable centralization was a lasting threat, to be countered by lasting vigilance. (Le Guin 96)

Furthermore, the relative autonomy of life on Anarres is bought at a steep cost; Anarres is functionally a mining colony for Urras. They export precious metals and imported "fossil oils and petroleum products, certain delicate machine parts and electronic components"—in other words, all the necessary commodities they cannot produce themselves. Because this deal works out to the advantage of both Anarres and Urras, it has remained stable despite occasional arguments in Anarresti assemblies. This stability does not prevent Anarres from looking like little more than an Urrasti mining colony. As Shevek's friend Tirin remarks, the truth of the matter may depend on which "hill one happens to be sitting on"—and, more to the point, on which planet (41).

The mining relationship between the planets complicates this system-level analysis. A reasonable argument can be made that the Anarresti society is merely a component in the Urrasti market system. Since Urrasti society does not depend on the importation of precious metals for its survival and the Anarresti rely a great deal on the importation of Urrasti items to maintain their way of life and standard of living, their relationship is decidedly unbalanced. However, Shevek discovers that these material exchanges between the planets are not the only points of contact.

Shevek moves to Abbenay in order to progress in his studies of theoretical physics and math. Through his professor, Sabul, he learns that the ships involved in importing and exporting often carry clandestine communiqués between Anarresti and Urrasti scientists. The Anarresti had long ago hermetically sealed off their borders. The Port of Anarres, where the import/export operations take place, is a closely monitored gateway in the "wall" between the planets; since the first-generation settlers were transferred to Anarres, no one else has been allowed to pass beyond the port. The literature exchanges function as unofficial technology transfers and act as an intellectual trading zone between the worlds. This trading zone is controlled and managed by the PDC, and Sabul acted as the consultant concerning communiqués to physicists.

Shevek's greatest hurdle both in his scientific work and in his socio-political efforts—which to Shevek are one and the same—is "the network of administration and management" known as PDC, Production and Distribution Coordination. Shevek explains its function to Oiie, an Urrasti, as follows: "they are a coordinating system for all syndicates, federatives, and individuals who do productive work. They do not govern persons; they administer production. They have no authority either to support me or to prevent me. They can only tell us the public opinion of [our Syndicate of Initiative]—where we stand in the social conscience" (76). As the mouth-piece of public opinion, the PDC functions as a crypto-governmental entity, Shevek's friend Bedap argues, in a society that supposedly has no leaders. The above quotation from Bedap concerns the efforts of Sabul and the PDC to oppose Shevek's scientific inquiry into temporal physics by preventing him from publishing his work. Shevek has apparently taken the maxim "publish or perish" much too literally as he admits to Bedap that he has "thought of suicide. A good deal" (164). What follows is an argument over the legitimacy of PDC and the checks and balances in place to prevent those who volunteer for and are lottery posted to serve on PDC from abusing their power. Even though Bedap, in moments, sounds like a conspiracy theorist, Shevek cannot deny his own frustrating experiences.

After learning Iotic, the language of A-Io, and reading smuggled copies of Urrasti scientific works, Shevek discovers that Sabul is little more than a plagiarist. As he explains to Bedap, "I read the sources. They're all Urrasti ideas. Not new ones, either. [Sabul] hasn't had a thought of his own for twenty years" (163). Moreover, Sabul "appropriated," as his own, the only book-length manuscript Shevek produced in his three years studying in Abbenay. The mechanisms in place to allow Shevek to engage in unfettered scientific inquiry are clearly dysfunctional. Shevek's access to a community of scientific practitioners—a system component necessary for scientific inquiry—is severely stifled both on Anarres and Urras. Therefore, the PDC appears to be a significant reverse salient, out of phase with Odonian thought.

However, classifying system components as reverse salients in *The Dispossessed* proves to be much more difficult than either *V for Vendetta* or *The Matrix*. Depending on where one stands—be it on Anarres, Urras, a Hainish starship, or on Terran soil at their embassy—any system-level perspective will be skewed. Furthermore, as Shevek comes to understand, how one understands a system in respect to its position on the temporal continuum of the past-present-future will also greatly affect what one considers to be out of phase.

V for Vendetta

The Norsefire government is called "The Head" and is composed of The Finger, The Mouth, The Eye, The Nose, and The Ears. "The Leader," Adam Susan, administers all of them and coordinates the Head's efforts with the unerring guidance of Fate, the central mainframe supercomputer. The directors of each department report directly to him. The Leader's goal is to "lead the country that I love out of the wilderness of the Twentieth century. I believe in survival. In the destiny of the Nordic Race. I believe in Fascism.... I will not hear talk of freedom. I will not hear talk of individual liberty. They are luxuries. I do not believe in luxuries" (Moore 37). So, the common goal of this system is to ensure survival of the "Nordic race" by strictly controlling the lives of its citizens. Because its early development is marked by atrocities such as concentration camps and high-risk medical trials on human subjects, it would seem that the architects of the Norsefire government will resort to any means they deem necessary to maintain their brand of ironclad fascism. V's violent terrorist acts can be seen as an equal and opposite reaction to these atrocities.

The Finger is the police; "Fingermen" are police-officers. They are highly feared and corrupt. Our first introduction to Fingermen comes when Evey is caught trying to sell her body for the ostensible purpose of being able to feed herself. They inform Evey, "you'll do anything we want and then we'll kill you. That's our prerogative" (Moore 11). The Finger has an advantage over the other members of The Head because they are directly feared by the people, a fear maintained through unchecked aggression and violence.

Another component in the system is the Voice of Fate, Lewis Prothero. Each day Prothero reads the report from the central computer over the citywide PA. The first page of *V for Vendetta* provides a vivid example of this ritual, exuding the cold logistics of fascist management. [Editor's note: graphic not included... see first page of *V for Vendetta*.]

Take particular notice of the precise weather reports. Because these reports are never wrong and are empirically confirmable by everyone, Fate would appear to be either omniscient, because it *knows* what the weather will be, or omnipotent, because it *causes* the changes in the weather. Fate's unimpeachable record on its weather reports lends even greater credence to its authority on resource management. Later on in the novel, the reader learns that the people of London believe that the Voice of Fate *is* the voice of the computer. V, of course, uses this belief to his advantage, as we shall see in the next section.

The Nose is under the leadership of Eric Finch, who is the only possible "nice guy" in the Head. He says early on: "I don't go much for this 'New Order' business. It's just my job, to help Britain out of this mess. You already know that, Leader." The Leader replies: "Indeed I do, Mr. Finch. You have expressed such sentiments before. That you are still alive is a mark of my respect for you and your craft" (30). The Nose is the investigative branch—a Central Intelligence Agency, if you will—and Finch is the most talented and top investigator. It is his job to learn to think like V in order to find him and stop him.

V, for all intents and purposes, is the most significant reverse salient within the infrastructure of New London. While at Larkhill, he was simply another component of the system, which, in many ways, helped Prothero and the others run the camp effectively. After he escapes, he becomes the system's greatest liability.

The Matrix

The common system goal of the Matrix is the generation and maintenance of the power source of "the Machines," human body heat.[1] This is why the idiomatic nickname "coppertop," as in Duracell™ batteries, is applied to those still plugged into the Matrix. To sustain life and maximize heat output, the Machines had to introduce a simulated reality to occupy their minds. Near the end of the film, we learn from Agent Smith that an earlier version of the Matrix failed because it was too perfect and was rejected by the human hosts. The Machines learned that they could not simply generate

---

1 Such a power source became necessary after humans had successfully blocked out sunlight in a last-ditch effort to cut the machines off from solar power. This clearly had serious, unintended consequences.

any surrogate reality; they had to simulate one containing the full spectrum of human experience from fear to love, from pain to pleasure, and everything in between. Therefore, the Machines decided to model the simulated world of the Matrix on an actual historical period, the late 20th century.

It is also important to note the reverse salients inside the Matrix. When Neo thinks he has déjà vu because he sees the same cat walk by twice, Trinity is quick to inform him that this "out of phase" experience is indicative of Agents changing something in the Matrix; cue fast-paced action sequence. Another reverse salient that becomes important in the second and third *Matrix* movies is Agent Smith himself.[1] The Oracle is another major reverse salient, as she exercises her autonomy from the system programming of the Matrix by aiding the rebellion. She has also taken into her care exceptional children who are candidates for removal from the Matrix. Because they are young, their minds are not as ingrained with the Matrix reality and will be more likely to accept the revealed "reality" of the outside. And, lastly, those who have been unplugged from the Matrix and rescued by the rebels of Zion represent a significant system liability to the perpetuation of the Matrix.[2] Only those who have been unplugged from the Matrix are able to jack-in to rescue others; freeborn citizens of Zion do not have the implants required to interface their consciousness with the Matrix.

Inside the Matrix, artificial intelligence programs, called Agents, try to prevent infiltrators, such as Morpheus and his crew, from freeing more minds. Agents have the ability to possess the virtual bodies of anyone hardwired into the Matrix. Once an infiltrator is located, agents often call for backup from the local police forces. Presumably, they can accomplish this easily by manipulating and controlling police communications. Because anyone in the Matrix can be possessed and/or controlled, there are no innocent bystanders.[3] This makes for a convenient black-and-white morality, which helps to justify the continually escalating level of violence in the film.

---

1 The first indication of this is when he is interrogating Morpheus while not wearing his characteristic Agent ear-piece. In the later movies he goes rogue and eventually possesses the entire Matrix in an attempt to destroy Neo once and for all.

2 Of course, this analysis gets turned on its head during "the Architect" scene near the end of the second movie, *Matrix: Reloaded*. In that scene, Neo and the audience codiscover the fact that Zion and the "One" are all part of the machines' greater scheme of system control. In fact, this is the sixth Matrix programming cycle. On all subsequent cycles the "One" chooses to sacrifice Zion in order to maintain a core of humanity to rebuild, thereby, starting the next cycle of the Matrix. This "One," whom we have grown to love, chooses to keep fighting a seemingly unwinnable battle.

3 Morpheus teaches Neo this lesson in a local simulation of the Matrix. A beautiful woman in a red dress distracts Neo, and Morpheus gets his attention. Then, Morpheus tells him to look again. Instead of the woman, there is an agent training a gun on Neo.

The Rebellion: The Seed of Revolution

> Anarchism is not, as some may suppose, a theory of the
> future to be realized through divine inspiration. It is a living
> force in the affairs of life, constantly creating new conditions.
> *The methods of Anarchism therefore do not comprise an iron-clad pro-*
> *gram to be carried out under all circumstances. Methods must grow out*
> *of the economic needs of each place and clime, and of the intellectual and*
> *temperamental requirements of the individual.* (Emphasis added)

> — Emma Goldman (63)

> Sacrifice might be demanded of the individual, but never
> compromise: for though only the society could give security
> and stability, only the individual, the person, had the power
> of moral choice—the power of change, the essential function
> of life. The Odonian society was conceived as a permanent
> revolution, and revolution begins in the thinking mind.

> — Ursula K. Le Guin from *The Dispossessed* (333)

> Turning and turning in the widening gyre
> The falcon cannot hear the falconer;
> Things fall apart; the centre cannot hold;
> Mere anarchy is loosed upon the world
> — from "The Second Coming" by William Butler Yeats[1]

Jacques Ellul writes in *Autopsy of Revolution*: "for *revolution* to be *necessary*, two conditions are requisite: first, man must sense to some degree that he cannot endure life as it is, even though he may not be able to explain why; secondly, the basic social structures must be blocked, that is, incapable of acting to satisfy express needs or of providing access to that satisfaction" (239). He goes on to clarify that this second condition exists in the structures of "technology and state" (239). The structures, or components of the system, which are "blocked," represent independent variables, sites where a protagonist's actions are entirely ineffective. This immediately brings to mind Hughes's seemingly irresistible "soft determinism" of large technological systems that have gained a good deal of "momentum." Rebelling against these systems is symptomatic of revolutionary desire, but rebellion does not *become* revolution; for a true "permanent revolution" to emerge, an Anarchist must dispense with rebellion. Or, in other words, rebellion must cease to be a means and become an end. Revolution, then, is equivalent to Goldman's "propagating uncompromising rebellion."

---

1 V quotes most of these words on page 196. A disembodied narrator voices the final line, "mere anarchy is loosed upon the world," as the authority of Norsefire rule dissolves into its final *climax.*

The Dispossessed: The Syndicate of Initiative

Laia Asieo Odo, 698–769

"To be whole is to be part; true voyage is return."

— Epitaph on Odo's tombstone (*The Dispossessed*, 84)

Shevek rebels against the social mores of the Anarresti people because he wants Anarres to open its borders to an inter-planetary exchange of information. Until Shevek and his Syndicate of Initiative built a station to exchange radio communication with the inhabitants of Urras, no one had ever *openly* sought discourse with the Urrasti beyond what was necessary for import/export exchanges. And, again, Shevek boldly defies convention, as embodied by the PDC, by leaving Anarres and traveling to Urras.

During the virulent debates preceding Shevek's departure, Le Guin offers particularly cogent discussions on Odonianism and Anarchy. While communicating with the Urrasti, Shevek and his Syndicate discover that there are "post-Settlement Odonians" on Urras who want to immigrate to Anarres. By proposing that some Urrasti be allowed in, they are accused of behaving "with total irresponsibility towards the society's welfare," which is exactly how "archist critics always predicted people would behave in a society without laws" (355).[1] Then Rulag, a vocal critique of The Syndicate, invokes the "Terms of the Settlement": "No Urrasti off the ships, except the Settlers, then, or ever. No mixing. No contact. To abandon that principle now is to say to the tyrants whom we defeated once, The experiment has failed, come enslave us!" (356). It is then that Shevek proposes that an Anarresti be allowed to travel to Urras.

By broadening the horizons of Anarresti culture, Shevek hopes to increase their ability to adapt to an uncertain future. Also, by allowing information to flow out of and into Anarres, he believes that other worlds may be positively influenced by their example. However, the crowning achievement of his rebellion is offering The Simultaneity Theory freely to all worlds.

Shevek's first major attempt to reach beyond the walls of Anarres, beyond even Urras, to the interplanetary community is a speech he delivers before the Council of World Governments soon after his arrival on Urras. It is "a plea for free communication and mutual recognition between the New World and the Old," and it is completely ineffective (84). In the words of Ellul, Shevek finds the avenue of direct diplomacy "blocked." Moreover, his access to the Urrasti public is "blocked" in that none of his speech is quoted in any newspaper. Some of the more "respectable weeklies" go so far to

---

1 The harshest criticisms against Shevek invariably came from Rulag, his estranged mother.

describe the speech as a "disinterested moral gesture of human brotherhood by a great scientist" (84). For Shevek to reach his goal, he clearly must find another way.

His second attempt at communicating his Anarchistic message to a broader audience is met with violence. He is co-opted into an ill-fated public demonstration of a group of so-called post-Settlement Odonians in A-Io. In direct contrast with his previous speech, where Le Guin provides her readers with *only* the audience response and the newspaper reports, Shevek speaks for three uninterrupted paragraphs. Before the audience even has time to cheer, military helicopters of the government of A-Io begin firing into the crowd. Shevek manages to barely escape this heinous act of state orchestrated mass murder. Fearing for his life, with virtually every other path closed to him, he seeks political asylum at the Terran embassy on A-Io.

Once at the embassy, Shevek explains his plan to disseminate his Theory of Simultaneity to the ambassador. "Do you not understand that I want to give this to you—and to Hain[1] and the other worlds—and to the countries of Urras? But to you all! So that one of you cannot use it...to get power over the others, to get richer or to win more wars. So that you cannot use the truth for your private profit, but only for the common good." The Terran ambassador responds, "In the end, the truth usually insists upon serving only the common good." Shevek replies, "In the end, yes, but I am not willing to wait for the end. I have one lifetime, and I will not spend it for greed and profiteering and lies. I will not serve *any* master" (*The Dispossessed* 345–346). Because Simultaneity Theory would make possible the development of an *ansible*[2] device, which would allow for instantaneous communication between any two points in space, it would revolutionize interplanetary communication and interplanetary politics. By sharing Simultaneity, Shevek takes the first steps toward creating a technological system to seamlessly *connect* distant societies across the farthest reaches of space.

V for Vendetta: The Land of Do-as-you-Please

[Editor's note: graphics in original; not included here]

Despite an almost fatal trial-and-error process, Shevek finds, in the Terran embassy, a political venue for satisfying his desire, the way *unblocked*. V, on the other hand, exists in a very different world—a world without embassies, a world without political asylum, a world without the possibility of justice.

---

1 The Hain are one of the oldest races of people. Because their starship technology is at an advanced stage of development, they are responsible for the majority of interstellar travel.
2 Ursula K. Le Guin's "ansible" shows up elsewhere in science fiction literature, such as Orson Scott Card's *Ender's Game* (1985).

This New London is a society governed by the cold hand (and Voice) of Fate. It too, like Anarres, was established in the hopes of ensuring survival in the face of a harsh and uncertain future. However, its order is maintained by surveillance, violence and threats of violence, imprisonment, and oppression. The cultural tyranny of the Anarresti society pales in comparison to the Norsefire regime.

In Book 1, Chapter 5: "Versions," a reader is offered two *versions* of "freedom" in New London. An internal monologue from the mind of Adam Susan, the "first version," is juxtaposed with the schizophrenic theatrics of V, the "second version," as he addresses the statue of Lady Justice atop the Old Bailey. One immediately obvious contrast is the silence attendant on Susan's procession into his command center versus V's dramatic vocal performance. This difference is brought into dynamic tension in each version's closing panels: Susan's monologue is punctuated by turning on Fate; V's is concluded with an explosion that demolishes the statue of Lady Justice.

This terrorist attack signifies that Justice, the "basic social structure" for balancing right and wrong, has become "blocked" under the fascist regime. In other words, the determinacy of Fate has trumped the intervention of Justice. In this context, V's Anarchistic terrorism becomes a *justified* mode of resistance.

From the beginning of the graphic novel, V is already aware of the intimate machinations of The Head. In fact, his primary goal is pedagogical in nature. By exposing the soft underbelly of the beast, he hopes to show the people of London how it can be killed, how enforced order can be brought to an end. He does so literally and figuratively by stealing the Voice of Fate, Lewis Prothero.[1] The next evening's broadcast by The Voice of Fate, Prothero's replacement, sounds queer to the ears of the people of London. They begin to doubt the omniscient, determining guidance of Fate.

It is implied that before the events of the graphic novel, V has insinuated himself into every component of the technological infrastructure—most notably the city surveillance cameras and the citywide PA system. Later in the story, the reader learns that V has accomplished all this by having his own proprietary access to Fate, the central computer system that controls all of London. He uses his limitless access to the departments of the Head to strategically plant bombs in key buildings. In one fell swoop, V disables the Head's surveillance systems.

In the prologue to *Book 3: The Land of Do-as-you-Please*, V has taken control of The Voice of Fate to tell the people of London of their recently acquired freedom:

---

1 Prothero was also, consequently, the former Commander at the Larkhill "resettlement camp."

The date, of course, is the 5th of November 1998, one year after V destroyed the Parliament building and almost 400 years after Guy Fawkes's failed attempt. So begins Book 3, Chapter 1: "Vox Populi," the voice of the people. V takes the Voice of Fate so that the voice of the people can be heard. Given the circumstances, this is not the dawning of a new age of democracy—or even Anarchy; it leads, instead, to a state of "Verwirrung." Chaos.

While not exactly depicting an "internal debate," the adjacent panels illustrate the semantic tensions and misrecognitions that make understanding "Anarchy" difficult. Evey questions V about the frantic voices coming over the police scanner falling into the common misconception of Anarchy as a state of Chaos. From V, the reader has already learned the difference between Justice and Anarchy, and now he offers a pithy lecture on the difference between Anarchy and chaos.

The Matrix: A World Where Anything is Possible

After Morpheus guides Neo through the painful process of realizing and understanding that his entire life to that point has been part of a computer simulation, he begins his "training." The training process entails uploading skills and abilities directly into his brain.[1] Neo's prodigious ability to assimilate all this data into his brain is implicitly linked to his hacking prowess. However, in his final test—leaping a great distance from the roof of one skyscraper to another—he fails, or falls, rather.

It is not until he understands "the spoon isn't really there"[2] that he fully understands: neither is his body. With this new self-awareness, Neo finds that not only can he make gravity defying leaps, but he can also dodge bullets. During his final showdown with Agent Smith, his "major technological transformation" is marked onscreen by a point-of-view shot from Neo's perspective in which he sees the green scrolling characters that signify the structure of the Matrix. Once he "sees" the Matrix, he realizes that he can manipulate it just like a computer program.

Neo and Trinity's violent assault on the building where the Agents are torturing Morpheus for information is nothing more than a cinematic smokescreen, a diversion from the true revolution. Had Neo continued to rely on what Ursula K. Le Guin calls "the mindless yell of weaponry, the meaningless word," he would have been killed (301). Once he becomes aware of the seams in the system, he can transcend his own bodily projection to interfere with the efficient integration of the system components and, as a result, the efficacy of the entire system.

---

1 Marked by that imminently quotable line, "I know Kung-Fu!"
2 This quotation comes from Neo's conversation in the Oracle's apartment with the young boy bending the spoon with his mind.

Conclusion

> More than any other idea, [Anarchy] is helping to do away with the wrong and the foolish; more than any other idea, it is building and sustaining new life.

> — Emma Goldman (49)

> A child free from guilt will grow up with the will to do what needs doing and the capacity for joy in doing it. It is useless work that darkens the heart. The delight of the nursing mother, of the scholar, of the successful hunter, of the good cook, of the skillful maker, of anyone doing needed work and doing it well—this durable joy is perhaps the deepest source of human affection, and of sociality as a whole.

> — from the writings of Odo (247)

The critical dystopia genre is particularly suited for exploring the ideology of Anarchism. Due to the prevalence of internal debate and open-ended conclusions, these works offer no clear answers. Instead, they offer heuristics for seeking our own conclusions. Furthermore, these works, as thought experiments, share an important quality of scientific experimentation: replicability. Each reader (or moviegoer) who follows the voyage of Shevek, considers the evolution of V, or traces the path of Neo replicates and recapitulates in a vital way the conceptual trappings of the thought experiment.

In the interest of not sounding like Neo, I will admit that the path of Anarchism does have a desired *end*: the proliferation of means. The greater the means we have at our disposal, the more adaptable we will be to a changing environment, increasing our chances for evolutionary success. Furthermore, any measure of evolutionary success will depend on environmental constraints and exigencies. This is precisely why the Divlab computers are necessary for Anarresti life, i.e., that they expand their capabilities without limiting free choice. This is why V turns off the cameras in dystopian London. This is why Neo's mind is freed from the Matrix.[1]

The most important lesson that Hughes's framework teaches Anarchists, and *experimental* Anarchists, is a simple one: the more momentum a technological system has the greater the effort required to re-direct it.

---

1 Even though Cypher offers an argument that Morpheus limited his free will by taking him out of the Matrix, I consider his discontent to be rooted in his own self-loathing, the resentment he holds against himself for choosing the red pill and not a desire for the lost *freedom* of "ignorance." Such a freedom is antithetical to the freedom of self-determination offered by Anarchism.

System intervention is most effective when a system is less integrated, less redundant, and still young. Technological momentum should always be tempered with flexibility. If Anarres was not closed off to immigration under the Terms of the Settlement, the violent clash between the A-Io government and the post-Settlement Odonians might have been prevented. If the Norsefire government had not systematically blocked and controlled virtually every public forum, then V may have never turned his back on Lady Justice. If humanity, prior to the Matrix, had treated artificially intelligent machines more equitably, allowing them greater freedom, the machines may never have revolted in the first place. By way of closing, I will now offer brief retrospectives on each of these thought experiments.

In the final pages of *The Dispossessed* the reader is not permitted to witness Shevek's return "home." However, Le Guin is kind enough to offer a stand-in: Ketho, the Hainish ship officer. Through Ketho—the first non-Anarresti to step beyond the "wall"—the reader is invited to participate in this Anarchistic way of life, but not on the surface of Anarres. Access to "permanent revolution" is granted by way of Ketho's refusal to accept another's experience as his own, his autodidactic dedication to a self-governed life: "my race is very old...we have been civilized for a thousand millennia. We have tried everything. Anarchism, with the rest. But I have not tried it. They say there is nothing new under any sun. But if each life is not new, each single life, then why are we born?" (*Dispossessed*, 385). Le Guin seems to reassure her readers sympathetic to Anarchistic ideals, that if millennia of Hainish exploration and civilization cannot eliminate the Anarchistic desire for self-actualization, self-governance, and freedom, then nothing ever will.

V for Vendetta ends after the rebellion. Moore leaves the future of New London open. Will Evey/V be able to sustain a state of "permanent revolution" in the city's ruins? Or, will another state institution fill the void of the fascist regime? The character of Evey/V does not promise a certain future; "new life" never does. It only offers a hope, a mere possibility, that freedom can be built and sustained for as long as we can will it so. On the final page of the graphic novel, Detective Eric Finch comes across Mrs. Helen Heyer huddled with some displaced "louts" next to a fire. She entreats him to help her "salvage something," that "given time we could build a small army. We could restore order" (265).[1] In other words, she desires to reestablish a government that can enforce conduct through the strength of its "small army" and restore the strict, inflexible "order" of fascism. Finch, however, is through with fascism; he pushes her away. The last panel is Finch walking down a deserted

---

1 Mrs. Heyer's sincerity is undercut by the fact that she calls Detective Finch "Edward" (265).

highway. Even though we do not know what he is walking toward, we do know what he is leaving behind.

The gross irony of the ending of *The Matrix* is the fact that "the world where anything is possible"—where one might, for instance, fly around like Superman—exists only within the Matrix. In this film, the audience is not permitted access to the *Holy Land* of Zion, the ultimate destination of those freed from the Matrix. Therefore, a viewer cannot discern the state of political affairs in this society. However, in the later films, the Wachowski Brothers backpedal on this promised "world without rules and controls." At the end of *The Matrix: Reloaded* Neo mysteriously develops telekinetic powers in the world of Zion, outside the Matrix. Even so, his newfound powers are limited by the constitution of his physical body, which does not seem to be the case for his virtualized avatar-self. In light of Neo's dependence on the technological infrastructure of the Matrix-world, his anarchism never extends beyond the scope of the present rebellion. Despite its clever title, *The Matrix: Revolutions* ends with Neo's martyrdom precisely because he fails to achieve a state of "permanent revolution." Instead, he *chooses* to preserve the power balance embodied in the technological infrastructure of the Matrix—in other words, he out-sources their present problems to the future generations of Zion.

References

Baccolini, Raffaella, and Tom Moylan, ed. *Dark Horizons: Science Fiction and the Dystopian Imagination*. New York: Routledge, 2003.

Brown, James Robert. "Thought Experiments." *Stanford Encyclopedia of Philosophy,*. March 25, 2007. Stanford University. Available: plato.stanford. edu. March 29, 2008.

Cox, Alex, and Abbe Wool. "Sid and Nancy." USA: Initial Pictures, 1986. 112 min.

Davis, Laurence, and Peter Stillman, ed. *The New Utopian Politics of Ursula K. Le Guin's the Dispossessed*. Lanham, MD: Lexington, 2005.

Fllul, Jacques. *The Technological Society*. Trans. John Wilkinson. New York. Vintage Books, 1964.

_____. *Autopsy of Revolution*. Trans. Patricia Wolf. New York: Alfred A. Knopf, 1971.

Goldman, Emma. *Anarchism and Other Essays with a New Introduction by Richard Drinnon*. New York: Dover, 1969.

Goodman, Paul. *Utopian Essays and Practical Proposals*. New York: Vintage Books, 1961.

_____. *Drawing the Line: The Political Essays of Paul Goodman*. Ed. Taylor Stoehr. New York: Free Life Editions, 1977.

Gould, Stephen Jay. "Kropotkin Was No Crackpot." *Natural History* 106 (1997): 9.

Hughes, Thomas P. "The Evolution of Large Technological Systems." *The Social Construction of Technological Systems: New Directions in the Sociology and History of Technology*. Ed. Wiebe Bijker, Thomas Hughes, and Trevor Pinch. Cambridge, MA: MIT Press, 1987. 51–82.

Kropotkin, Peter. *Selected Writings on Anarchism and Revolution*. Ed. Martin A. Miller. Cambridge, MA: The MIT Press, 1970.

_____. *Mutual Aid: A Factor of Evolution*. Ed. Paul Avrich. New York: New York University Press, 1972.

_____. *The Conquest of Bread*. Ed. Paul Avrich. New York: New York University, 1972.

_____. "Evolution and Environment." *The Collected Works of Peter Kropotkin*. Ed. George Woodcock. Vol. 11. New York: Black Rose Books, 1995.

Le Guin, Ursula K. "An Interview with Ursula K. Le Guin." *Across the Wounded Galaxies*. Ed. Larry McCaffery. Chicago: University of Chicago Press, 1990.

_____. *The Dispossessed*. 1974. New York: Perennial, 2003.

Longo, Robert. "Johnny Mnemonic." Written by William Gibson. USA: Sony Pictures, 1995. 96 mins.

Mach, Ernst. *Knowledge and Error: Sketches on the Psychology of Enquiry*. Trans. Thomas J. McCormack and Paul Foulkes. Boston: D. Reidel, 1976.

McTeigue, James. "V for Vendetta" (film). Written by Larry and Andy Wachowski. Warner Bros., 2006. 132 mins.

Moore, Alan. Art by David Lloyd. *V for Vendetta*. Canada: DC Comics, 1989.

Mumford, Lewis. "Authoritarian and Democratic Technics." *Technology and Culture* 5.1 (1964): 1–8.

Sargent, Lyman Tower. "Us Eutopias in the 1980s and 1990s: Self-Fashioning in a World of Multiple Identities." *Utopianism/Literary Utopias and National Cultural Identities: A Comparative Perspective*. Ed. Paola Spinozzi. Bologna: University of Bologna, 2001. 221–32.

Schmid, Alex Peter, and A. J. Jongman. *Political Terrorism: A New Guide to Actors, Authors, Concepts, Data Bases, Theories, and Literature*. New Brunswick, USA: Transaction Publishers, 2005.

Wachowski, Larry and Andy. "The Matrix." Written by Larry and Andy Wachowski. USA: Warner Bros., 1999. 136 mins.

_____. "The Matrix: Reloaded." Written by Larry and Andy Wachowski. USA: Warner Bros., 2003. 138 mins.

_____. "The Matrix: Revolutions." Written by Larry and Andy Wachowski. USA: Warner Bros., 2003. 129 mins.

Ward, Dana. *Anarchy Archives: An Online Research Center on the History and Theory of Anarchism.* 1995–2008. Available: dwardmac.pitzer.edu. March 2008.

Zamyatin, Yevgeny. *We.* Trans. Clarence Brown. New York: Penguin Books, 1993.

9. STAGING ANARCHY: ON ANARCHISM AND DRAMA

Jeff Shantz

Anarchist author, playwright, critic, and theorist Paul Goodman suggests by the last decades of the late twentieth century literature had become a minor art, more significant than pottery, but less than graphic arts. Cinema, radio, television, illustrations and music (of certain types) are now the arts of the greater public (56). Yet, in metropolitan centers, the stage remains a popular art. At the same time Goldman worries that it is no longer a literary stage. The emphasis has shifted overwhelmingly to the sp ectacle, the stars, the music, and production (56). Interestingly, those literary works that become objects of mass audiences tend to be dramatic—those that are cinematic in character (and destined to be made into movies, like *Harry Potter*). The vast *oeuvre* of Stephen King is but one potent illustration.

Anarchists have long used the means of drama to express opposition to values and relations characterizing advanced capitalist societies while also expressing key aspects of the alternative values and institutions proposed within anarchism. Among favored themes are anarchist critiques of corporatization, prisons and patriarchal relations as well as explorations of developing anarchist positions on polysexuality, non-monogamy and mutual aid.

At first glance it might seem odd to associate anarchism and drama, especially given the negative media portrayal of contemporary anarchists as street fighting vandals in response to "black bloc" actions at anti-globalization demonstrations. Lost in sensationalist accounts, however, are the creative and constructive practices undertaken daily by constructive anarchist activists seeking a world free from violence, oppression and exploitation. Yet an examination of some of constructive anarchist projects shows drama to be part of a holistic approach to everyday resistance, providing insights into real world attempts to develop peaceful and creative social relations in the here and now of everyday life. In various anarchist movements, drama plays a rich part, as brief look at ongoing anarchist histories show.

As anarchists, commentators like Emma Goldman and Paul Goodman hold strongly to the affirmation of community. Theatre is a big part of this community expression. Unlike cinema, in which the editor, the one who constructs the montage, is paramount, the timing of theatre is based on a collaboration of three—the actor, director, and dramatic poet (Goodman 115). Plays are inherently expressions of community. To be a proper playwright is to be in a company. Scenes can be tailored at rehearsals so that the actors (who are known to the playwright) might shine.

Anarchists have preferred theatre because of its collaborative nature and its dependence on a certain social capital (not financial) to be produced. As well, it is art that evokes, indeed requires, a public response. For Goodman, the play is neither something done by others while some watch, nor is it something that does something to the watchers. As an anarchist he prefers accomplices. As numerous anarchists argue, people will always make plays. It is an expression of freedom and playfulness. Children of very young ages put on shows for adults to watch.

The Anarchist Cometh: Anarchy and O'Neill

The intersection of anarchism and drama is shown significantly in the works of Eugene O'Neill. Indeed anarchism is the primary overtly referenced ideological influence on O'Neill's perspective. While O'Neill initially showed some sympathy for social anarchist movements, and looked favorably upon the writings of prominent social anarchist Emma Goldman, his primary personal commitment was to philosophical anarchism, which remained the greatest ideological influence on his thinking. Perhaps the strongest direct influence on O'Neill's anarchist perspective was Benjamin R. Tucker, the editor of the important anarchist journal *Liberty*. Tucker was the first prominent American thinker to identify himself as an anarchist. He would become the central figure in the emergence and development of philosophical or individualist anarchism in the U.S., introducing the works of Pierre-Joseph Proudhon and Max Stirner, among others, to North American audiences. Tucker was himself influenced by Stirner, being the first to publish an English-language version of Stirner's work. O'Neill was introduced to Tucker as an eighteen year old and spent much time at Tucker's Unique Book Shop in New York City.

The eclectic collection at Tucker's bookstore exposed O'Neill to experimental and provocative works of philosophy, politics and art that were not available anywhere else in the U.S. Many of the works had been translated and/or published by Tucker himself. Tucker was the first to publish in North America Max Stirner's individualist classic, *The Ego and Its Own*, a book that was quite influential on the development of O'Neill's political consciousness. Tucker published the important libertarian journals *Radical Review* and the highly influential *Liberty*, which became regarded as the best English-language anarchist journal. Tucker was admired by writers including Bernard Shaw and Walt Whitman.

A distinction is sometimes drawn between individualist, or philosophical, anarchism, with its emphasis on individual liberty and personal transformation, or communist anarchism, with its emphasis on equality and collective mobilization for broad social change. Philosophical anarchism places greater emphasis on individual freedom to act unfettered by the constraints of social mores and norms. Philosophical anarchism also differs from social anarchism in its distrust of social organization, including the mass organizing for radical or revolutionary social change preferred by socialists and social anarchists.

Philosophical anarchists understand anarchism not as a revolutionary establishment of something new, a leap into the unknown, or as a break with the present. Rather, they regard anarchism as the realization of anti-authoritarian practices of mutual aid and solidarity that are already present in society but which have been overshadowed by state authority. Anarchism is the extension of spheres of freedom until they make up the majority of social life. Starting from this perspective contemporary anarchists seek to develop non-authoritarian and non-hierarchical relations in the here-and-now of everyday life. It is philosophical anarchism, with its emphasis on personal innovation and creativity that has inspired artists such as Eugene O'Neill.

Tucker's anarchism, unlike that of anarchist communist contemporaries Goldman and Berkman, was based on gradual, non-violent, rather than revolutionary, social and cultural change. In place of force, Tucker advocated the liberation of the individual's creative capacities. Tucker looked to gradual enlightenment through alternative institutions, schools, cooperative banks and workers' associations, as practical means to enact change.

Social change, for Tucker, required personal transformation first and foremost, a perspective that O'Neill himself claimed as a great influence on his own outlook. At the same time, while rejecting force, which he termed domination, Tucker did assert the right of individuals and groups to defend themselves against.

O'Neill was convinced to abandon socialism for anarchism by his friends Terry Carlin and Hutchins Hapgood. O'Neill studied at the Ferrer Center in New York City, an alternative school organized and frequented by numerous anarchists, in 1915. That year he also served an apprenticeship at the anarchist magazine *Revolt* published by Hippolyte Havel.

A friend of O'Neill's Havel is portrayed as Hugo Kalmar in *The Iceman Cometh*, in what one commentator identifies as "a rather nasty caricature" (Porton 12). Kalmar (Havel) is given to jovial, inebriated rants, as in his "soapbox denunciations" ("Capitalist swine! Bourgeois stool pigeons! Have the slaves no right to sleep even?," *Iceman*, 11) which begin as wild declamations and wind down into sound and sudden sleep. He offers this view of the anarchist future: "Soon, leedle proletarians, ve vill have free picnic in the cool shade, ve vill eat hot dogs and trink free beer beneath the villow trees!" (*Iceman*, 105).

O'Neill draws attention to Kalmar's concern with maintaining a fashionable and neat appearance, "even his flowing Windsor tie" (*Iceman*, 4), and the actual poverty of his material existence as reflected in his "threadbare black clothes" and shirt "frayed at collar and cuffs" (*Iceman*, 4). Havel's life displayed the duality that has often characterized anarchist existence. In Havel, the aesthetic dreams of a new world, reflected in the cafes and salons was juxtaposed with the reality of poverty and precarious work as a dishwasher and short order cook.

Born in 1869 in Burowski, Bohemia, and educated in Vienna, Hippolyte Havel was a prominent organizer, essayist, publisher and raconteur within the international anarchist movement. Now a largely forgotten figure, even among anarchist circles, Havel was, during his time, at the center of the artistic and political avant-garde in Greenwich Village.

Among Havel's innovations was the development of creative spaces in which anarchist ideas could be presented and discussed, beyond the didactic form of political speeches. Influenced by the salons and cabarets he had experienced in Paris, Havel set about establishing such venues in New York, on an anarchist basis. Havel gave particular attention to nurturing performances of various types. Havel viewed such spaces as crucial to the creation of anarchist solidarity and community. Indeed this emphasis on the development of a sense of anarchist community distinguished him both from individualist anarchists, who stressed personal uniqueness, and anarchist communists who focused on class struggle.

For Havel, cafes, salons, dinner parties and theater were crucial for the development of solidarity among and between anarchists and artists. Havel viewed artists and anarchists as natural allies who challenged the bounds of conventional thought and action, a challenge necessary both for creative development as well as social change. He advocated the idea that art was revolutionary, not strictly on a realist basis, as would be the case for the socialist realists who would follow, but through experimentation and abstraction as well.

O'Neill also shared Nietzsche's disdain for state socialist politics, inasmuch as its collective forms expressed the resentment of the herd. Nietzsche disparaged the anarchists and socialists of his day who were motivated by a spirit of revenge or personal weakness and fear. Speaking with indignation at their lack of rights, such anarchists and socialists were, in his view, too lazy or fearful to see that a right is a power that must be exercised, their suffering rested in a failure to create new lives for themselves. Socialism stood as a new religion, a new slave morality, in Nietzsche's phrase. As in the case of Christianity, Nietzsche opposed the self-limiting, self-sacrificing characteristics of socialism that marked it as a new religion.

These criticisms are themes that appear in O'Neill's writings and statements on socialism, and anarchist communism, and are also reflected in his portrayals of these political movements in works such as *The Iceman Cometh* and *The Hairy Ape*. The slave mentality or sense that the powerless are more virtuous and thus must wait for an imagined salvation is reflected starkly in the hopeless longing of the characters in Harry Hope's bar in *The Iceman Cometh*.

O'Neill was also inspired by Nietzsche's views on art and theater and influenced by Nietzsche's view of Greek tragedy as Apollo's harnessing of Dionysus, the emotional element in life and art. Greek tragedy stood as the epitome of the creative force directing the passions (Dionysus).

Anarchists on Drama: The Critical Works of Emma Goldman and Paul Goodman

Among the important theoretical influences on anarchism and drama was Emma Goldman, the most prominent American anarchist. "Red Emma," whose works influenced O'Neill and who was herself influenced by Nietzsche, contributed important reflections on the relationship of drama and anarchy. So influenced by modern theatre, especially the works of Ibsen, was the influential anarchist Emma Goldman that her pioneering biographer Richard Drinnon was led to suggest that her anarchism was as influenced by the works of Ibsen as by the political writings of Kropotkin. Indeed, so interested was Goldman in the political potential of theater as a means for spreading and encouraging revolutionary ideas that her article "The Drama: A Powerful Disseminator of Radical Thought" makes up the longest entry in her best known work *Anarchism and Other Essays*. In fact "The Drama" easily eclipses other, supposedly more political works, as "Majorities versus

Majorities," "The Traffic in Women," and "The Psychology of Political Violence" that stand as recognized anarchist classics.

Beyond merely its length, the character of the article reveals the great value Goldman finds in theater as a possibly crucial aspect of "the tremendous spread of the modern, conscious social unrest" (Goldman 241). Indeed Goldman glimpses in the modern drama "the strongest and most far-reaching interpreter of our deep-felt dissatisfaction" (Goldman 242). For Goldman, drama allows for a greater appreciation of social unrest than can be gained from what she calls "propagandistic literature." More than this, however, the development of social unrest into a widespread and conscious movement necessarily gives rise to creative expressions, such as dramatic theater, "in the gradual transvaluation of existing values" (Goldman 242).

The anarchist critic and theorist Paul Goodman was himself an active playwright who produced numerous works in his lifetime. His output of plays includes *The Young Disciple, Faustina, and Jonah as well as several cubist plays.* Many were put on by the Living Theatre. Goodman expresses his love for theatre in deeply personal terms (which express a collective aspect): "To me, writing for the theatre is the only kind of writing that is not lonely" (140). Goodman speaks against babbling in plays and disdains prosy essays in plays that explain too much. That the speech happens to be about something is no excuse.

Paul Goodman admires especially the Japanese noh-plays. Whereas the movement of Western drama is an action, a character coming to an act, the movement of noh is enlightenment, a coming to awareness (for the character as well as for the audience). In the dancer is reflected the corresponding change from an apparent to an actual state (62). There is a state of realization, a subtle and indirect process of initiation leading to a moment of awareness. The anarchists generally prefer the progressive seeking and explaining of revelation to the unambiguous, and uncontestable, assertions of socialist realism.

Goodman even refers to his own poems as noh-plays (in a nod to Ezra Pound's suggestion that the noh-play is a long imagist poem). As in the noh-play, Goodman suggests that in distraction from the world, one can reach the intrinsic character of things (65). Goodman quotes approvingly from the opening couplet of *Atsumori*: "Life is a lying dream, he only wakes/ who casts the World aside" (65). At the same time, Goodman marvels at poetry that becomes drama: "the actual awareness turns into stage, properties, actors" (221).

While critical of the rigidity of social realism and the hardening of artistic production into format (sanctioned by bureaucrats), Goodman affirms a positive realism within his work. For Goodman: "There is no art without the real, and there is no excitement without the real" (65). In this, Goodman echoes the great anarchist theorist Peter Kropotkin. For Kropotkin: "In a good work of art the actions of heroes are evidently what they would have been under similar conditions in reality; otherwise it would *not* be good art. Therefore they can be discussed as facts of life" (311). This playful realism or realist imaginary is a key part of the work of the literary artist. According to Goodman: "The artist sets before us, and we attend to, what is lifelike, true, recognizable, like ourselves. But all this is set in motion again, in play in the medium, with freedom and imagination, and according to the laws of poetic justice. Then we are moved: what is out there becomes actual to us here and now, sensory and alive" (110). Drama offers a meeting of the imaginary and the real. Unlike the avant-garde playwrights, and postmodern commentators, Goodman "has not given up on fatherhood, community, vocation, rational politics, benevolent nature, the culture of the Western world" (141). As a social anarchist, he sought to maintain and extend the decent qualities of human interaction, such as mutual aid, while extending those qualities throughout expanding realms of human relationship and activity.

Contemporary Drama and Anarchy

Through the years anarchists have shared the enthusiasm for drama expressed by Goldman and Goodman as well as their belief that theatre is an important part of anti-systemic movements. Perhaps the most famous, and longstanding, anarchist theatre project is the Living Theatre which has been operating for more than 60 years. Goodman was a close collaborator with the Living Theatre. His engagement with the theatre included both the production of his plays as well as theoretical debates over the direction of new and community theatre. Founded in 1947 by Judith Malina and Julian Beck, the Living Theatre continues to produce and perform works that uses experiments in theatre to pursue themes centered around the interaction of political processes and forces of love and mutual aid. Addressing issues of authoritarianism, oppression and resistance in social and personal relations, the Living Theatre remains focused "on humanity's millennial dream of uniting these aspects of life in a cosmically inspired fusion that transcends the quotidian contradictions that have fostered the alienation that separates most people from the realization of their highest potential."[1] As an experimental political project the Living Theatre has directly confronted and contested these issues. Throughout the 1950s, in the climate of McCarthyism in the US, the Living Theatre's venues were repeatedly closed by authorities. As result

---

1 This quote comes from the Sixth Annual Montreal Anarchist Bookfair, May 21, 2005. During the book fair the Living Theatre gave two performances and was celebrated for its contributions to anarchism and other social movements.

the Living Theatre developed as a nomadic and collective effort pioneering new forms of nonfictional acting rooted in actors' physical commitment to using the theatre as an agent for social change. Dedicated to reaching the broadest of possible audiences, and committed to taking theatre beyond segregated specialist spaces, the Living Theatre has performed at the gates of Pittsburgh steel mills, at prisons in Brazil, in the poorest sections of Palermo and in New York Schools.

Among more recently organized anarchist theatre projects, the "Trumbull Theater Complex" or "Trumbullplex" in Detroit is one particularly interesting example. Located in the low-income "Cass Corridor" in downtown Detroit, the "Trumbullplex" houses a co-operative living space, temporary shelter, food kitchen and lending library. The former carriage-house has been converted into a live performance space. In addition to staging more traditional forms of theatre the Trumbullplex hosts experimental performances as well as providing a space for touring anarchist and punk bands and for public lectures. Recently the Trumbullplex has expanded adding a building in another part of the city. Significantly the Trumbull members uses theatre as a way to make connections with the working class residents of the Cass Corridor, offering a space for shared creative activities as well as a venue for spreading anarchist ideas and practices beyond the anarchist "scene." The activists and artists of the "Trumbullplex" are literally "building the new society in the vacant lots of the old," to quote a popular anarchist saying.

As exhibited in the activities of the Trumbullplex, anarchist theatres are liminal sites, spaces of transformation and passage. As such they are important sites of re-skilling, in which anarchists prepare themselves for the new forms of relationship necessary to break authoritarian and hierarchical structures. Participants also learn the diverse tasks and varied interpersonal skills necessary for collective work, play and living. This collective skill sharing serves to discourage the emergence of knowledge elites and to allow for the sharing of all tasks, even the least desirable, necessary for social maintenance.

Speech Acts and Censorship

By nature the arts are action-speech rather than simply speech about. The arts instruct in order to move, even if they initially move feelings. For Goodman, art moves and teaches, but it "does not move in order to teach, like sugar-coating a pill or seducing" (133). Speech is an act. It is a presence, a force, for Goodman.

In liberal democracies freedom of speech is taken to mean freedom to talk about. It is not meant to imply saying as action (Goodman 102). In heated circumstances in which there might be incitement to riot the freedom is curtailed. According to Goodman: "Pornography is forbidden because it is the nature of detailed sexual reporting that it leads to physiological reactions and likely acts. Blasphemy and obscenity are forbidden because they are acts as such, for they break a taboo in their very utterance, as well as presumably undamming what is held in repression by the taboo" (102).

Goodman suggests that the arts have been generally considered the greatest influence in education, in forming attitudes, and in shaping character (102). This leaves them more liable to be targets of censorship than, say, sociological reports or political analysis.

The central action of theatre is to tear away the mask of political, moral, and religious hypocrisy. According to Goodman: "It is the role of poetry and other humane philosophy to eradicate our superstitions and make us stop avoiding, skirting, shutting our eyes. To open our eyes" (75).

Goodman notes that "of the literary arts, it is the stage that has been the most heavily censored" (103). He finds the reasons for this to be instructive on the issue of saying as action. He argues:

> First, the theatre gives more material stimulation than the book: the offensive thing is not only spoken, it is acted out in the flesh. (The shadows of cinema, also heavily censored, are both more and less stimulating: more because they are direct fantasies, close to day-dreams; but less because they are therefore more simply masturbatory, less socially troublesome, private safety-valves.) Secondly, and more important, the actor on the stage is a representative figure for the audience, and he has already dared and broken the taboo: if my model here can do it, then I can and even ought to. Actors are intensely conscious of this responsibility, and it is often with the greatest difficulty that one can find a professional actor to play certain roles, for he must protect his reputation, as if he could not distinguish between himself in the play and in society. But most important of all, I think, is that the stage plays to a public audience not isolated readers; the audience shares the risk, the excitement, and the guilt, and it responds with the mutual permissiveness and seduction of mass-psychology that easily displaces the super-ego. (103)

Within contemporary liberal democracies and capitalist economies, censorship is less official than financial. Censorable works do not find producers. Even more the recognized likelihood that they will not be produced means that they often are not written in the first place (Goodman 105).

There is a concern that the work will result in a loss of sponsors and that theatre owners will pass on the work. The centralization of communication in corporate media means that criticism can be deployed to discourage censorable works. In some cases, fire marshals suddenly become concerned about the code in a fairly selective way.

Creative impulses are pressed upon by technologies and organizations that tend to conformity. The artists do not stir up the hidden or speak the unheard of and the audience puts its money to trivial fare (Goodman 106). The stage is rendered as "mere entertainment" (Goodman 106).

Even the great potential of the Internet is used up in cat videos, pornography, and online gambling. Satirical comedy currently consists of detached sketches and unconnected gags. One might only look at the last several seasons of *Saturday Night Live* or *Mad TV* to see the extent of this decline of satire. Comedy avoids mocking the key thing and thus cannot really mock anything.

Do It Yourself: Anarchism, Drama, and Arts Funding

A key component of anarchist perspectives is the belief that means and ends must correspond. Thus in anarchist drama as in anarchist politics, a radical approach to form is as important as content. Anarchist theatre joins other critical approaches to theatre in attempting to break down divisions between audience and artist, encouraging all to become active participants in the creative process. Anarchist gatherings, conferences and book fairs regularly include workshops on DIY theatre. Typically performances, often impromptu, are put on in the neighborhoods (often literally in the streets) in which such gatherings are held.

The DIY anarchist theatres survive according to their own voluntary labor, working in smaller or larger venues as available. They offer engaged non-commercial environments and opportunities to work with interesting material. Producing unfamiliar works, they are limited in receiving a mass or popular response. Without major reviews notice has to be built by word of mouth. This takes time and puts additional financial stresses on the production.

Anarchists reject the common liberal remedy for the problem of funding for the arts—money from government. As Goodman suggests: "Since the arts, like the poor, are worthy and neglected, there must be an Arts Council in Washington and a direct government subsidy" (125). For anarchists, government funding is a threat to new art. It also provides a misleading sense of the nature of both government (beneficent) and the arts (dependent). According to Goodman: "At best, officially sponsored theatre would be sanitary, uplifting, or mass entertaining; it could not be corrosive, political, or intimately vulgar and popular. Artistically, official support of *new* theatre would in all probability be positively damaging" (125).

The anarchist Living Theatre has been tirelessly committed to new theatre working to advance the art through often trying conditions without financial reward. Over the years the Living Theatre lost production spaces due to default on rent and taxes due to the costs of production (and Equity pay) and the desire to keep prices low. The Living Theatre sought to keep half of its seats available at one dollar to allow attendance by students, artists, poor people, and beats or hippies (Goodman 123). Throughout its history, right up to the present, the Living Theatre has benefitted through the donation of space rent-free. The Living Theatre held non-profit classification and sought support from foundations—which was generally not forthcoming. Goodman offers a guess why not: "It was rumoured that the Living Theatre's connection with the Worldwide General Strike for Peace put the foundations off; Julian Beck and Judith Malina (Mrs. Beck, the directors, were in and out of jail on this issue and civil rights; also the theatre itself was a resort of known pacifists, potheads, poets, and other punks" (124).

Goodman turns a sociological eye to the question of how social structures impact alternative and innovative ventures like the Living Theatre. He outlines the situation as follows:

> The essence of our modern problem, as I see it, is that the growth of mass communications, the centralized decision-making in the big media, their heavy capitalization, their concentration by continual mergers, the inflated costs for overhead, public relations, and highly organized labor, and the vast common-denominator audiences sought and created for the efficient and profitable use of such investments— these things pre-empt the field and make it impossible for small, new, or dissenting enterprises to get a start and a fair hearing. Even more important, the big mass media interlock in their financing and echo one another in content and style; with one tale to tell, they swamp and outblare, and they effectually set definite limits to what can "normally" be thought, said, and felt. (125–126)

Some call for the government publishing of classical national literature or the defense of state broadcasters. Anarchists suggest that while this may be suitable for some standard fare it does not address the issue of production of the critical, controversial, and innovative. Government consensus impedes the production and dissemination of the controversial and novel. Even more significantly it removes decision-making from the artists and their communities and centralizes it in undemocratic fashion in statist (and corporate) hands.

Anarchists note that justified suspicion of government power usually serves as apology for support for the expansion of private powers (capital) that are more powerful and even less accessible to democratic oversight. Such is the unfortunate situation of libertarian positions in the US and their drift toward the Republican Party and support for an unfettered capitalist market. Thus anarchists assert instead the importance of workplace and community self-determination and autonomy. This is expressed in calls for do-it-ourself production and participatory decision-making. Goodman insists on the necessity of cultural worker organizing. He argues at length:

> Let me insist that the principle of total theatre unionism, including Equity, seems to me to be correct. This is simply because of the nature of the theatre arts and crafts. Our city abounds in people of artistic talent, eager to exercise their separate talents. By disposition such people are free-lances; and the state of serious art in our society is such that, until they make a lot of money, free artists have little status or security and cannot easily maintain their rights and dignity. As a group, then, they are peculiarly subject to be taken advantage of and exploited by producers who can give them any work at all; and when taken advantage of, they act effectually as scabs and lower the standards of honest employment. That is, it is precisely the intrinsic virtues of the talented, their hunger to work and their solitariness, that makes them socially weak and liable to lower social standards. Poor gifted musicians, painters, poets, dancers, and actors are severally weak indeed; by insisting, even inflexibly and intransigently, on their union, one can give them collectively some strength. (118–119)

Here the anarchist concern with workers' rights meets the conditions of alternative cultural production. This is a concern that has motivated a range of anarchist alternative economic projects.

Conclusion

In the face of capitalist alienation and mediation of creativity, one of the options left is "to begin *right now immediately* live as if the battle were already won, as if *today* the artist were no longer a special kind of person, but each person a special sort of artist" (Bey, 43). So, anarchists make insurrections now rather than wait for their desires to be revealed to them at some later date. For anarchists this immediacy contributes to a widening of the circle of pleasure and un-alienated work.

Goodman reflects on his own position as such: "It is in this unhappy plight that I make a pathetic pitch for community in all my books, and also in these plays. I refuse to concede that out community does not exist.

Presumably, if it existed, it would solve my dilemma. But I'm certainly not getting any younger." (141)

Opponents of anarchism typically respond to it by claiming that it rests upon a naive view of "human nature." The best response to such criticisms is simply to point to the diversity of anarchist views on the question of human nature. There is little commonality between Stirner's self-interested "egoist" and Peter Kropotkin's altruistic upholder of mutual aid. Indeed, the diversity of anarchist views regarding "the individual" and its relation to "the community" may be upheld as testimony to the creativity and respect for pluralism which have sustained anarchism against enormous odds. Anarchists simply stress the capacity of humans to change themselves and the conditions in which they find themselves. Social relations, freely entered, based upon tolerance, mutual aid, and sympathy are expected to discourage the emergence of disputes and aid resolution where they do occur. There are no guarantees for anarchists and the emphasis is always on potential.

References

Bey, Hakim. *Immediatism: Essays by Hakim Bey*. Edinburgh: AK Press, 1994.

Goldman, Emma. "The Modern Drama: A Powerful Disseminator of Radical Thought." *Anarchism and Other Essays*. New York: Dover, 1969, 241–271.

Goodman, Paul. *Creator Spirit Come: Literary Essays*. New York: Free Life Editions, 1977.

Kropotkin, Peter. *Russian Literature: Ideals and Realities*. Montreal: Black Rose, 1991.

Porton, Richard. *Film and the Anarchist Imagination*. London: Verso, 1999.

10. What Things Could Come? *Xenogenesis* and Post-Anarchist Feminism

Michelle Campbell

How does one build a theory? In the sciences the standard procedure, broadly speaking, is to start with a hypothesis, build an experiment, test the hypothesis, and then refine the preliminary hypothesis if needed. Of course, then this procedure begins anew. How does one build a theory in the humanities? Often, we look to human behaviors, cultural artifacts, institutionalized structures, or "texts" in the general postmodern sense because we believe these things encode essential parts of the human experience from which we can draw conclusions. For anarchist studies, classical theorists like Bakunin, Kropotkin, Proudhon, and de Cleyre drew upon their personal experiences, the cultural codes of conduct they observed, and the institutions or formal structures which enforced these behaviors. Many contemporary anarchist theorists and activists still use this sound method of grounding their theory in the actions and events of the every day.

But what happens when we want, or even need, to theorize a world or community that does not necessarily follow from that which is within our grasp? In developing a theory of post-anarchist feminism (PAF), a theory that draws upon the fields of postmodernism, feminism, anarchism, post anarchism, and the intersections of these fields, I came to the conclusion that one of the only ways to draw out a theory whose aim it was to break open a schism that created an imagining of new ways of becoming was to turn to a world that simply does not exist. It was for this primary reason that I turned to science fiction literature to develop a theory of PAF. This chapter represents only a portion of the theory of

PAF, a theory that is still in its stages of infancy, and a theory whose lines of flight I hope will be taken up by others so that it can be expanded, beaten back, and formed in a rigorous critical debate. This chapter explores part of a theory of PAF using Octavia Butler's *Xenogenesis* trilogy.

An Introduction to Post-Anarchist Feminism

I originally set out to connect post-anarchism and feminism because both theoretical approaches have similar ideas about identity, the constructed nature of reality, and resistance (or revolution). Putting (post)anarchism and feminism in conversation with each other has yielded some very interesting points for consideration. Utilizing feminism within post anarchist studies has helped me to think about where post anarchism fails to extend its reach. Although post anarchism has produced sexuality-related thought, such as queer anarchism, it has, up until now, mostly ignored any traditionally feminist issues both in the historical anarchist movement (which some theories proclaim one the purposes of post anarchism is to interrogate classical anarchism) as well in contemporary (post)anarchist thought and activism. Issues of gender, sex, and sexuality are ignored, whether willfully or simply by the nature of the movement, within contemporary anarchist and post anarchist circles. In many revolutionary movements, "women's issues" are put aside to focus on the emancipation of the whole, but I argue that the whole can never be emancipated unless these issues are interrogated. Gender, sex, and sexuality are not women's issues; they are people's issues. They need to be at the table in our post anarchist conversations and our post anarchist scholarship. Introducing feminism into the field of contemporary anarchist and post anarchist thought has yielded new venues of research and lines of inquiry that need to be explored.

Bringing post anarchism to feminist thought has also yielded interesting results. By and large, much of the field of anarchist studies has had a bent toward certain militant or radical methodologies and conclusions. While there are certainly many feminist thinkers who are radical and revolutionary, certain strands of feminist scholarship back away from radicalism or radical solutions in favor of international approaches in regards to gender, sex, and sexuality. Post anarchism brings to feminism a sense that radicalism is back on the table, and perhaps, suggests to feminist inquiry that the only way to confront issues of gender, sex, and sexuality *is* in a radical manner. When I was thinking about how to name this theoretical approach, I had to think carefully about the implications of noun and adjective placement. I could have named this theory "post-feminist anarchism," with "anarchism" as the root noun and "feminist" as the modifier (which also would have allayed the theory with the post-feminist approach I rejected earlier), but I decided on "post-anarchist feminism." I chose "feminism" as the noun and "anarchism" as the modifier because the root of this theory rests in an augmented inquiry of gender, sex, and sexuality, to which anarchism and post anarchism bring new theoretical frameworks to help us consider how to look at gender, sex, and sexuality as possibilities for revolution, resistance, subversion, and other radical actions.

These ideas comprise the beginning of a theory of PAF, a theory that is emerging, but still not completely formulated at this time. The blending of post-anarchism and feminism to produce a new theoretical approach borrowing critiques and arguments from both yielded an interesting amalgamation of questions highlighted by SF literature. All of these ideas have one common spirit, and that is the spirit of possibility. Whether we seek to uncover the possibilities in our bodies, our sexuality, or the ways we can resist or revolt, these possibilities are shaped by both our relations and our ability to understand resistance.

The Happy Partnership of Anarchism and Literature: Genre Conventions and SF

Because I choose to operate specifically within the genre of SF literature in this chapter, it is important to situate Butler's texts in the genre history of SF as well as in contemporary SF. Darren Harris-Fain, in his book *Understanding Contemporary Science Fiction: The Age of Maturity 1970–2000*, provides an overview of the genre of SF and some of the unique features the genre can support. Traditionally, SF includes fantastical elements, but Harris-Fain is careful to explain the differences between SF and fantasy: "It is here that we are able to make our first real distinction. In noting that science fiction is not realistic, in the sense that it includes elements that neither exist in the present nor have existed in the past, science fiction is not an example of realism (either contemporary or historical) but of the fantastic" (3–4). He continues to explain that we should think of the fantastic as the major genre, which then encapsulates the subgenres of both fantasy and SF, respectively. This is because "Both are nonrealistic forms of fiction, but apart from their shared fantastic natures, the two are significantly different" (Harris-Fain 4). To this end, Harris-Fain contends, "By contrast, science fiction includes elements that do not exist and have not existed in the past, but that plausibly could exist in the future (or even, in cases as alien-contact or disaster stories, in the present) or could have existed in the past if the direction of history had been altered" (4). This distinction is important to note because it means that SF is grounded in events that could happen or in a realistic extension of events as they currently are, rather than in things that defy existing realities.

For example, while Butler writes of cataclysmic disasters (i.e. nuclear war), which are certainly fantastic, nowhere in the trilogy are elements of fantasy, such as magic or mythical creatures. The aliens Butler depicts are well within the possibilities of what we currently know about science and living organisms. But SF's unique features are not just in its contradistinction to fantasy.

Harris-Fain argues that SF's strengths lie in that it utilizes both the conventions of fiction as well as other genre-specific tools, such as scientific fact, extrapolation, and imagination (6). Writers in the genre are able to employ these methods to engage with sociological, historical and psychological factors within their texts. One result of these methods is a text that is at the same time historical fiction and SF. Extrapolation and imagination, Harris-Fain contends, "[have] led writers to explore the manifold ways in which the future might develop (which also helps to explain the abundance of futures to be found in science fiction, including contradictory visions)" (6–7). With such techniques used in conjunction with alternate history, "this extrapolation takes place using historical events, and with science fiction stories set in the present, writers imagine how the intrusion of some possible or at least plausible event might change the world as we now know it" (Harris-Fain 7). SF has the ability to create a simulation of what could happen or what could have happened if only certain factors or events had turned out differently, whether that difference is slight or significant.

This assessment of the genre of SF is similar to that of Robert Scholes, who argues in *Speculations on Speculation: Theories of Science Fiction* that SF changes with the concerns of society. Scholes explains, "In works of structural fabulation the tradition of speculative fiction is modified by an awareness of the nature of the universe as a system of systems, a structure of structures, and the insights of the past century of science are accepted as fictional points of departure" (214). At the same time, however, "structural fabulation is neither scientific in its methods nor a substitute for actual science. It is a fictional exploration of human situations made perceptible by the implications of recent science" (Scholes 214). As we see with the *Xenogenesis* trilogy, "its favorite themes involve the impact of developments or revelations derived from the human or physical sciences upon the people who must live with those revelations or developments" (Scholes 214). Butler's texts engage with this idea of an alternate history (or alternate present), depending on when readers read the novels. While Butler's texts presumably take place approximately two hundred years in the future, they could be possibly construed as an alternate present. Butler's trilogy allows us to experience a future based upon two significant events: nuclear holocaust and alien salvation.

As a final point in regards to the uniqueness of using the genre conventions of SF in general and why it is particularly useful to the project of developing anarchist theories in general, it is important to note the impact of creating alternative histories, presents, and futures in an attempt to effectively promote radical thought. Harris-Fain argues the radicalizing aspect of the subgenre of alternative historical fiction is important because "like other forms of science fiction, it provides a response to the question, What if?" (107). Specifically, "this question [in SF] concerns some matter in the present or usually in the future that touches in some way upon scientific or technological factors, or at any rate upon the notion of radical change" (Harris-Fain 107). Science fiction, as a genre, is particularly apt at describing and portraying radical change. This is certainly because the genre conventions, unlike regular fiction, do not require the author to stay within the realm of what has happened; rather, the author is able to branch out into what could have happened in the past or what could happen in the future. Thus, SF is perfect for experimenting with social conventions and constrictions, for questioning the way things are and the way they could or should be. Moreover, this experimentation with radical change, in terms of sociology, psychology, history, and other relational concerns, is particularly marked in utopic/dystopic and post apocalyptic sub-genres of science fiction.

Utopian and Dystopian SF

One of the primary reasons that the *Xenogenesis* trilogy is particularly well-suited to radical inquiry is that it includes elements of both utopian and dystopian narratives. In her recent critical work *In Other Worlds*, Margaret Atwood coins the term "Ustopian," referring to the intersection of utopian and dystopian literature. She writes, "*Ustopia* is a word I made up by combining utopia and dystopia—the imagined perfect society and its opposite—because, in my view, each contains a latent version of the other" (Atwood 66). Atwood explains that utopias are thought to be "good" places and no places, possibilities that may never exist; on the other hand, dystopias are thought to be "bad" places. Although utopias and dystopias are different sides of the same coin, they are, as Atwood argues, latent versions of each other. Utopias are places or worlds where everything has become perfect, or at least as perfect as possible. But whose perfect world? Utopias, when looked at from other positions or points of view, transform into dystopias. It could be argued that the general population in *Brave New World* was experiencing an unrestrained and drug-induced utopia, whereas, for the reader and the "other," the world depicted was a horrific dystopia. The intersection of utopian and dystopian literature shows that the line between the two merely rests on a subject position: it depends on where the subject is and what s/he believes to be particularly good rather than what actually is universally good, if such an abstract quality could even be defined.

As utopian/ustopian visionaries of the future, Butler imagines and ventures into new societies organized by other means than previously found in the history of civilization. Dunja Mohr, author of *Worlds Apart? Dualism and Transgression in Contemporary Female Dystopias* contends, "Feminist utopias significantly differ in terms of narrative content from male utopias. Thematically, feminist utopias shift the focus to female reality and to everyday life; they restructure the distribution of power within society *and* family and reject sex-segregated labor" (24). This is especially true of this trilogy because Butler's work is centered on Lilith's family and her place within the community. Mohr offers that feminist utopias "particularly emphasize gender equality, communitarian goals, decentralization, consensual decision-making, cooperation, education, and ecological issues, and they discard the classical utopian notion of growth and the domination of nature. These non-aggressive, non-hierarchical, and hence classless future societies challenge patriarchy" (24). These aspects of feminist utopias are seen in the way in which Butler's alien Oankali operate through sensory/chemical attachment to make decisions and strengthen communal as well as familial bonds. The end result of these radical practices is the creation of societies in which the protagonists put the health of the community before the wealth of the individual. Although the texts are utopian in regards to cooperation and strong communal bonds that emphasize the equalization of power, they also have dystopian elements.

The differences between utopian and dystopian narratives are marked. Mohr points out: "...dystopia reverses, mistrusts, and parodies the ideal of a perfectly regulated utopian state, often unintentionally inclined towards totalitarianism. Where utopia uplifts the reader, dystopia holds up a hellish mirror and describes the worst of all possible futures" (27). In other words, while dystopias highlight the continuation of the worst realities, utopias uplifts the reader by showing the positive possibilities for the future. Although utopias and dystopias have dissimilar methods, their endgame, Mohr argues, is the same: "Using opposed strategies, both utopia and dystopia, however, share the same objective: sociopolitical change by means of the aesthetic representation of a paradigm shift" (28). *Xenogenesis* depicts hellish as well as ideal conditions. Autonomy and freedom are compromised in favor of safety and security. In the end, however, the narrative leaves the characters and readers with uncertainty. What happens when humanity exists only as part of the genetic makeup of a new alien species? What rights do humans have when they are "proven" to be flawed and, therefore, are supposedly careening toward death rather than the continuation of life? These representations of the two sides of the utopian/dystopian coin allow the authors to complicate the possible futures that could extend from the present. Not only does Butler use ustopian (both utopian and dystopian) genre conventions in an attempt to show how current sociopolitical conditions can shape the future of earth, she also uses post apocalyptic genre conventions to highlight the concept detailing opportunities to start over after everything has seemingly been lost.

Post Apocalyptic SF

The use of post apocalyptic genre conventions in these two bodies of work is important because it sets up a fictional simulation in which new communities develop. This is important to thinking about PAF because it allows us to imagine the limitations of society and social relations and new lines of flight, which could offer possibilities of resistance, subversion, or escape.[1] In short, these works allow us to explore gender and social politics in an effort to see what happens when we try to start over. Author of *Postapocalyptic Fiction and the Social Contract: We'll Not Go Home Again*, Claire P. Curtis argues, "Postapocalyptic fiction provides flesh to the usual hypothetical imaginings of the state of nature and post apocalyptic fiction is written with an eye not to the academy but to the life of the ordinary reader" (4). Curtis focuses on the social contract, and on thinkers such as Hobbes, to explicate the interaction between socio-psychology and post apocalyptic genre conventions. I argue that there are two reasons to use post apocalyptic genre conventions in fiction, and Curtis details these two reasons:

> First, it works out the imaginative hypothetical of social contract thinkers in rich detail, although with little analysis. While fictional, post apocalyptic novels fill in the details of the state of nature scenario. Hobbes describes what the consequences of living in the state of nature are, but he does not fully describe who lives there or what the details are of their lives. [....]. The second advantage to using post apocalyptic fiction to think through the social contract is that it is written with an eye to the reader—the life of an ordinary

1 "Lines of flight" is a term borrowed from Deleuze and Guattari in *A Thousand Plateaus: Capitalism and Schizophrenia* used to describe an assemblage, such as a text. Lines of flight for Deleuze and Guattari mean the "movements of deterritorialization and destratification" (3). By lines of flight, I mean the possibilities of deconstructing realities, possibilities, and alternatives to determine what has happened and what could happen in the future. Butler's and SF does just this in order to show a different view of the way things could have occurred; this, too, is a goal of PAF when it comes to the constructions of gender, sex, and sexuality.

person on the ground. Postapocalyptic fiction is not written for an academic audience assessing the character of the state of nature and the potential contract that might emerge from it. It is written for a variety of reasons, not least of which might well be to sell books, but as a particular niche of fiction post apocalyptic fiction is often grounded in the day to day. (4–5)

This distinction between science fiction and post apocalyptic fiction as a subgenre of SF is important to a theory of PAF because such a theory involves a detailed look at the constraints and allowances of the social contract. Insofar as post apocalyptic fiction is not written for an academic audience, using it to develop a theory of PAF allows the theory to echo a non-hierarchical ethic: because the theory is developed from literature written for a general audience, the theory, in part, is rooted in the quotidian rather than in academia, which is important for a theory dealing in the questioning of hierarchies, established conventions, and power structures.

The Texts

Octavia E. Butler's *Xenogenesis* trilogy, published in the late 1980s, concerns an alien resuscitation of the human race after a nuclear holocaust. The first book, *Dawn*, follows the journey of Lilith Iyapo, a black woman who has been awakened on an alien ship two hundred years after the nuclear war that destroyed the world. [1] She learns about the Oankali, an alien race that seeks to "trade" with the humans; in return for the human's genetic material, they save what is left of the human race, cure diseases such as cancer, and intend to breed out their "contradiction." This contradiction, according to the aliens, is that humans possess both intelligence and an innate need for hierarchical social organization. It is the interaction of these two drives that have, according to the Oankali, led to the self-destruction of the human race and will lead to self-destruction again unless it is bred out. Once awoken, Lilith is trained to become the mother of the new race of Oankali-human constructs,[2] but first she is tasked with awakening many other humans who

---

1 It is important to note that much of critical and secondary literature concerning the *Xenogenesis* trilogy centers around issues of race, ethnicity, and slave narratives. Although I acknowledge that these are critical areas of importance and that Butler's texts are rich ground for these types of analyses, this chapters scope is informed but not directed by this aspect of race; instead, I focus on the sexual and familial interactions between the alien other and humans. These would be interesting questions for an offshoot of anarchist studies that deals with race and colonial/postcolonial intersections. This chapter *does* focus on post-anarchist feminism, which involves different but overlapping issues of agency, freedom, sexuality, and reproduction.
2 These Oankali-human constructs are the hybrid species resulting from the mating of the Oankali and humans, which involve a five person family: a female

have been saved from earth. These humans are trained to live in a newly altered and healed earth, an earth that has been regenerated with many new species of plants and animals after the nuclear holocaust by the Oankali. They are eventually going to be the foremothers and forefathers of a new race of Oankali-human beings. The Oankali, Lilith learns, are an advanced communal society whose space-ship is a living creature. The Oankali live in discreet family units, but are connected through the living ship; they can communicate through the ship's neural network. The Oankali have a special epidermic skin chemical that allows them to grow or reduce the ship (create door-ways, sleeping platforms, etc.), and thus they exist in a symbiotic relationship with each other and their vehicle. At the end of the first book, Lilith's partner, Joseph, has been killed by other humans, and Lilith's third-sexed ooloi impregnates her against her will with Joseph's child.

Book two, *Adulthood Rites*, follows Lilith's Oankali-human construct child, Akin. As a child, Akin, who looks human, is kidnapped by the Resisters—people who have chosen to live on earth without the Oankali. Because the Resisters do not want to take part in the formation of a new species, they are sterilized. Akin grows up with the Resisters, but he also misses very important bonding time with his paired sibling and the rest of his family—hindering his maturation as an adult. As Akin matures, he begins to see the injustices perpetrated against the humans, especially the Resisters, on the part of the Oankali. Akin advocates to the Oankali for the construction of a colony on Mars where the humans who do not want to breed with the Oankali can live and reproduce. Although the Oankali (through a consensus-based decision process) allow Akin to begin the Mars colony, they warn him that he is only killing the human race again because, with its contradiction, it is inevitable that the human race will once again destroy itself.

The third book, *Imago*, details the life of Jodahs, an Oankali-human construct ooloi. The ooloi are the Oankali's third-sex population, which has some very special talents. Jodahs is able to heal both humans and Oankali, and, when it matures, it is able to store vast amounts of genetic information from which it can draw to create new life. [1] Unlike other ooloi, Jodahs discovers that *its* form is unstable once it begins to mature. *It* is truly a gender and species shape-shifter. Luckily, *it* finds human mates, but its sibling is not so lucky. The human mates and the ooloi siblings travel to a Resister outpost where the people are still fertile, but have awful genetic diseases.

---

human, a male human, a female Oankali, a male Oankali, and a third-sexed Oankali called an ooloi.

1 I refer to the ooloi, or third-sex beings, as "*it*" because they do not fit with a heterosexual human gender binary. Additionally, Butler uses "it" in her text, and thus I also use it for the purpose of consistency. To avoid ambiguity and confusion, I have put the third person non-gendered "*it*" in italics as it refers to the ooloi.

The ooloi siblings are able to find fertile humans, and after being held captive and healing the people, are eventually trusted by them. At the end of the trilogy, the two ooloi and many of the fertile Resisters decide to stay on the earth, plant a new home, and become the ancestors of a full-fledged, new Oankali-human race.

This trilogy is rich with themes, issues, and tropes that may be of particular interest to PAF. The characters, relations, and tropes used by Butler in *Xenogenesis* expose conflicts within the matrices of a post anarchist theory, and each of these three aspects are in some way affected by gender or sexuality. For example, the character of Lilith is depicted, at first, as being a powerless captive, akin to an animal kept for breeding; however, as the narrative continues, Lilith gains more power and agency over herself, her Oankali family, and the future of the human race. Likewise, her son, Akin, problematizes the ethics of productive power when he is granted a colony on Mars for the human resisters who do not want to participate in the Oankali-human trade. Tropes, like that of the shapeshifter, as embodied by the Oankali-human construct and third-sexed character of Jodahs, represent an exploration of post-anarchist's *anarchy of the subject* through an *anarchy of becoming*, specifically in terms of the way in which gender or sex is constructed for purely reproductive means.[1] Because *Xenogenesis* presents a range of challenges and problems with reference to both post-anarchism and feminism (including queer theory), it is fecund material against which to test a post-anarchist feminist theory. Butler's work will also help to complicate the theory in an effort to provide avenues for reconsideration

Post-Anarchist Feminism and Butler's Xenogenesis Trilogy

Because Butler's science fiction (SF) texts are pieces of art I view as cultural artifacts, they reveal preoccupations and contemporary explorations of societal values. There is more than a twenty-year span between when Octavia E. Butler wrote the *Xenogenesis* trilogy and when post-anarchist theory became visible, with Butler's texts appearing in the 1980s and post-anarchist theory coming on the scene as a popular mode of inquiry in the 2000s. Curiously, that means that post anarchist and post-anarchist feminist thought may have existed in art—and probably in the general consciousness— well before a theory of it was articulated in any depth because Butler's texts are consistent with the interests of PAF. Butler's *Xenogenesis* trilogy is an important text against which to test, and complicate, a theory of PAF. As I discussed in the beginning of this chapter, SF literature is particularly useful

---

1 In his book *Postmodern Anarchism* (2002), Lewis Call uses these philosophical concepts to develop his theory of postmodern anarchism.

to develop a theory concerned with social issues, such as power, gender, sex, and sexuality, because it allow us to explore and experiment with different ways of living. Patricia Melzer, in her work "Beyond Binary Gender: Queer Identities and Intersexed Bodies in Octavia E. Butler's *Wild Seed* and *Imago* and Melissa Scott's *Shadow Man*," argues that SF literature is unique in that it offers other ways of looking at sexual identities and gender politics (220). Specifically, Melzer looks at Butler's queering of sexual politics through third sex and shapeshifter tropes in Xenogenesis, arguing that "Butler's ambiguous representations of the sex/gender/sexuality relationship destabilize power that relies on a naturalized heteronormativity" (241). This makes Butler's trilogy especially fertile ground for post-anarchist feminist theory.

At heart, the *Xenogenesis* trilogy is about the erasure of one civilization to ensure the survival of another. The *Oxford English Dictionary* defines "xenogenesis" as the "[supposed] production of offspring permanently unlike the parent." This is in contradistinction to the term heterogenesis, which is the production of offspring similar to the parent. Broken down into its component parts, "genesis" as a component of a word is defined as "forming nouns with the sense 'origin or development (of the thing or a kind specified by the first element)'" ("Xenogenesis"). "Xeno," as a prefix, can mean foreign, strange, or dissimilar; thus, while the term "xenogenesis" can mean the production of offspring dissimilar to the parent, it can also mean the origin or development of a foreign or strange species. Both definitions are accurate for Butler's trilogy, as Lilith's children are both permanently unlike her and the origin of a foreign species.

This term may have come from the hard SF Butler read while a budding writer. The *Oxford English Dictionary* gives the known first usages of the word "xenobiologist." All three usages come from SF texts Butler probably read, or at least knew about, and the *Oxford English Dictionary* traces the early usages of this term. The first is Heinlein's 1954 usage in the *Magazine of Fantasy and Science Fiction*, the second is Pohl's 1979 usage in *Jem*, and then in Asimov's 1984 *Banquets of Black Widowers*. All three use the term xenobiologist to describe the study of other life, life dissimilar or foreign to their own characters' lives. As an author, Butler is giving the reader the role of xenobiologist in her *Xenogenesis* trilogy, where we study not only foreign life, but foreign ways of living and interacting with other sentient beings. It is this experiment with foreign life and foreign ideas that gives us the perfect breeding ground to inspect our own naturalized conceptions, as well as seemingly foreign ideas (such as the offshoots of anarchism), within a controlled environment.

The setting for this experiment takes us to two worlds very different than our own: the Oankali Mothership and the Oankali-human colony on the restored earth. After she is rescued by the Oankali, Lilith becomes familiar with their culture aboard the Mothership. After the Oankali teach her how to train other humans to live with the Oankali on the restored but altered Earth, she starts a blended family, which produces Akin and Jodahs, both Oankali-human constructs who explore different avenues of power, humanity, alienness, and sexuality. As Lilith discovers when she is awakened on the Oankali Mothership, it is nothing like she has ever seen before. The ship is alive, and the Oankali and the ship have a symbiotic relationship. As Jdahya, the Oankali who awakes Lilith, explains, "There is an affinity, but it's biological—a strong, symbiotic relationship. We serve the ship's needs and it serves ours. It would die without us and we would be planetbound without it" (*Dawn* 28, 33). To Lilith, the ship outside of her room looks like a huge tree. When she emerges out of Jdahya's home on the Mothership, she sees that the rest of the ship looks like a huge tree whose limbs are heavy with fruit. Lilith discovers from Jdahya, that the food produced from the tree meets the Oankali's (and Lilith's) nutritional needs (*Dawn* 29). As she and Jdahya navigate the ship, Lilith sees doorways open and close with the touch of Jdahya's tentacles; she asks if the ship is intelligent, and she finds that the ship does have intelligence, but that part is dormant now; however, it can be chemically induced to perform certain functions, like growing openings, platforms, and rooms (*Dawn* 33).

When Lilith is sent to earth with the other humans and her Oankali family, her housing is an immature ship planted by the Oankali. When Tino, Lilith's eventual mate, finds her gathering food in the forest, she takes him back to her village. There, Tino berates Lilith and the others for living as primitive savages, but he does not realize that their primitive dwellings are actually an Oankali construct, similar to the Mothership. Lilith explains to Tino that their village is "a kind of larval version of the ship. A neotenic larva. It can reproduce without growing up. It can also get a lot bigger without maturing sexually" (*Adulthood Rites* 34). Like the mothership, the people of the village are able to control the walls of the houses. Eventually, in Butler's last book of the trilogy, *Imago*, we learn that these larval versions of the ship will one day grow into Motherships to take a new species of Oankali-human constructs to the stars—but only after ravaging earth to provide resources for growth and maturity. It is in these two major settings that Butler depicts the experiment of creating and navigating a new species and a new culture—a Xenogenesis.

Lilith and Sexuality

The character of Lilith is interesting to examine using post-anarchist feminist theory. Through Lilith, a post-anarchist feminist reading establishes that sexuality is not exempt from the reaches of authoritarian power. This is especially easy to detect in the interactions between Lilith and the Oankali. When Lilith first becomes aware of her imprisonment on the Oankali ship, Butler compares Lilith to an "experimental animal": "She was intended to live and reproduce, not to die. Experimental animal, parent to domestic animals? Or...nearly extinct animal, part of a captive breeding program?" (*Dawn* 58). The Oankali explain that the "trade" (of new genetic material for the Oankali in exchange for saving the human race) will make both species stronger and better; however, the Oankali have bred out of humans the thing that almost annihilated them the first time, which the Oankali consider to be their tragic downfall, namely the need for hierarchy. In this process, the Oankali have "fixed" the humans (which the Oankali consider an improvement) they rescued from post apocalyptic earth: the Oankali cure diseases and deformities and have extended the lifespan of the humans. For Lilith, this means curing her cancer at a genetic level to ensure it never reappears.

Lilith's sexuality and reproductive functions are beyond her control in this environment because she is controlled by the Oankali. Lilith first meets Nikanj when Jdahya brings her to his living space aboard the Mothership from her confinement in another part of the ship. Nikanj is a child ooloi when they first meet—a child who is close to reproductive age and who needs to find a mate to bond with. At first, Lilith does not understand this, but as she spends more time with Nikanj, they grow closer and intimate, sleeping together on the same bed platform and connecting with Nikanj's sensory tentacles. This intimacy is not necessarily consensual, and it is very possible that Lilith is suffering from a type of Stockholm syndrome, where she begins to see her captors as friends instead of adversaries. I address the implications of this later when considering issues of authority and power regarding intimacy, reproduction, and sexual acts.

As an ooloi, Nikanj is able to take DNA from different partners and intentionally "mix" the genetic formation of a fetus. The ooloi then implants the fertilized material into a female (either human or Oankali) to grow. Not only does Lilith become intimate with Nikanj without total autonomy or consent, for she is little aware of the impact or meaning of such a contract, but she has little reproductive choice or control when Nikanj impregnates Lilith without her consent. At the end of the first book, *Dawn*, Lilith's lover Joseph dies at the hand of humans who hate Lilith, but when Lilith reflects on his death, Nikanj explains that *it* has made her pregnant. Joseph was a man who was rescued from earth and awakened on the ship. Joseph and Lilith banded together as friends, and then as lovers, when the other humans had been awakened. When Nikanj confides in Lilith that *it* has made her pregnant, Lilith exclaims "I am not ready! I will never be ready!" (*Dawn* 246). *It* explains to her that she is ready to have a child, but Lilith is still horrified by the idea, and the concept that the child she will have will not be human, that "it will be a thing. A monster" (*Dawn* 246). Lilith is horrified at the idea of having a construct child (a child of both Oankali and human genetic make-up), and Nikanj's act of impregnating Lilith without her knowledge can be read as rape. While Nikanj insists that, although Lilith could not have voiced her desire for the child, she does want it—but the reader never hears that from Lilith, voiding any clear indication of consent. Lilith is forced to reproduce without her consent, thus showing that sexuality and reproduction, too, can be regulated by authoritarian power.

The familial, sexual, and reproductive assemblages Lilith finds in the Oankali community of which she becomes a part of falls in line with what I would call a post-anarchist feminist critique of representations and acts of sex within anarchist communities. A PAF theory explores issues of socio-political representations that subvert and invert the boundaries and barriers of normative behavior and practice. The Oankali, in many ways, are representational of an anarchist community, and their society can be read as a representation of radical politics. According to Hoda Zaki, "Among the Oankali, true consensus, non-hierarchical communitarianism, and truthful communication can be found" (242–243). The Oankali are only able to arrive at a decision through consensus-based decision making, they all live together without apparent hierarchy on the Mothership, and their communication using biology and chemicals instead of vocalized communication inhibits deception. For many anarchist theorists, these are markers of a radical anarchist society: one that values the input of all the members of the society and does its best to promote harmony and avoid coercion.[1] Furthermore, Zaki explains that "[a]dults communicate non-verbally by way of their tentacles, a mode of communication which does not allow for deceit for ambiguity; and they achieve consensus by totally coalescing with one another, after which they resume their separate individualities" (242–243). Zaki's analysis of the Oankali society is significant because it shows us that it is the Oankali's ability to communicate with each other like bees in a hive (without deception or ambiguity) that leads to a non-hierarchical, communitarian society that can be read as radical and anarchist. Practical anarchist tactics

---

1   An example of a communal or collectivist anarchist is Mikhail Bakunin and his creation of the First International discussed in the introduction of my work. He asserts in his document that "[e]quality does not mean the levelling down of individual differences, nor intellectual, moral and physical uniformity among individuals. This diversity of ability and strength, and these differences of race, nation, sex, age and character, far from being a social evil, constitute the treasure-house of mankind" (Bakunin 76). In fact, the members of Bakunin's new society, regardless of difference, had the right to provide consensus and direction in the community.

used today include non-hierarchical consensus building and, in some strains of anarchism, communitarianism, where the needs of the community are usually put before the needs of the individual. Additionally, although the Oankali originally destine the resisters to live a long, unfertile life on earth, through consensus, they allow Akin to learn about the humans as a child. Then, the Oankali acquiesce to his decision to create a Mars colony and restore reproductive function (without the Oankali) to the resisters. As a consequence of such an integrated society, however, the humans are left only with a representational politics rested squarely on the shoulders of Akin, who is "a kin" to humans but also part Oankali. It is from this consensus-based, internally non-hierarchical society in which Lilith is thrust as she is awoken from her stasis.

After Lilith becomes somewhat accustomed to the Oankali environment, she learns about the Oankali family structure. The Oankali have a tripartite family structure: male, female, and ooloi. The familial structure to create new human race includes five: Oankali male, Oankali female, ooloi, human male, and human female. The ooloi is extremely important when it comes to reproduction. Males and females, whether they are Oankali or human, succumb to the material of the ooloi, thus rendering the heterosexual pairs repulsive to touching each other. Lilith first experiences a tri-sexual union when she is mated with Joseph. The ooloi, Nikanj, lies between the male and female, merging with their central nervous systems. The narrator describes the sexual experience as delightful: "They moved together, sustaining an impossible intensity, both of them tireless, perfectly matched, ablaze in sensation, lost in one another. They seemed to rush upward. A long time later, they seemed to drift down slowly, gradually, savoring a few more moments wholly together" (163). During this sexual act, the ooloi is able to heal as well as abscond with genetic material in order to form a fertilized embryo for implantation in either an Oankali female or a human female. Lilith is aware of this when she is first impregnated by Nikanj, but she thought they had an understanding that she would only become pregnant when she was ready to do so. The Oankali-human fashion of reproduction requires trust and faith that the ooloi will not impregnate the female when she does not want to be—and this would seem to coincide with the Oankali's inability to deceive; however, as we see with Lilith, Nikanj impregnates her when it thinks she is ready, not when she voices consent. While this is not necessarily deceptive, it is coercive and defies a mutual understanding of informed consent and autonomy. Nikanj's decision and act of impregnating Lilith also suggests that the ooloi knows Lilith better than she knows herself.

Butler's creation of these familial structures and sexual assemblages are at the core of a PAF critique of sexual representation. While the family structure seems foreign because of the ooloi third-sex as well as the alien and human mating pairs, there is still an outstanding level of normativity both within the human relations as well as within the Oankali relations. As such, although the family and sexual relations of these pairings subvert some boundaries, they also create an anarchonormativity—meaning these relations are normative, albeit within a subversive context. For example, although a three or five member reproductive community is strange in terms of both human and Oankali practice, both pairs of humans and Oankali are heterosexual. There is little room for non-heteronormative sexual relations within the subversive structure, save for the third-sexed ooloi. Furthermore, the families are in a committed polyamorous relationship. Once an ooloi has mated with a pair of humans or Oankali, they are chemically bound to each other—and the ooloi suffers, and could even die, from lack of contact with its mates. This is an interesting invention, as it prevents the degradation of the family structure. These are family bonds that certainly cannot be broken without dire consequences. Although the family structure is subversive because it incorporates more than two people and more than two sexes or genders, the normative structure of a committed family with defined social and sexual interactions is still a requirement of such relations. While PAF theory is helpful for examining the imposition of reproduction, familial, and sexual structures in the text, Butler's texts contain marked challenges to some of the precepts of PAF that I established earlier concerning issues of agency, manipulation, and the influence of traditions from modern Western thought within the text.

Lilith encounters several problematic situations whereby manipulation is used to inhibit her agency. One example is when Lilith is told by Nikanj that she must undergo a procedure to alter her brain chemistry so she will remember things better. Lilith is already a prisoner on the living ship, but she is allowed some freedoms. Nikanj gives her a choice, and somewhat respects her agency, although the assumption is that the choice should be easy to make: through violation, Lilith will become a more perfect being. Nikanj gives Lilith the illusion of choice, although she knows that the procedure will happen eventually, and, according to Nikanj, it will modify her brain chemistry (*Dawn* 74). This is significant because the alteration of her brain chemistry makes Lilith less human and more like the Oankali; in a way, Lilith is becoming a *cyborg*—a fusion of human DNA improved with alien technology. Lilith forces herself to make the decision, and she allows Nikanj to perform the procedure on her (*Dawn* 78). The problem is that Lilith did not have a choice, and, although the procedure was for the "betterment" of her life, it was done through unethical means, which the Oankali do not seem to find problematic in their nonhierarchical and powerfully acquisitive society (Butler 39). Other examples include the mating Lilith undergoes with Nikanj, not understanding the full implications when *it* would inject substances in her body that would biologically link them together for the rest of their lives. Lilith is unable to make an informed decision about the procedure because she was not aware of the full implications; it is not until after the procedure that she begins to realize what Nikanj failed (or perhaps was not able to) reveal, namely that she and *it* would be biologically linked until death. Agency is also a problem when Nikanj impregnates Lilith without her knowledge and explicit consent, even though Nikanj argues that Lilith really did want to carry Joseph's child. It is through manipulation, and the illusion of choice, that Lilith's agency is compromised.

Butler purposefully uses the name Lilith for her main female character in this trilogy, and it is a name that comes with the weight of tradition and several implications. The archetype of and allusion to the name "Lilith" has a long-standing history in the western tradition. According to Michele Osherow in "The Dawn of a New Lilith: Revisionary Mythmaking in Women's Science Fiction," the Lilith archetype is an allusion to the first wife of Adam in Judaic biblical tradition. Osherow argues that the archetype of Lilith often oscillates between "images of wicked temptress and fond mother," but also that, through Lilith, "women's science fiction presents a new feminine image, one reflecting a diversification of women's roles in contemporary culture" (68). As Adam's first wife, Lilith was created from the earth and refused to be unequal to Adam. Because Lilith valued "independence above male companionship," she left "Adam and Eden" (Osherow 70). While Lilith is often depicted as evil because, as legend states, she "joined forces with Satan and gave birth to armies of devil children," Osherow argues that Lilith takes the form of an alien archetype because she is "immortal, powerful, strong, feared, [and] sexual" (Osherow 70-71). Osherow explains that representations of Lilith, especially in SF literature, help to create a more complex female character. She writes:

> The Liliths we meet in [SF] works are not ideal as mothers, lovers, or alien others. Instead, they demonstrate women's ambition and ability to support others without sacrificing or disempowering themselves. These new myths move Lilith into a respected and essential category of female representations that is difficult to dismiss [.....] Thus, the myth of Lilith continues to indicate the history of the age in which it is given shape. For the first time, however, Lilith depicts an era of women who are ambitious yet human, independent yet social, and by and large, splendidly complex. (81)

In other words, authors like Butler uses revisions of archetypes imbedded in traditional Western thought in order to subvert or invert the boundaries concerning gender expectations. It is by engaging with the demonized "Lilith" archetype that Butler can show another way of becoming a woman enmeshed within a strange, but familiar, network of manipulative power relations that hinder agency. Furthermore, the symbolic weight the archetype of "Lilith" brings to the table allows Butler to leave many things unsaid. Although the Oankali want Lilith to be the mother of a new race and to retrain humans to live in a rehabilitated earth, she finds it difficult to live up to the Oankali's expectations for her to take on the roles of nurturance and leadership. In addition, she finds that her efforts to help the human survivors adjust to their new lives often create resentment and anger toward her. Her best advice to her fellow humans is to "learn and run," something she finds difficult to do herself, just as the archetypal Lilith ran from Adam and Eden (*Dawn* 248). It is not until the later books that Lilith seems to be somewhat accustomed to her living arrangements with her Oankali-human family, but Butler never really returns to Lilith's point of view for the reader to be able to determine if Lilith has accepted her role as mother and sex-mate, or if she has simply acquiesced to the role due to lack of choice.

Akin and Productive Power

Similar to the character of Lilith, the character of her Oankali-Human construct son Akin helps us think about PAF. The character of Akin demonstrates two veins of a post-anarchist feminist theory: the reaches of authoritarian power in sexuality and an *anarchy of sexuality* through an *anarchy of becoming*. Akin realizes the reaches of authoritarian power into the sexual lives of the human resisters after he is left to live with them for many years during his childhood. Tate, a resister, explains to Akin why their worlds have fallen into violence after the Oankali "rescue." She suggests that "[t]hey got sick of one pointless, endless existence and chose another," and Akin responds, "Pointless because resisters can't have children?" (*Adulthood Rites* 157-158). Tate confirms this when she replies, "That's it. It means a lot more than I could ever explain to you. We don't get old. We don't have kids, and nothing we do means shit" (*Adulthood Rites* 158). For the human resisters who have been sterilized by the Oankali, not having children gives them no future and nothing to look forward to unlike their "Trade-Village" human counterparts, who live with the Oankali and raise construct children. After this exchange, Akin realizes the Oankali have sterilized the human resisters to prevent another holocaust. The Oankali solution to the problem of the human resisters, to sterilize them so they cannot continue having children that will one day destroy themselves, is cruel. Butler writes:

> Who among the Oankali was speaking for the interests of resister Humans? Who had seriously considered that it might not be enough to let Humans choose either union with the Oankali or sterile lives free of the Oankali? Trade-village Humans said it, but they were so flawed, so genetically contradictory that they were often not listened to. [Akin] did not have their flaw. He had been assembled within the body of an ooloi. He was Oankali enough to be listened to by other Oankali and Human enough to know that resister Humans were being treated with cruelty and condescension. (*Adulthood Rites* 159)

Akin's realization that the humans are being treated inhumanely is the catalyst for his request to create a Mars colony where humankind could start over. His request is granted through a consensus-based decision making process with the Oankali Mothership. Now, humans have a choice to live and mate with the Oankali or live on the Mars colony, which will leave them free to reproduce, but will be a hard life with no promises. These life choices for the humans are regulated purely through sexuality and reproduction—do they want to have construct children or human children? This is significant because the humans continue to have little agency after the Mars colony is created. Instead of having more choice, it is only the illusion of choice that is expanded for them. And it is through this choice that the authoritarian Oankali use their power to regulate the lives, sexuality, and reproductive choices of the human race. What remains problematic for people in this position is the role of responsibility, guilt, and free-will. Does the illusion of choice negate guilt of a restrictive authoritarian regime? Is responsibility for an individual's well-being shifted back to the individual, or does it remain vested with the authoritarian regime?

Akin also represents an *anarchy of becoming* through an *anarchy of sexuality*. Although Akin is male, he is also a construct—a combination of both Oankali and Human genetics. An ooloi subadult explains to him: "You're more Oankali than you think, Akin—and far more Oankali than you look. Yet you're very Human. You skirt as close to the Contradiction as anyone has dared to go. You're as much of them as you can be and as much of us as your ooan dared make you. That leaves you with your own contradiction" (*Adulthood Rites* 233). [1,2] Akin is one of the first male constructs who grew up with human looks, and his time with the human resisters helped him to

---

1 A subadult is an Oankali, or an Oankali-human construct, that has gone through the first phase of metamorphosis, but not the second. Although some characters in the book compare this stage to human adolescence, others counter that it is not entirely accurate as a subadult cannot reproduce like a human adolescent can.

2 In the Oankali family structure, an ooan is the ooloi parent. The ooloi is responsible for assembling the genetic make-up of the children before it is implanted in a female body to develop into a fetus.

become more sympathetic to humans than he would have growing up with his family composed of humans and Oankalis. The ooloi continues to tell Akin, "You aren't flawed. I noticed even before I went to my parents that there was a wholeness to you—a strong wholeness. I don't know whether you'll be what your parents wanted you to be, but whatever you become, you'll be complete. You'll have within yourself everything you need to content yourself. Just follow what seems right to you" (*Adulthood Rites* 223). Akin is unsure of his place and his identity, but the ooloi reassures him that these things are inconsequential: he has everything he needs to become a full-functioning adult. His uncertainties stem from his multiplicity, because he is both alien and human, but not exactly either. Akin represents an *anarchy of becoming* because he is one of the first male Oankali-human construct children to be born and grow up. Furthermore, because of his time spent in captivity with the human resisters, he struggles to find himself between his Oankali and human composition. This translates into an *anarchy of sexuality* when he learns that, because of his development of becoming something different than either his Oankali or human parents, he no longer needs to fit into an Oankali familial relation to survive. Akin is a loner; he literally can survive on his own. This is unheard of for the Oankali, who have a very normative stance on how sexuality should operate within a structure of family relations. Akin's *anarchy of sexuality* through an apparent asexuality (or at the very least the ability to be asexual, which other Oankali appear not to be able to engage with), allows Akin to subvert the normative Oankali behaviors of sexual relations within family structures.[1] By asexuality, I mean that Akin is able to live his life without finding a mate with whom to bond, and he is not genetically driven to reproduce or exercise his sexuality in any manner. Arguably, Akin's ability to be sexually anarchic affords him extreme agency not normally found in an Oankali society; therefore, he is able to administer productive power that allows the human resisters to live as ethically as possible on the Mars colony, albeit within the constraints of the Oankali authoritarian regime.

Akin problematizes an ethics of productive power, resistance, and an Oankali-produced ontology of the human race when he is granted the ability to construct a colony on Mars for the human resisters who do not want to

---

1 In terms of anarchist theory, this split between communal sexuality and asexuality mirrors two different strains of anarchist theory. The first, communal anarchy, requires that the individual consent to the legitimate authority of the community, and she or he abides by communal decisions, often putting the community's needs before the needs of the individual. The second, individualist anarchism, heralds the authority of the individual before all others. In Akin's case, he is can survive outside of the community, making him an individualist anarchist, and is able to put his individuality before that of any community or familial group.

participate in the Oankali-human trade. Because of Akin's use of productive power to aid in human resistance to the Oankali authoritarian regime and subvert Oankali ontology of the Contradiction, Akin shows the connections between power and sexuality. I argue that the basis of the Oankali's authoritarianism rests in the fact that they have totalizing control over the humans' reproduction, although Butler makes it clear that that the Oankali do not feel what they are doing is coercive. By creating the Mars colony, Akin subverts the ontology of the Contradiction and restores the choice of human reproduction to the colonizers in a creative act of making them fertile again. This restoration of fertility embraces resistance and subversion of oppression. By examining the character of Akin, we can see that his character can give us some ideas to flesh out and complicate PAF, like his innovative resistance against the hegemonic force of the Oankali collective. PAF needs to encompass issues of productive power, resistance, and ontology within its framework because they are critical to understanding sex, gender, and sexuality.

Jodahs the Shapeshifter

Arguably, the character of Jodahs, from the third book *Imago*, has the most to offer a theory of PAF. Like Lilith and Akin, Jodahs experiences the reaches of authoritarian power into the realm of sexuality because of the threat of exile to the Mothership of the Oankali upon the realization that *it* would grow up to be an ooloi construct. As an Oankali-human construct, Jodahs realizes that it is the first ooloi construct to be born. Before Jodahs, the other Oankali-human constructs developed into either females or males. Jodahs, however, will develop into a third-sexed individual like Nikanj. Because *it* is the first third-sex construct, *its* metamorphosis is unknown, and, because ooloi have powers to heal through radically changing body chemistry, the Oankali fear that Jodahs could be dangerous. Metamorphosis for the construct children is like going through adolescence: they mature and develop sexually. Jodahs could be dangerous after *it* experiences metamorphosis because *it* will have additional powers that could be used to hurt others. Because Jodahs could be dangerous, they want to send *it* to the Mothership before it experiences metamorphosis. There, the Oankali can ensure *its* safety as well as the safety of those around *it*. Jodahs explains, "If, someday, Nikanj saw that I needed mates more than I needed my family, Nikanj would send me to the ship no matter what I said" (*Imago* 32). The danger represented by Jodahs's sexual development trumps its autonomy. Still, Jodahs does not want to leave earth: "It was only the thought of going to Chkahichdahk [the Mothership], and being kept there, that made me feel caged and frantic" (*Imago* 91). Curiously,

Jodahs is not being exiled from earth for any other reason than *it* represents a dangerous sexuality, a sexuality that, until *it* has been proven that it can operate successfully within the established societal organization, must be contained and guarded. It is Jodahs's non-normative sexuality as a third-sex Oankali-human construct that exemplifies the ways in which authoritarian power regulates sexualities deemed dangerous or subversive to the social organization.

Jodahs's character enables a critique of the representations and acts of sex within the Oankali's anarchist community. Jodahs's sexuality represents danger to the Oankali because they do not know exactly what will happened when it matures sexually: *its* sexuality subverts and inverts the boundaries and barriers of normative behavior and practice. For example, *its* mates Tomás and Jesusa are brother and sister, a relationship which subverts normative behavior. Normally, a sexual mating between a brother and sister would be considered incestuous and, if not morally wrong, socially repulsive; however, since the pair come from a society where incest is needed for the survival of the community, and their fears of having deformed children are put to rest by the fact that Jodahs will 1) genetically craft future children and 2) facilitate in sexual relations in which the brother and sister will never touch, incest becomes socially acceptable. Not only does Jodahs facilitate a critique of the representation of normative behavior within an anarchist community, *its* relationship with Tomás and Jesusa exemplifies what I am calling "erotic productive power."

Although many writers use the term "erotic power" in critiques of the power inherent in sexual relations, desires, and exchanges of passion, it is uncertain whether there is a clear definition of this term. What I mean by the term "erotic power" are the power relations inherent, assumed, or created concerning sexual and/or reproductive acts. Erotic productive power, then, would borrow the Foucauldian post-anarchist capillaristic and rhizomatic conceptualization of power in order to describe how power relations concerning erotic acts could be both productive and destructive. This also implies that mechanisms of resistance can be employed through erotic acts, thus destabilizing barriers and boundaries meant to regulate normative behaviors. Thus, erotic productive power is important to a post-anarchist feminist project because it is another line of flight to examine, critique, resist, and perhaps change current socio-political relations.

Relations of erotic productive power come into play when Jodahs "saves" Tomás and Jesusa because their three-member relationship employs mechanisms of resistance through erotic acts. The siblings had run away from their resister community to avoid forced marriages. Each member of the tripartite relationship is using the relationship to resist something different, although each person's resistance is to a normative structure or authoritarian power. For example, Jodahs employs sexual relations with Tomás and Jesusa in order to subvert the authoritarian power of the Oankali that wants to exile him to the Mothership. Tomás participates in sexual relations with Jodahs and his sister, Jesusa, because he understands it is a way to subvert the dictums of his community, a place he describes as "[f]ull of pain and sickness and duty and false hope" (*Imago* 163). Tomás is healed from his disfiguring genetic disease through mating with Jodahs, and he also sees the mating as a way to stay connected with his sister, thus saving her from a life of forced motherhood in their community. Like Tomás, Jesusa also benefits from the relationship with Jodahs because *it* heals her genetic deformities. Jesusa also views the mating as a way to not be forced into a reproductive relationship that would most likely produce children who would die young or live with genetic disorders due to the incest within the home community. Therefore, it is through sexual acts that Jodahs, Tomás, and Jesusa employ mechanisms of resistance against oppression that would limit their agency.

Furthermore, the character of Jodahs exemplifies *anarchy of sexuality* through *anarchy of becoming*. Although Jodahs is a third-sex Oankali-Human construct, *it* is an example of the shapeshifter trope. This trope, commonly found in SF literature, describes a character who changes all or some of her or his identifying characteristics, often taken on the shape or identity of another character in the text. Jodahs can literally *become* anything, and, unless *it* forms relations with others to keep *it* stable or *it* becomes mature enough to control the shapeshifting, *it* will be constantly immersed in a river of becoming (Call 22). The shapeshifter trope of Jodahs is extremely important in understanding of an *anarchy of sexuality* through an *anarchy of becoming* because he experiences sexuality through multiple identities and in a way that denatures the hierarchy of sexuality we usually experience.[1]

Acts of sex within the Oankali and construct relations are also emblematic of an *anarchy of sexuality*. In thinking through an *anarchy of sexuality*, it is helpful to look at the radical metaphor of the *dildo*. Another useful metaphor for exploring the possibilities of PAF is the *dildo*. Lena Eckert connects the metaphor of the *dildo* from Beatriz Preciado's *Contrasexual Manifesto* with that of Haraway's *cyborg*. Eckert explains "One of the preconditions is that we have to accept the *cyborg* as our ontology; the *cyborg* is a means by which we can study our existence, just as the *dildo* is the means by which we can

---

1 By "denature," I mean the process or act of destabilizing or altering the assumed structure of a particular concept. For example, by enacting an *anarchy of sexuality*, one is able to alter the assumed structure of heterosexuality, thus placing it in a paradigm rather than regarding it as the natural default mode of sexuality in humans.

interrogate our desires. The *cyborg* is genealogy as is the *dildo*" (italics in original 84). It is when the *cyborg* needs to interrogate not simply gender, but also sexuality, that the metaphor of the *dildo* as an enabling device of contrasexuality is precise in delving into the possibilities of breaking dualisms, social constructions, and performativity in search of desire and pleasure. In short, according to Eckert, "The *cyborg* is the *contrasexual* citizen, which becomes its own genealogy" (84). But what can the metaphor of the *dildo* add to the development of a theory of PAF?

The *dildo* is the marker of the deconstruction and reconstruction of the boundaries and barriers of sexuality, pleasure, and desire. Previously, the boundaries of pleasure and desire in terms of sexual acts were ruled by the phallus, or the penis. The *dildo*, Eckert argues, comes before the penis; thus, "The invention of the *dildo* is the end of the penis as a marker of sexual difference—everything can become *dildo*! The subversive repetition of the quotation of the *dildo* on any kind of body part proves and represents its performativity" (78–79). Because "everything can become *dildo*!" the phallus is unseated from its position within a hierarchy of desire, thereby removing the power of the phallus and replacing it with the power of the *dildo*, a noun that can literally be any *thing* or any *one*. It is the *dildo* that translates an anarchist project of creating a rhizomatic network of productive erotic power simply because the *dildo* has become a "multiple, dispersed, and schizophrenic" object of perceived pleasure or desire by a posthuman subjectivity.[1][2]

Additionally, Eckert explains that the *dildo* is effective in undermining "hegemonic structures of desire, pleasure and bodies when applied as a subversive quotation. Quoting the dildo on any body part (or the entirety of the body) means to question the body as a sexual contest; it questions the possibility of framing or defining the context" (81). By quoting, Eckert means mapping the *dildo* on any part of the body, in effect showing anything really can become *dildo*. The "non-coherent narrative" of the *dildo* stems from it "being non-organic, detached from the body, but at the same time as being able to become any part of the body or the body in its entirety" (Eckert 81). Because it can be mapped on the body in a plethora of ways, the *dildo* is versatile and difficult to pin down. The *dildo* is an effective metaphor to explore the possibilities of subverting a discourse of hierarchy

---

1 A rhizomatic network of productive erotic power is a system of sexual power relations without hierarchy or origin. The metaphor of the *dildo*, which anything can become, shatters any hierarchy (including that of the phallus), thus creating a rhizome of equalized sexual relations.

2 By "posthuman subjectivity," I mean the subject perceived as a posthuman. A posthuman is no longer tied to the ideals of humanism and is able to go beyond the standard limitations of what it means to be "human." The quintessential example of a posthuman subject is Donna Haraway's *cyborg*.

and boundaries about desire and pleasure because it allows us to explore nomadic sexualities. If everything can become *dildo*, then the metaphor can help us think about a range of sexualities; however, the metaphor of the *dildo* can be problematic, too. Because the *dildo* is a representation of the phallus, there is some hesitation to using the metaphor to think about the possibilities of sex, gender, and sexuality. This hesitation stems from a concern of the power of the phallus in Western culture, a concept which could contaminate the playful perversity of using the *dildo* as a metaphor to explore sexualities beyond those controlled by the hierarchy of patriarchy— or the rule of the phallus. But why are the *cyborg* and the *dildo* important metaphors to consider for an anarchist politics, specifically a post-anarchist feminist politics?

The deconstruction of "naturalized" practices acts as a catalyst to explore a nomadic sexuality are important for PAF because this deconstruction allows for sex, gender, and sexuality to avoid remaining static and fixed. The instability of sex, gender, and sexuality is key to PAF because, as Eckert writes, "The reclaiming of the body as a non-hierarchical structure might enable us to re-figure body parts with equal functions or characteristics in relation to erotogenicity, desire and pleasure" (88.) Not only could the *dildo* enable a restructuring of the boundaries of erotogenicity, desire, and pleasure, but as Eckert suggests, "The discourses which are linked to a heterosexualised/ gendered and naturalized hegemonic position are substantial [...]. But in rewriting their history we might be able to reconstruct a materializing discourse which does not rely on identitarian, naturalizing narratives of subjectivities, bodies and desires" (88). Reconstructing this materializing discourse is important to PAF because it opens up the possibilities suggested by the metaphor of the *dildo* as well as a range of different sexualities and sexual acts that thwart the hierarchical stabilization of sexuality and sex. By using the metaphor of the *dildo* to explore the possibilities of sexuality, we may be able to enact a revolution that allows subjects to go beyond static or fixed ways of practicing sexuality. This is significant because the metaphor of the *dildo* may be the concept that helps the postmodern individual reject a fixed or static subjectivity in favor of a multiple and dispersed nomadic sexuality. This would be one of the goals of PAF because it rejects the concept of identity politics in favor of radically revolutionizing our ontologies instead of simply shifting the paradigm of the structures under which we operate.

In his article "Utopia, Dystopia, and Ideology in the Science Fiction of Octavia Butler," Eric White recognizes the nuances of sexuality in the *Xenogenesis* trilogy. He explains that the Oankali sex in Butler's texts is significant:

Undoing the privileging of genital over other erogenous zones, alien sex is polymorphously perverse. Erotic intensity is evenly dispersed across the surface of the body. Oankali sensory experience in general is acentric in just this way. The aliens neither privilege the faculty of sight over the other senses nor concentrate perception and sensation in discrete sensory organs, relying instead on the multifarious tentacles that cover them everywhere. Finally, in alien sex, the nervous systems of all the partners are connected, so that each experiences not only its own but the other's pleasure as well. (White 404)

Just as the metaphor of the *dildo* denatures the hierarchy of the phallus, the Oankali's sexual acts and other sensory acts denature the hierarchy of erogenous and sensory zones of the body. The acts of sex between the aliens (or between humans if an ooloi is present) exemplify a nonhierarchical experience in which pleasure is neither given nor received, but rather experienced and shared equally through a circuit connecting all bodies involved. This is important because, as Eric White finds, "the aliens can abolish the dualism of self and other. The species as a whole, in fact, periodically links up to form a single nervous system in order to deliberate on matters of general concern" (404). This is significant because the Oankali are able to extend their communitarian modes of communication to sexual polyamorous encounters. Because these sexual acts denature a hierarchy of desire and pleasure between bodies, organs, and sensory zones, the characters enact an *anarchy of sexuality*. The fact that Jodahs is a shapeshifter is important to this aspect of post-anarchist feminist theory as well.

Jodahs represents the possibility of a multiple, dispersed, and schizophrenic subjectivity, which then translates into this role in erotic acts (Call 22). White notes that the cancer cells the Oankali harvested from humans, like Lilith, enable them to become shapeshifters, and this ability can be found in ooloi like Jodahs, Lilith's child (405). I find this particularly interesting because it insinuates that the ability to become a shapeshifter is extrapolated from our humanity, not an attribute introduced by a foreign species. One implication of the connection between the ability to change shape and humanity is that, as humans, we all have the ability to exist with a flexible identity, perhaps while also experiencing a flexible sexuality. Although a person may not desire to partake in sexual acts with a same-sex or same-gender partner (or multiple partners), most people are physically able to do so if they chose that course of action. Throughout *its* metamorphosis, Jodahs changes drastically depending on who or what *it* is around. When *it* is around *its* siblings, *it* looks more human, but when *it* is in the woods alone, *it* begins to form a bald scaly head and face with claws instead of hands (*Imago* 92-94). Furthermore, when Jodahs is around a man, *it* begins to look more feminine; when *it* is around a woman, *it* begins to look more masculine. Around humans, at least, Jodahs transforms into the opposite gender, arguably the result of the other individual's sexual preference. This, of course, is problematic because it implies that Butler only sees Jodahs as filling in as an "other" counterpart in an otherwise heterosexual relationship. Jodahs transforms into a feminine figure in the presence of a masculine individual in an apparent biological effort to attract a mate.

Even though Butler does not let us explore non-heterosexual transformations with Jodahs beyond that of his adventures in the forest, the fact that Jodahs can traverse the social construction of genders and species is truly interesting. White affirms that "Butler thus imagines a revised economy of repetition and difference in which difference is neither persecuted as a threat to identity nor interpreted as subordinate [...] The advent of shapeshifters able to transform themselves at will enables maximally flexible and innovative responsiveness to heterogeneous situation" (406). Thus, it is through the shapeshifter trope exemplified by Jodahs that we can begin to imagine a world in which "identity has been contrived as a historically situated response to a particular set of circumstances" (White 406). Identity, then, as well as sexuality, becomes malleable instead of fixed. Approaches to identity construction like White's are the catalyst that could allow us to experiment with an *anarchy of becoming* and an *anarchy of sexuality* in our own practices.

The character of Jodahs, as a third-sex shapeshifter, creates a critical awareness of the construction of gender for reproductive means. An old resister, Francisco, even goes as far to state that if there had been more constructs like Jodahs, or more ooloi who could traverse a heteronormative human gender binary as a shapeshifter, then he doubted there would have been human resisters at all. Francisco explains, "My god, if there had been people like you around a hundred years ago, I couldn't have become a resister. I think there would be no resisters" (*Imago* 214). It is because of construct ooloi like Jodahs who have the power to traverse the gender binary through shapeshifting that the human resisters' xenophobia is expelled. Jodahs is a welcomed alternative to the tentacled, slug-like Oankali ooloi, which seems very foreign and alien. Jodahs's shapeshifting abilities help to quell this xenophobia because it can look attractive to humans instead of repulsive. This is caused, in part, by the fact that the humans can categorize Jodahs within their gender binaries, even though it is still a third sex. This gap between gender and sex does not seem to repulse the humans; this signifies that we may not be as connected to rigid parallels between constructions of sex and gender as may have been previously thought. The major implication here is that difference or alienness is not really important if humans can identify in some way with the other or if the other is able to outwardly construct an identity that falls within the preexisting normative structures.

This is significant because it demonstrates that erotic productive power can only be employed if gender is constructed appropriately by the (alien) other for the (human) subject. In other words, relating back to a post-anarchist feminist theory, a *dildo* can only work if it fills the hole left by the phallus-cy of the penis.

Contributions of Xenogenesis to PAF

The characters of Lilith, Akin, and Jodahs help to both exemplify and add to a theory of PAF. Lilith brings forth questions of agency, manipulation, and the role of traditions of Western thought in subverting relations. Akin adds critical components concerning productive power, resistance, and ontology. Finally, Jodahs creates a space for considering the construction of gender for reproductive means. Developing PAF using post apocalyptic American SF has led me think further about the relationship between power and resistance. While the classical anarchists saw power as gathering in specific terminal ends: the church, the lumber baron, the president, or the male head of house, postmodern anarchism recognizes that power is capillaristic. This, of course, means that power is present in all social relations, not just those that are the most visible, and it also means that opportunities for resistance are present in all of our social relations as well. Thus, one does not have to assassinate a banking institution's CEO to illustrate resistance (as Alexander Berkman's failed assassination attempt of businessman Henry Clay Frick); it could simply be a matter of standing up to sexual discrimination led by a coworker in the workplace. It would be a mistake, however, to think that a capillaristic conception of power means that the power in all social relations is equal to that in all other social relations. Because post-anarchist feminism asks us to examine the limitations of possibility in the hopes of 1) finding them and 2) changing them, we need to examine power and resistance and the role privilege and hierarchy plays in each. If not all power relations are equal, are all acts of resistance equal? Who gets to place a value on each of these, and, more importantly, what purpose does such a valuation serve?

This chapter is only the first imaginings of a theory of post-anarchist feminism, and it illustrates how literature can be used to further fields like anarchist studies. Perhaps, in the years to come, it will continue to provide a basis for questions such as those raised herein about the connections between feminism, anarchism, and postmodernism. The questions and theoretical arguments brought up about sex, gender, sexuality, power, resistance, authority, domination, and other themes belong to many fields including feminist studies, anarchist studies, literary theory, cultural theory, and philosophy. They deserve to be brought up in light of these disciplines, viewed through their looking glasses, and interrogated by the foundations of each. Doing so will hopefully produce challenging vistas and exciting lines of inquiry leading to other such projects.

References

Atwood, Margaret. *In Other Worlds: SF and the Human Imagination*. New York: Doubleday, 2011. Print.

Butler, Octavia E. *Adulthood Rites*. New York: Warner, 1988. Print.

_____. *Dawn*. New York: Warner, 1987. Print.

_____. *Imago*. New York: Warner, 1989. Print.

Call, Lewis. *Postmodern Anarchism*. Lanham: Lexington, 2002. Print.

Curtis, Claire P. *Postapocalyptic Fiction and the Social Contract: We'll Not Go Home Again*. Maryland: Lexington, 2010. Print.

Deleuze, Gilles and Félix Guattari. *A Thousand Plateaus: Capitalism and Schizophrenia*. Minneapolis: University of Minnesota Press, 1987. Print.

Eckert, Lena. "Post(-)anarchism and the Contrasexual practices of Cyborgs in Dildotopia Or 'The War on the Phallus'." *Anarchism and Sexuality: Ethics, Relationships and Power*. Eds. Jamie Heckert and Richard Cleminson. New York: Routledge, 2011. 69-92. Electronic.

Harris-Fain, Darren. *Understanding Contemporary American Science Fiction: The Age of Maturity, 1970–2000*. Columbia, S.C.: University of South Carolina UP, 2005. Print.

Melzer, Patricia. "Beyond Binary Gender: Queer Identities and Intersexed Bodies in Octavia E. Butler's *Wild Seed* and *Imago* and Melissa Scott's *Shadow Man*." *Alien Constructions: Science Fiction and Feminist Thought*. Austin: University of Texas Press, 2006. Print.

Mohr, Dunja M. *Worlds Apart: Dualism and Transgression in Contemporary Female Dystopias*. Jefferson, N.C.: McFarland & Co, 2005. Print.

Osherow, Michele. "The Dawn of a New Lilith: Revisionary Mythmaking in Women's Science Fiction." *NWSA Journal* 12.2 (2000): 68-83. PDF.

Scholes, Robert. "The Roots of Science Fiction." *Speculations on Speculation: Theories of Science Fiction*. Eds. James E. Gunn and Matthew Candelaria. Lanham, Maryland: Scarecrow, 2005. 205-218. Print.

White, Eric. "The Erotics of Becoming: Xenogenesis and 'The Thing.'" *Science Fiction Studies* 20.3 (1993): 394-408. PDF.

"Xenobiologist." *Oxford English Dictionary*. 3rd Ed. 2013. Electronic.

"Xenogenesis." *Oxford English Dictionary*. 3rd Ed. 2013. Electronic.

Zaki, Hoda. "Utopia, Dystopia, and Ideology in the Science Fiction of Octavia Butler." *Science Fiction Studies* 17.2 (1990): 239-251. PDF.

List of Contributors

James Brown, University of Minnesota
Agathe Brun, Université Nice–Sophia Antipolis
Michelle Campbell, Purdue University
Scott Drake, Douglas College
Max Haiven, NSCAD University
Michael D. Gilliland, Independent Scholar
Bryan L. Jones, Oklahoma State University
Taylor Andrew Loy, Independent Scholar
Josephine A. McQuail, Tennessee Technological University
Jeff Shantz, Kwantlen Polytechnic University

Printed in the United States
By Bookmasters